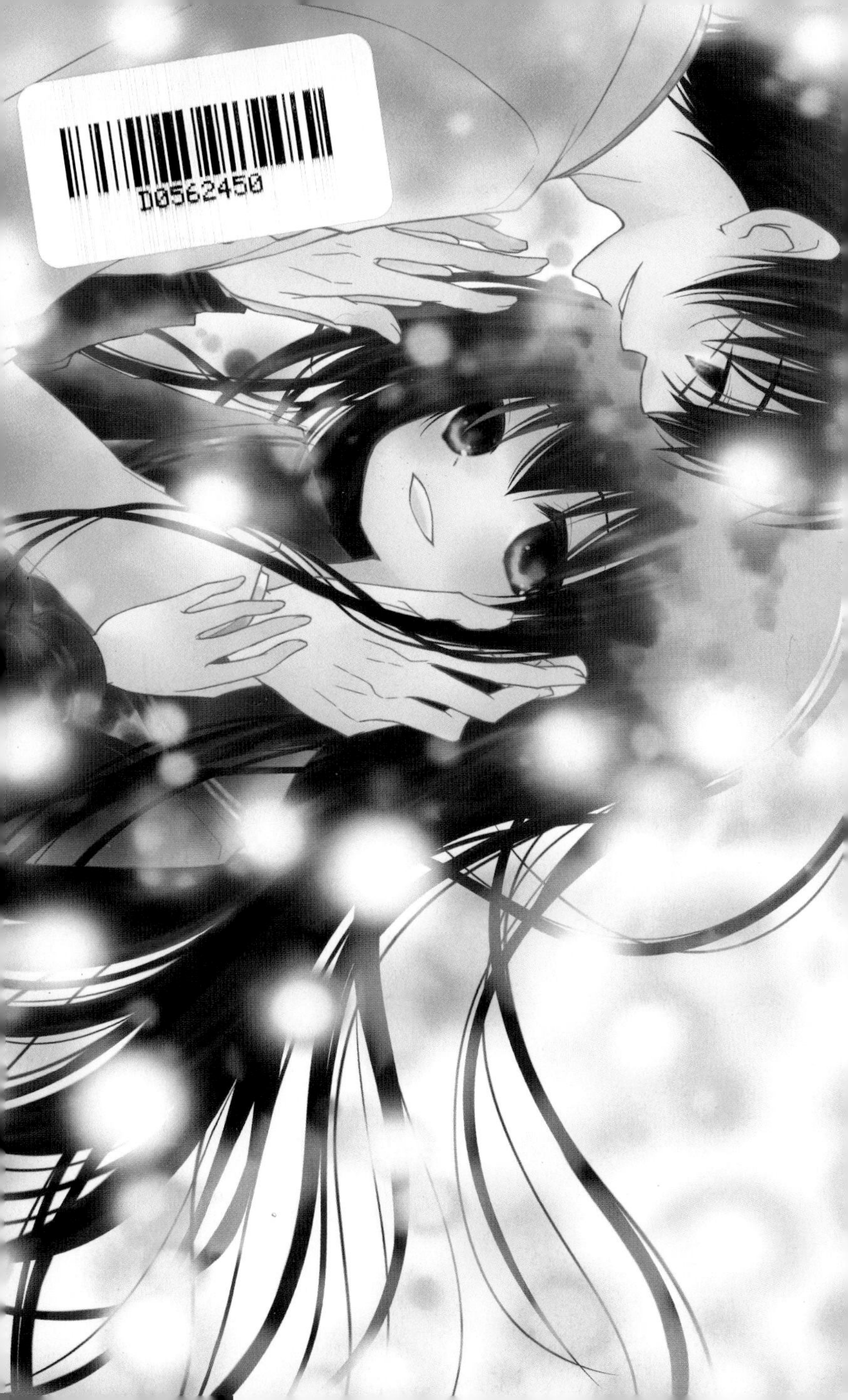

[Ani-Imo]

Big Brother becomes Little Sister;
Little Sister becomes Big Brother.

Ani-Imo

(5)

[Ani-Imo]

Big Brother becomes
Little Sister;
Little Sister becomes
Big Brother.

Haruko
Kurumatani

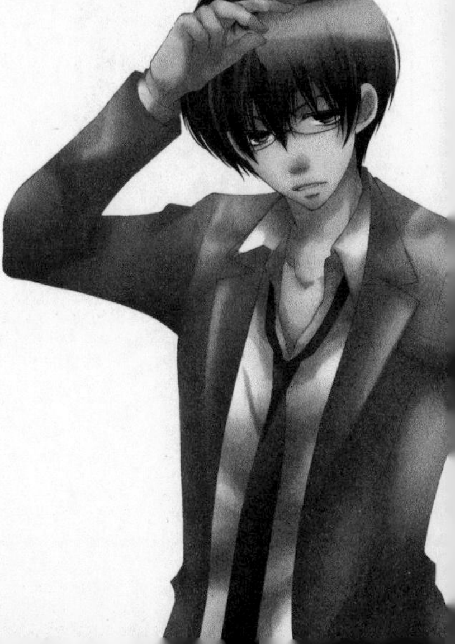

CHARACTERS

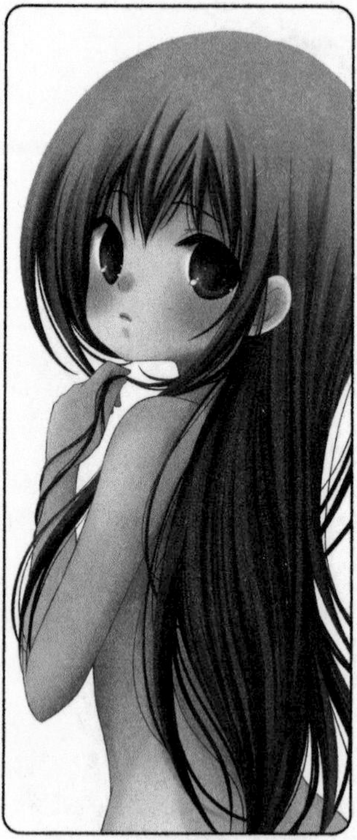

Youta Koizumi

A first-year in high school. Has Hikaru's body but is in fact Youta on the inside. Hikaru is his precious little sister, but he can't accept how she feels about him.

NOW BACK TO NORMAL!

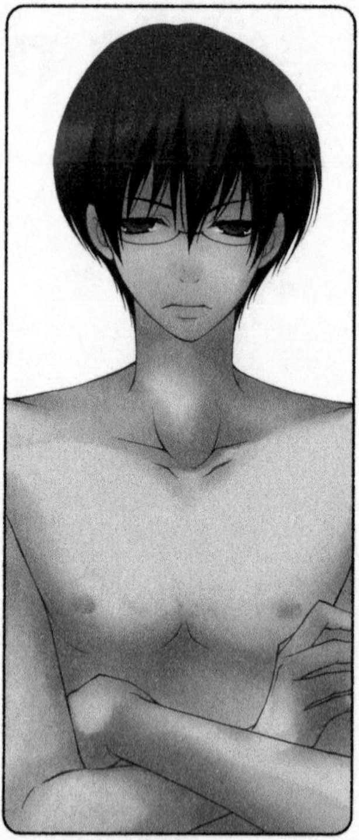

Hikaru Koizumi

A first-year in high school. Outwardly appears to be Youta but is Hikaru on the inside. Her feelings for her brother are very serious and only became all the more so when they switched bodies.

Kakeru Mayama

Has Yurika's body but is Mayama on the inside. A ditzy classmate who can't accept reality for what it is.

Yurika Oda

Has Mayama's body but is Yurika on the inside. Hikaru and Youta's classmate. She is Yurika-sama, the merciless lesbian.

Chisato Ichijou

Hikaru and Youta's doctor. Sadistic and brutal at heart. Despite this, he has taken an interest in the Koizumi siblings.

STORY

I'm Youta Koizumi.
One day, I switched bodies with my precious little sister, whom I've protected my whole life!!!!! Before I could recover from the shock, my once adorable little sister went completely sadistic on me, and I fell for her ploy to get me to go out with her. Then the lesbian babe, Oda-san, and our innocent, clueless classmate, Mayama, switched bodies too! In search of a way to get back to normal, the four of us embarked on a steamy hot springs trip! Ichijou-sensei suggested we make the journey so that we could meet two body-swapping "senpais" who'd switched twenty-five years earlier. These two experienced swappers told us they had decided to stay in their switched bodies and had even abandoned looking for a way to get back to normal......Not long after, I found myself looking at Hikaru like she was any other girl. But quite suddenly and beyond my control, we accidentally bonked heads and successfully reverted back to our original bodies!!! Now we can finally go back to how things used to be. Or so I think!?

CONTENTS

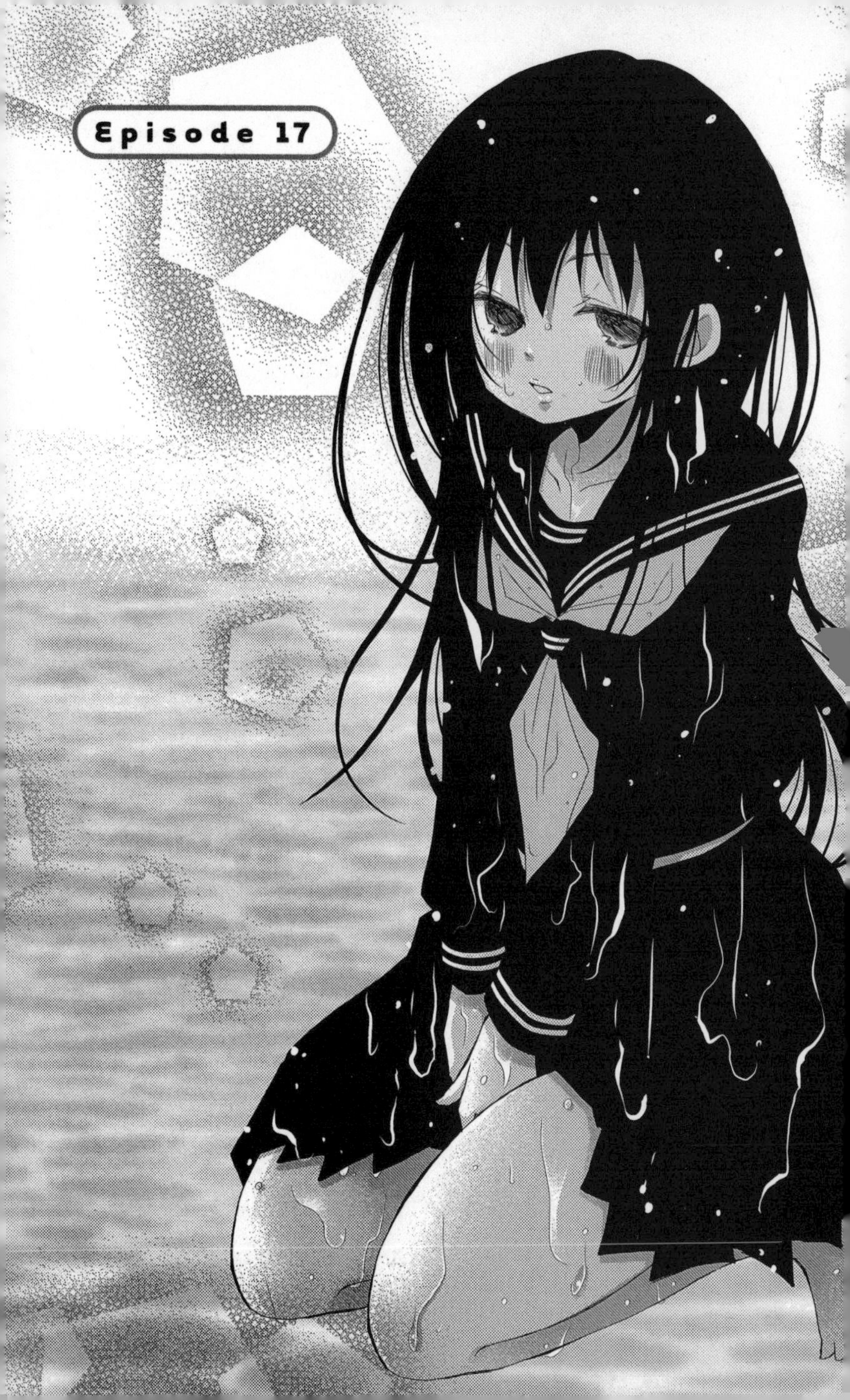
Episode 17

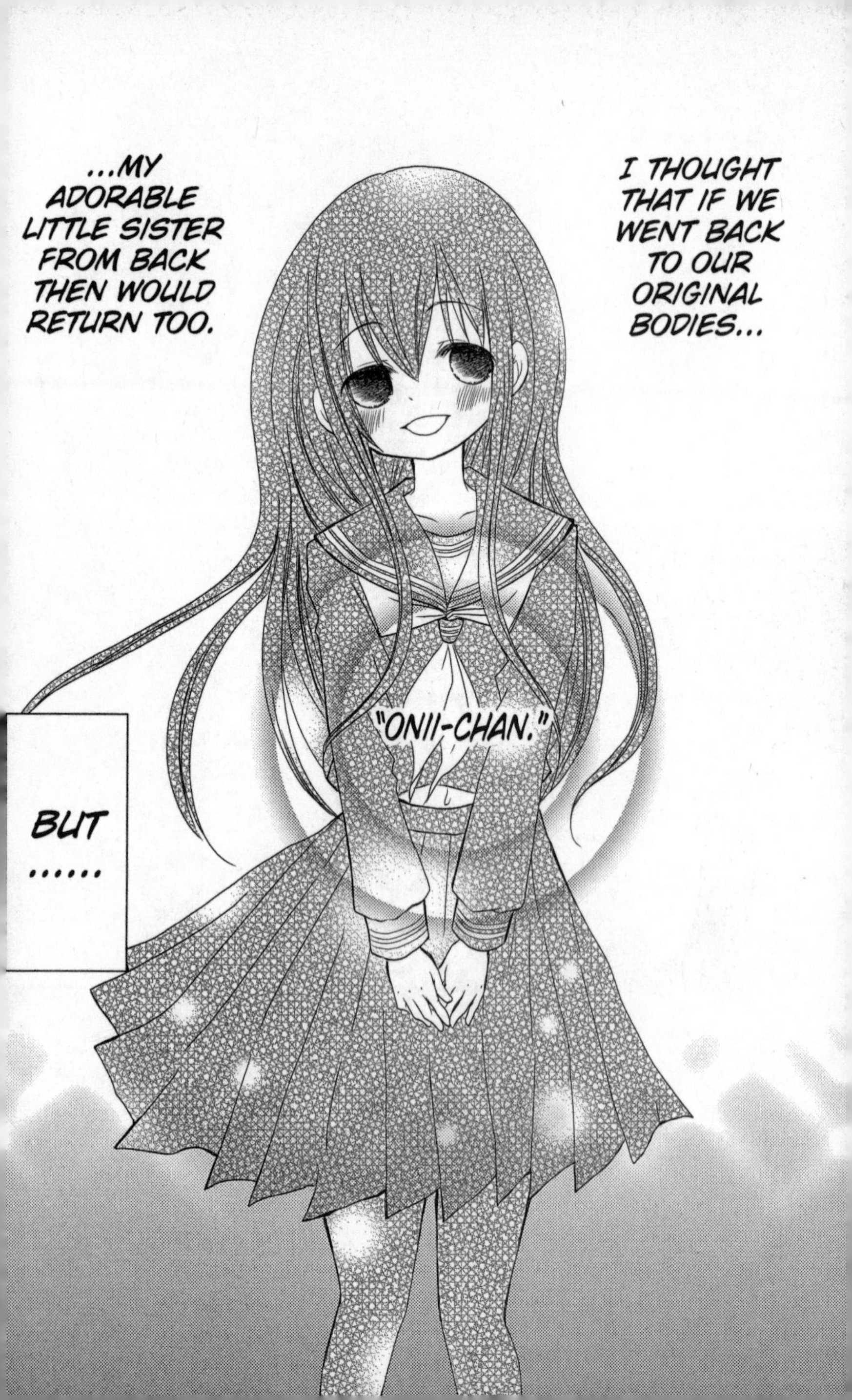
I THOUGHT THAT IF WE WENT BACK TO OUR ORIGINAL BODIES...
...MY ADORABLE LITTLE SISTER FROM BACK THEN WOULD RETURN TOO.
"ONII-CHAN."
BUT ......

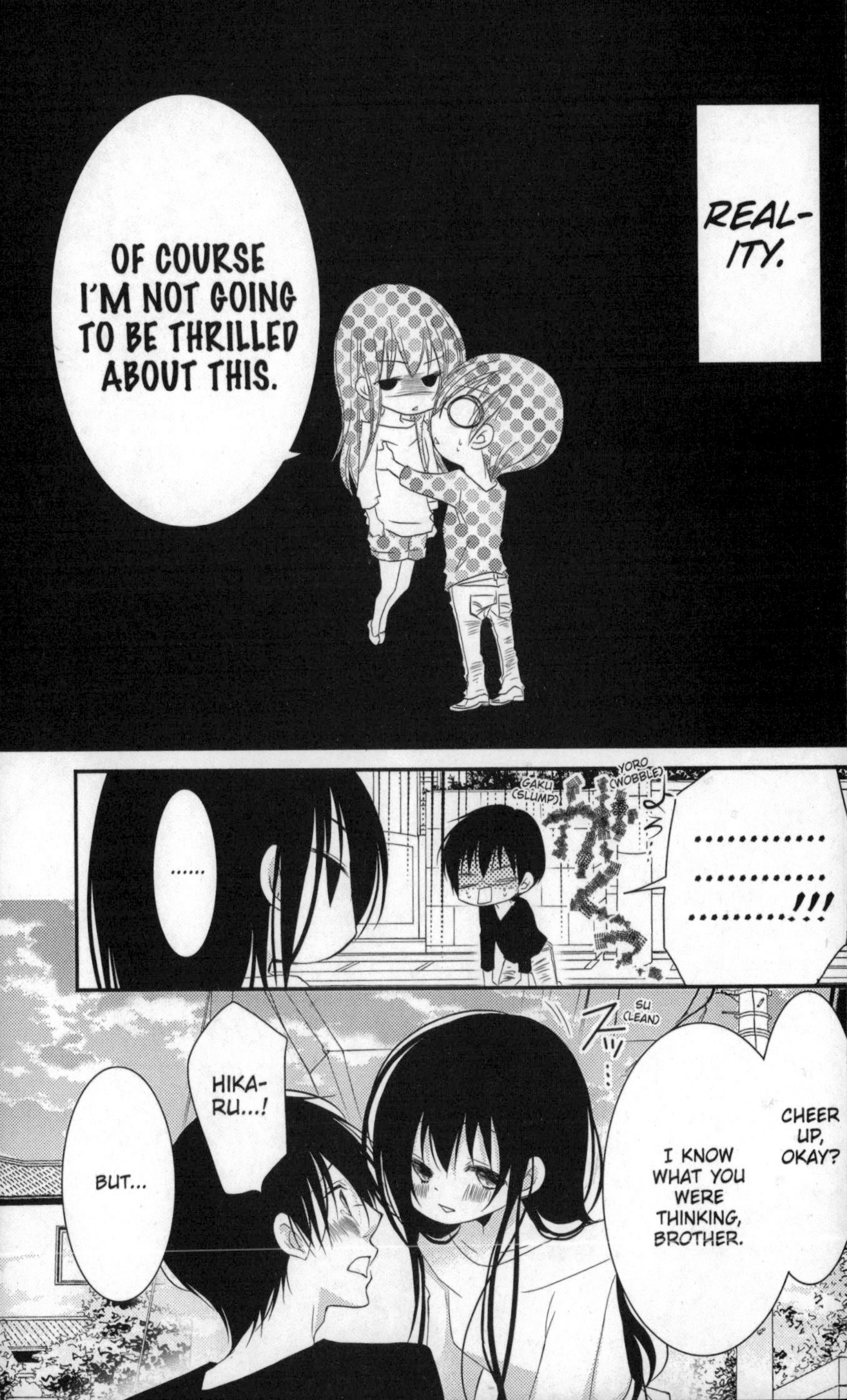
REAL-ITY.
OF COURSE I'M NOT GOING TO BE THRILLED ABOUT THIS.
....!!!
YORO (WOBBLE)
GAKU (SLUMP)
......
CHEER UP, OKAY?
I KNOW WHAT YOU WERE THINKING, BROTHER.
SU (LEAN)
HIKA-RU...!
BUT...

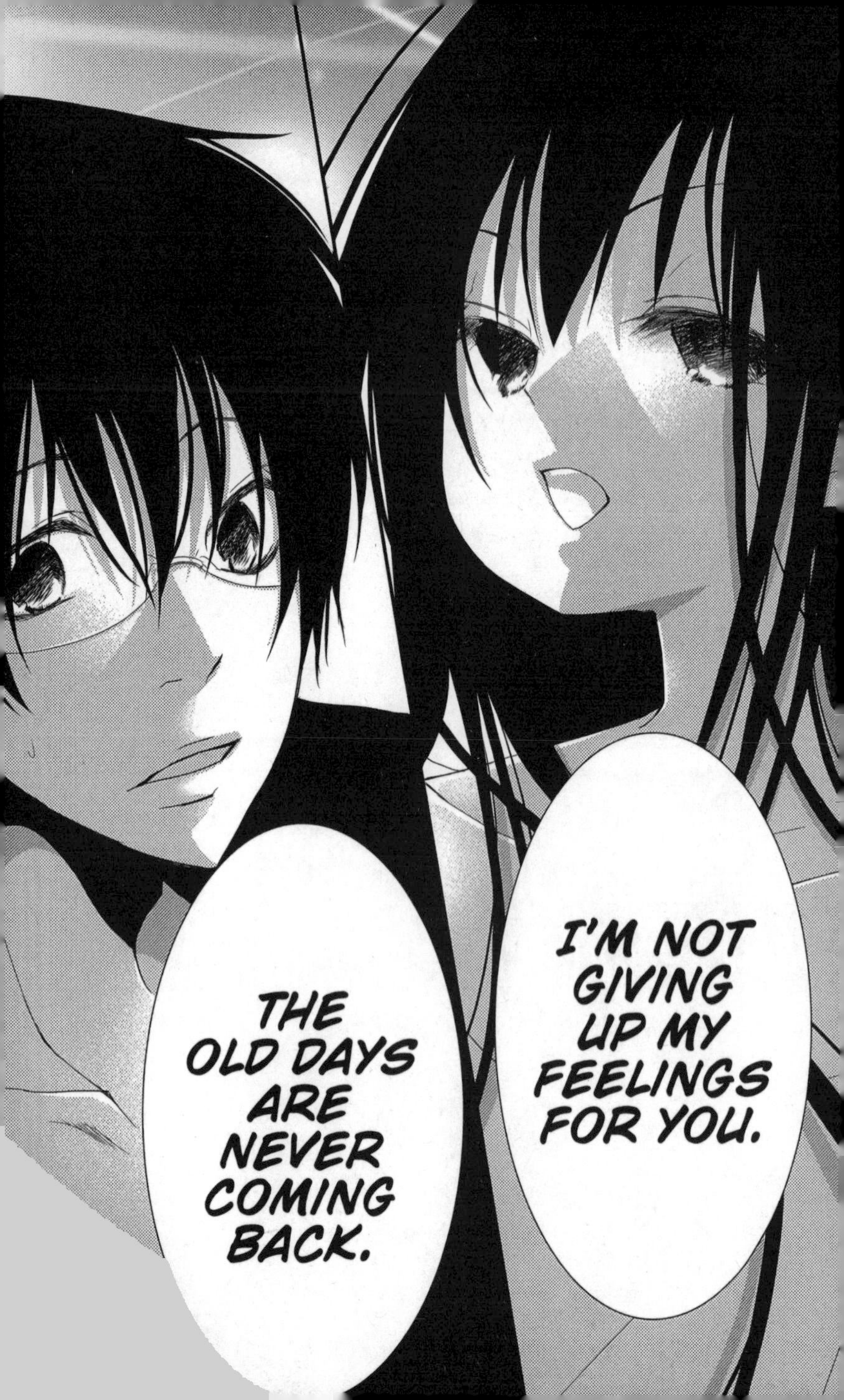
I'M NOT GIVING UP MY FEELINGS FOR YOU.
THE OLD DAYS ARE NEVER COMING BACK.

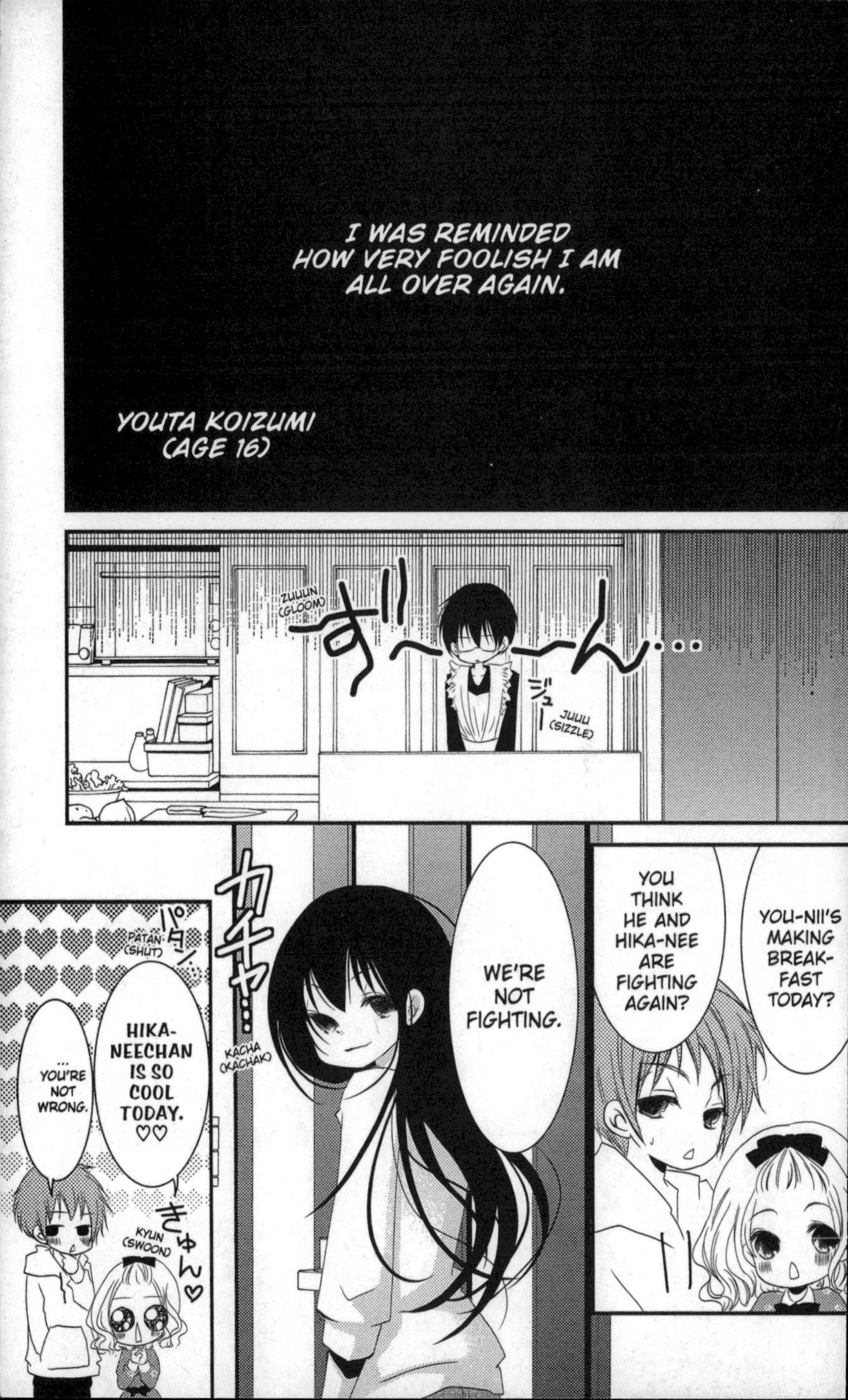
I WAS REMINDED HOW VERY FOOLISH I AM ALL OVER AGAIN.
YOUTA KOIZUMI (AGE 16)
ZUUUN (GLOOM)
JUUU (SIZZLE)
YOU-NII'S MAKING BREAK-FAST TODAY?
YOU THINK HE AND HIKA-NEE ARE FIGHTING AGAIN?
WE'RE NOT FIGHTING.
KACHA (KACHAK)
PATAN (SHUT)
HIKA-NEECHAN IS SO COOL TODAY. ♡♡
... YOU'RE NOT WRONG.
KYUN (SWOON)

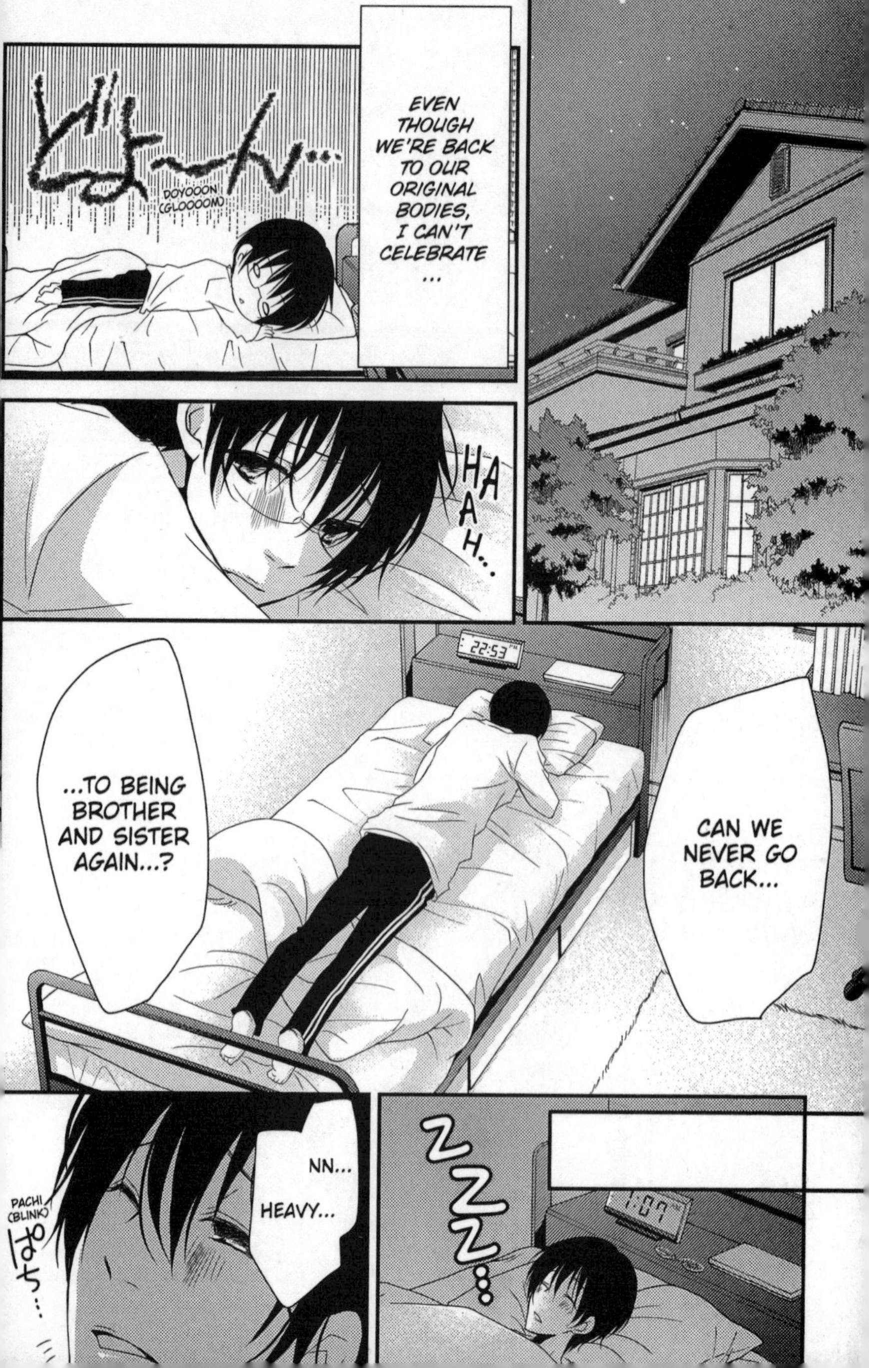
EVEN THOUGH WE'RE BACK TO OUR ORIGINAL BODIES, I CAN'T CELEBRATE ...
どよ〜ん…
DOYOOON (GLOOOOM)
HAAH...
CAN WE NEVER GO BACK...
...TO BEING BROTHER AND SISTER AGAIN...?
ZZZ...
NN...
HEAVY...
PACHI (BLINK)
ぱち…

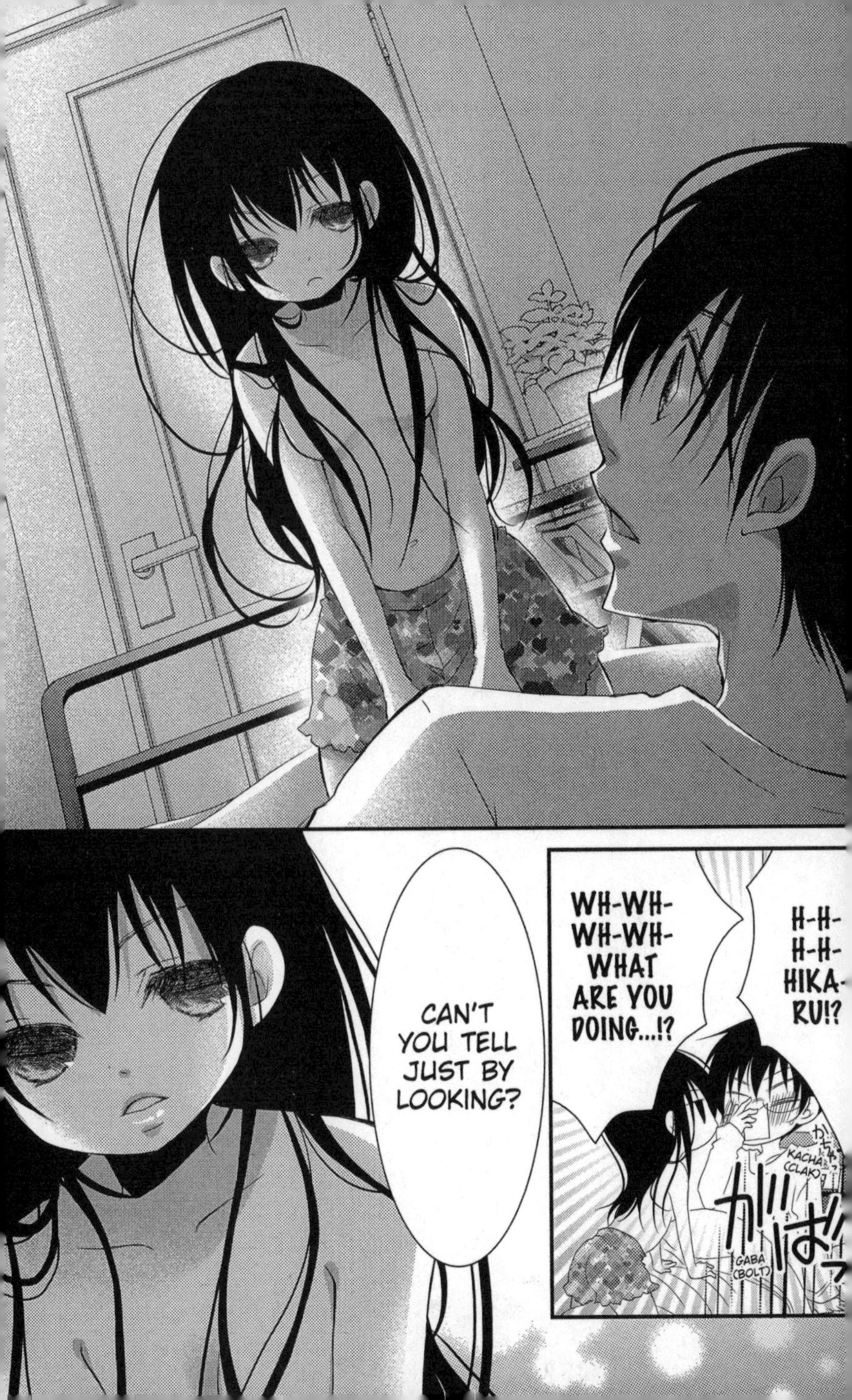
H-H-H-H-HIKARU!?
WH-WH-WH-WH-WHAT ARE YOU DOING...!?
KACHA (CLAK)
GABA (BOLT)
CAN'T YOU TELL JUST BY LOOKING?

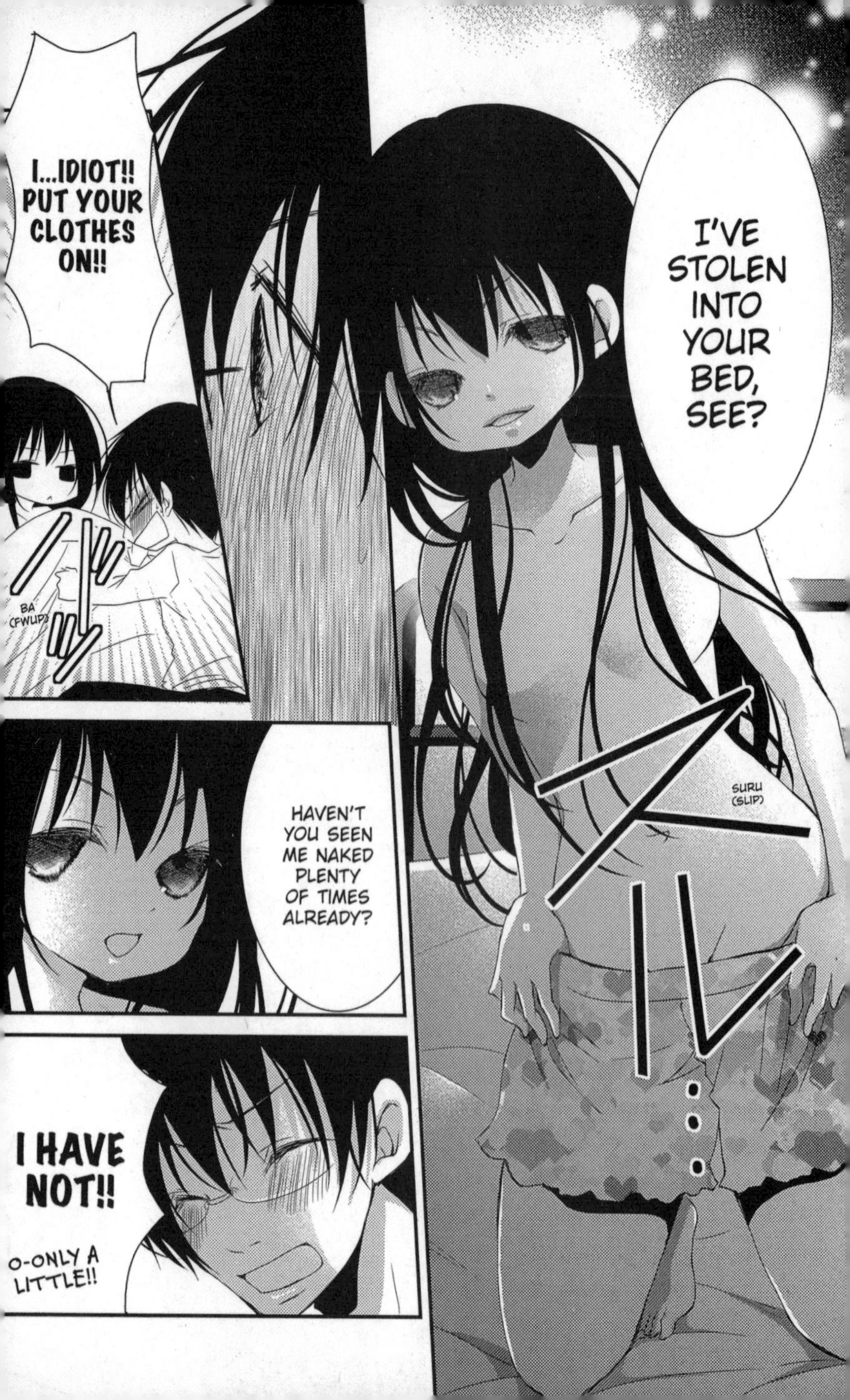
I'VE STOLEN INTO YOUR BED, SEE?
SURU (SLIP)
I...IDIOT!! PUT YOUR CLOTHES ON!!
BA (FWUP)
HAVEN'T YOU SEEN ME NAKED PLENTY OF TIMES ALREADY?
I HAVE NOT!!
O-ONLY A LITTLE!!

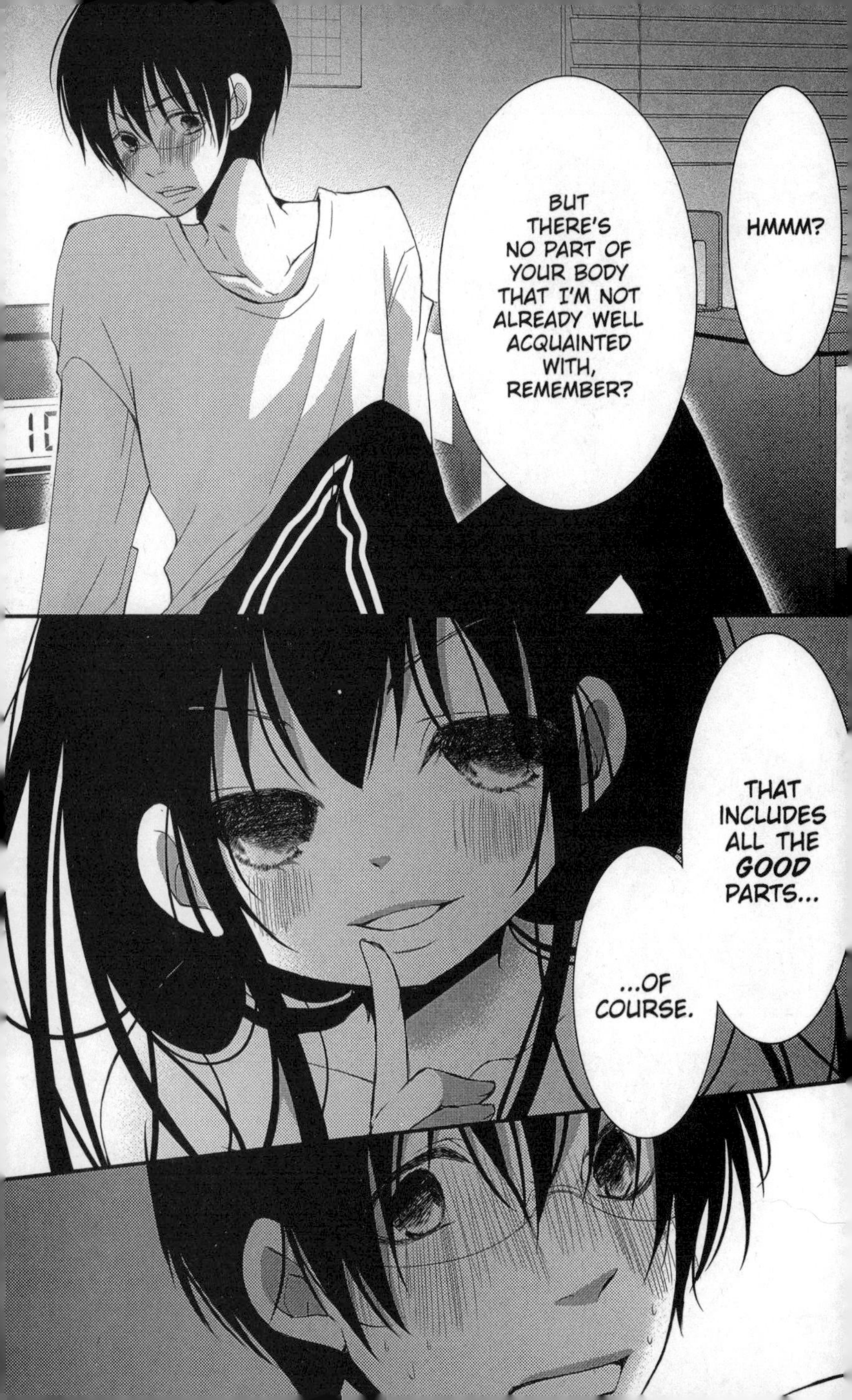
HMMM?
BUT THERE'S NO PART OF YOUR BODY THAT I'M NOT ALREADY WELL ACQUAINTED WITH, REMEMBER?
THAT INCLUDES ALL THE GOOD PARTS...
...OF COURSE.

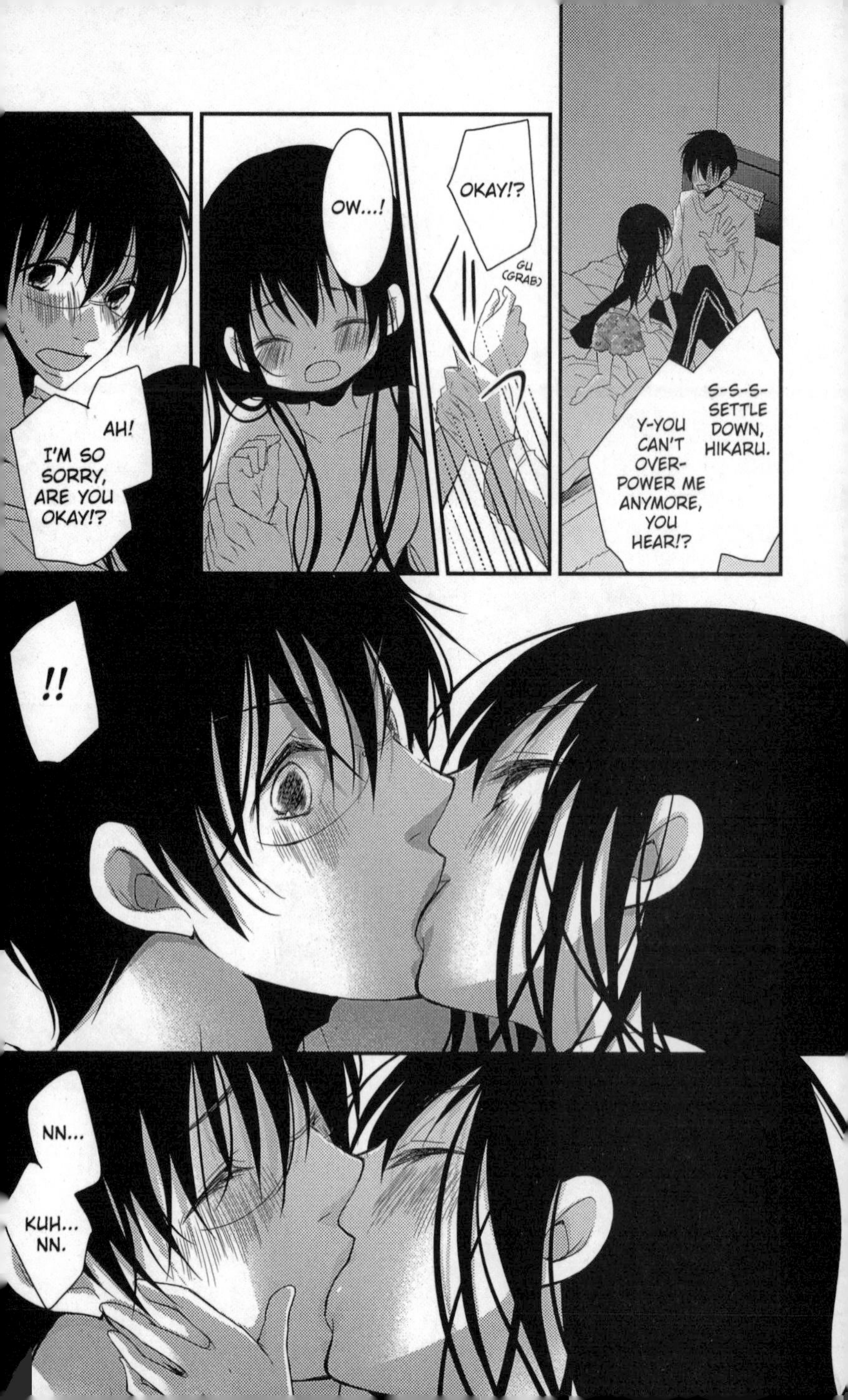
S-S-S-SETTLE DOWN, HIKARU.
Y-YOU CAN'T OVER-POWER ME ANYMORE, YOU HEAR!?
OKAY!?
GU (GRAB)
OW...!
AH! I'M SO SORRY, ARE YOU OKAY!?
!!
NN...
KUH... NN.

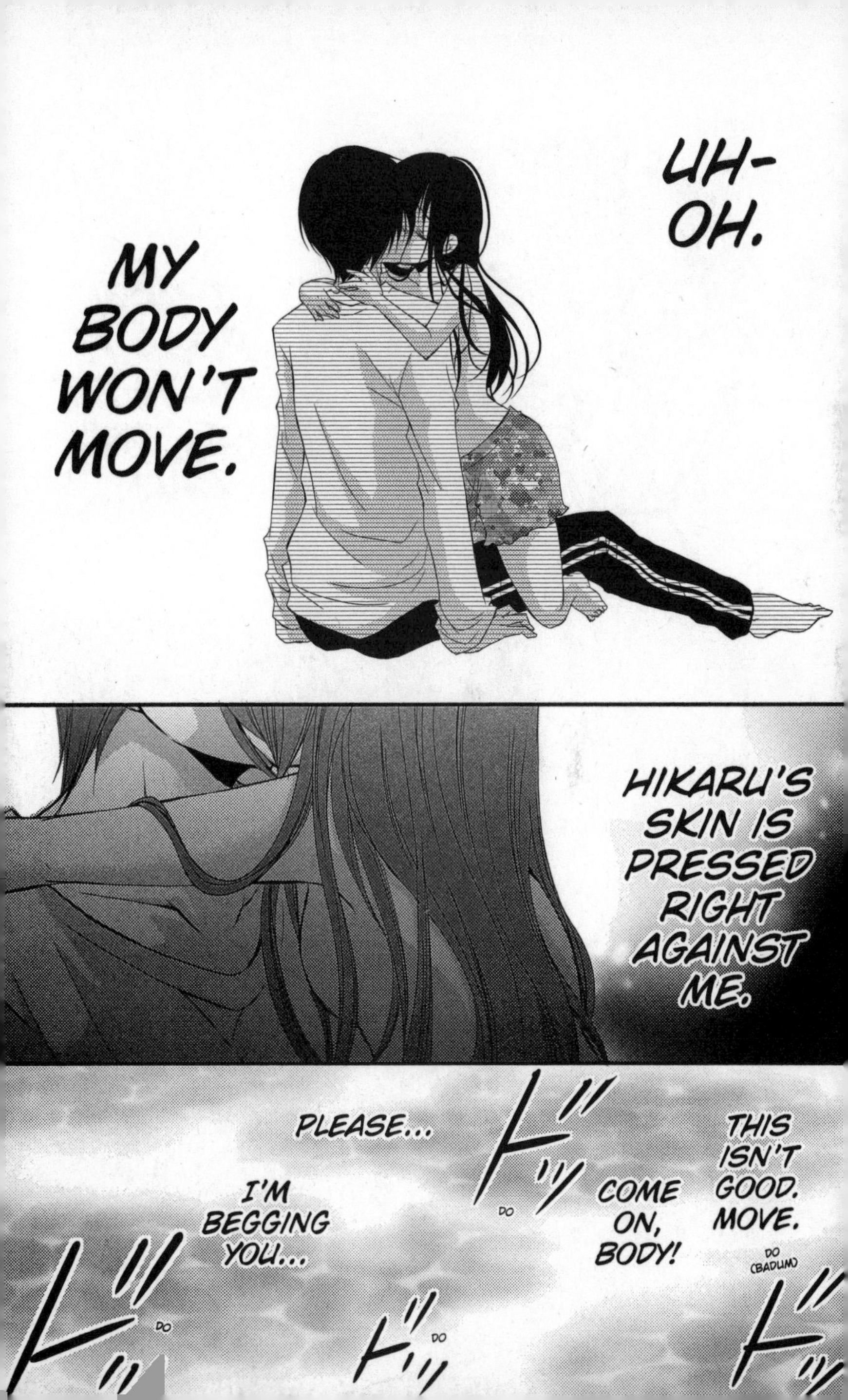
UH-OH.
MY BODY WON'T MOVE.
HIKARU'S SKIN IS PRESSED RIGHT AGAINST ME.
THIS ISN'T GOOD. MOVE.
DO (BADUM)
COME ON, BODY!
DO
PLEASE...
I'M BEGGING YOU...
DO
DO

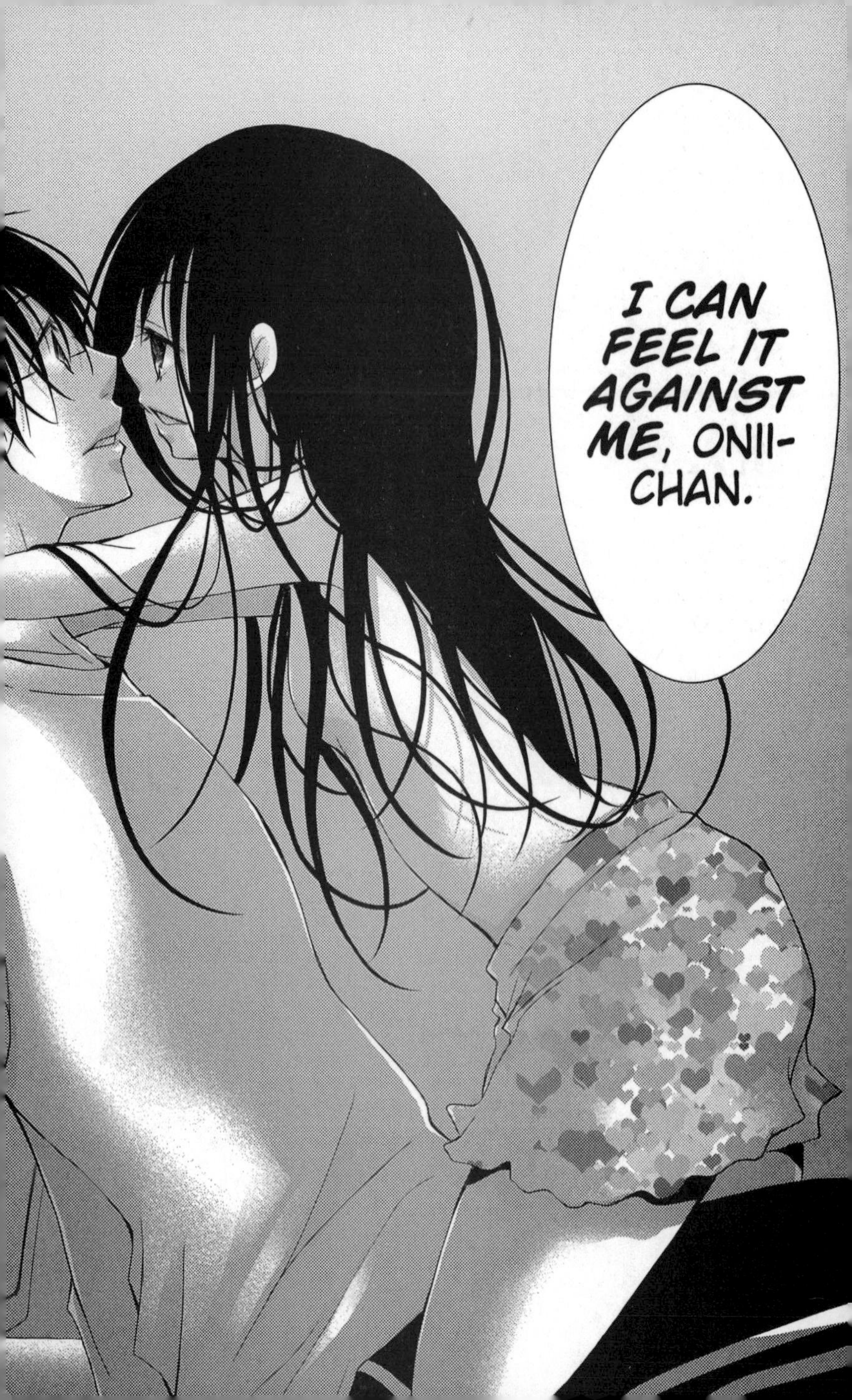
I CAN FEEL IT AGAINST ME, ONIII-CHAN.

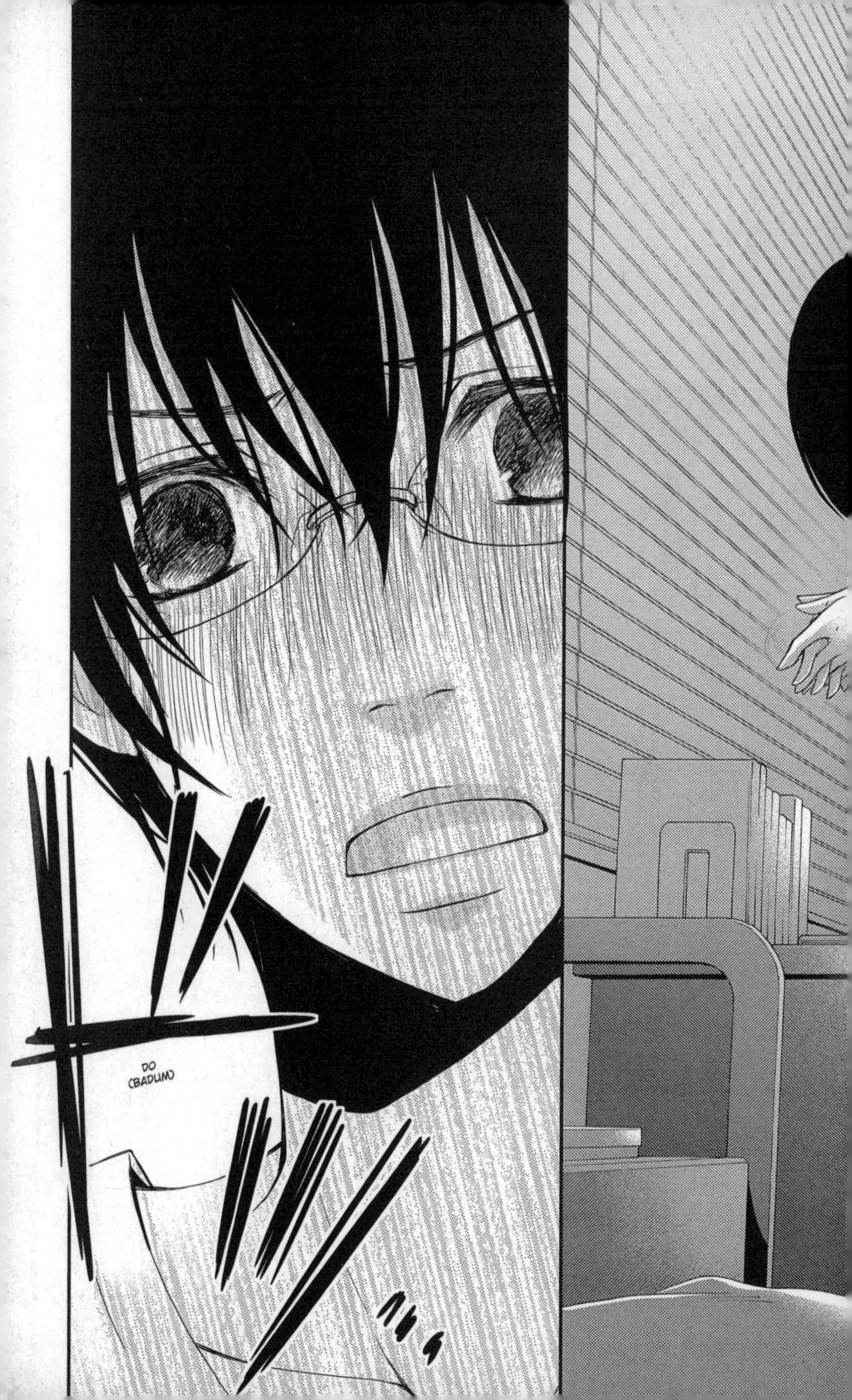
DO
(BADUM)

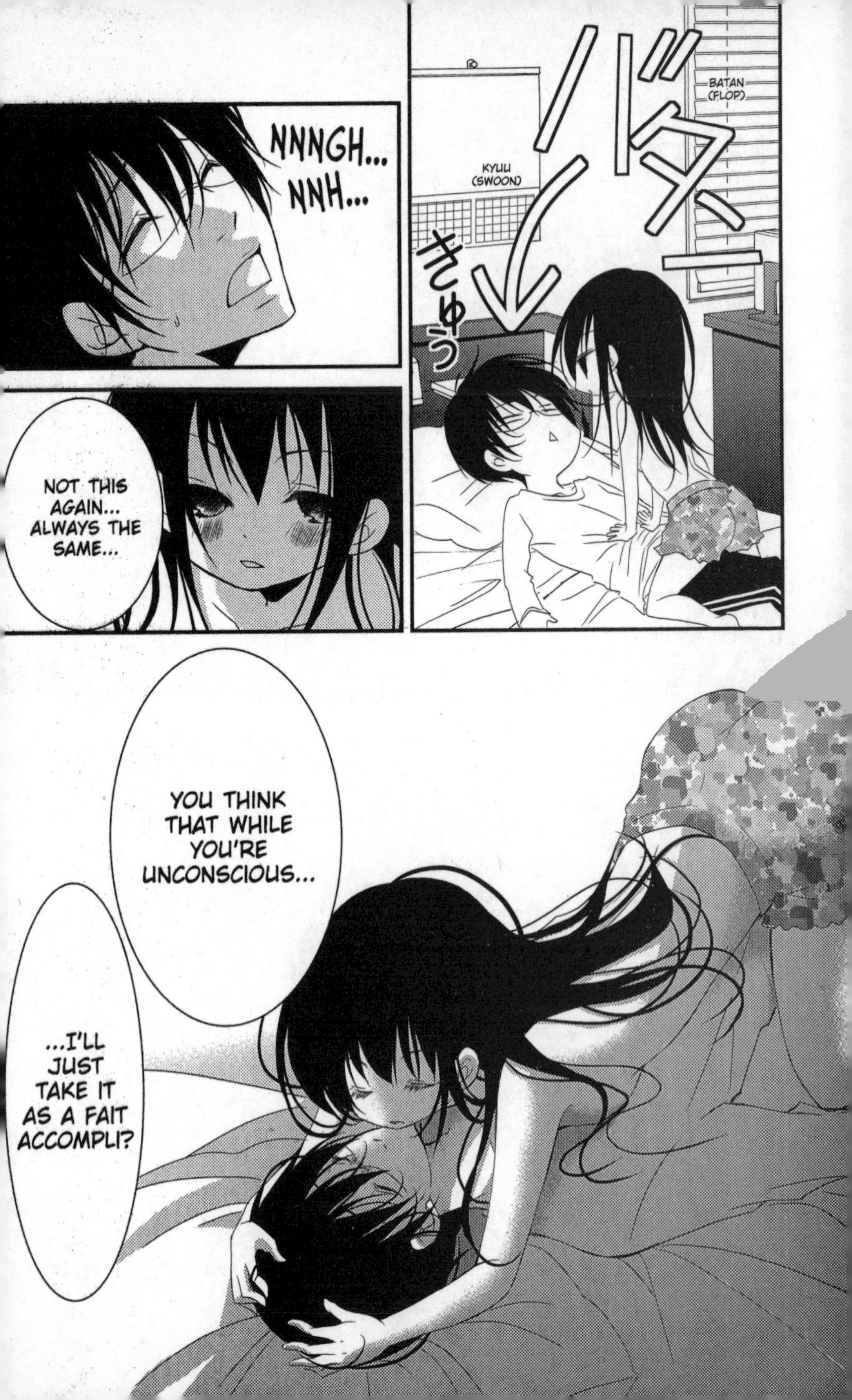

バタ
BATAN (FLOP)
きゅう
KYUU (SWOON)
NNNGH... NNH...
NOT THIS AGAIN... ALWAYS THE SAME...
YOU THINK THAT WHILE YOU'RE UNCONSCIOUS...
...I'LL JUST TAKE IT AS A FAIT ACCOMPLI?

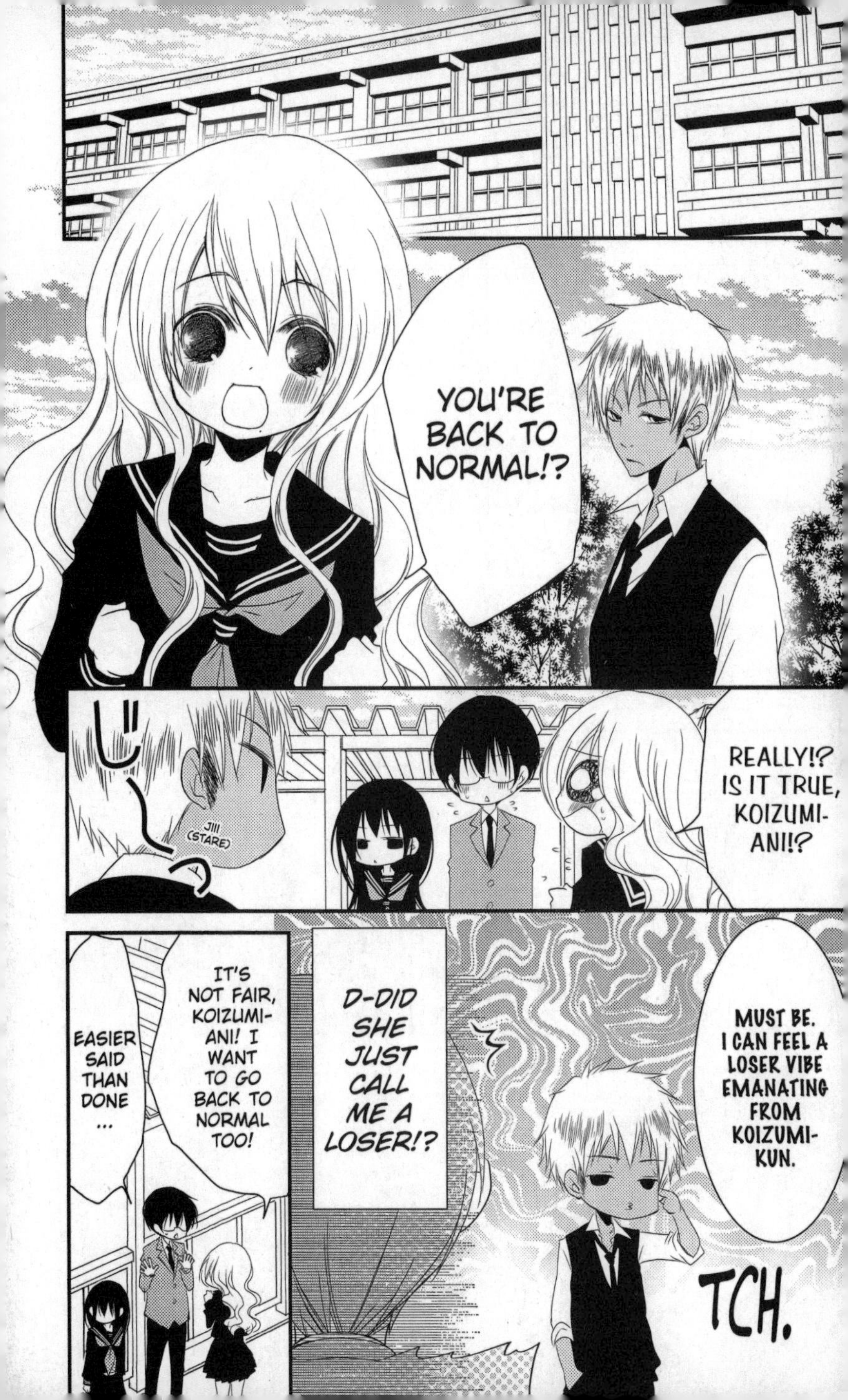
YOU'RE BACK TO NORMAL!?
REALLY!? IS IT TRUE, KOIZUMI-ANI!?
JIII (STARE)
MUST BE. I CAN FEEL A LOSER VIBE EMANATING FROM KOIZUMI-KUN.
TCH.
D-DID SHE JUST CALL ME A LOSER!?
IT'S NOT FAIR, KOIZUMI-ANI! I WANT TO GO BACK TO NORMAL TOO!
EASIER SAID THAN DONE...

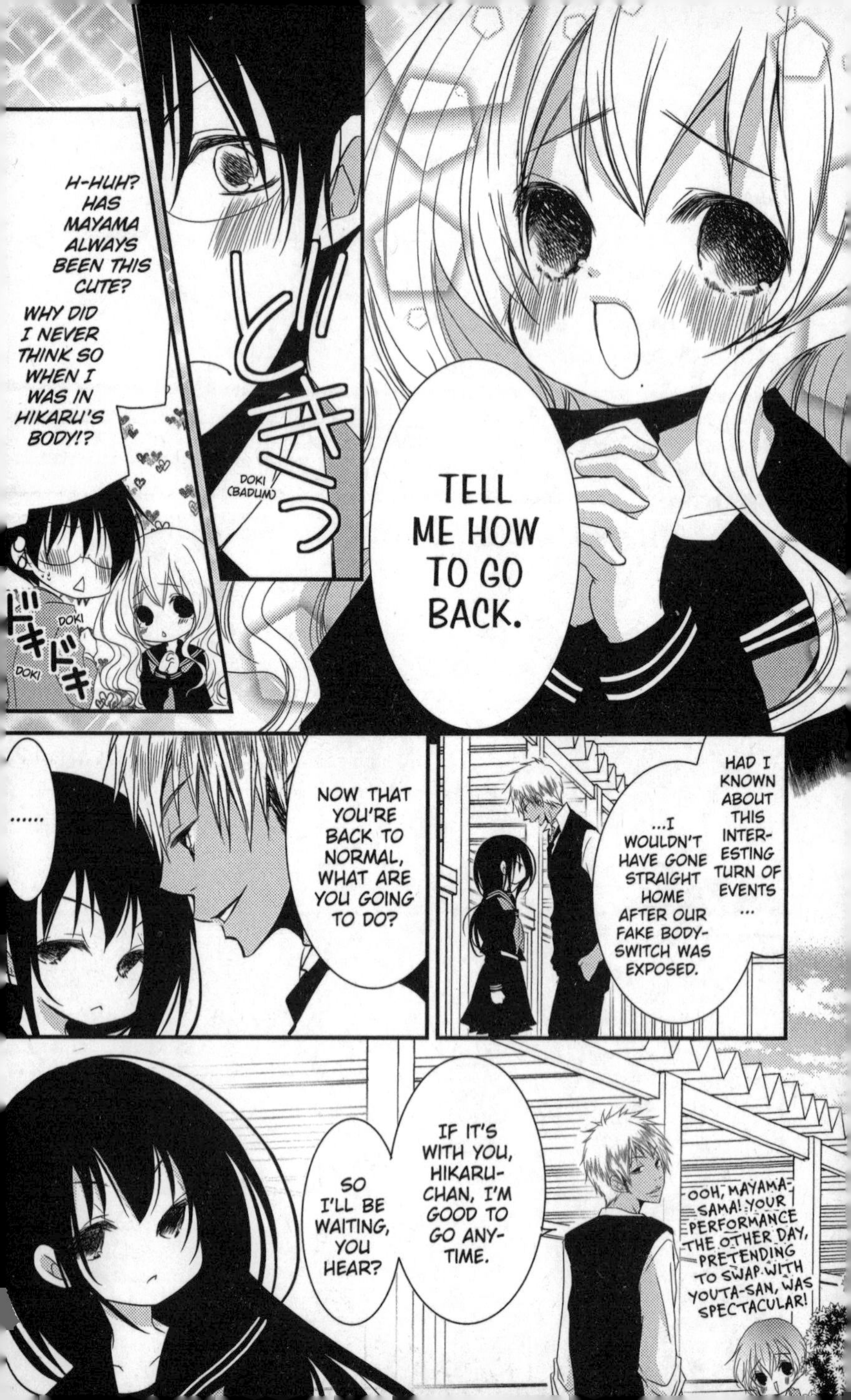
TELL ME HOW TO GO BACK.
H-HUH? HAS MAYAMA ALWAYS BEEN THIS CUTE?
WHY DID I NEVER THINK SO WHEN I WAS IN HIKARU'S BODY!?
DOKI (BADUM)
DOKI
DOKI
HAD I KNOWN ABOUT THIS INTERESTING TURN OF EVENTS...
...I WOULDN'T HAVE GONE STRAIGHT HOME AFTER OUR FAKE BODY-SWITCH WAS EXPOSED.
NOW THAT YOU'RE BACK TO NORMAL, WHAT ARE YOU GOING TO DO?
......
OOH, MAYAMA-SAMA! YOUR PERFORMANCE THE OTHER DAY, PRETENDING TO SWAP WITH YOUTA-SAN, WAS SPECTACULAR!
IF IT'S WITH YOU, HIKARU-CHAN, I'M GOOD TO GO ANY-TIME.
SO I'LL BE WAITING, YOU HEAR?

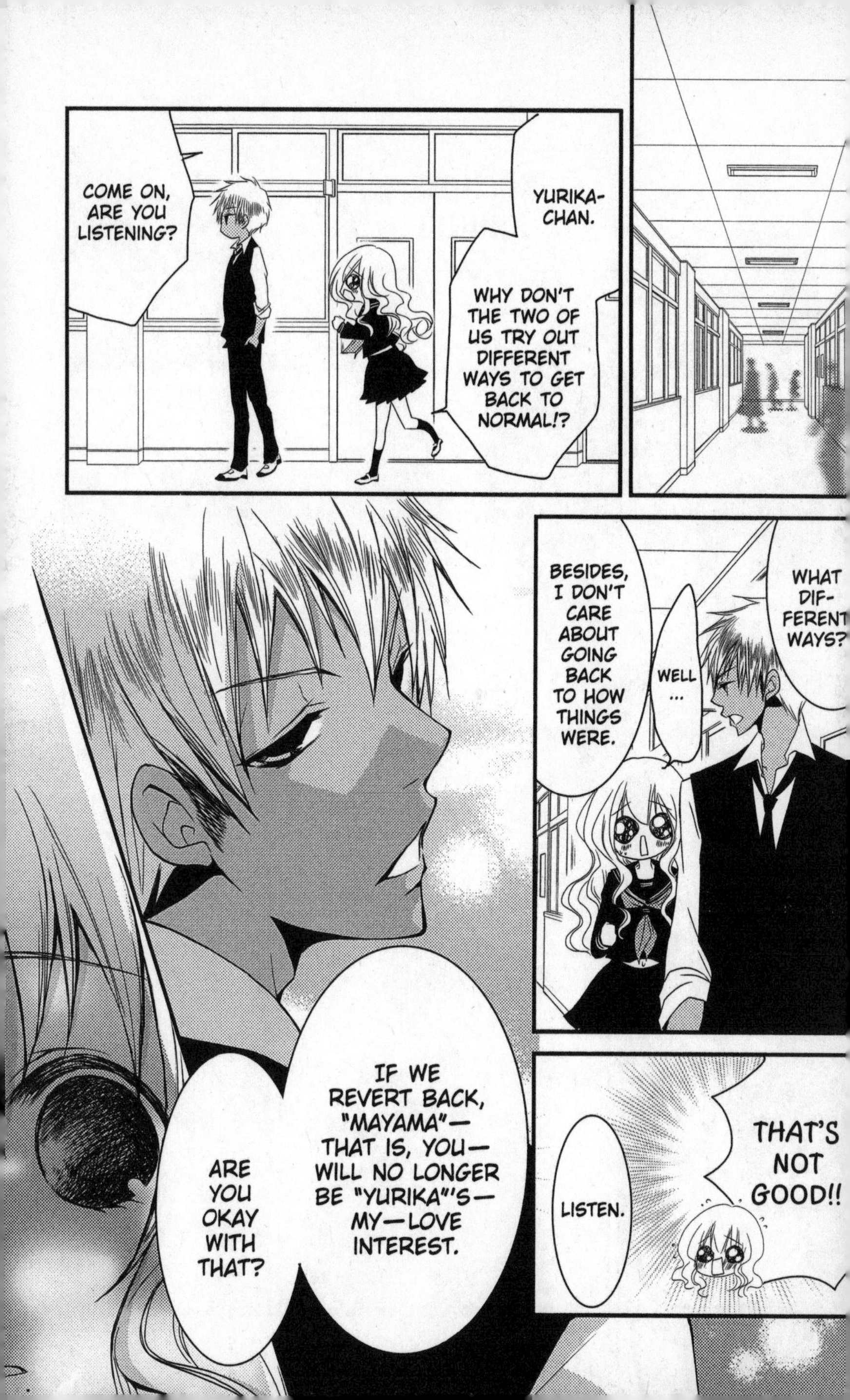
YURIKA-CHAN.
WHY DON'T THE TWO OF US TRY OUT DIFFERENT WAYS TO GET BACK TO NORMAL!?
COME ON, ARE YOU LISTENING?
WHAT DIF-FERENT WAYS?
WELL ...
BESIDES, I DON'T CARE ABOUT GOING BACK TO HOW THINGS WERE.
THAT'S NOT GOOD!!
LISTEN.
IF WE REVERT BACK, "MAYAMA"—THAT IS, YOU—WILL NO LONGER BE "YURIKA"'S—MY—LOVE INTEREST.
ARE YOU OKAY WITH THAT?

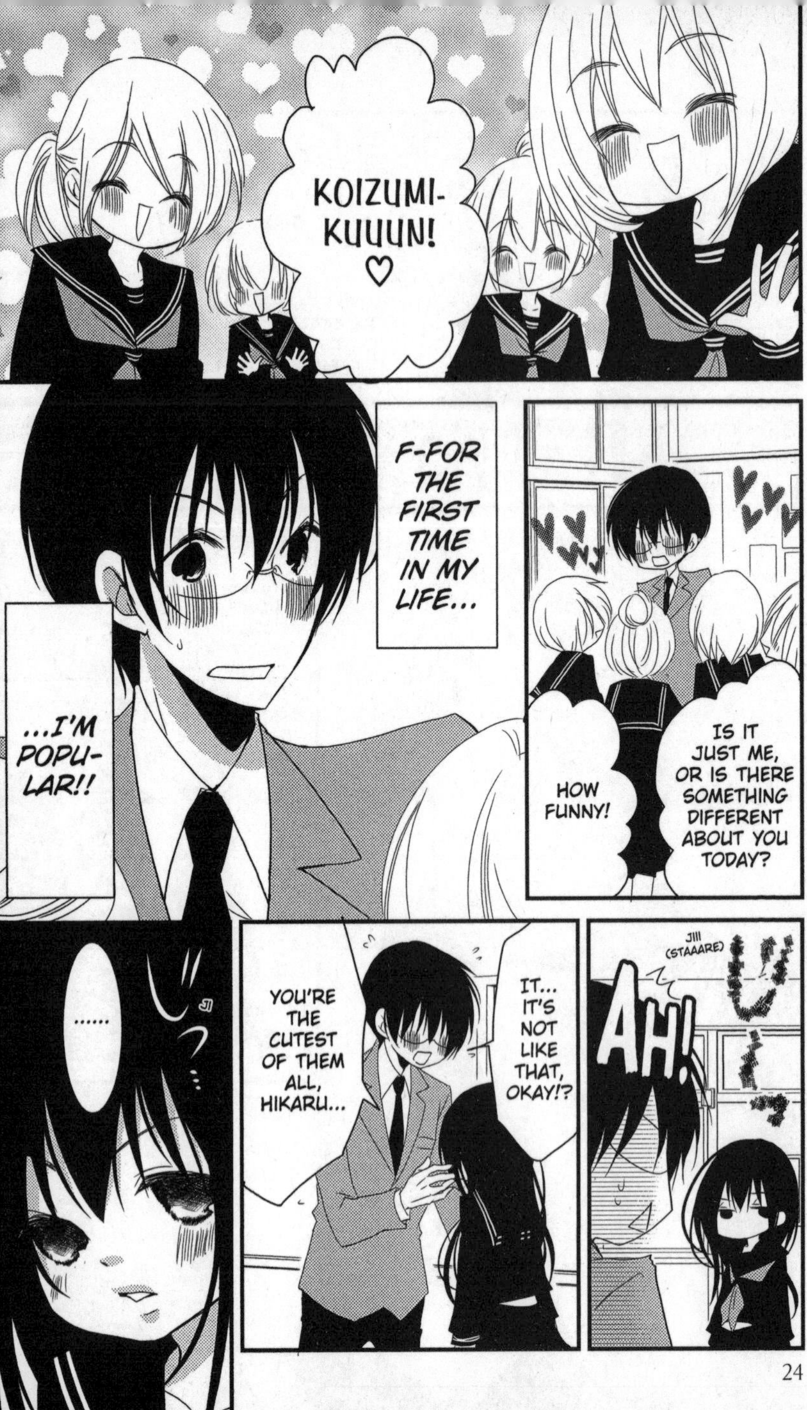
KOIZUMI-KUUUN! ♡
IS IT JUST ME, OR IS THERE SOMETHING DIFFERENT ABOUT YOU TODAY?
HOW FUNNY!
F-FOR THE FIRST TIME IN MY LIFE...
...I'M POPU-LAR!!
JIII (STAAARE)
AH!
IT... IT'S NOT LIKE THAT, OKAY!?
YOU'RE THE CUTEST OF THEM ALL, HIKARU...
......

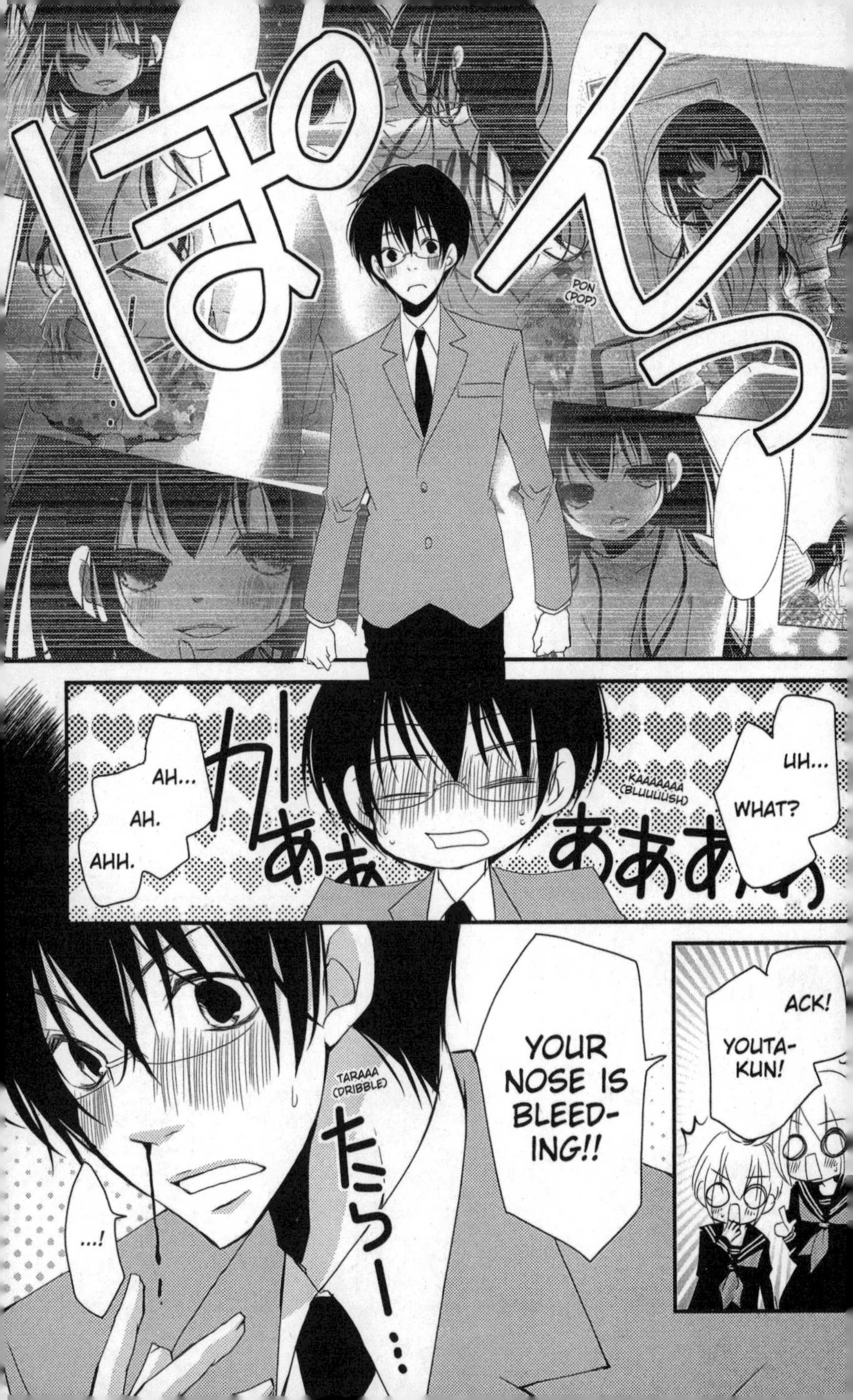
ぽんっ
PON (POP)
UH... WHAT?
KAAAAAAA (BLUUUUSH)
AH... AH. AHH.
ACK! YOUTA-KUN!
YOUR NOSE IS BLEED-ING!!
TARAAA (DRIBBLE)
たらー…
...!

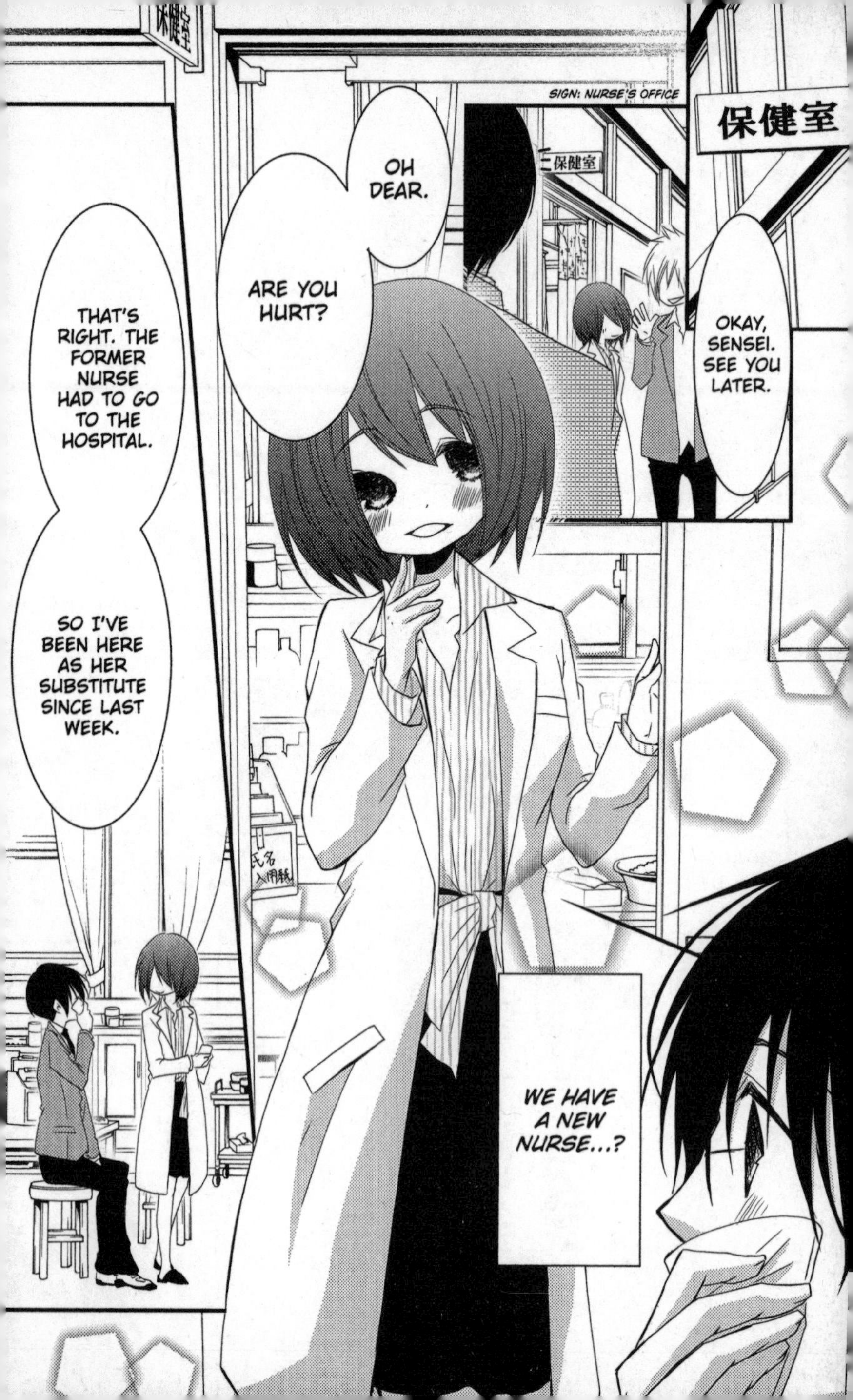

SIGN: NURSE'S OFFICE
保健室
OKAY, SENSEI. SEE YOU LATER.
OH DEAR.
ARE YOU HURT?
WE HAVE A NEW NURSE...?
THAT'S RIGHT. THE FORMER NURSE HAD TO GO TO THE HOSPITAL.
SO I'VE BEEN HERE AS HER SUBSTITUTE SINCE LAST WEEK.

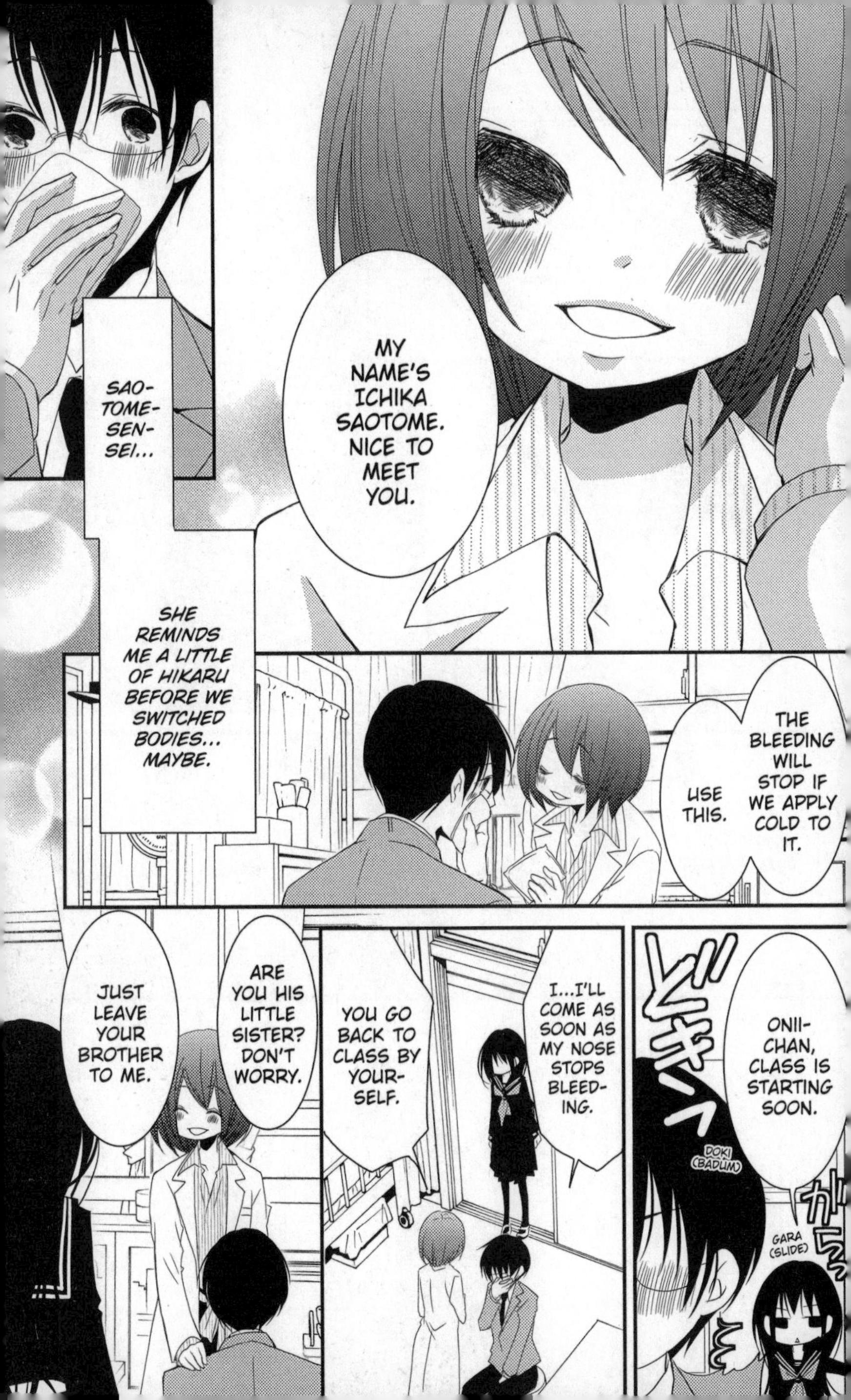
MY NAME'S ICHIKA SAOTOME. NICE TO MEET YOU.
SAO-TOME-SEN-SEI...
SHE REMINDS ME A LITTLE OF HIKARU BEFORE WE SWITCHED BODIES... MAYBE.
THE BLEEDING WILL STOP IF WE APPLY COLD TO IT.
USE THIS.
ONII-CHAN, CLASS IS STARTING SOON.
DOKI (BADUM)
GARA (SLIDE)
I...I'LL COME AS SOON AS MY NOSE STOPS BLEEDING.
YOU GO BACK TO CLASS BY YOURSELF.
ARE YOU HIS LITTLE SISTER? DON'T WORRY.
JUST LEAVE YOUR BROTHER TO ME.

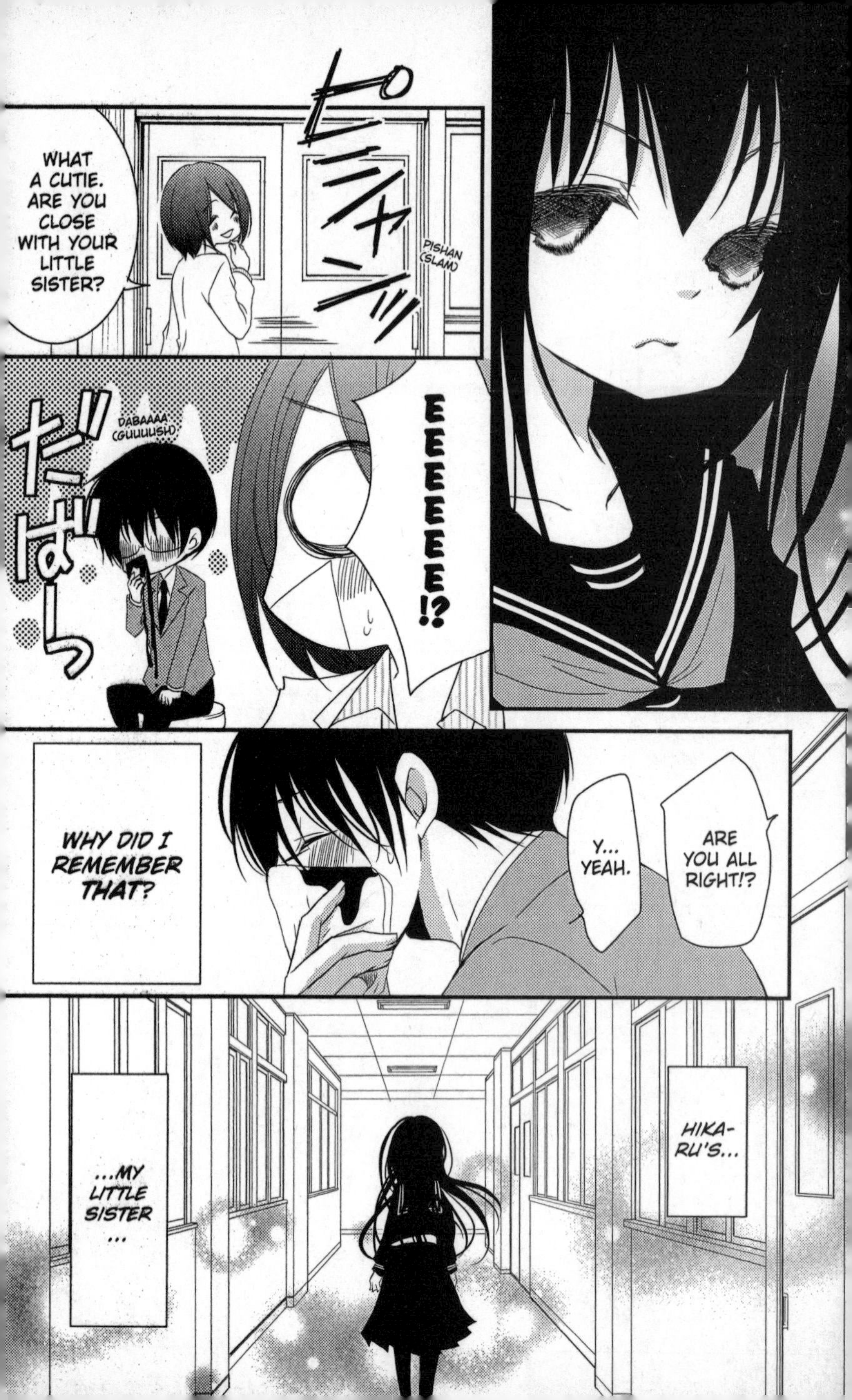
PISHAN (SLAM)
WHAT A CUTIE. ARE YOU CLOSE WITH YOUR LITTLE SISTER?
EEEEEEE!?
DABAAAA (GUUUUSH)
ARE YOU ALL RIGHT!?
Y... YEAH.
WHY DID I REMEMBER THAT?
HIKA-RU'S...
...MY LITTLE SISTER...

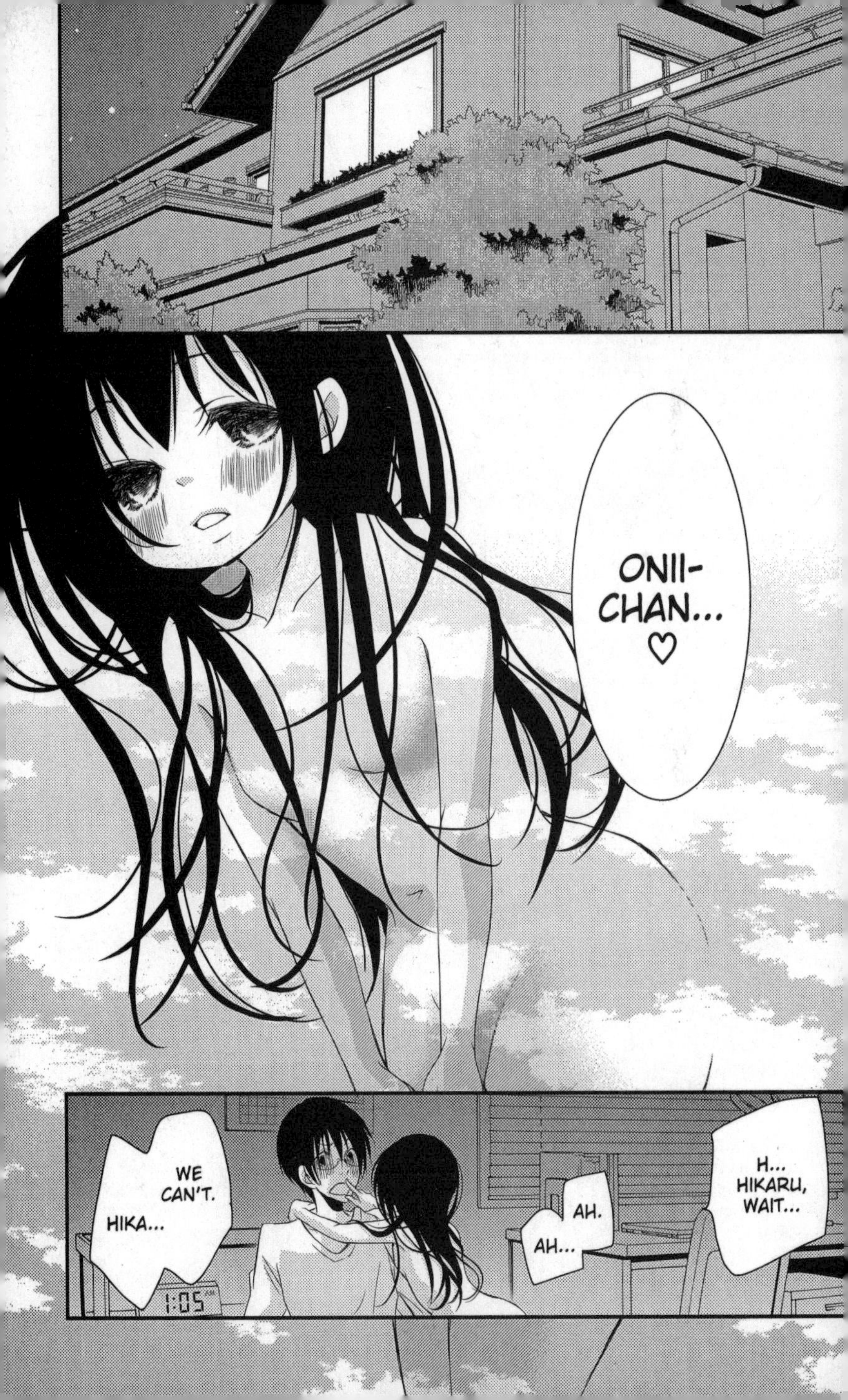
ONII-CHAN... ♡
H... HIKARU, WAIT...
AH. AH...
WE CAN'T. HIKA...
1:05

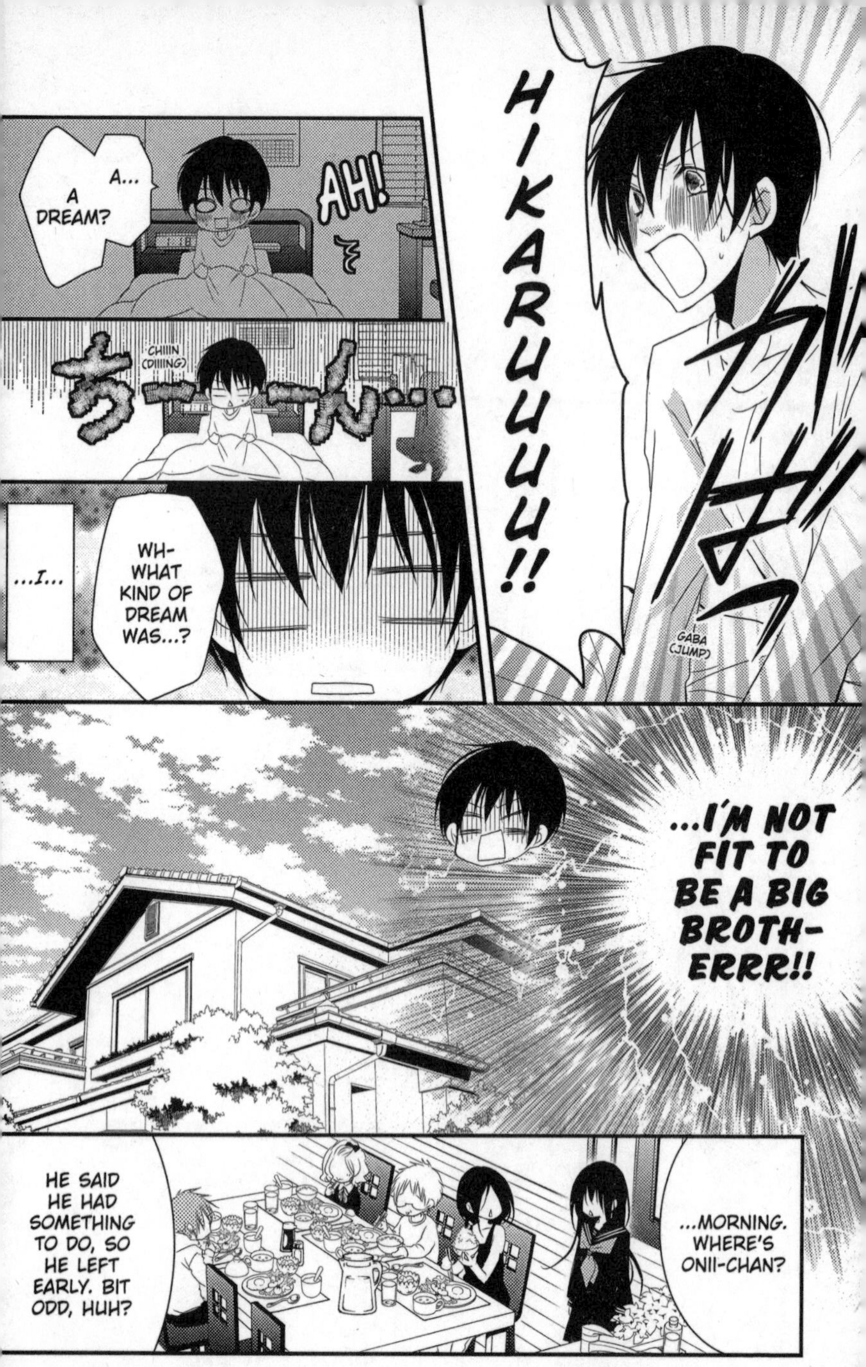
HIKARUUUUU!!
GABA (JUMP)
AH!
A... A DREAM?
CHIIIN (DIIIING)
WH- WHAT KIND OF DREAM WAS...?
...I...
...I'M NOT FIT TO BE A BIG BROTH- ERRR!!
...MORNING. WHERE'S ONII-CHAN?
HE SAID HE HAD SOMETHING TO DO, SO HE LEFT EARLY. BIT ODD, HUH?

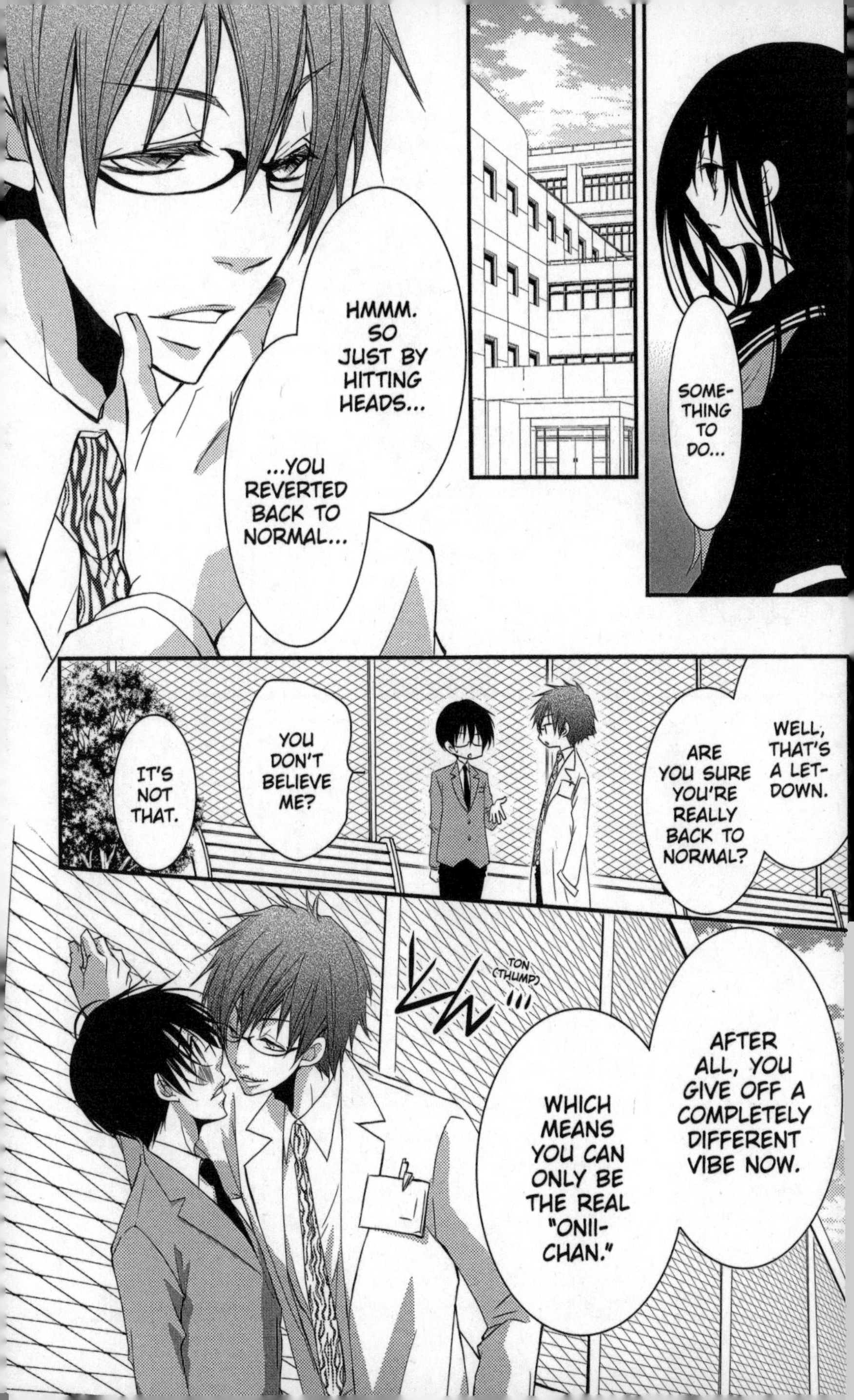
SOME-THING TO DO...
HMMM. SO JUST BY HITTING HEADS...
...YOU REVERTED BACK TO NORMAL...
WELL, THAT'S A LET-DOWN.
ARE YOU SURE YOU'RE REALLY BACK TO NORMAL?
YOU DON'T BELIEVE ME?
IT'S NOT THAT.
TON (THUMP)
AFTER ALL, YOU GIVE OFF A COMPLETELY DIFFERENT VIBE NOW.
WHICH MEANS YOU CAN ONLY BE THE REAL "ONII-CHAN."

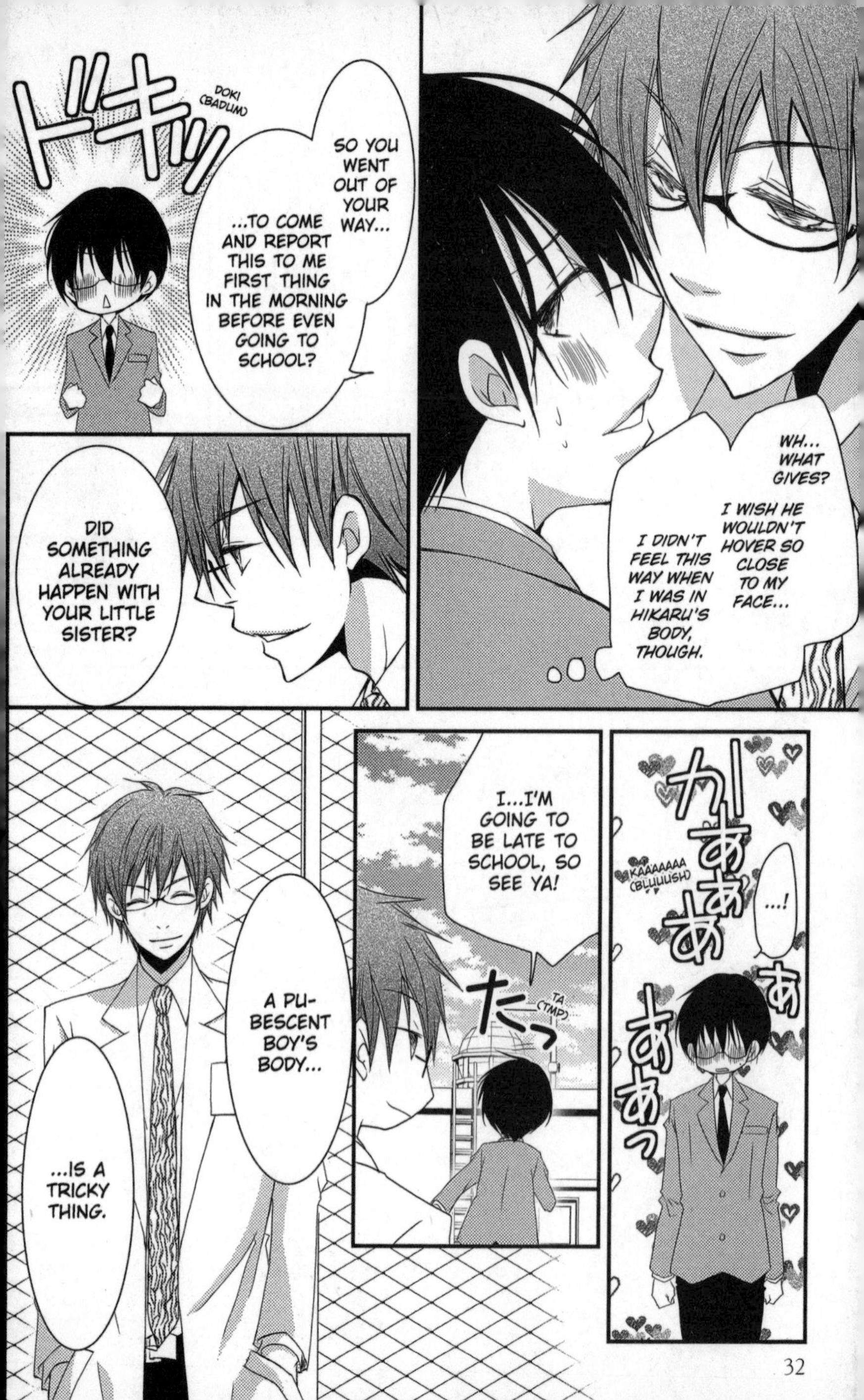
WH... WHAT GIVES?
I WISH HE WOULDN'T HOVER SO CLOSE TO MY FACE...
I DIDN'T FEEL THIS WAY WHEN I WAS IN HIKARU'S BODY, THOUGH.
ドキッ
DOKI (BADUM)
SO YOU WENT OUT OF YOUR WAY...
...TO COME AND REPORT THIS TO ME FIRST THING IN THE MORNING BEFORE EVEN GOING TO SCHOOL?
DID SOMETHING ALREADY HAPPEN WITH YOUR LITTLE SISTER?
かぁぁぁぁあああっ
KAAAAAAA (BLUUUSH)
...!
I...I'M GOING TO BE LATE TO SCHOOL, SO SEE YA!
たっ
TA (TMP)
A PU-BESCENT BOY'S BODY...
...IS A TRICKY THING.

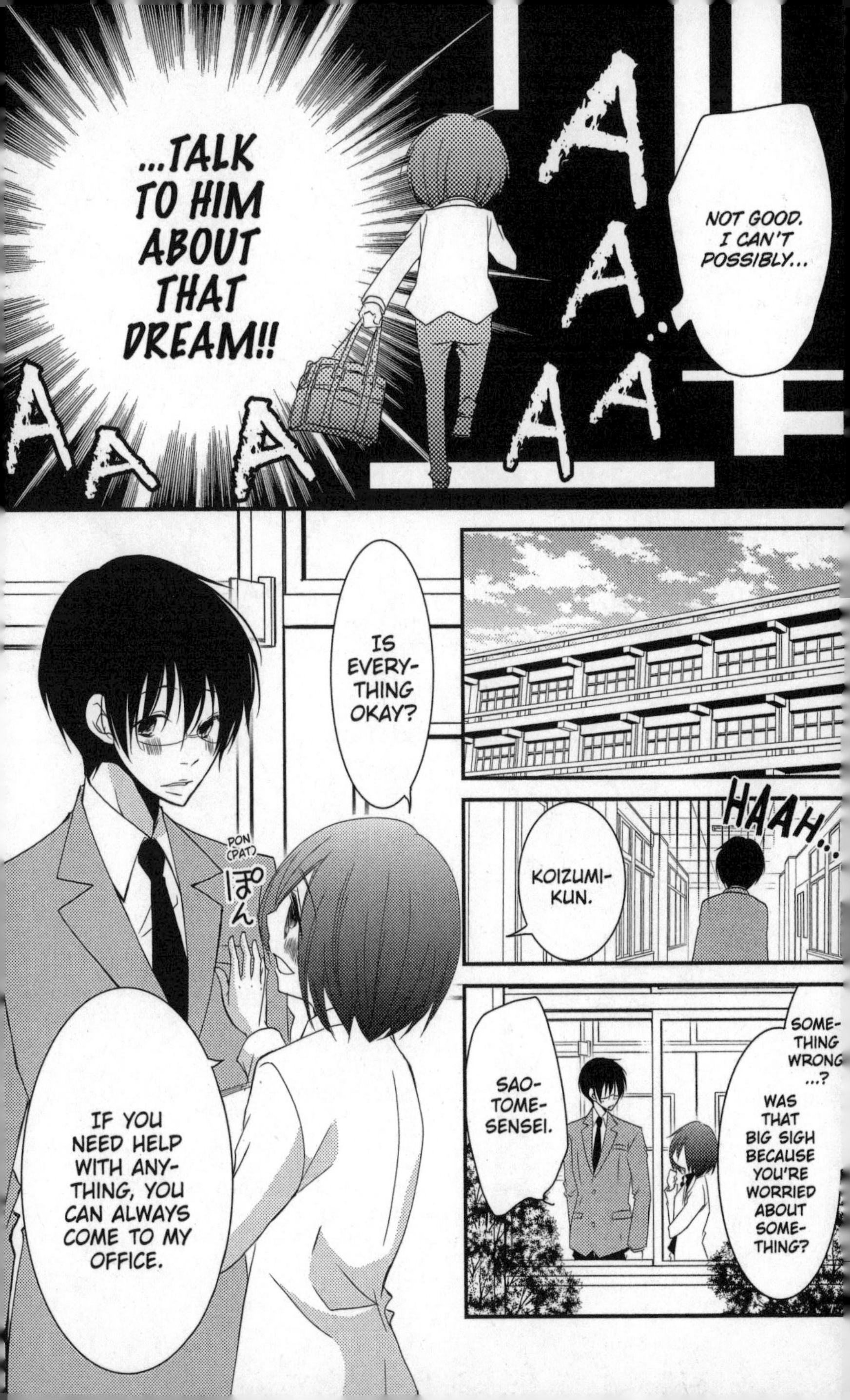
NOT GOOD. I CAN'T POSSIBLY...
AAAAAA
...TALK TO HIM ABOUT THAT DREAM!!
HAAAH..
KOIZUMI-KUN.
SOMETHING WRONG...?
WAS THAT BIG SIGH BECAUSE YOU'RE WORRIED ABOUT SOMETHING?
SAOTOME-SENSEI.
IS EVERYTHING OKAY?
PON (PAT)
ぽん
IF YOU NEED HELP WITH ANYTHING, YOU CAN ALWAYS COME TO MY OFFICE.

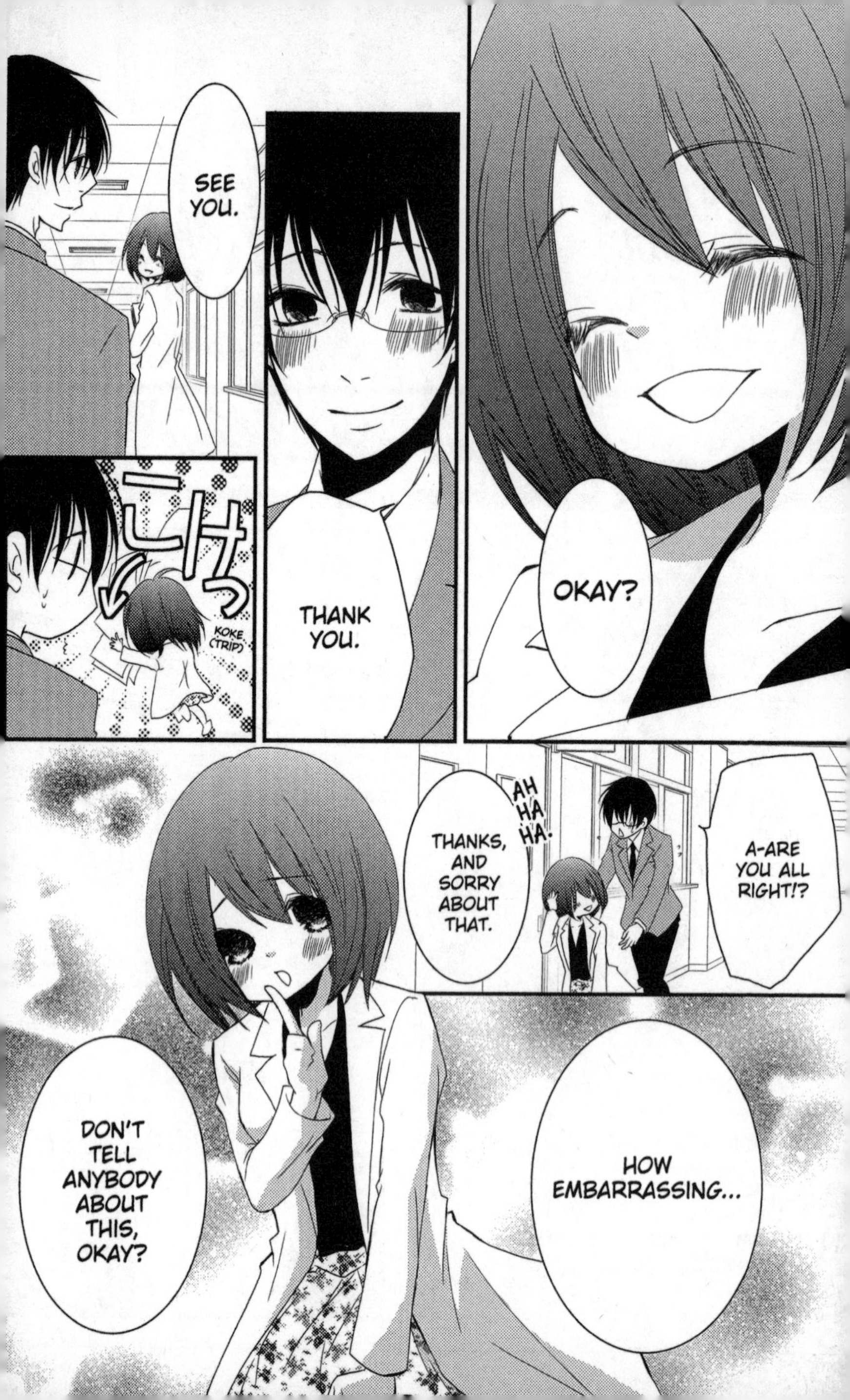
OKAY?
THANK YOU.
SEE YOU.
こけっ
KOKE (TRIP)
A-ARE YOU ALL RIGHT!?
AH HA HA.
THANKS, AND SORRY ABOUT THAT.
HOW EMBARRASSING...
DON'T TELL ANYBODY ABOUT THIS, OKAY?

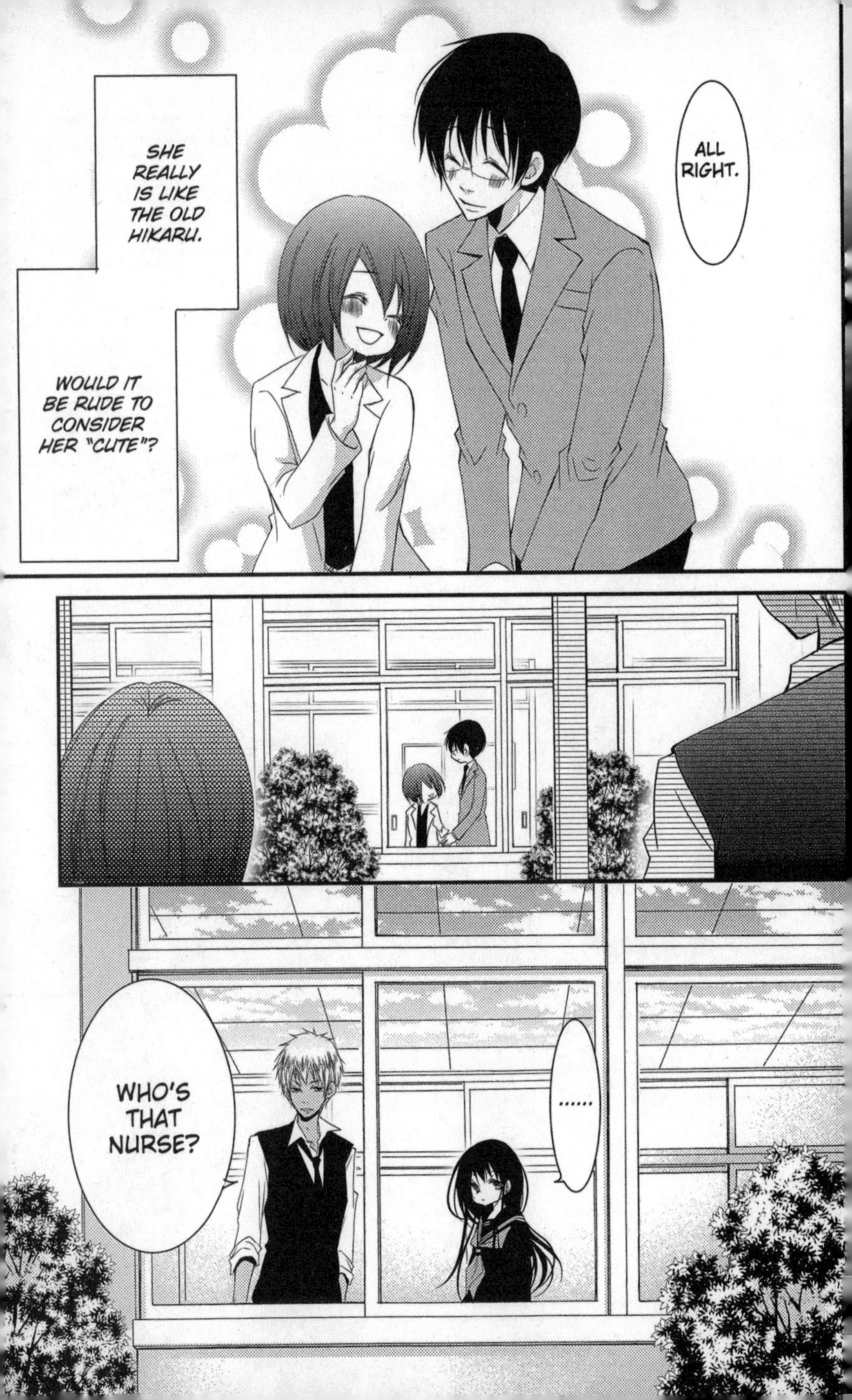
ALL RIGHT.
SHE REALLY IS LIKE THE OLD HIKARU.
WOULD IT BE RUDE TO CONSIDER HER "CUTE"?
......
WHO'S THAT NURSE?

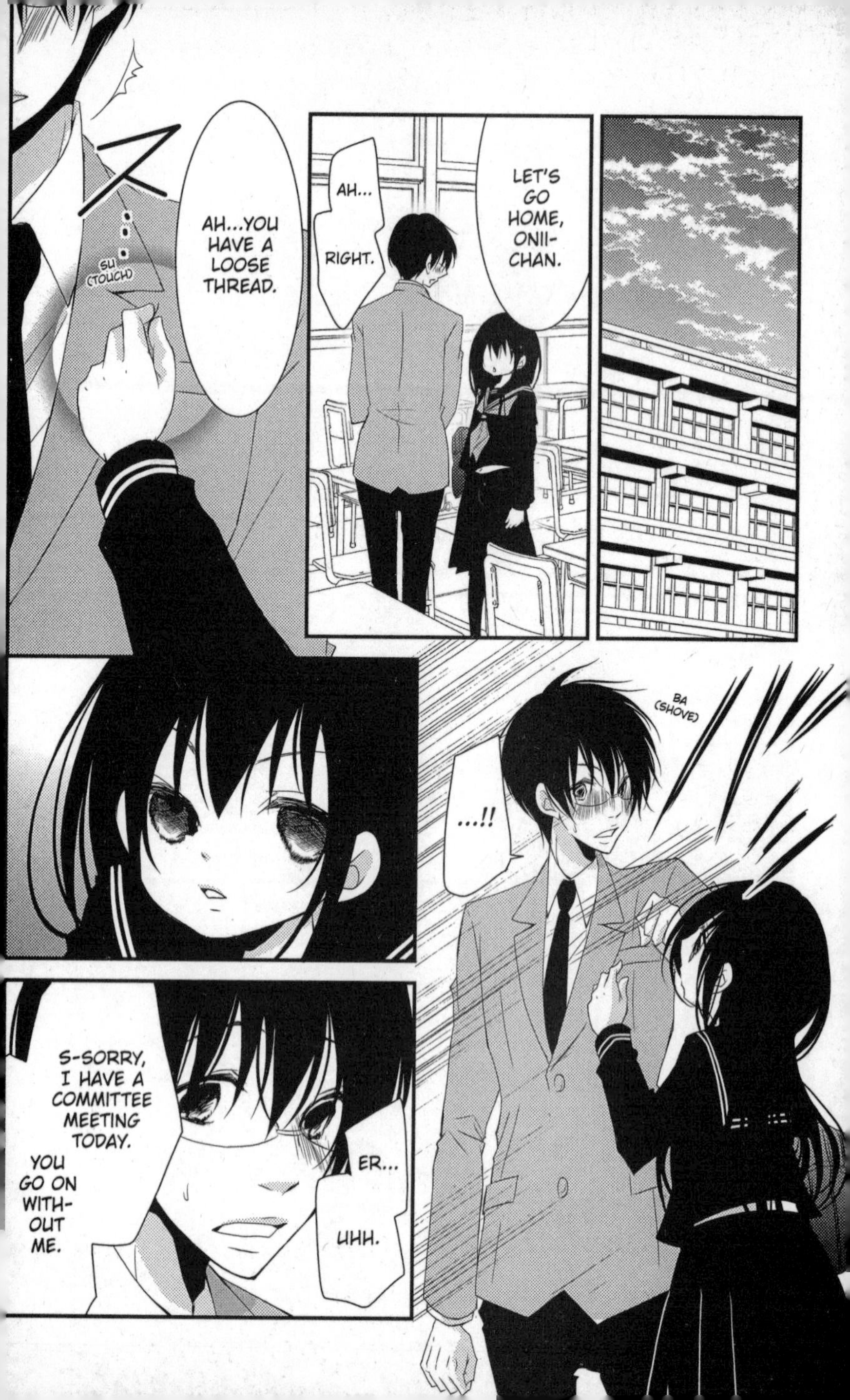
LET'S GO HOME, ONII-CHAN.
AH...
RIGHT.
AH...YOU HAVE A LOOSE THREAD.
SU (TOUCH)
BA (SHOVE)
...!!
ER...
UHH.
S-SORRY, I HAVE A COMMITTEE MEETING TODAY.
YOU GO ON WITH-OUT ME.

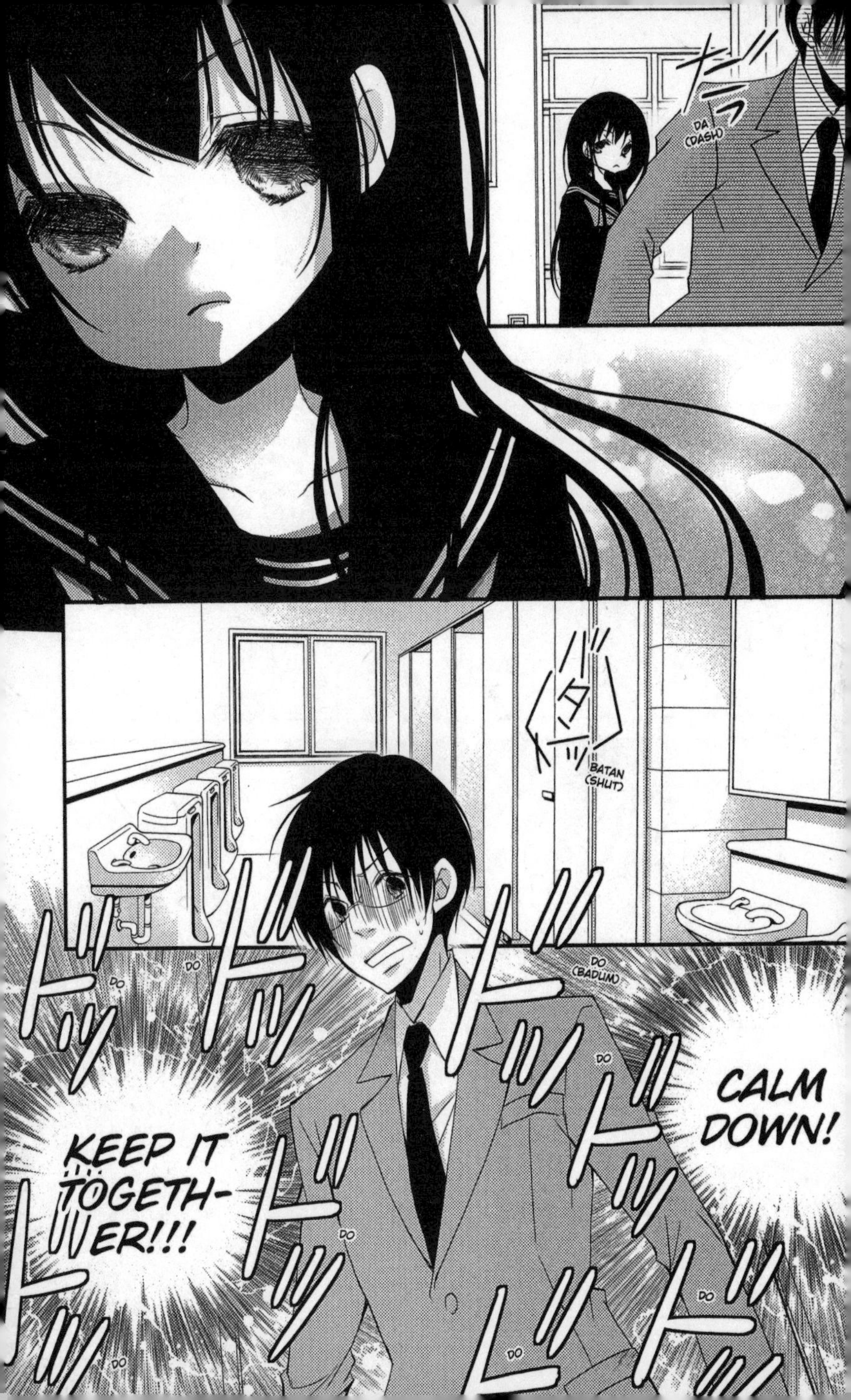

DA (DASH)
BATAN (SHUT)
DO (BADUM)
DO
DO
CALM DOWN!
KEEP IT TOGETH-ER!!!
DO
DO
DO
DO

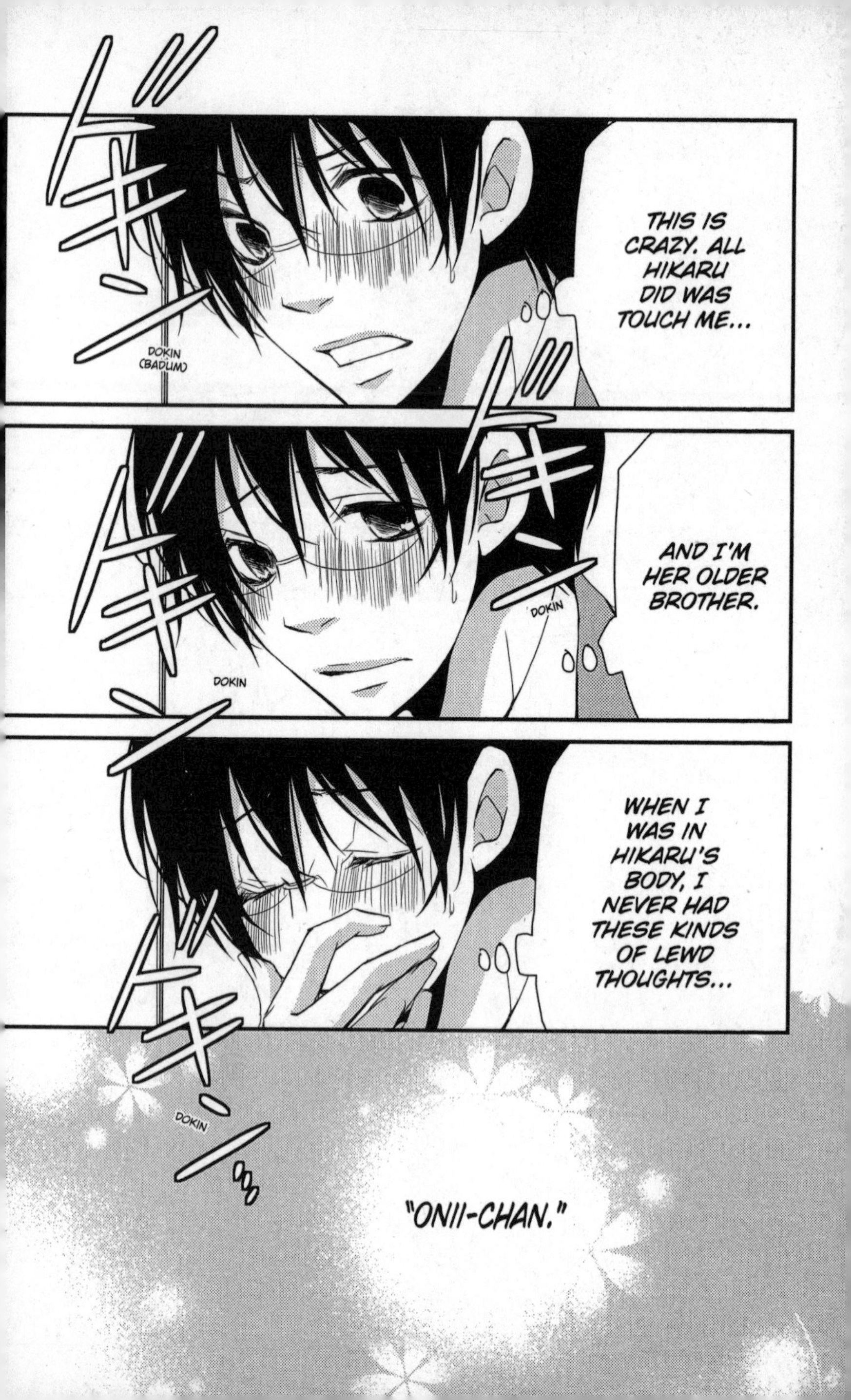
THIS IS CRAZY. ALL HIKARU DID WAS TOUCH ME...
DOKIN (BADUM)
AND I'M HER OLDER BROTHER.
DOKIN
DOKIN
WHEN I WAS IN HIKARU'S BODY, I NEVER HAD THESE KINDS OF LEWD THOUGHTS...
DOKIN
"ONII-CHAN."

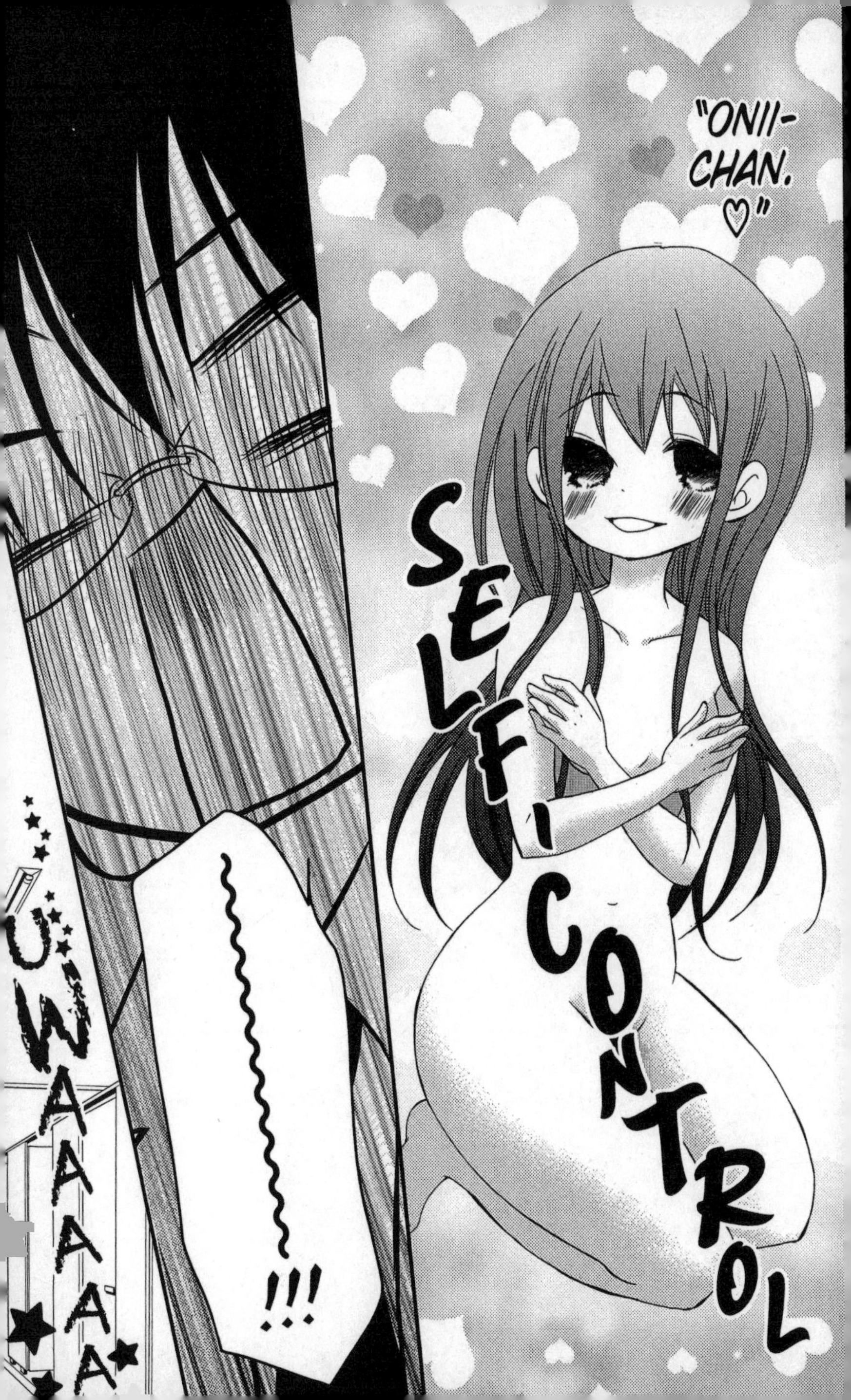
"ONII-CHAN. ♡"
SELF-CONTROL
——!!!
UWAAAAA

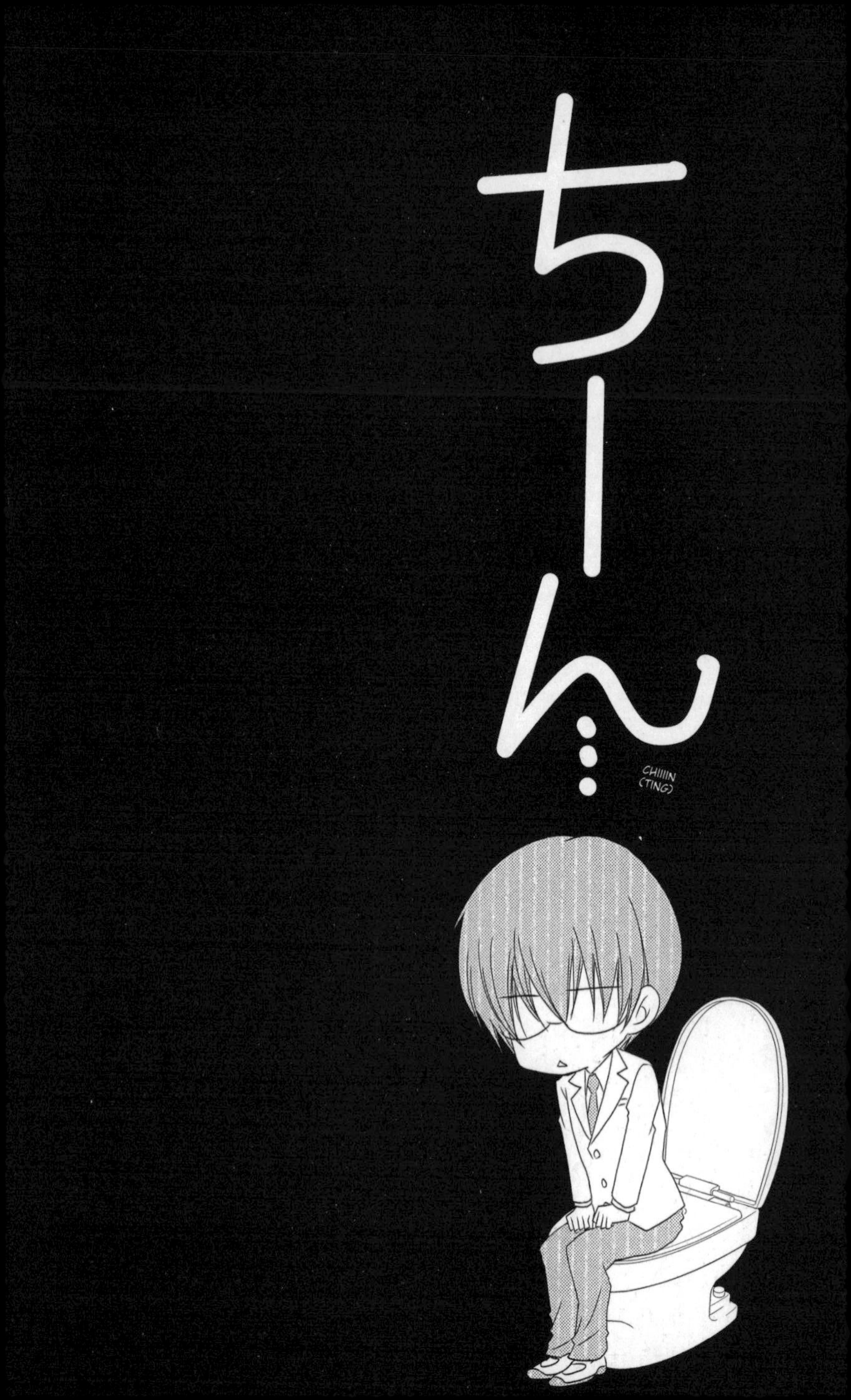
ちーん…
CHIIIIN (TING)

IT WAS
THE FIRST
TIME I'D
EVER
WANTED
TO DIE IN
THE BATH-
ROOM.

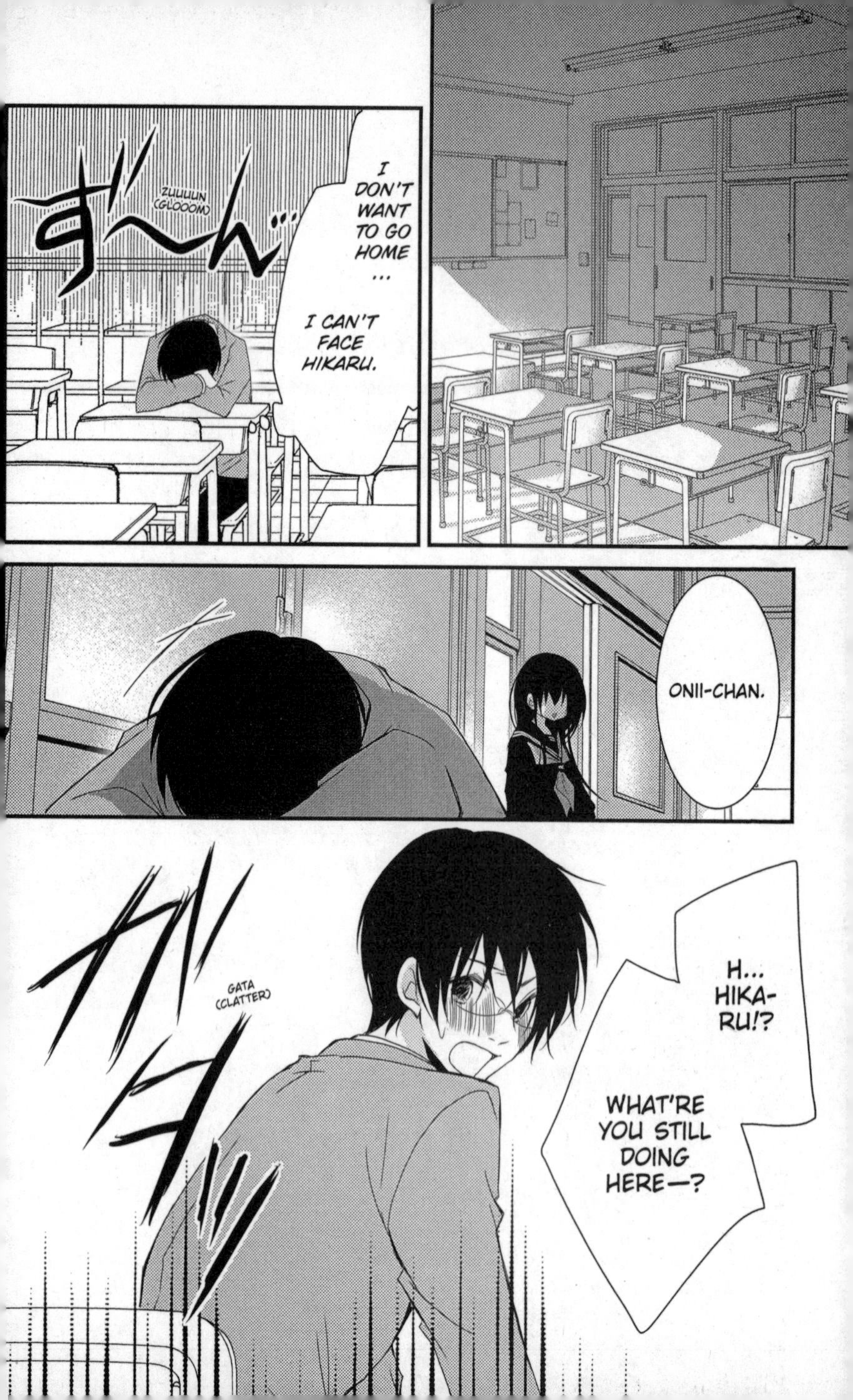
ZUUUUN (GLOOOM)
I DON'T WANT TO GO HOME ...
I CAN'T FACE HIKARU.
ONII-CHAN.
GATA (CLATTER)
H... HIKA-RU!?
WHAT'RE YOU STILL DOING HERE—?

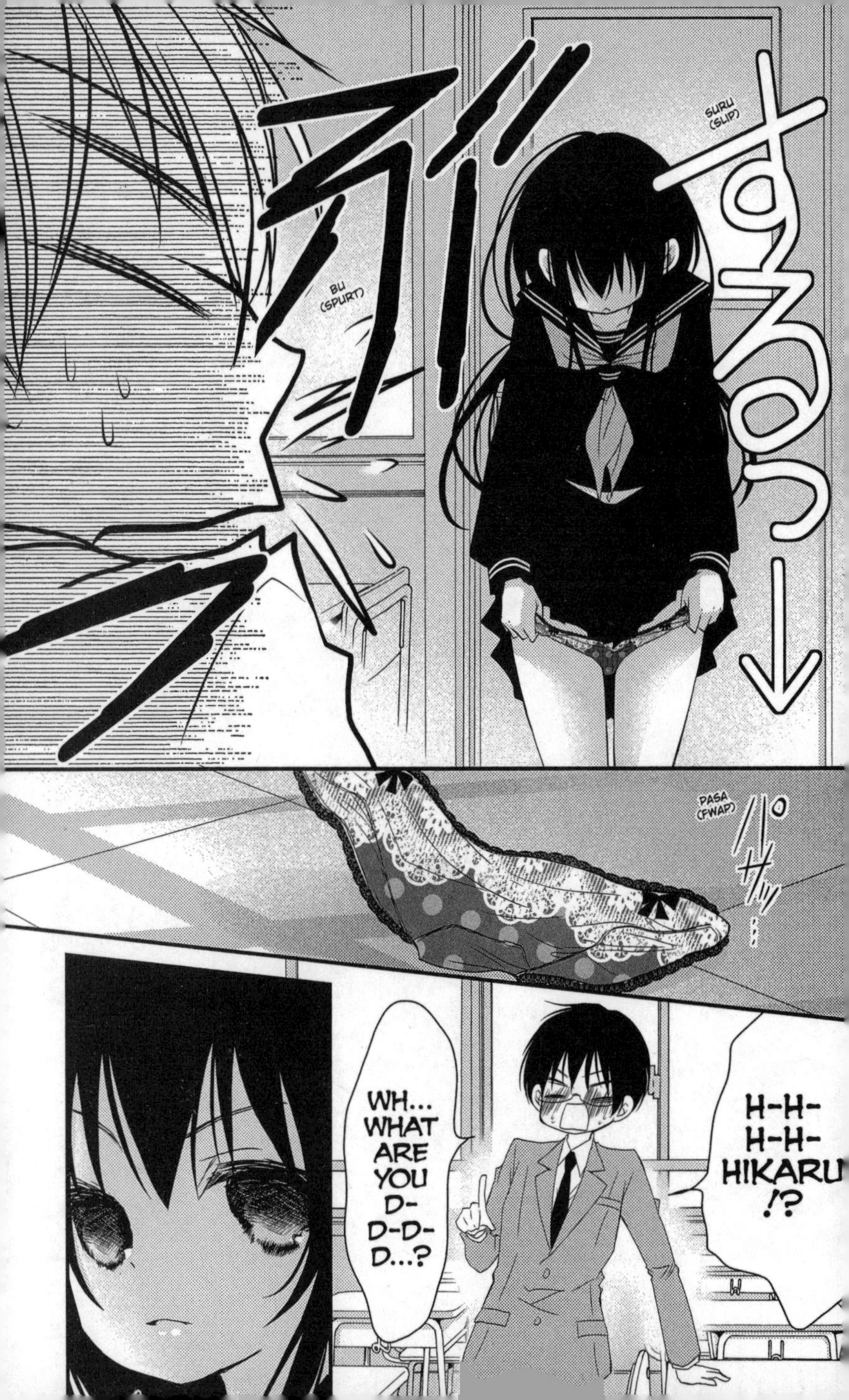
SURU (SLIP)
BU (SPURT)
PASA (FWAP)
H-H-H-H-HIKARU!?
WH... WHAT ARE YOU D-D-D-D...?

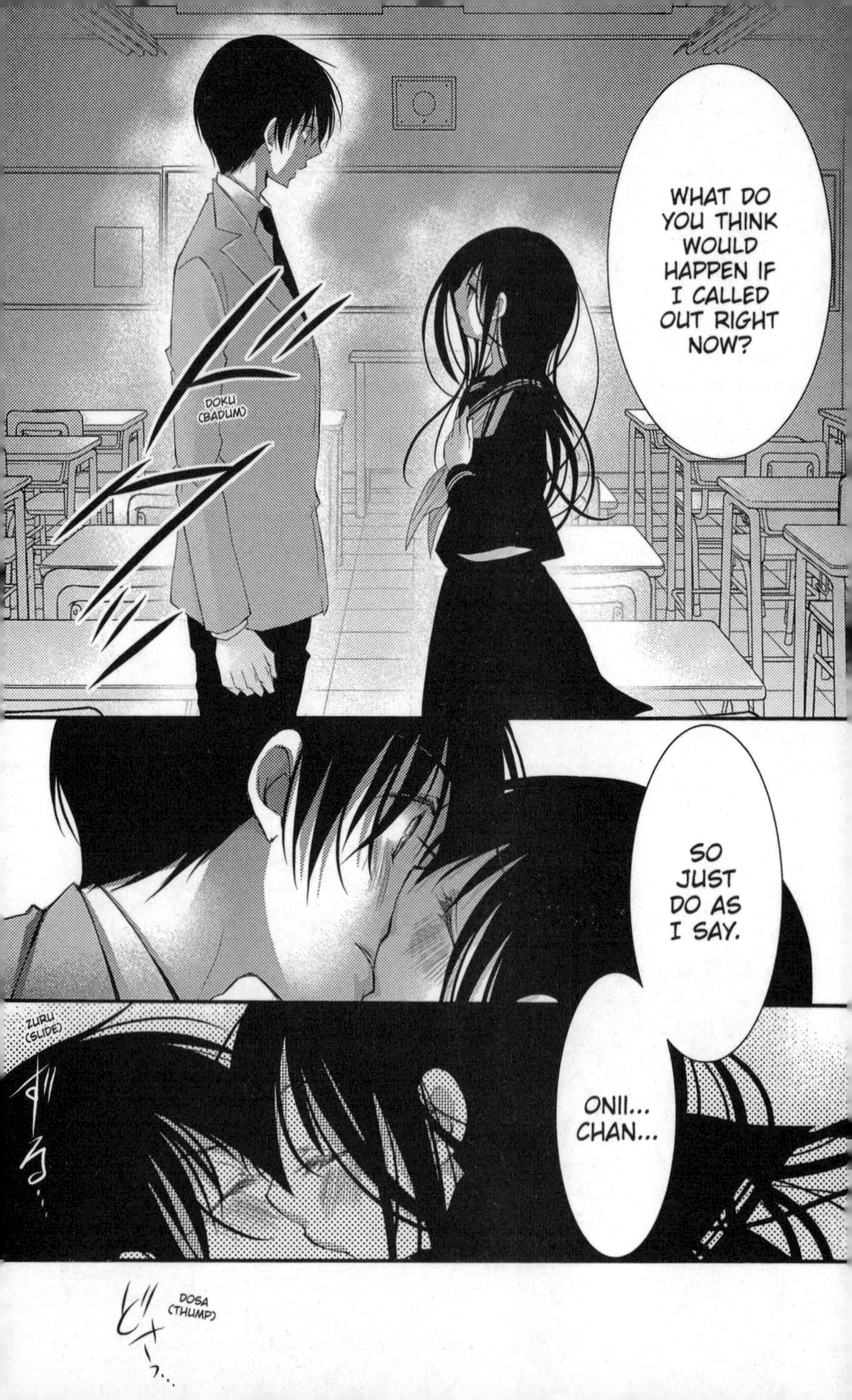
WHAT DO YOU THINK WOULD HAPPEN IF I CALLED OUT RIGHT NOW?
DOKU (BADUM)
SO JUST DO AS I SAY.
ONII... CHAN...
ZURU (SLIDE)
DOSA (THUMP)

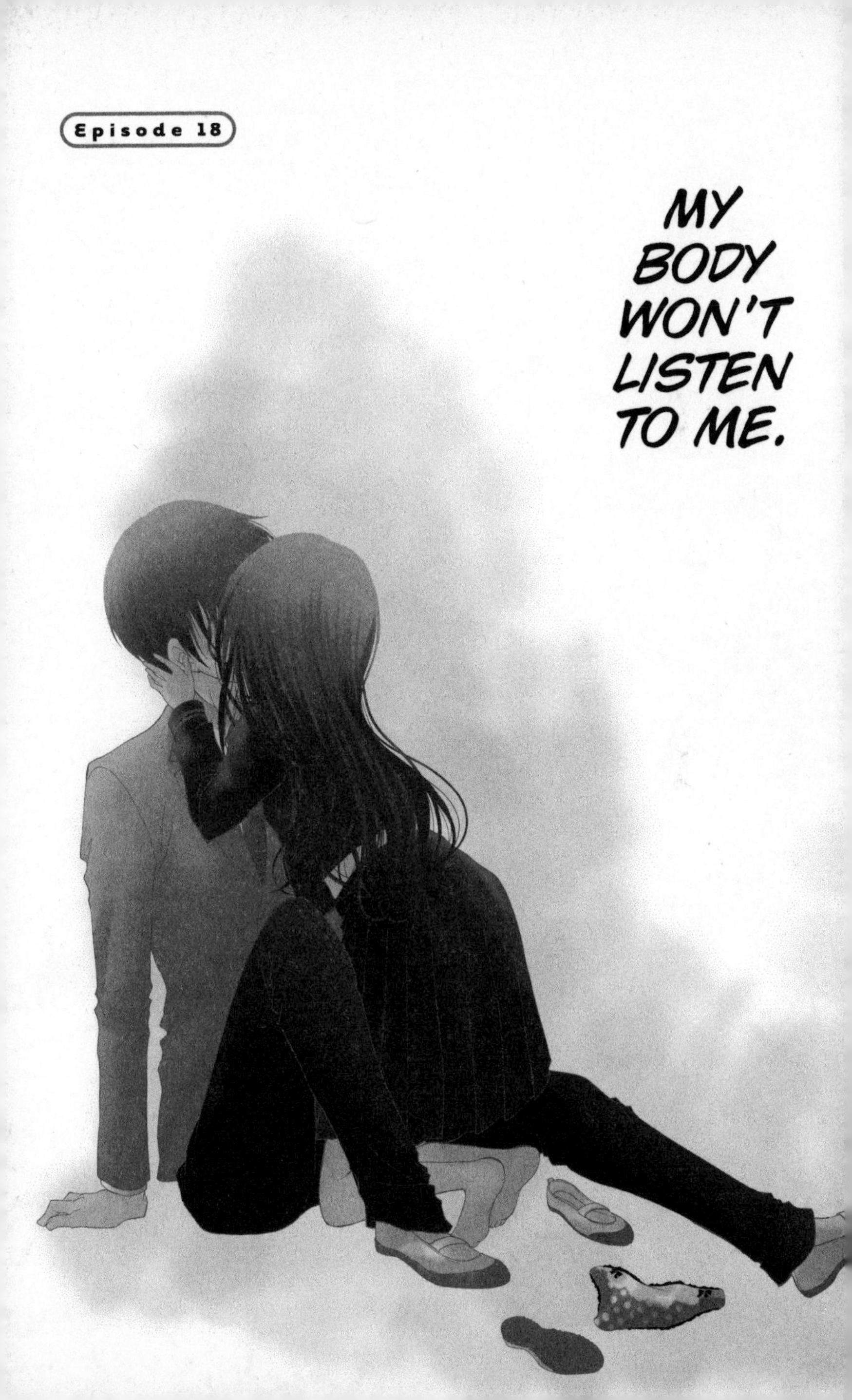
Episode 18
MY BODY WON'T LISTEN TO ME.

Episode 18

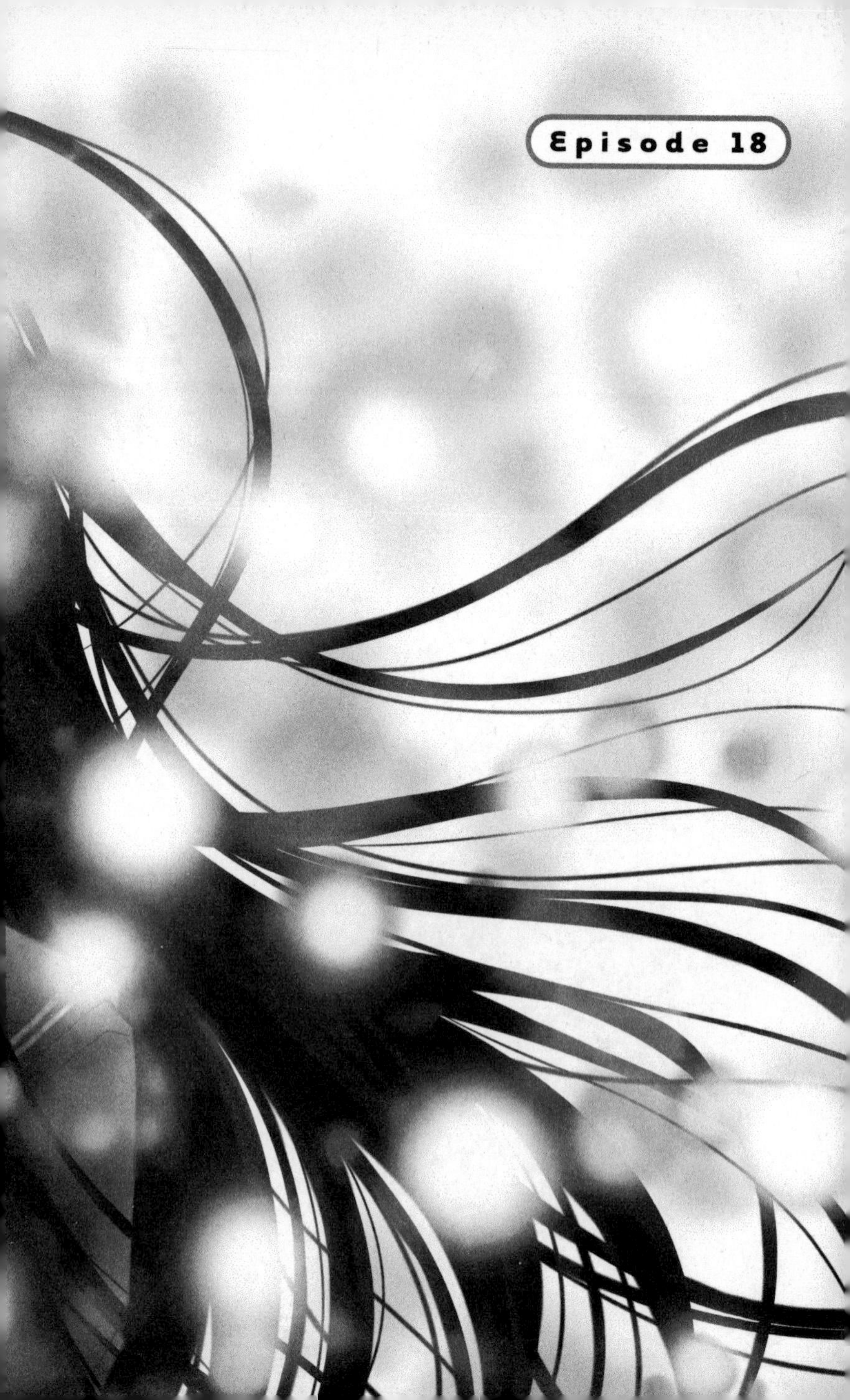

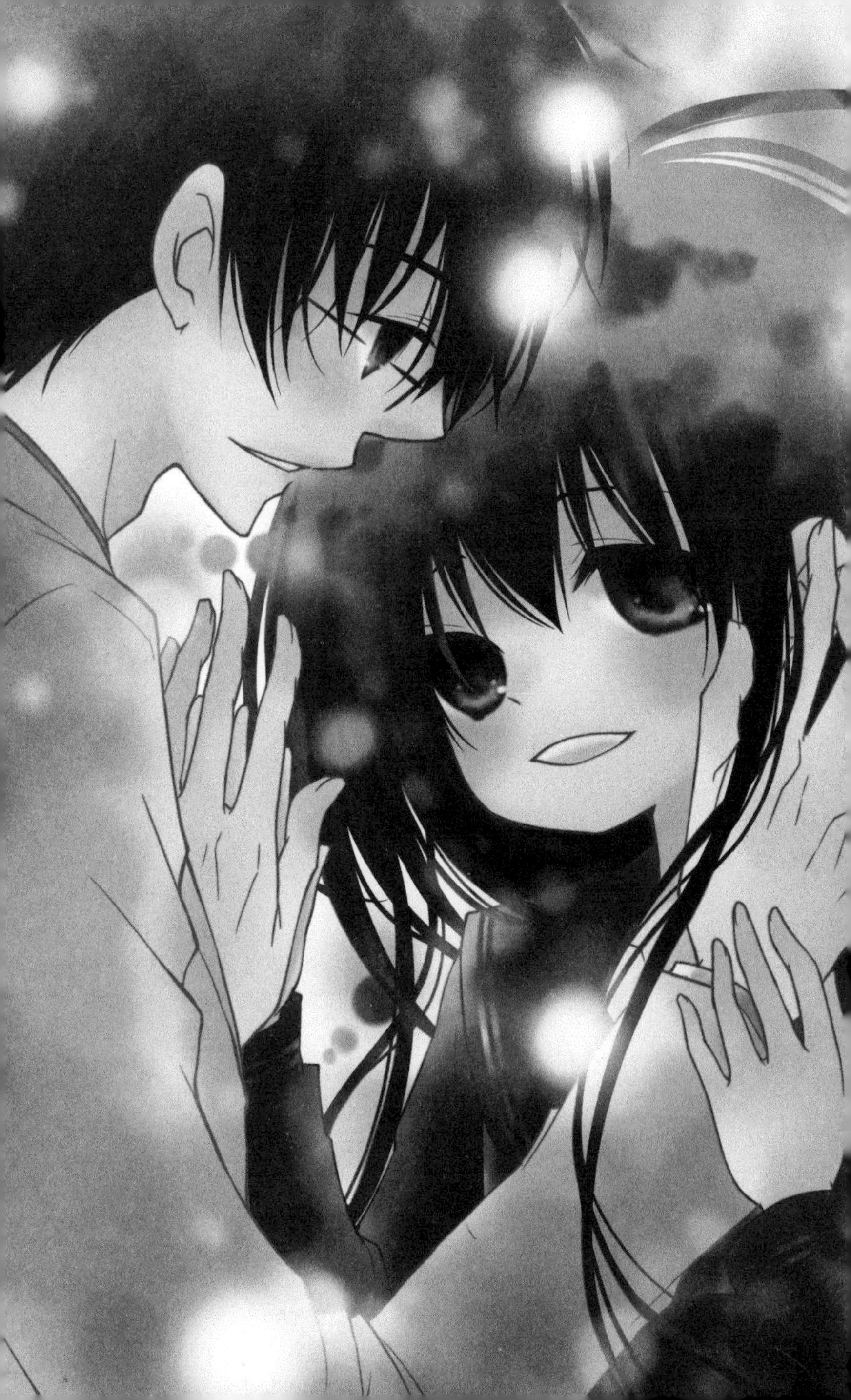

[Ani-Imo]

Big Brother becomes Little Sister;
Little Sister becomes Big Brother.

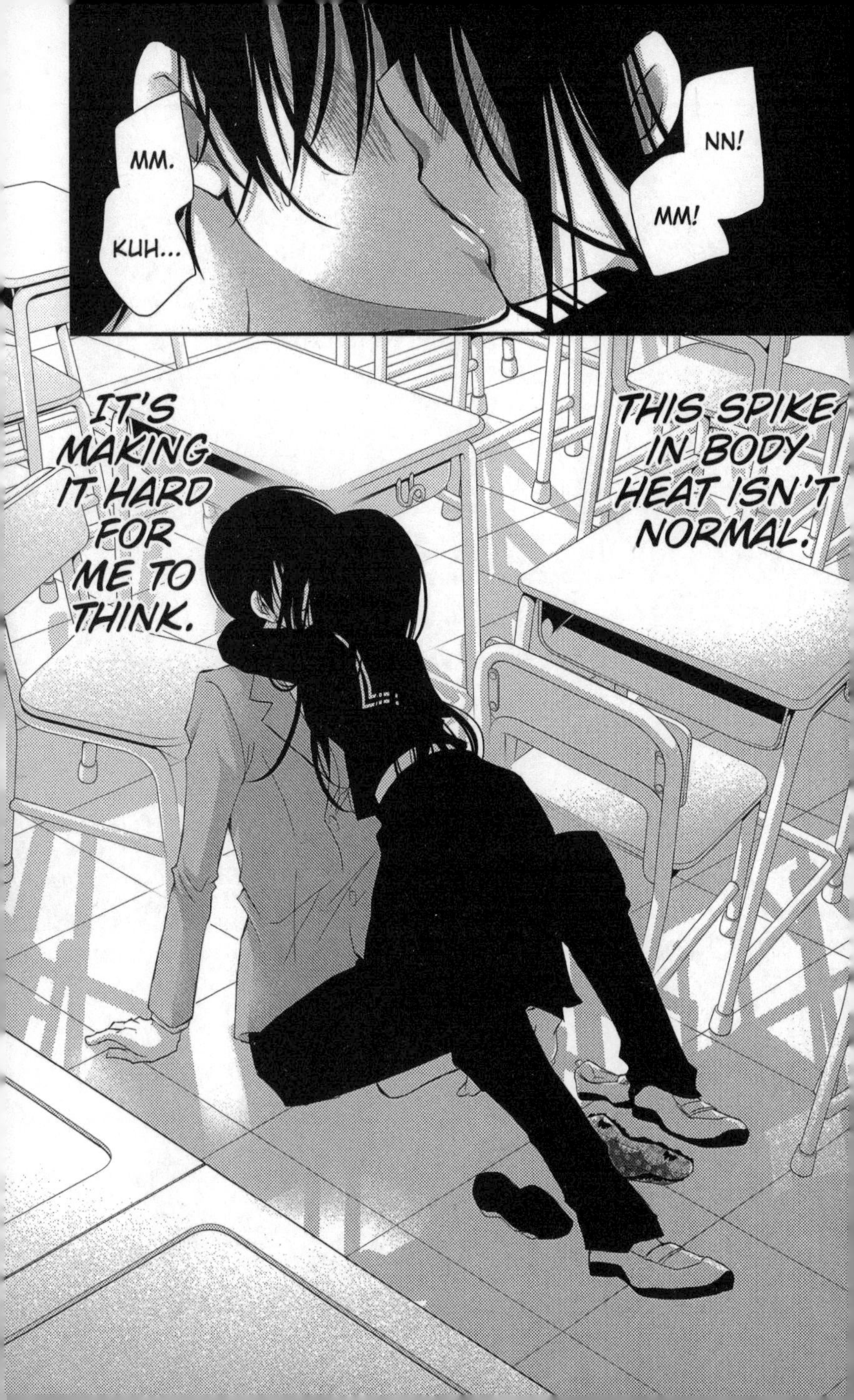
NN!
MM!
MM.
KUH...
THIS SPIKE IN BODY HEAT ISN'T NORMAL.
IT'S MAKING IT HARD FOR ME TO THINK.

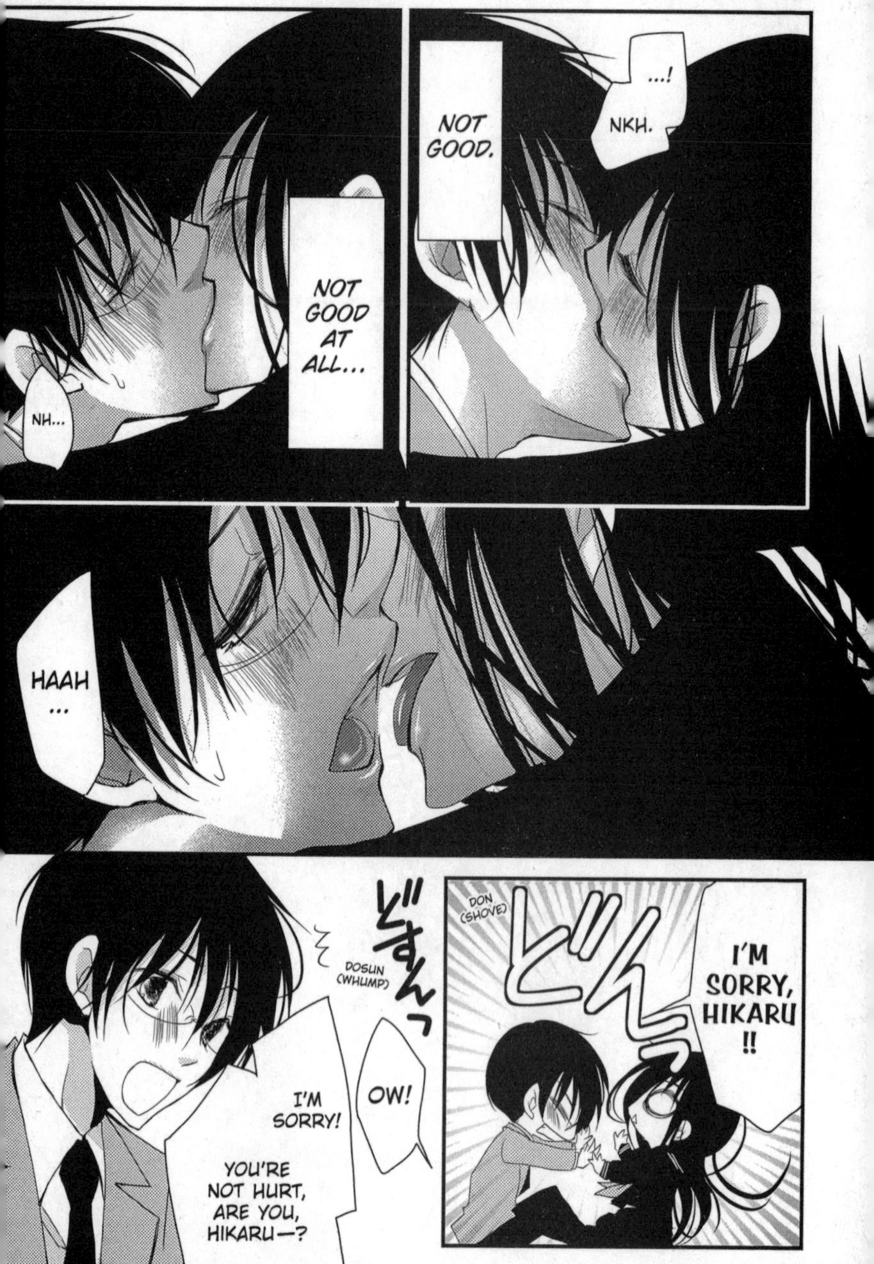
...! NKH.
NOT GOOD.
NOT GOOD AT ALL...
NH...
HAAH ...
どんっ
DON (SHOVE)
I'M SORRY, HIKARU !!
どすんっ
DOSUN (WHUMP)
OW!
I'M SORRY!
YOU'RE NOT HURT, ARE YOU, HIKARU—?

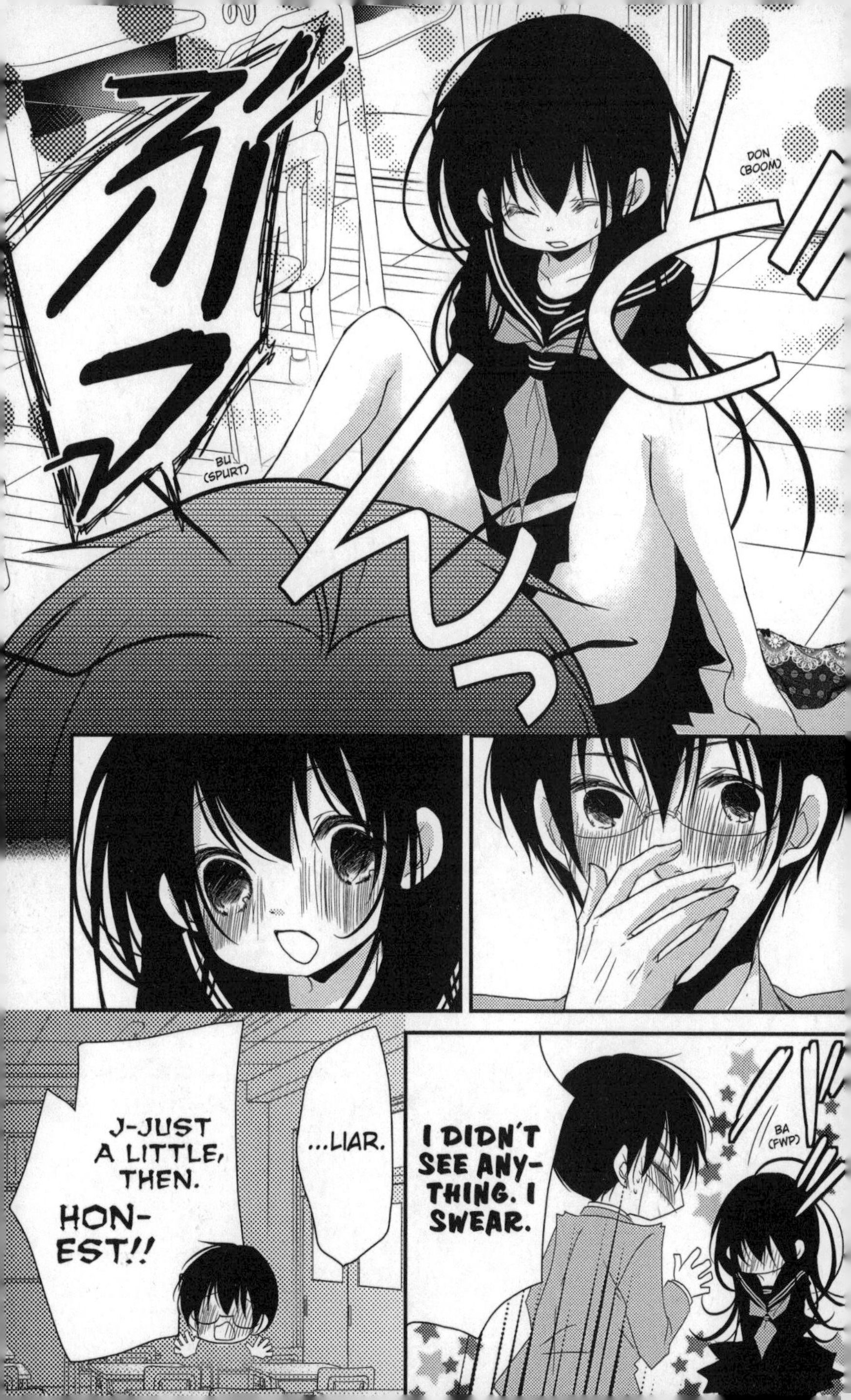
DON (BOOM)
BU (SPURT)
BA (FWP)
I DIDN'T SEE ANY-THING. I SWEAR.
...LIAR.
J-JUST A LITTLE, THEN.
HON-EST!!

YOU SAW...
...A LITTLE, DIDN'T YOU...?
...UH.
HUH?
EVEN THOUGH SHE'S BEEN THE AGGRESSOR THIS WHOLE TIME...
...AND FORCED ME TO SEE HER NAKED...
...HOW COME...
...HER CHEEKS ARE SO RED NOW...?
DOKIN (BADUM)

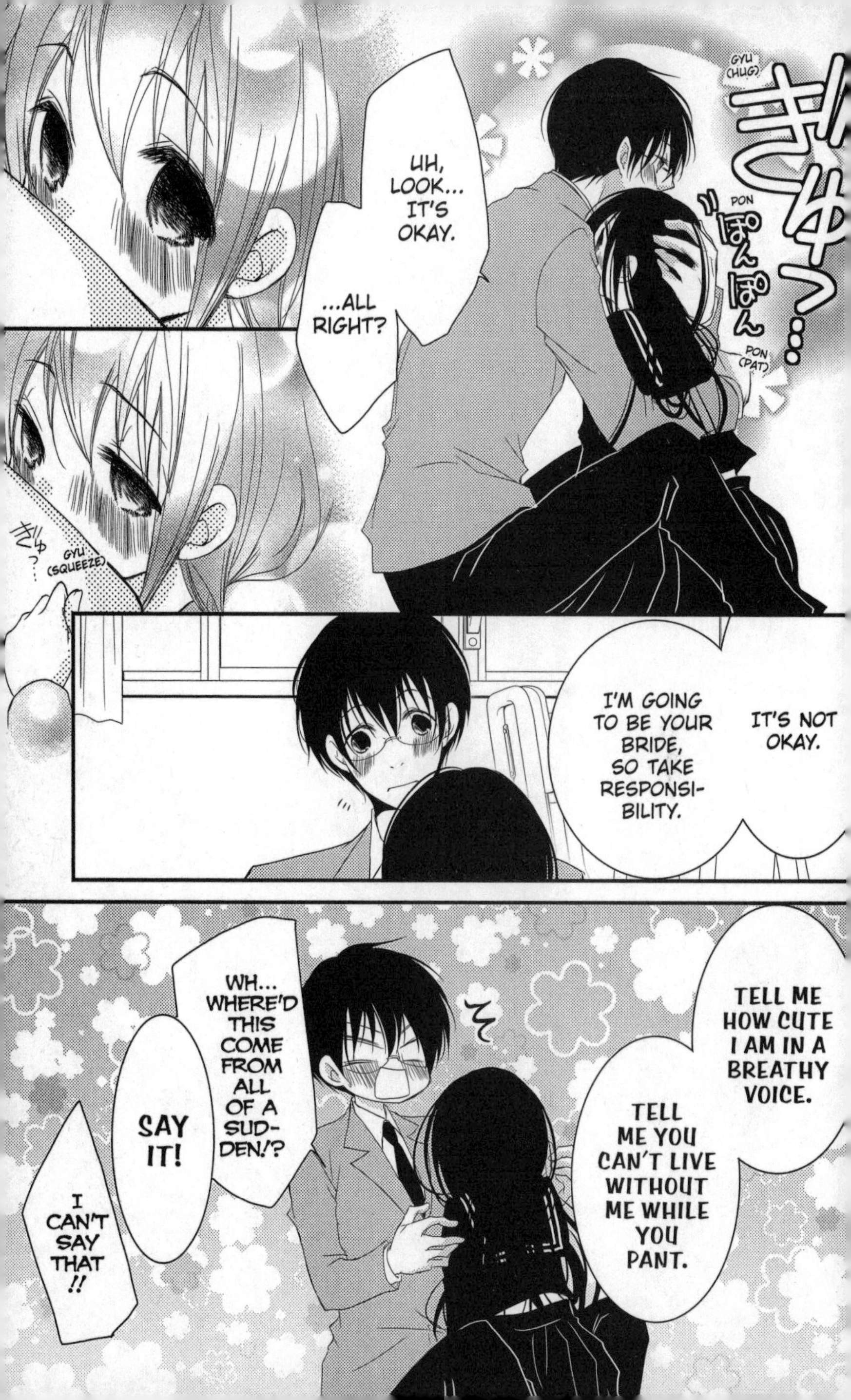
きゅっ…
GYU (HUG)
ぽんぽん
PON PON (PAT)
UH, LOOK... IT'S OKAY.
...ALL RIGHT?
きゅっ…
GYU (SQUEEZE)
IT'S NOT OKAY.
I'M GOING TO BE YOUR BRIDE, SO TAKE RESPONSI-BILITY.
TELL ME HOW CUTE I AM IN A BREATHY VOICE.
TELL ME YOU CAN'T LIVE WITHOUT ME WHILE YOU PANT.
WH... WHERE'D THIS COME FROM ALL OF A SUD-DEN!?
SAY IT!
I CAN'T SAY THAT!!

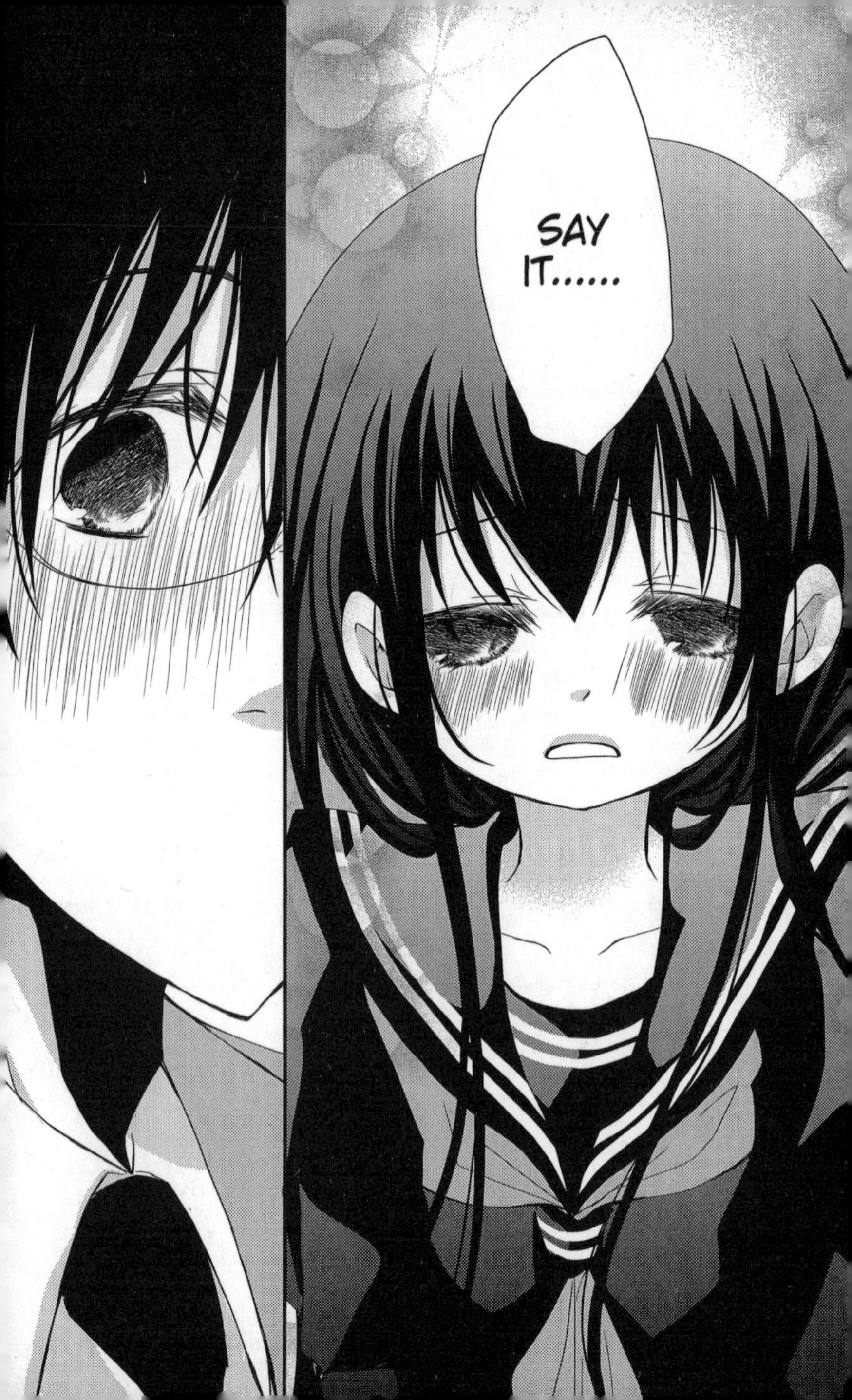
SAY IT......

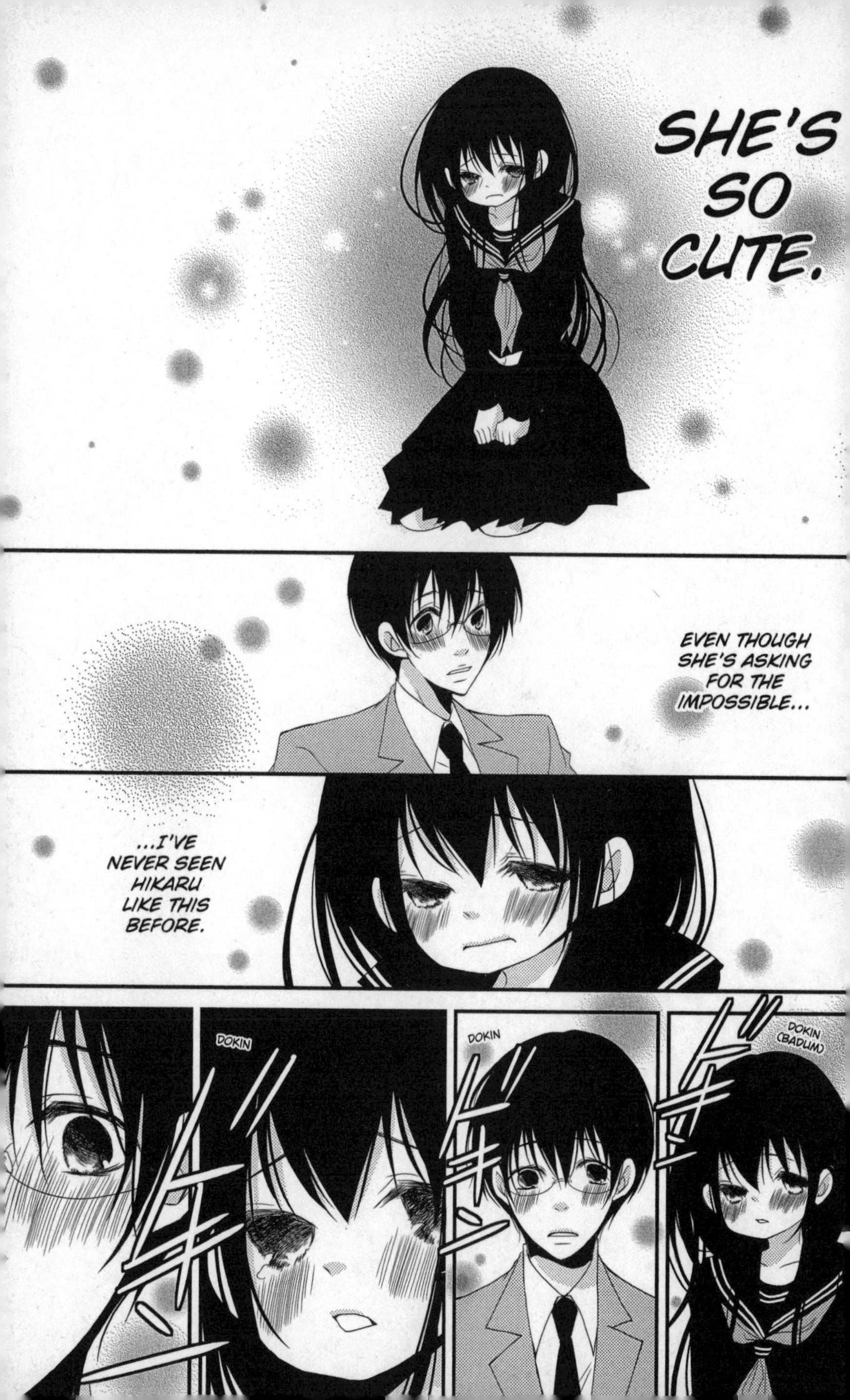
SHE'S SO CUTE.
EVEN THOUGH SHE'S ASKING FOR THE IMPOSSIBLE...
...I'VE NEVER SEEN HIKARU LIKE THIS BEFORE.
DOKIN (BADUM)
DOKIN
DOKIN

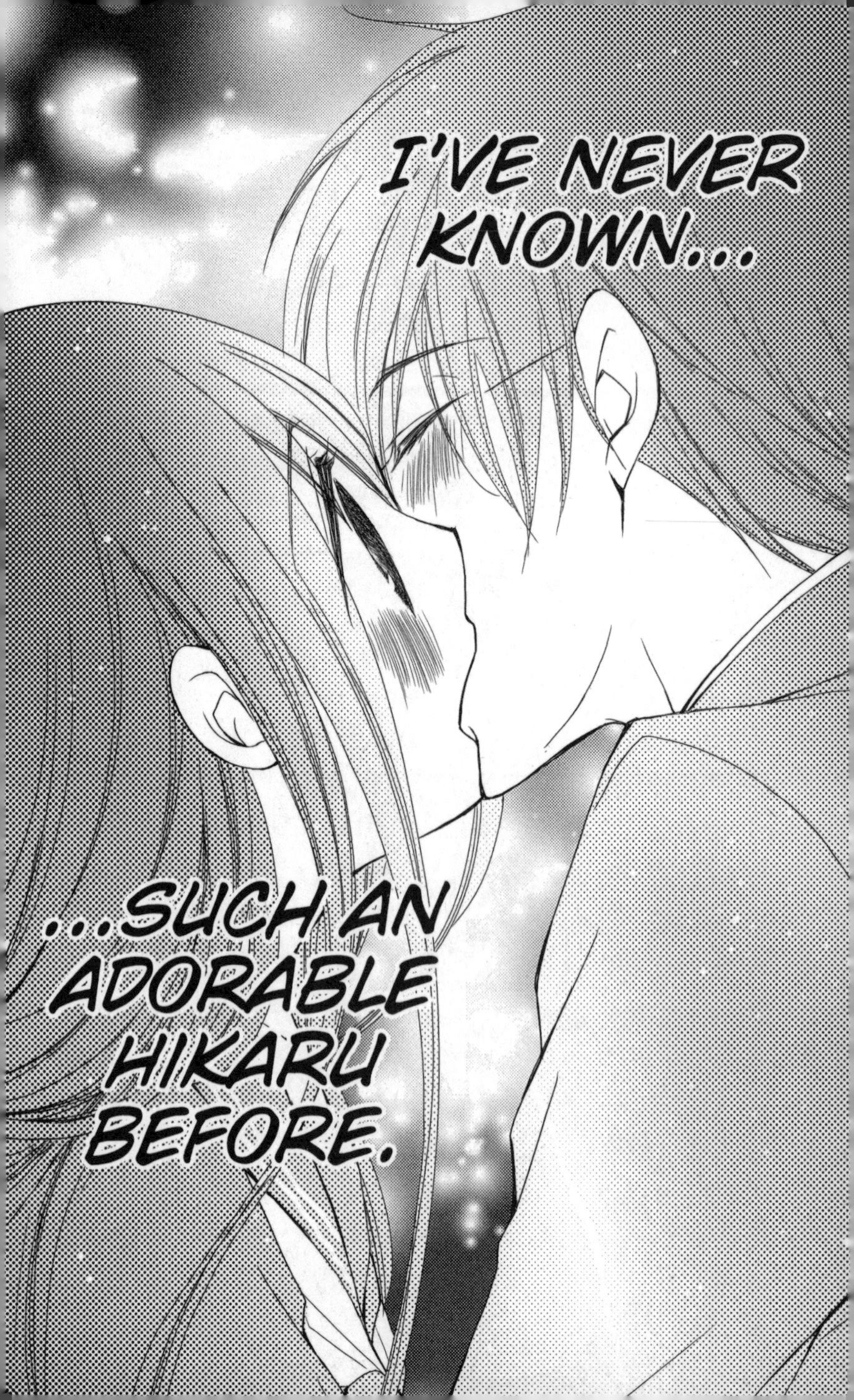
I'VE NEVER KNOWN...
...SUCH AN ADORABLE HIKARU BEFORE.

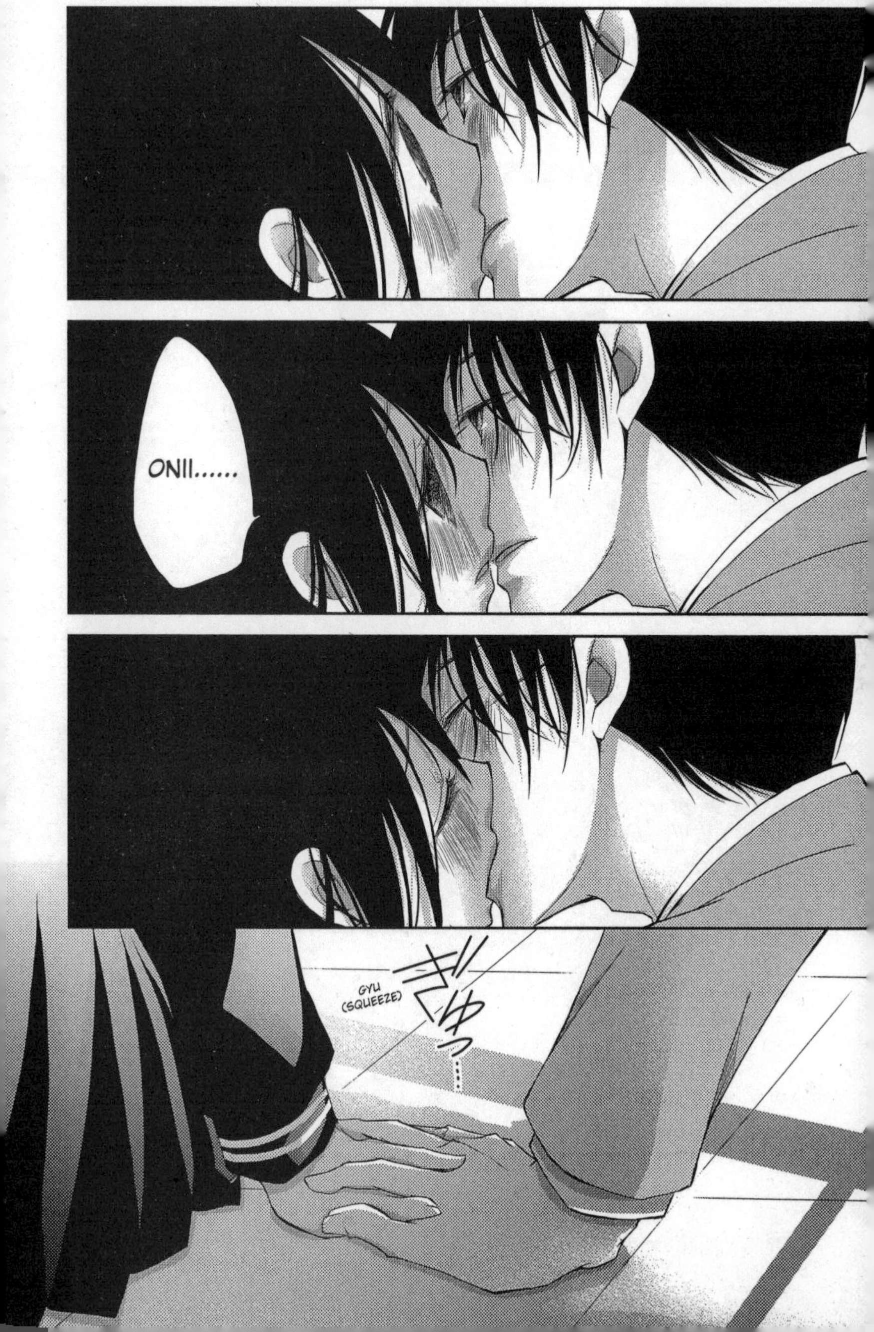
ONII......
ぎゅっ……
GYU (SQUEEZE)

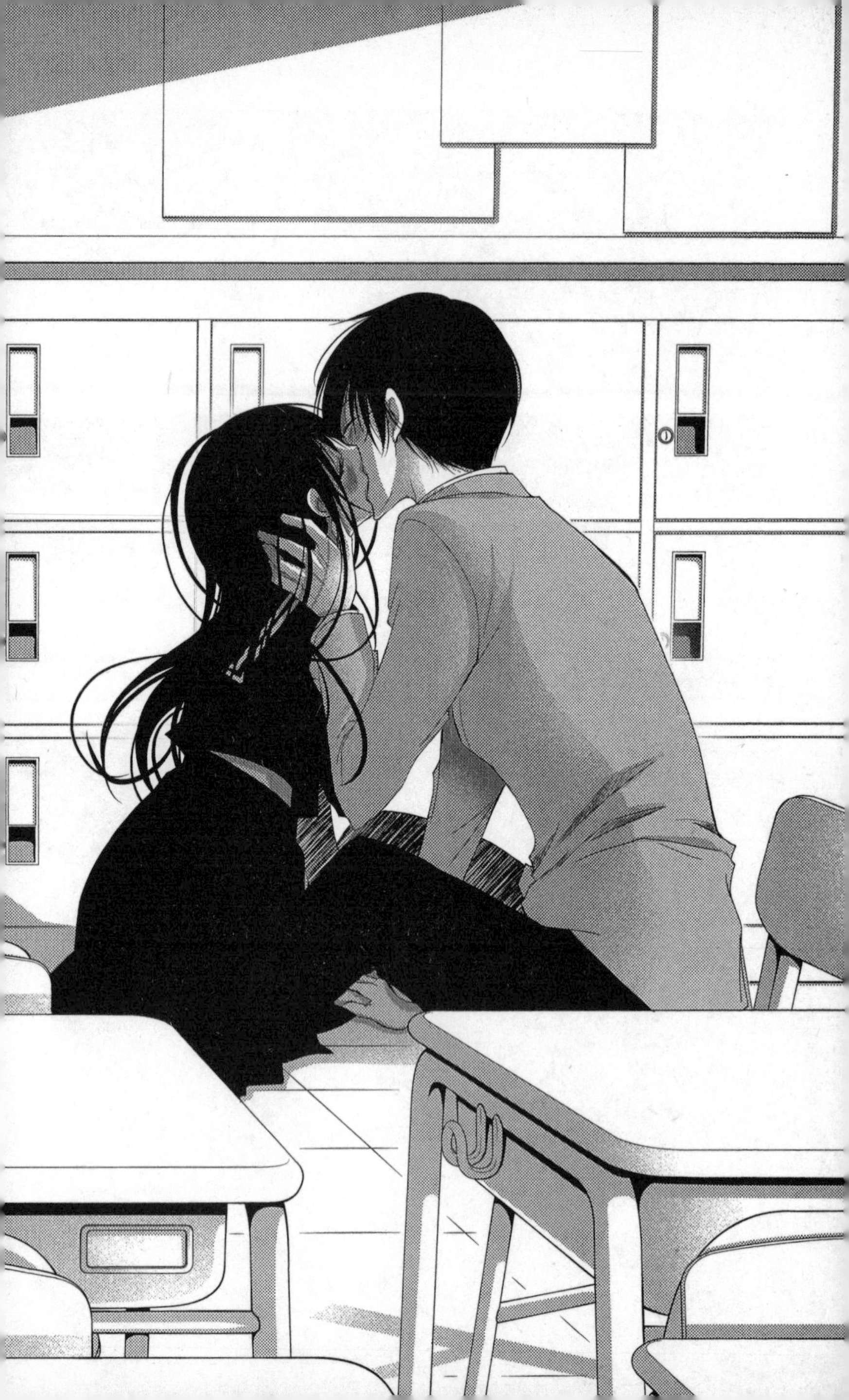

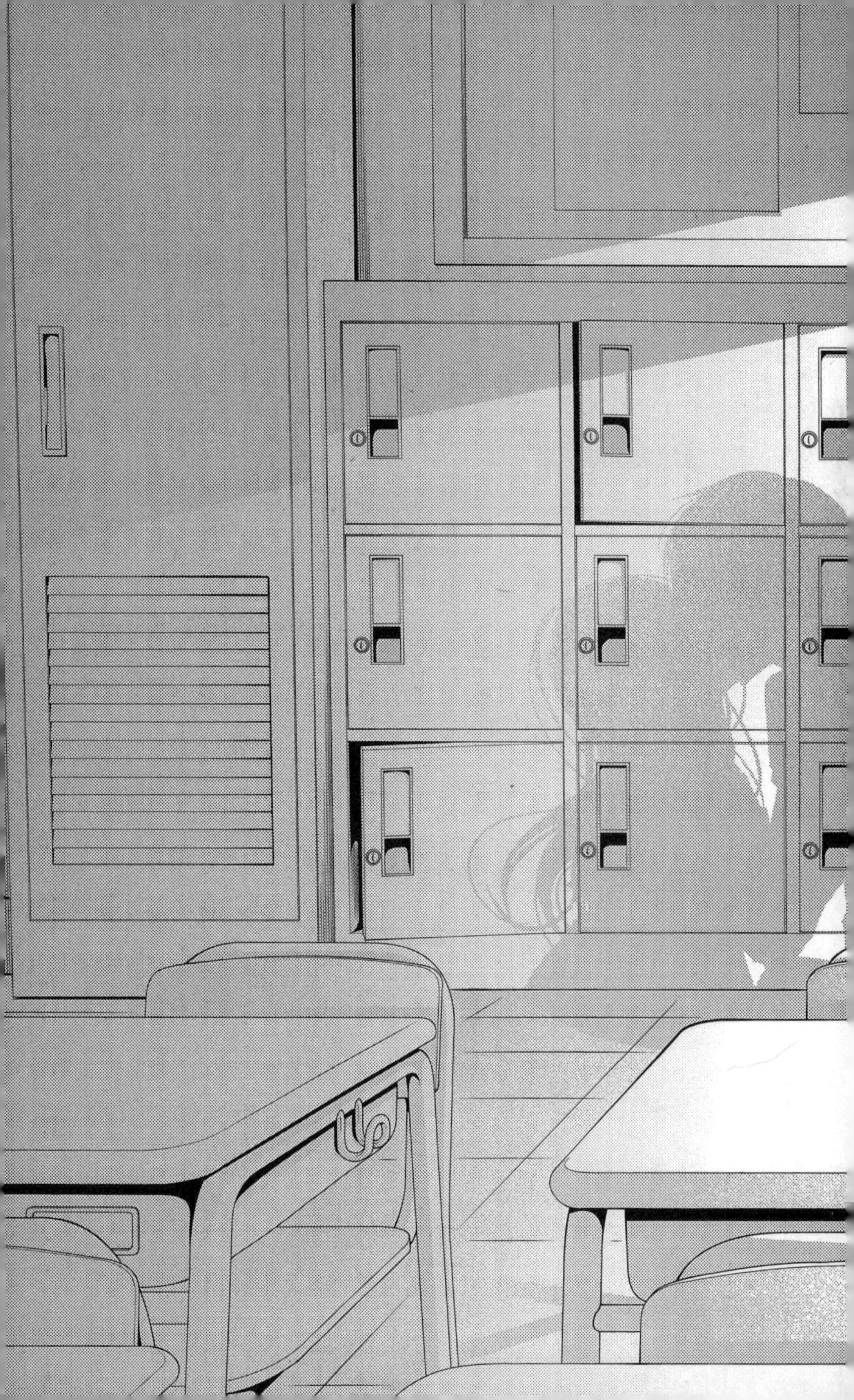

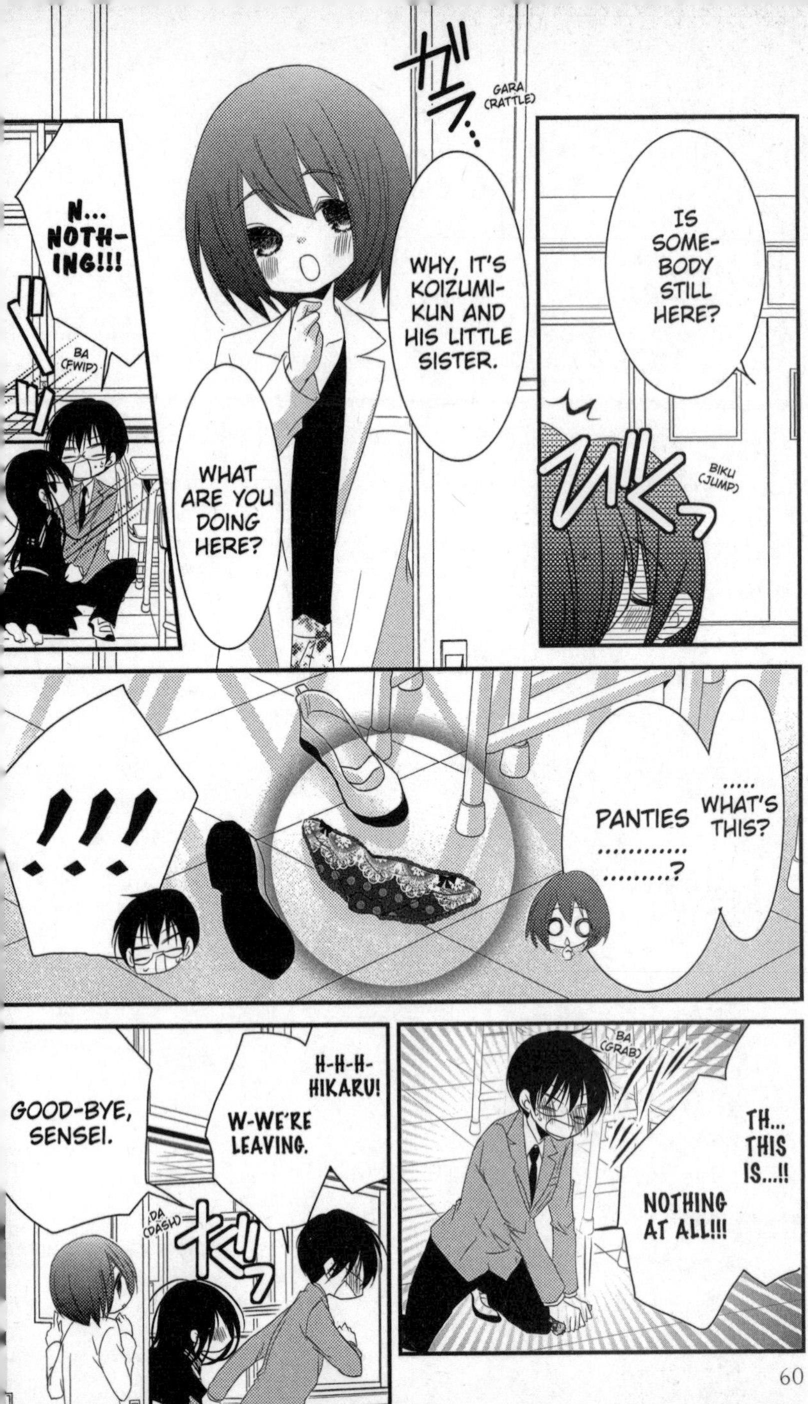

GARA (RATTLE)
IS SOMEBODY STILL HERE?
BIKU (JUMP)
WHY, IT'S KOIZUMI-KUN AND HIS LITTLE SISTER.
WHAT ARE YOU DOING HERE?
N... NOTHING!!!
BA (FWIP)
..... WHAT'S THIS?
PANTIES ....?
!!!
BA (GRAB)
TH... THIS IS...!!
NOTHING AT ALL!!!
H-H-H-HIKARU!
W-WE'RE LEAVING.
DA (DASH)
GOOD-BYE, SENSEI.

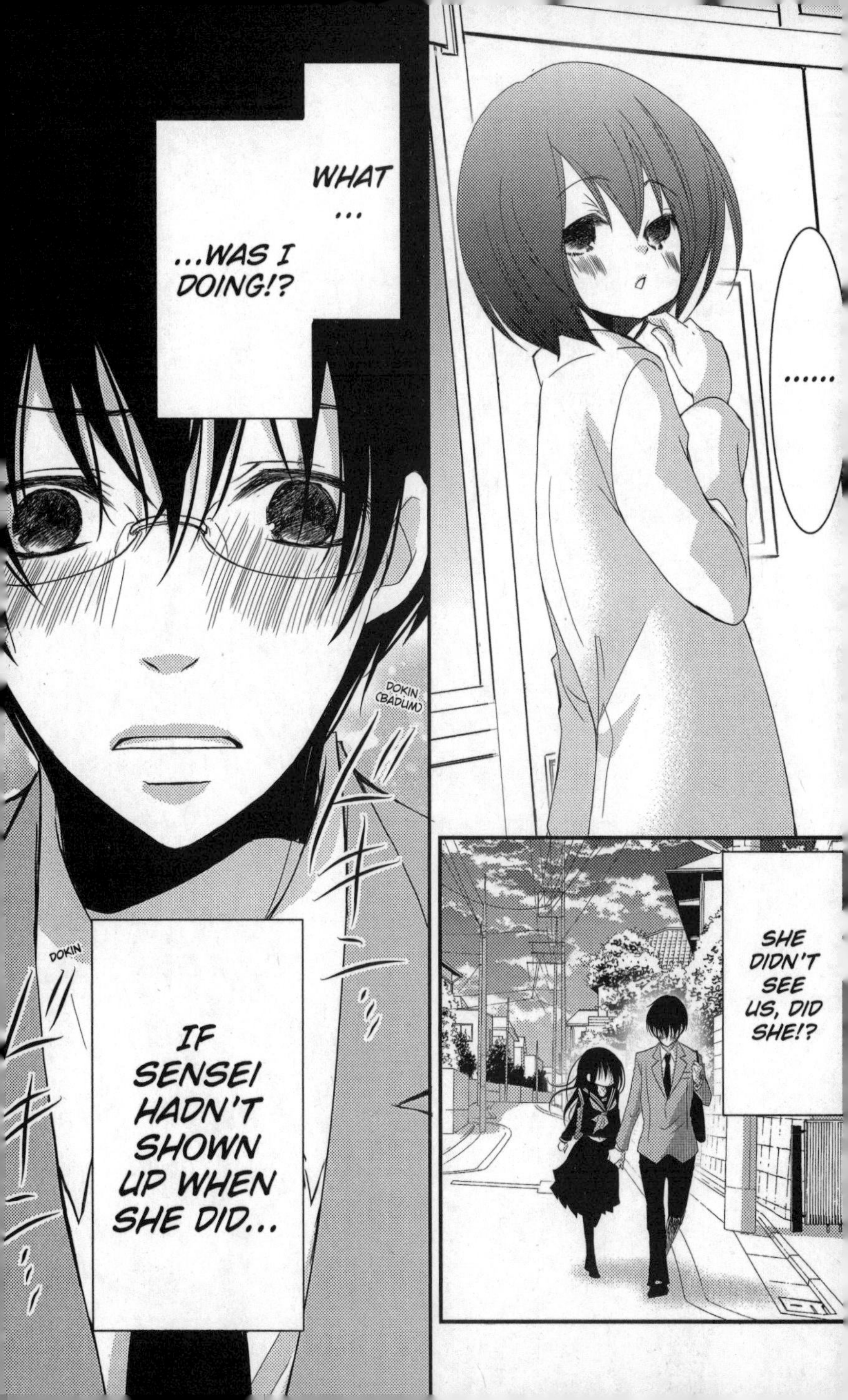
......
SHE DIDN'T SEE US, DID SHE!?
WHAT ...
...WAS I DOING!?
DOKIN (BADUM)
DOKIN
IF SENSEI HADN'T SHOWN UP WHEN SHE DID...

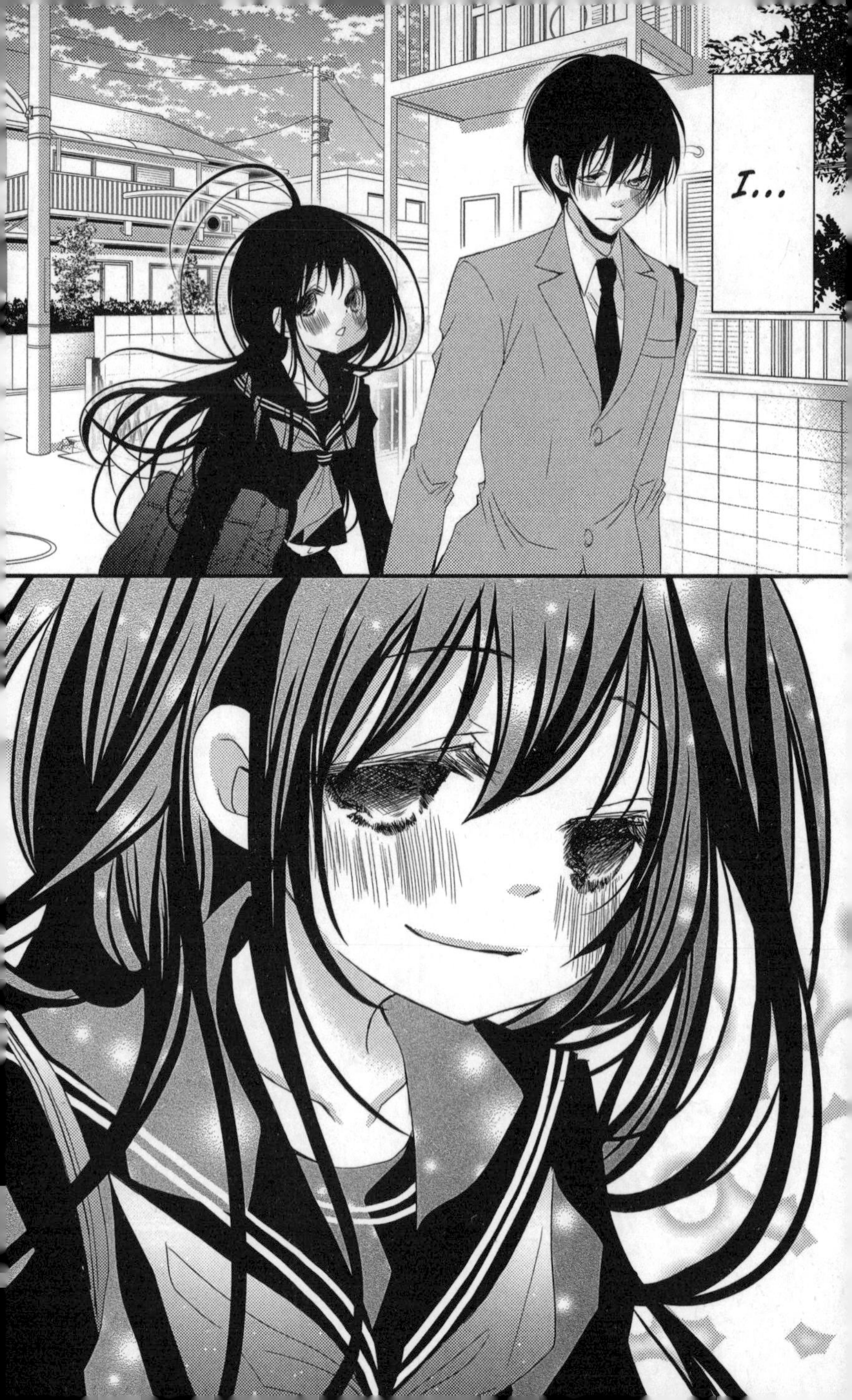
I...

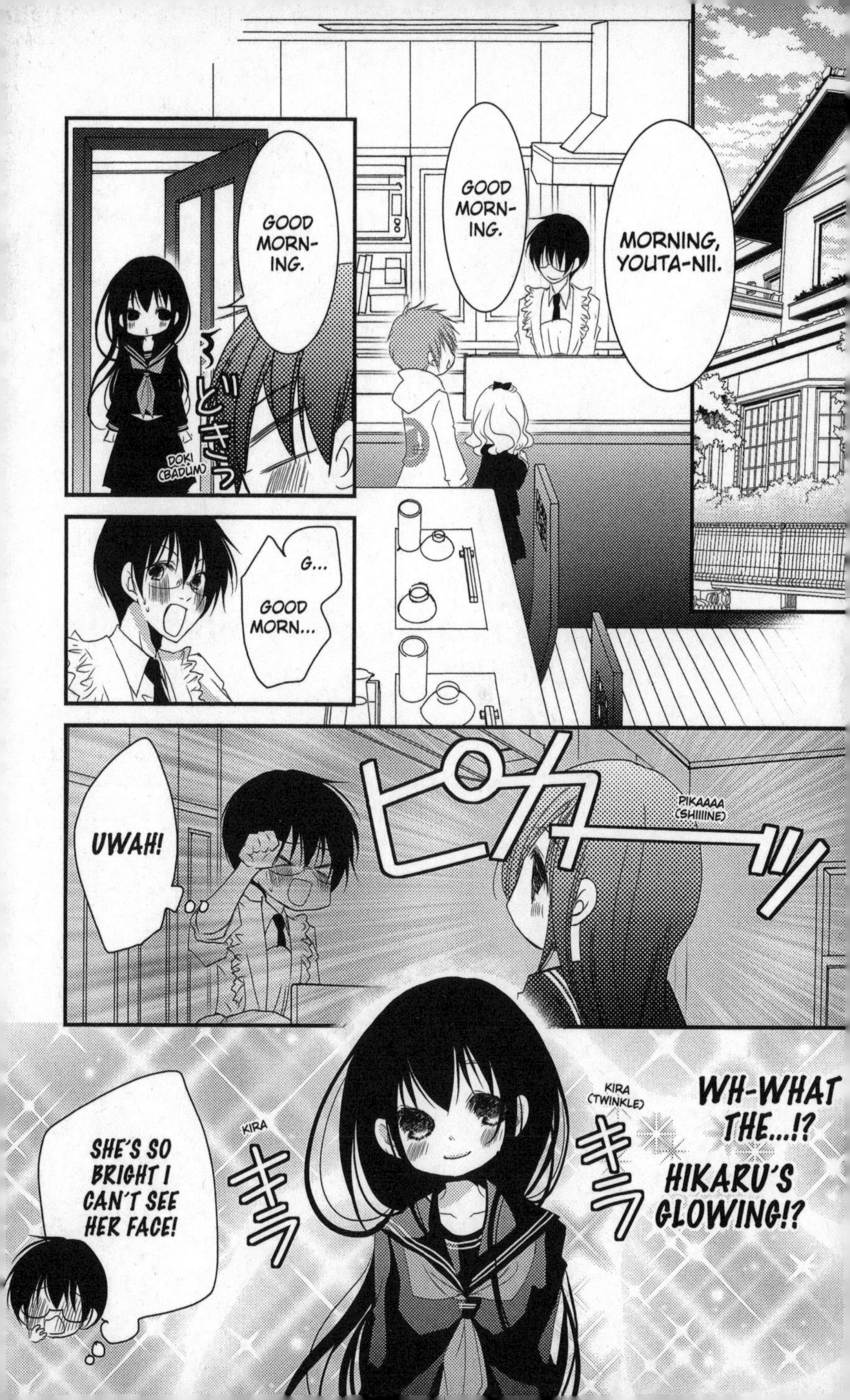
MORNING, YOUTA-NII.
GOOD MORN-ING.
GOOD MORN-ING.
DOKI (BADUM)
G... GOOD MORN...
PIKAAAA (SHIIINE)
UWAH!
WH-WHAT THE...!? HIKARU'S GLOWING!?
KIRA (TWINKLE)
KIRA
SHE'S SO BRIGHT I CAN'T SEE HER FACE!

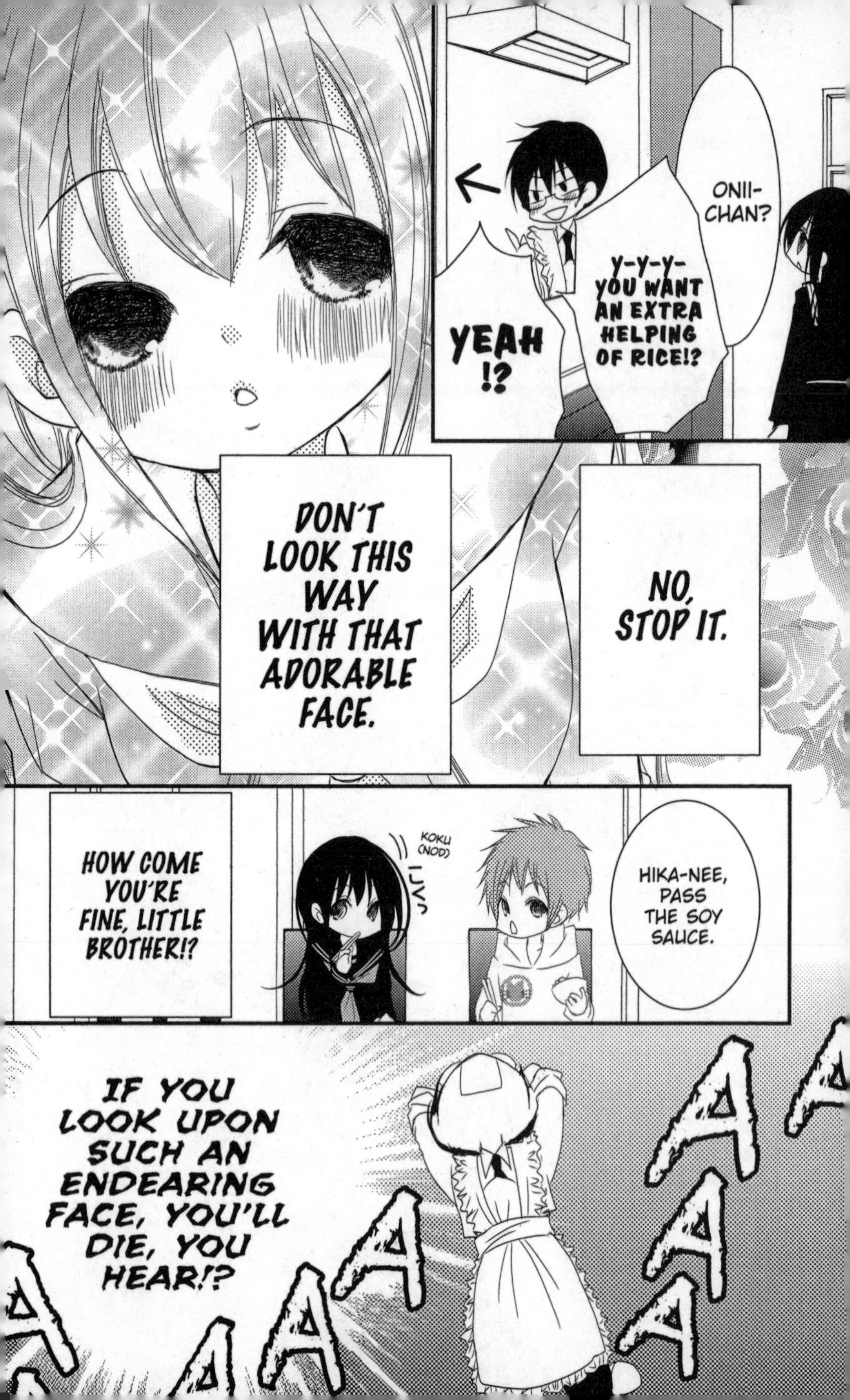
ONII-CHAN?
Y-Y-Y-YOU WANT AN EXTRA HELPING OF RICE!?
YEAH!?
NO, STOP IT.
DON'T LOOK THIS WAY WITH THAT ADORABLE FACE.
HIKA-NEE, PASS THE SOY SAUCE.
KOKU (NOD)
HOW COME YOU'RE FINE, LITTLE BROTHER!?
IF YOU LOOK UPON SUCH AN ENDEARING FACE, YOU'LL DIE, YOU HEAR!?
AAAAAAAAA

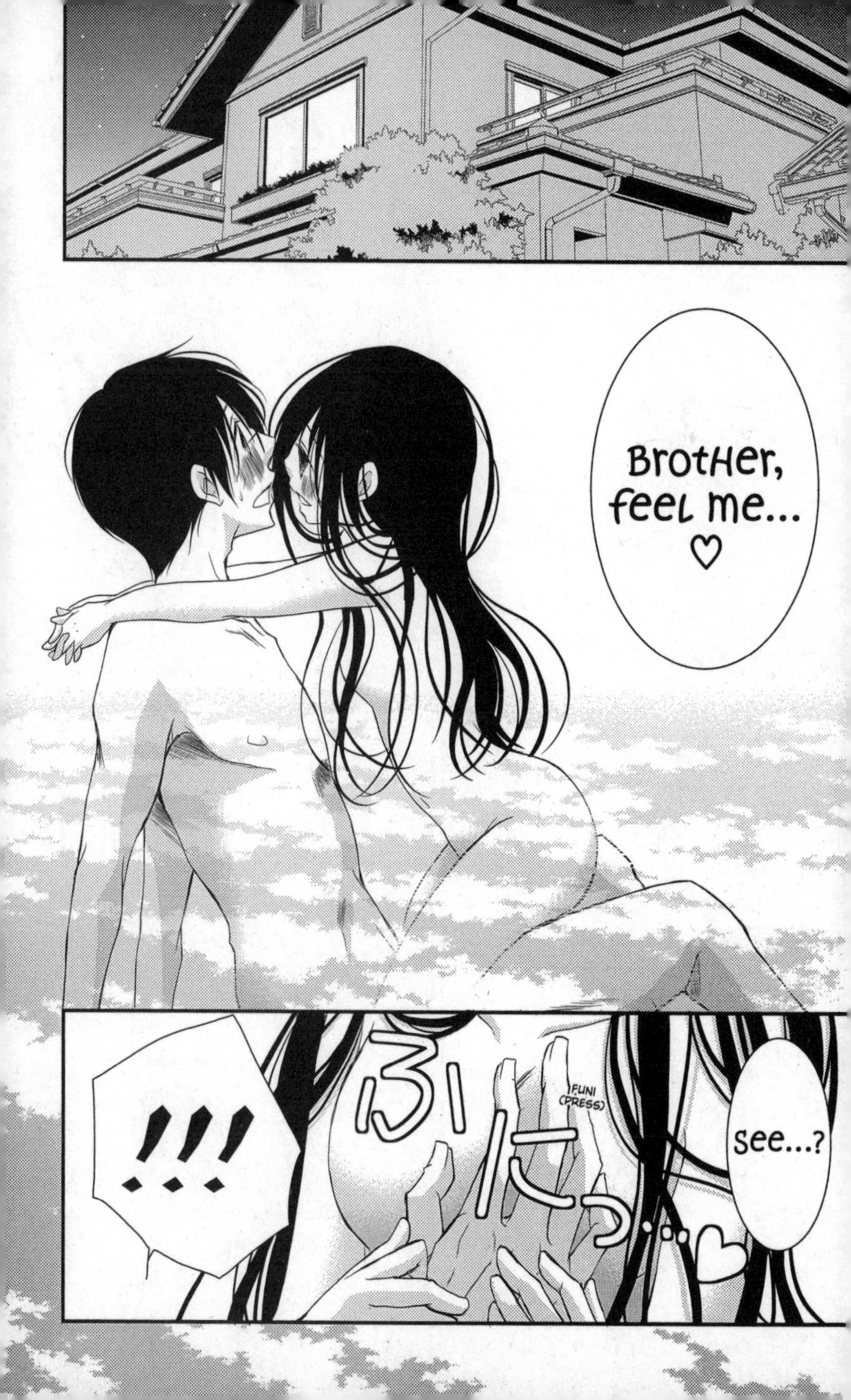
Brother, feel me... ♡
see...?
ふにっ…♡
FUNI (PRESS)
!!!

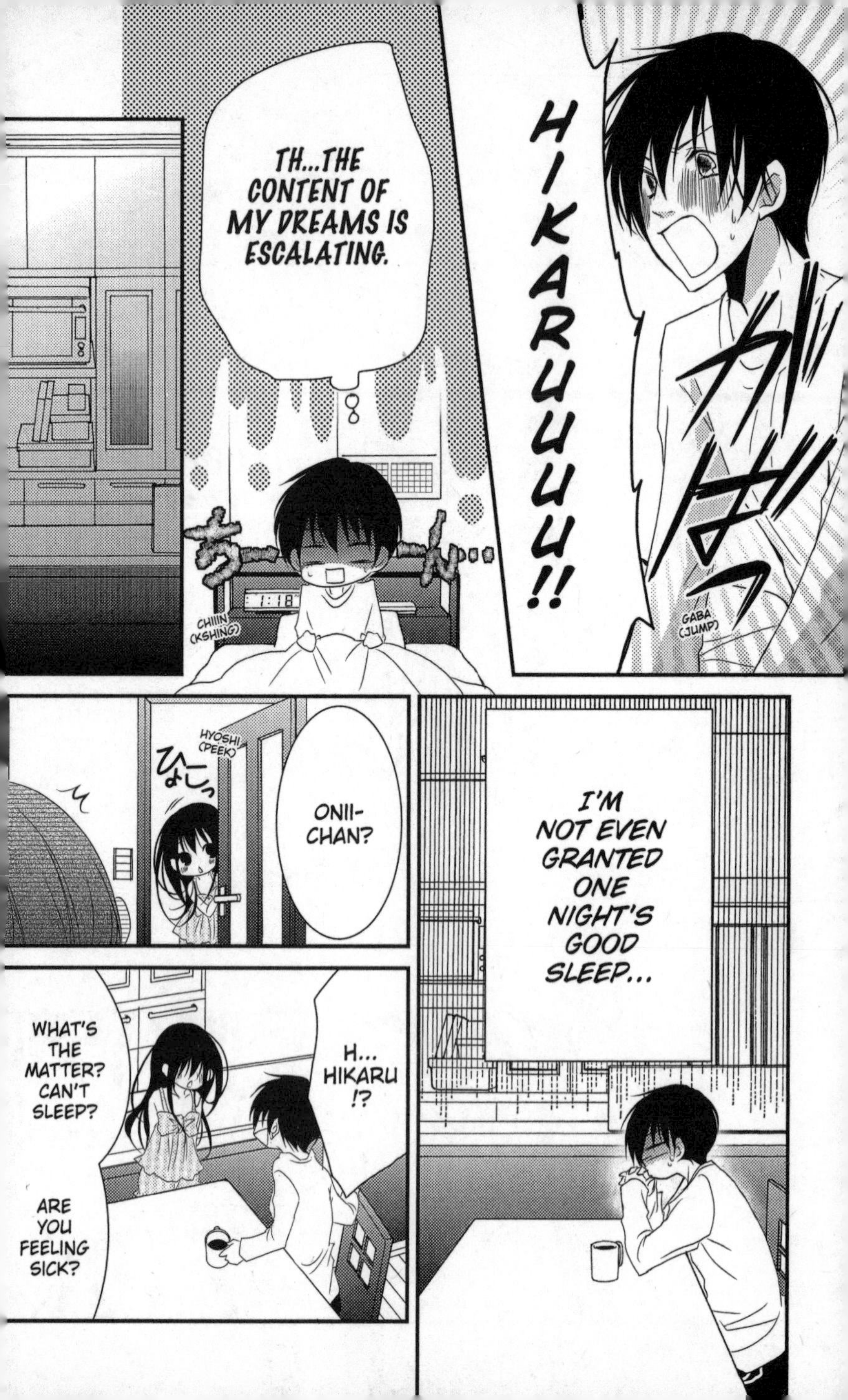
HIKARUUUUU!!
GABA (JUMP)
TH...THE CONTENT OF MY DREAMS IS ESCALATING.
CHIIN (KSHING)
1:18
I'M NOT EVEN GRANTED ONE NIGHT'S GOOD SLEEP...
HYOSHI (PEEK)
ONII-CHAN?
H... HIKARU!?
WHAT'S THE MATTER? CAN'T SLEEP?
ARE YOU FEELING SICK?

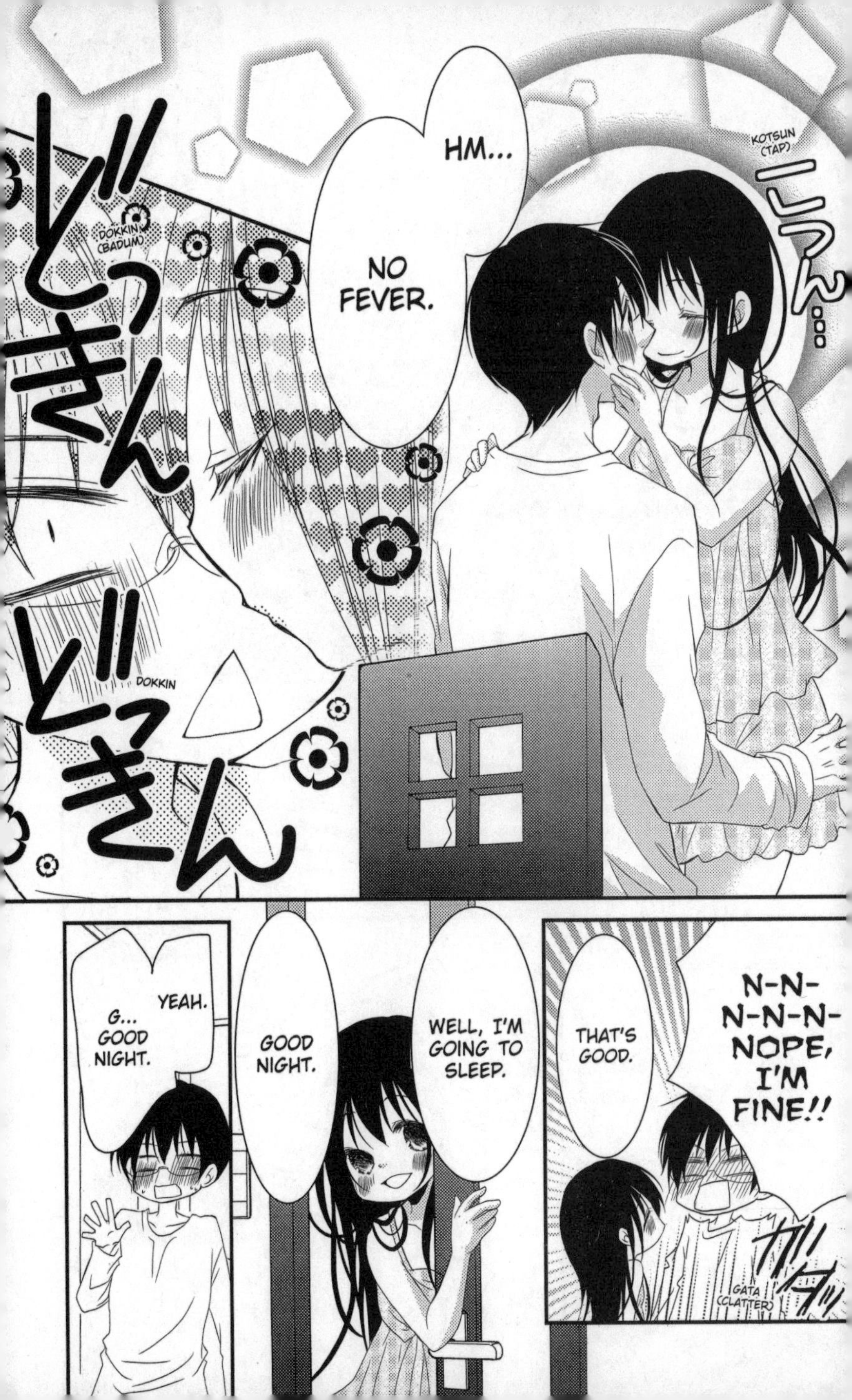
こつん…
KOTSUN (TAP)
HM...
NO FEVER.
どっきん
DOKKIN (BADUM)
どっきん
DOKKIN
N-N-N-N-N-NOPE, I'M FINE!!
THAT'S GOOD.
GATA (CLATTER)
WELL, I'M GOING TO SLEEP.
GOOD NIGHT.
YEAH.
G... GOOD NIGHT.

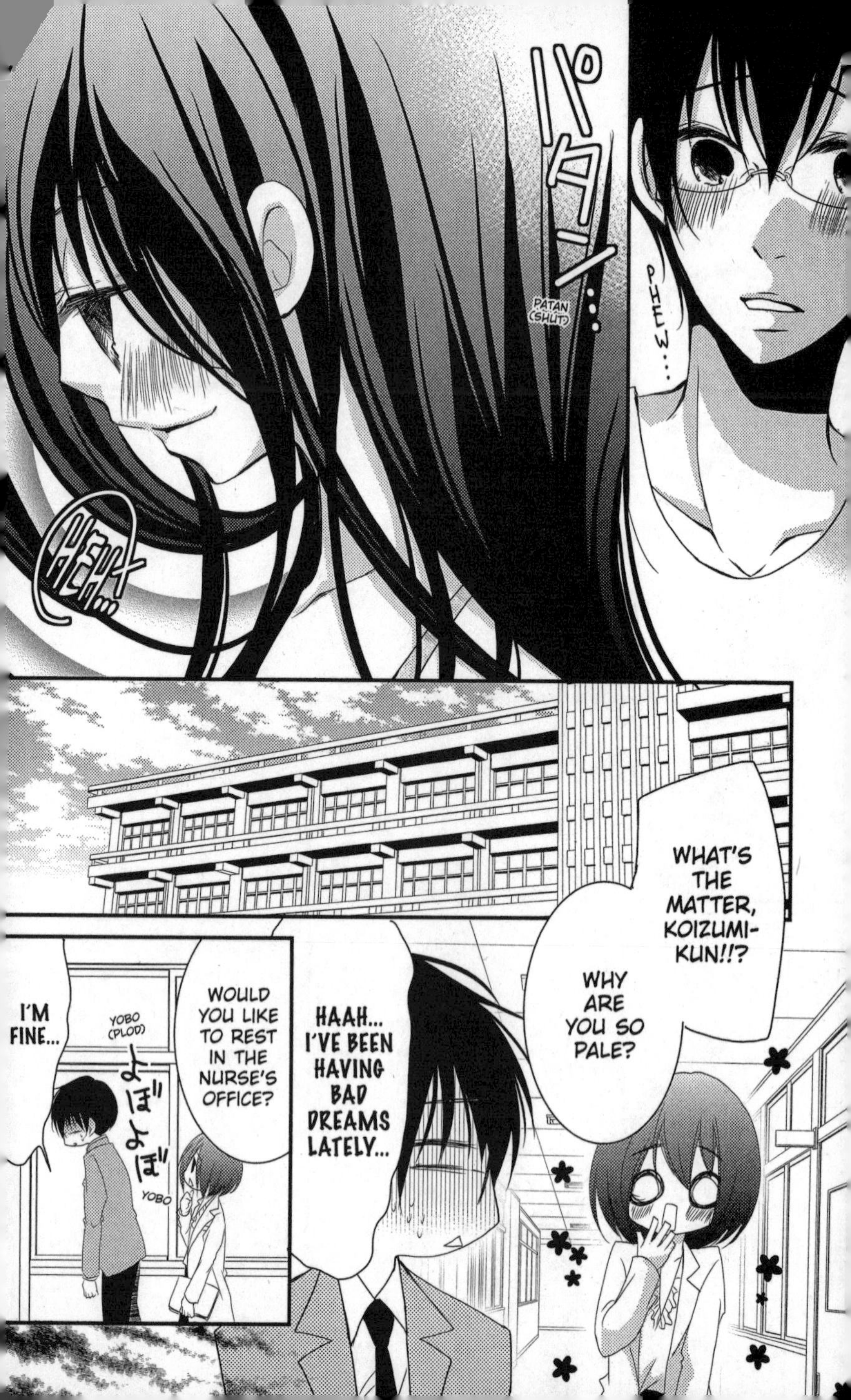
PHEW...
パタン…
PATAN (SHUT)
PHEW...
WHAT'S THE MATTER, KOIZUMI-KUN!!?
WHY ARE YOU SO PALE?
HAAH... I'VE BEEN HAVING BAD DREAMS LATELY...
WOULD YOU LIKE TO REST IN THE NURSE'S OFFICE?
よぼよぼ
YOBO (PLOD)
YOBO
I'M FINE...

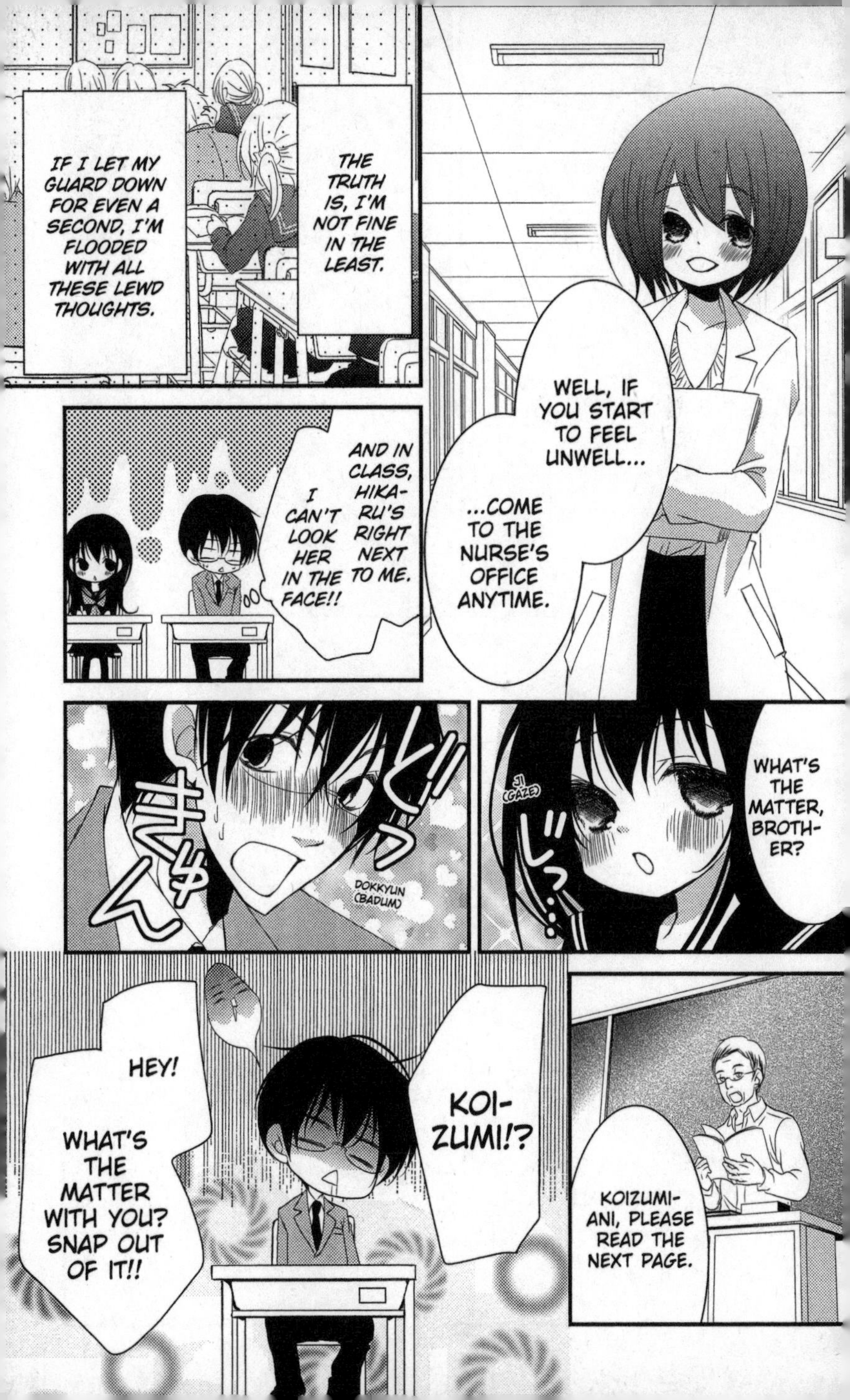

WELL, IF YOU START TO FEEL UNWELL...
...COME TO THE NURSE'S OFFICE ANYTIME.
THE TRUTH IS, I'M NOT FINE IN THE LEAST.
IF I LET MY GUARD DOWN FOR EVEN A SECOND, I'M FLOODED WITH ALL THESE LEWD THOUGHTS.
AND IN CLASS, HIKARU'S RIGHT NEXT TO ME.
I CAN'T LOOK HER IN THE FACE!!
WHAT'S THE MATTER, BROTHER?
JI (GAZE)
DOKKYUN (BADUM)
KOIZUMI-ANI, PLEASE READ THE NEXT PAGE.
KOI-ZUMI!?
HEY!
WHAT'S THE MATTER WITH YOU? SNAP OUT OF IT!!

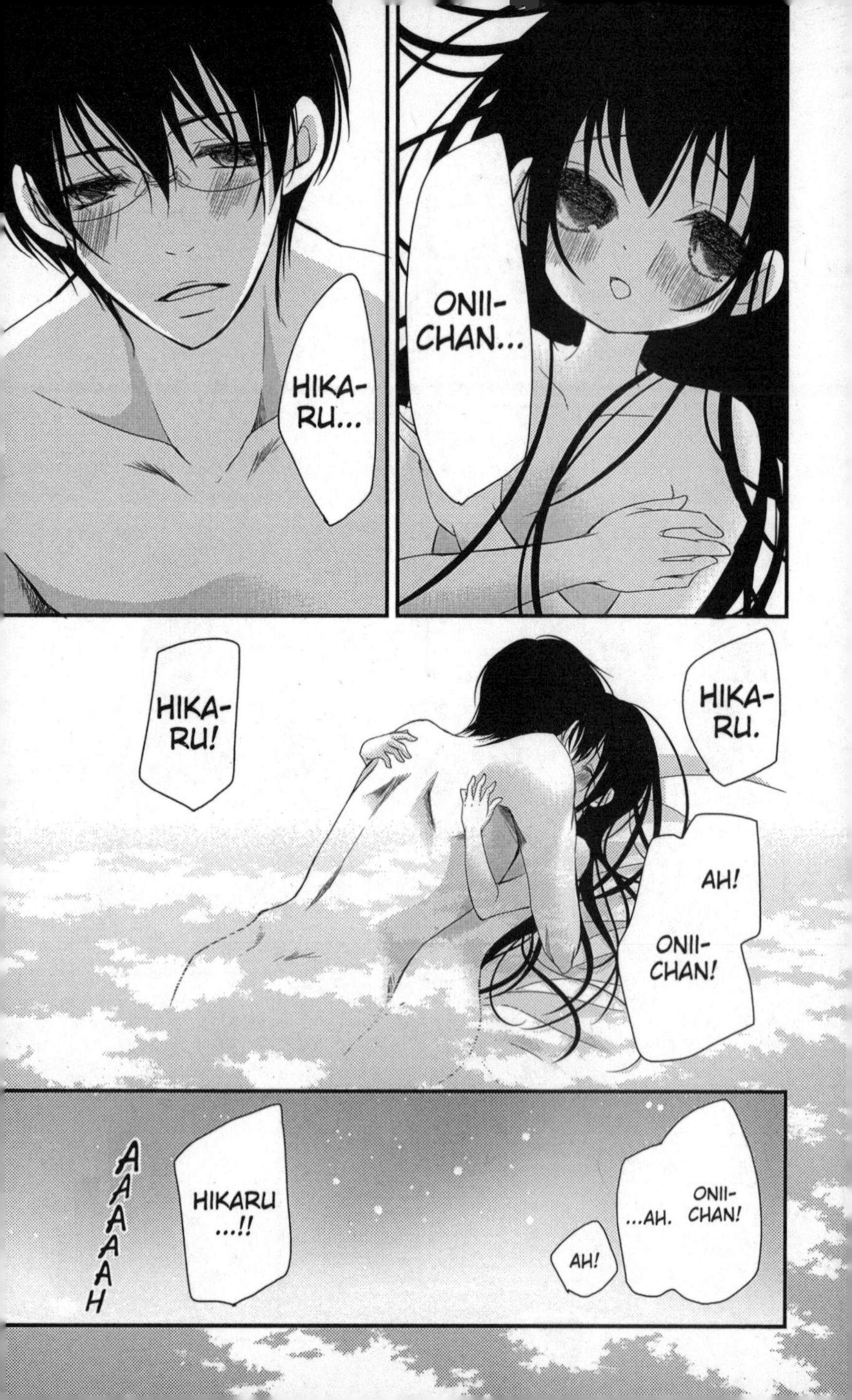
ONII-CHAN...
HIKA-RU...
HIKA-RU.
AH!
ONII-CHAN!
HIKA-RU!
ONII-CHAN!
...AH.
AH!
HIKARU ...!!
AAAAAAH

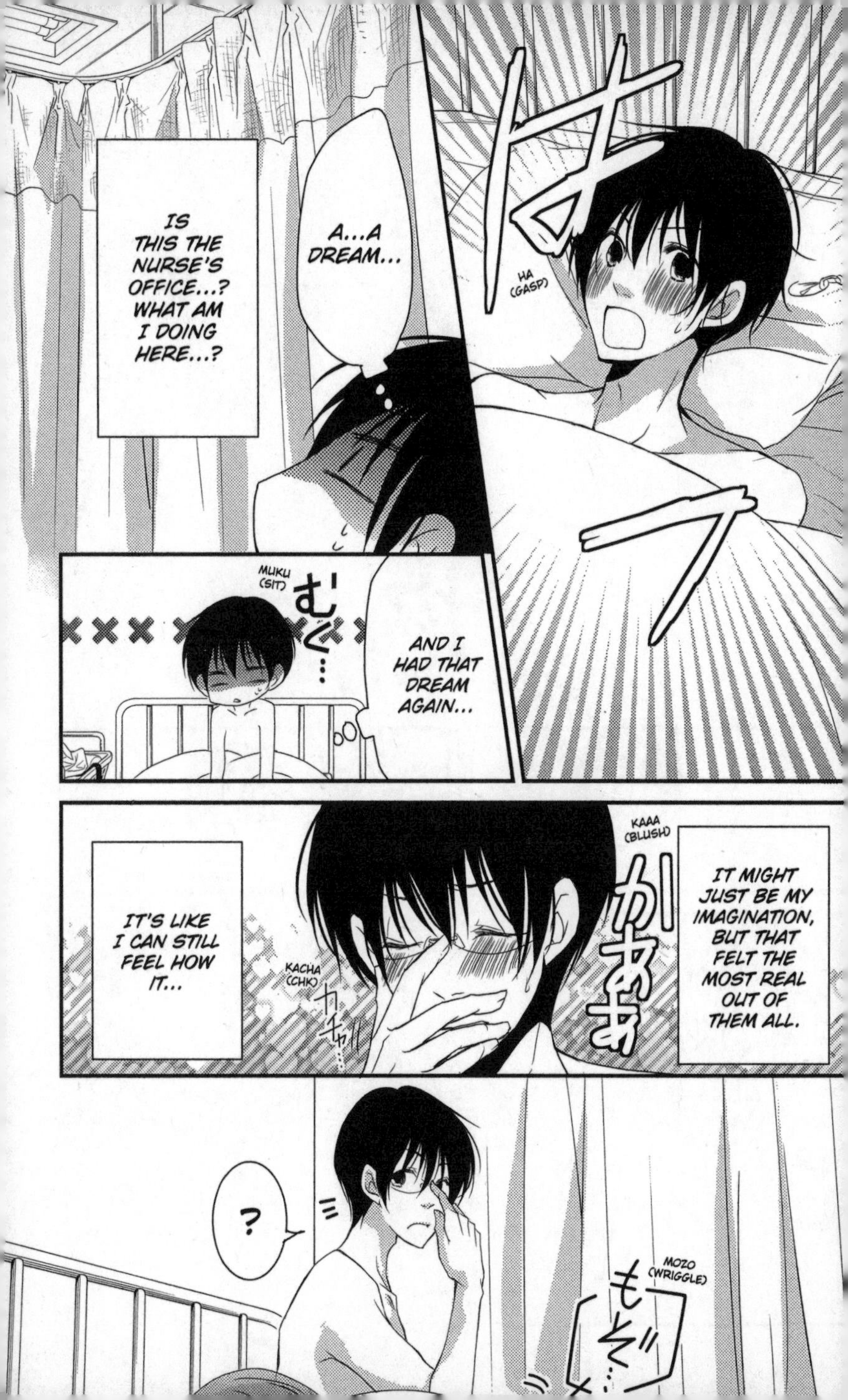
HA (GASP)
A...A DREAM...
IS THIS THE NURSE'S OFFICE...? WHAT AM I DOING HERE...?
MUKU (SIT)
AND I HAD THAT DREAM AGAIN...
KAAA (BLUSH)
IT MIGHT JUST BE MY IMAGINATION, BUT THAT FELT THE MOST REAL OUT OF THEM ALL.
KACHA (CHK)
IT'S LIKE I CAN STILL FEEL HOW IT...
MOZO (WRIGGLE)
?

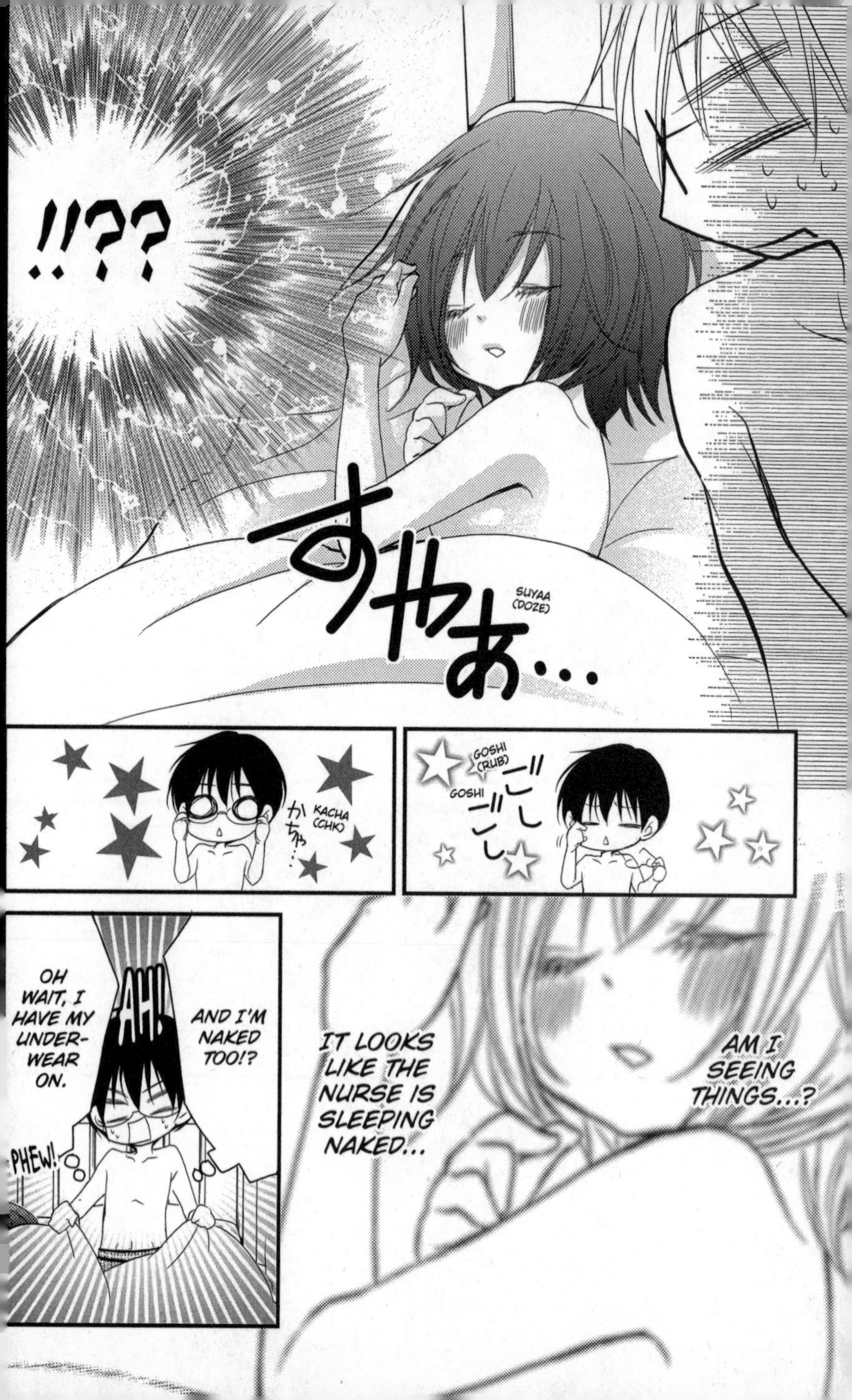
!!??
すやぁ…
SUYAA (DOZE)
ごしごし
GOSHI (RUB) GOSHI
かちゃ…
KACHA (CHK)
AM I SEEING THINGS...?
IT LOOKS LIKE THE NURSE IS SLEEPING NAKED...
AND I'M NAKED TOO!?
AH!
OH WAIT, I HAVE MY UNDER-WEAR ON.
PHEW!

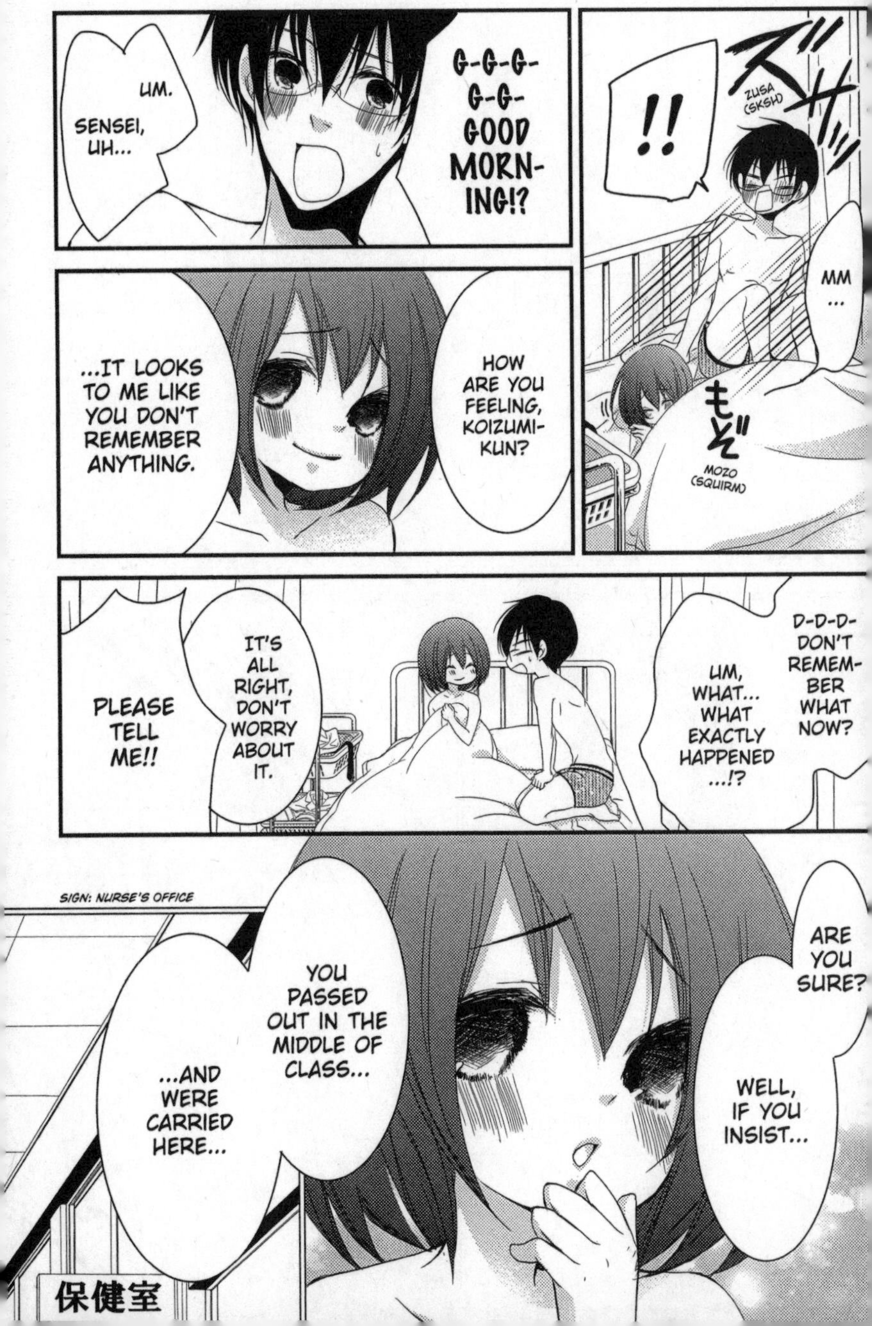
ズザッ
ZUSA (SKSH)
!!
MM ...
もぞ
MOZO (SQUIRM)
G-G-G-G-G-GOOD MORNING!?
UM. SENSEI, UH...
HOW ARE YOU FEELING, KOIZUMI-KUN?
...IT LOOKS TO ME LIKE YOU DON'T REMEMBER ANYTHING.
D-D-D-DON'T REMEMBER WHAT NOW?
UM, WHAT... WHAT EXACTLY HAPPENED ...!?
IT'S ALL RIGHT, DON'T WORRY ABOUT IT.
PLEASE TELL ME!!
ARE YOU SURE?
WELL, IF YOU INSIST...
YOU PASSED OUT IN THE MIDDLE OF CLASS...
...AND WERE CARRIED HERE...
SIGN: NURSE'S OFFICE
保健室

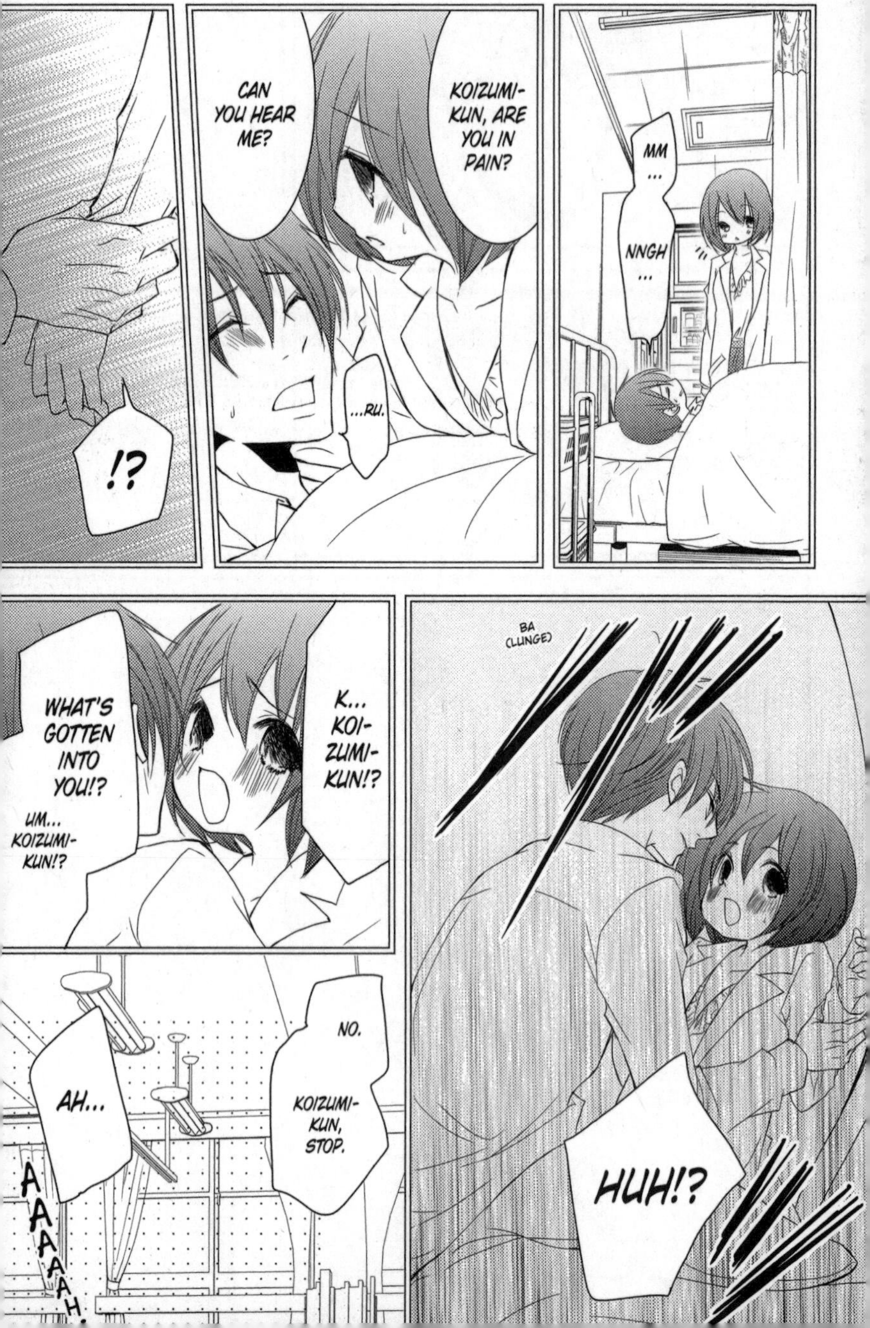
MM ...
NNGH ...
KOIZUMI-KUN, ARE YOU IN PAIN?
CAN YOU HEAR ME?
...RU.
!?
BA (LUNGE)
HUH!?
K... KOI-ZUMI-KUN!?
WHAT'S GOTTEN INTO YOU!?
UM... KOIZUMI-KUN!?
NO.
KOIZUMI-KUN, STOP.
AH...
AAAAAAH.

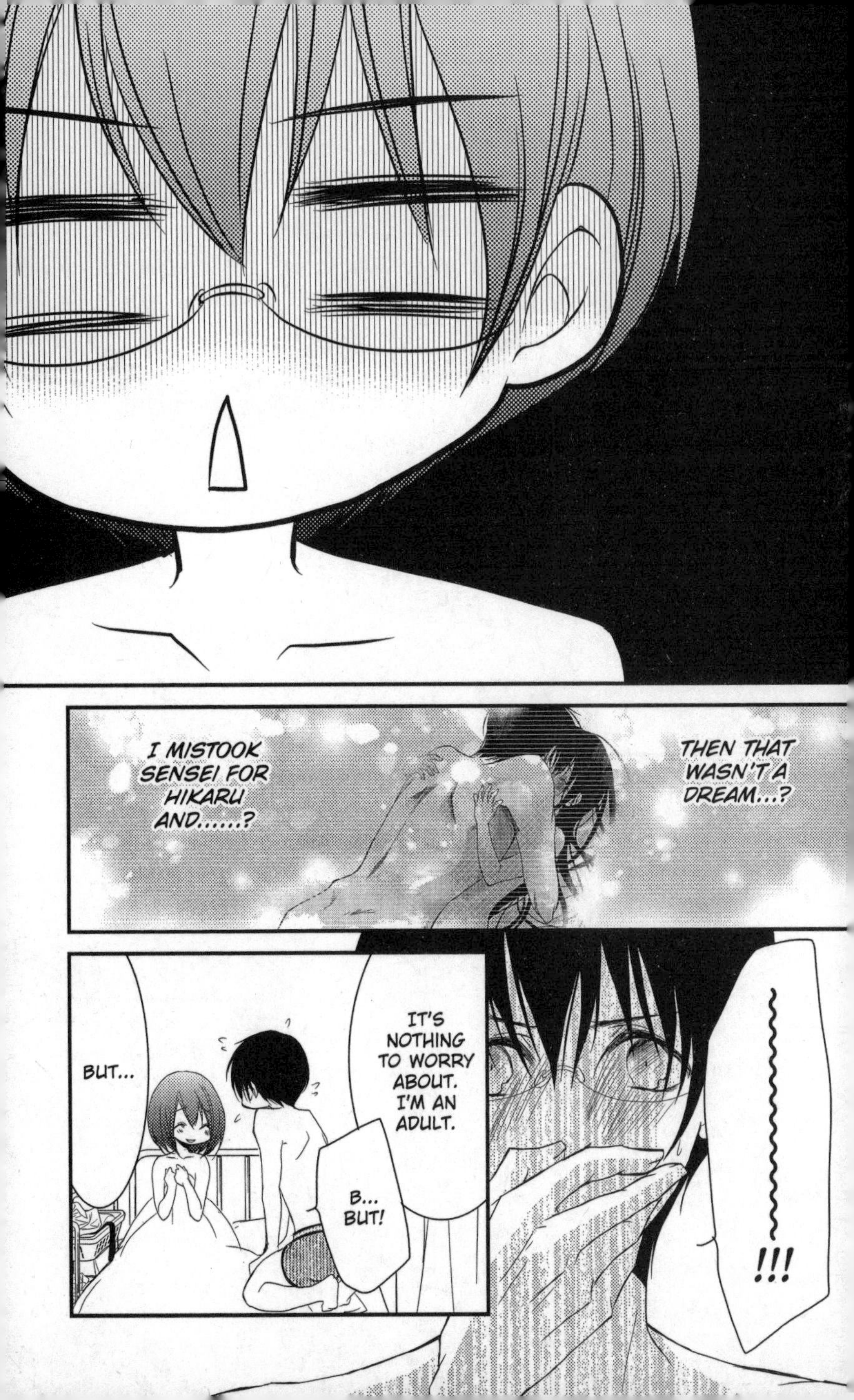

THEN THAT WASN'T A DREAM...?
I MISTOOK SENSEI FOR HIKARU AND......?
!!!
IT'S NOTHING TO WORRY ABOUT. I'M AN ADULT.
B... BUT!
BUT...

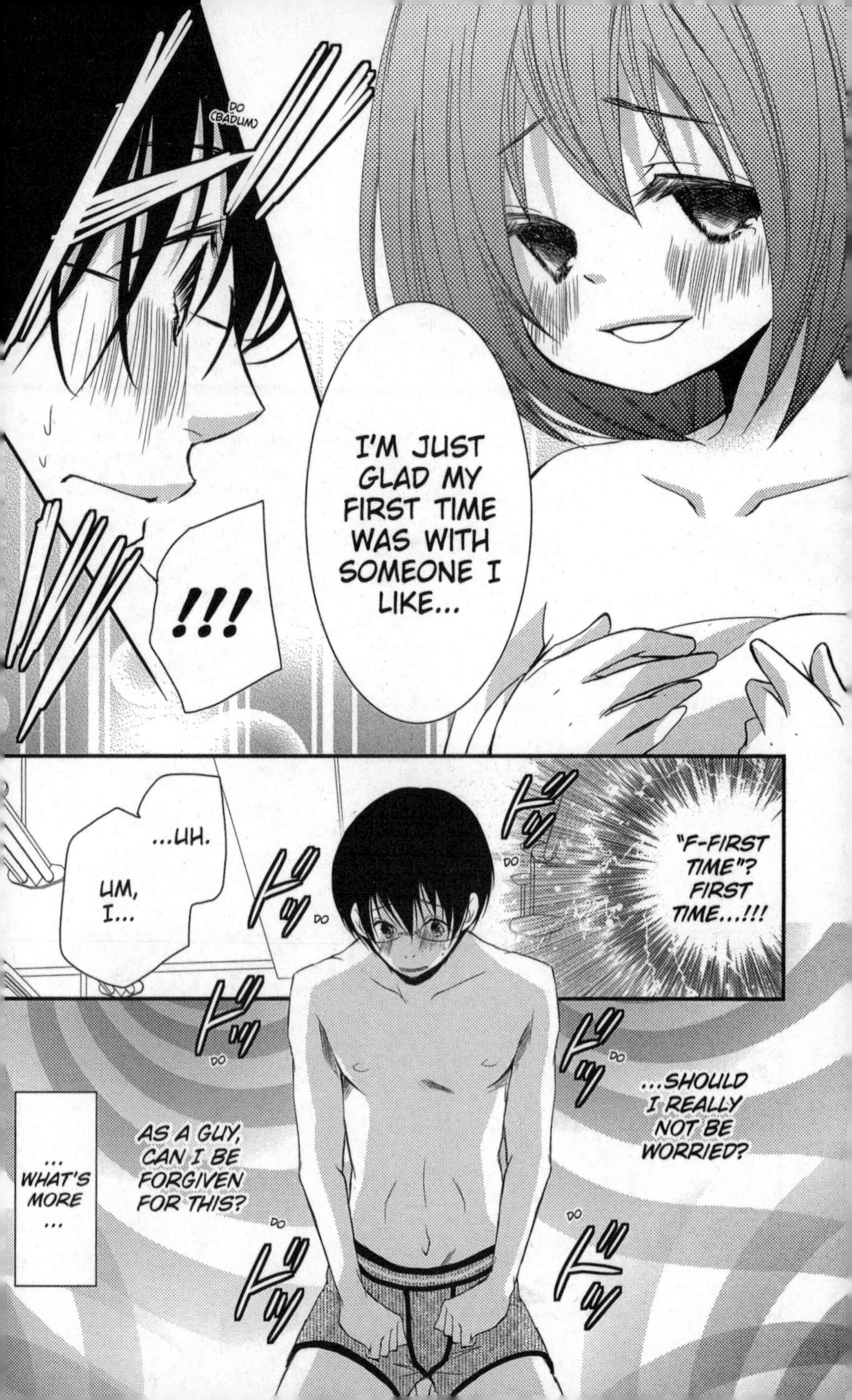
I'M JUST GLAD MY FIRST TIME WAS WITH SOMEONE I LIKE...
DO (BADUM)
!!!
DO
"F-FIRST TIME"? FIRST TIME...!!!
DO
...UH.
UM, I...
DO
DO
...SHOULD I REALLY NOT BE WORRIED?
AS A GUY, CAN I BE FORGIVEN FOR THIS?
DO
DO
... WHAT'S MORE ...

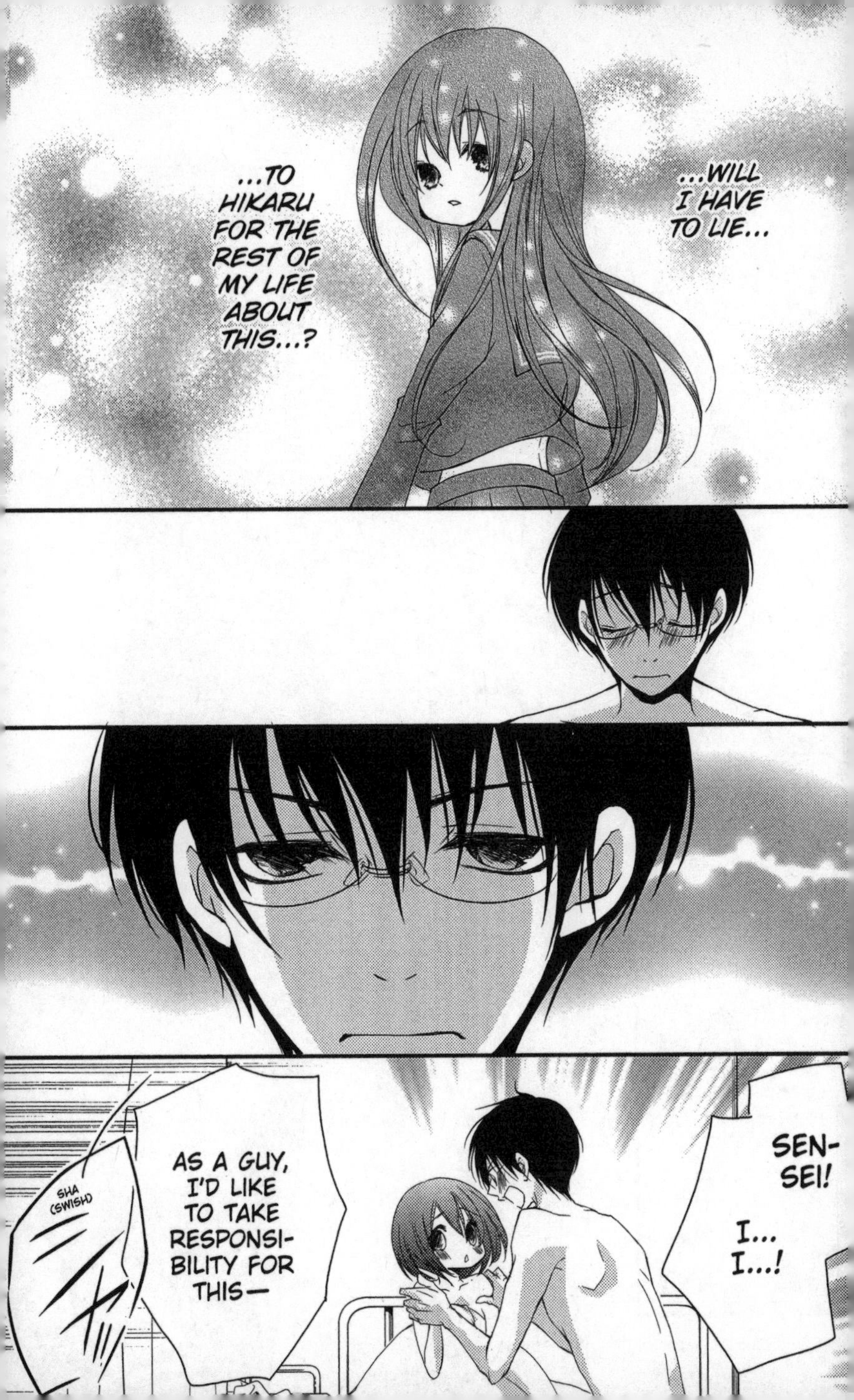
...WILL I HAVE TO LIE...
...TO HIKARU FOR THE REST OF MY LIFE ABOUT THIS...?
SENSEI!
I... I...!
AS A GUY, I'D LIKE TO TAKE RESPONSIBILITY FOR THIS—
SHA (SWISH)

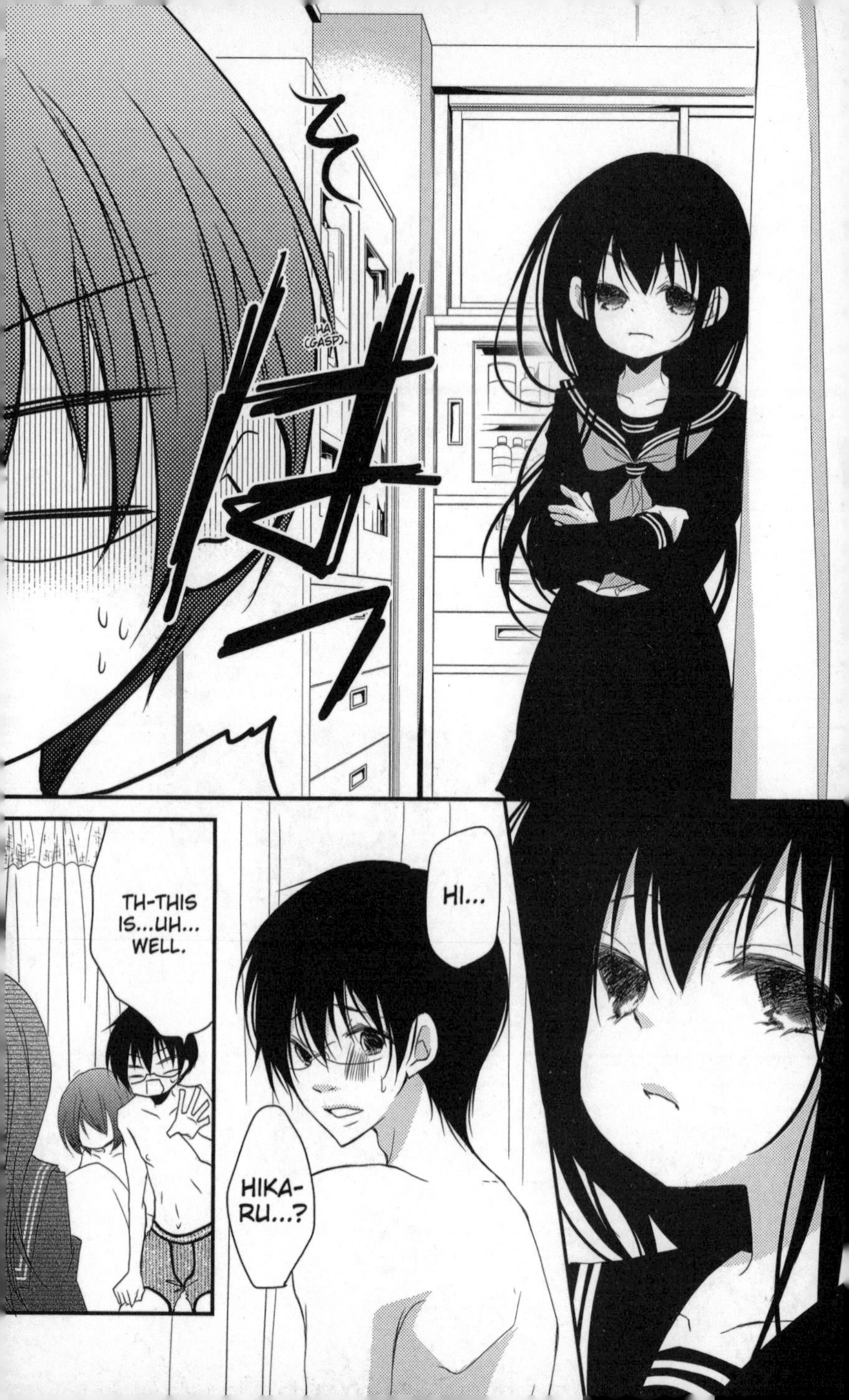
HA (GASP)
TH-THIS IS...UH... WELL.
HI...
HIKA-RU...?

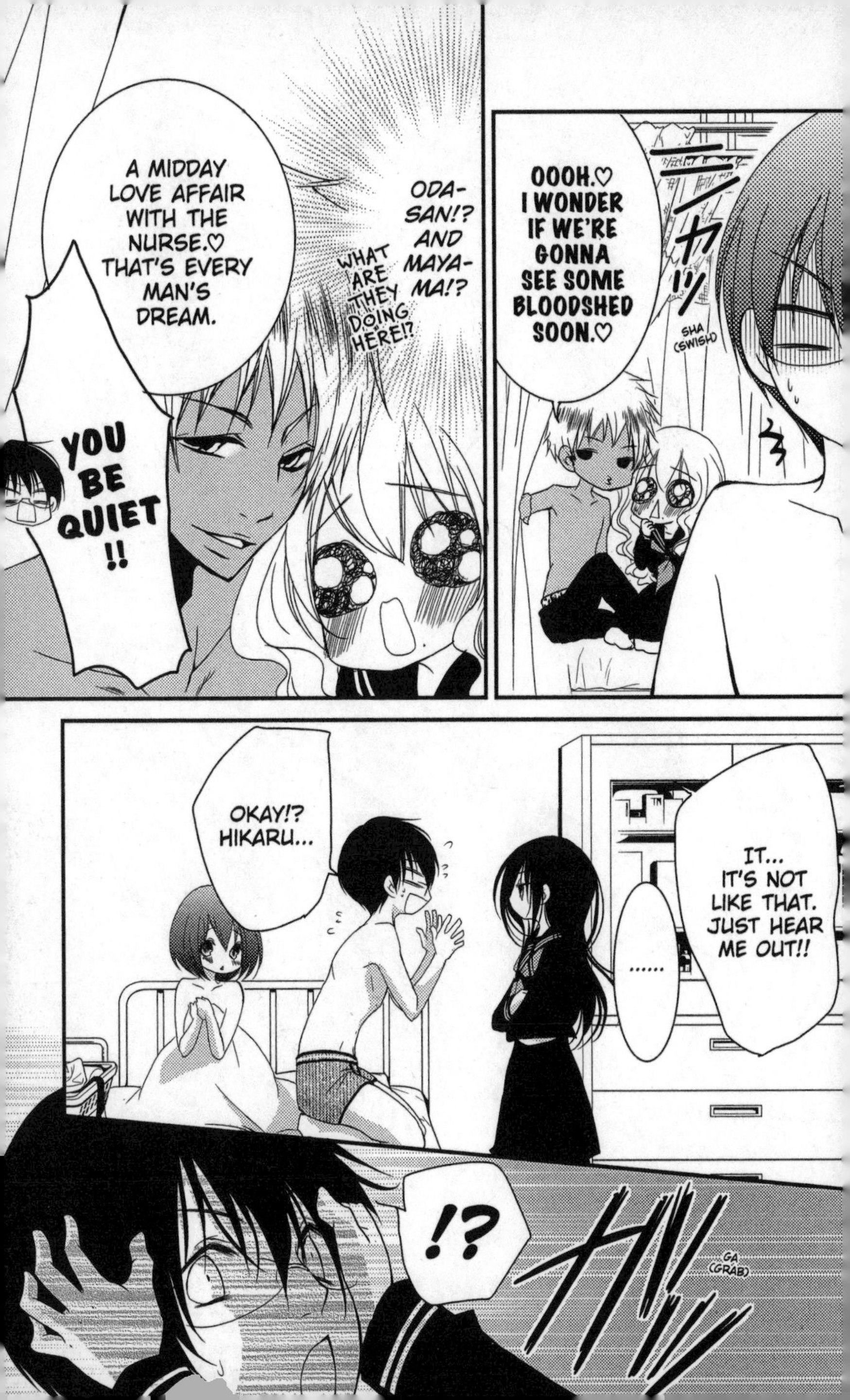
SHA (SWISH)
OOOH.♡ I WONDER IF WE'RE GONNA SEE SOME BLOODSHED SOON.♡
ODA-SAN!? AND MAYAMA!?
WHAT ARE THEY DOING HERE!?
A MIDDAY LOVE AFFAIR WITH THE NURSE.♡ THAT'S EVERY MAN'S DREAM.
YOU BE QUIET!!
IT... IT'S NOT LIKE THAT. JUST HEAR ME OUT!!
......
OKAY!? HIKARU...
GA (GRAB)
!?

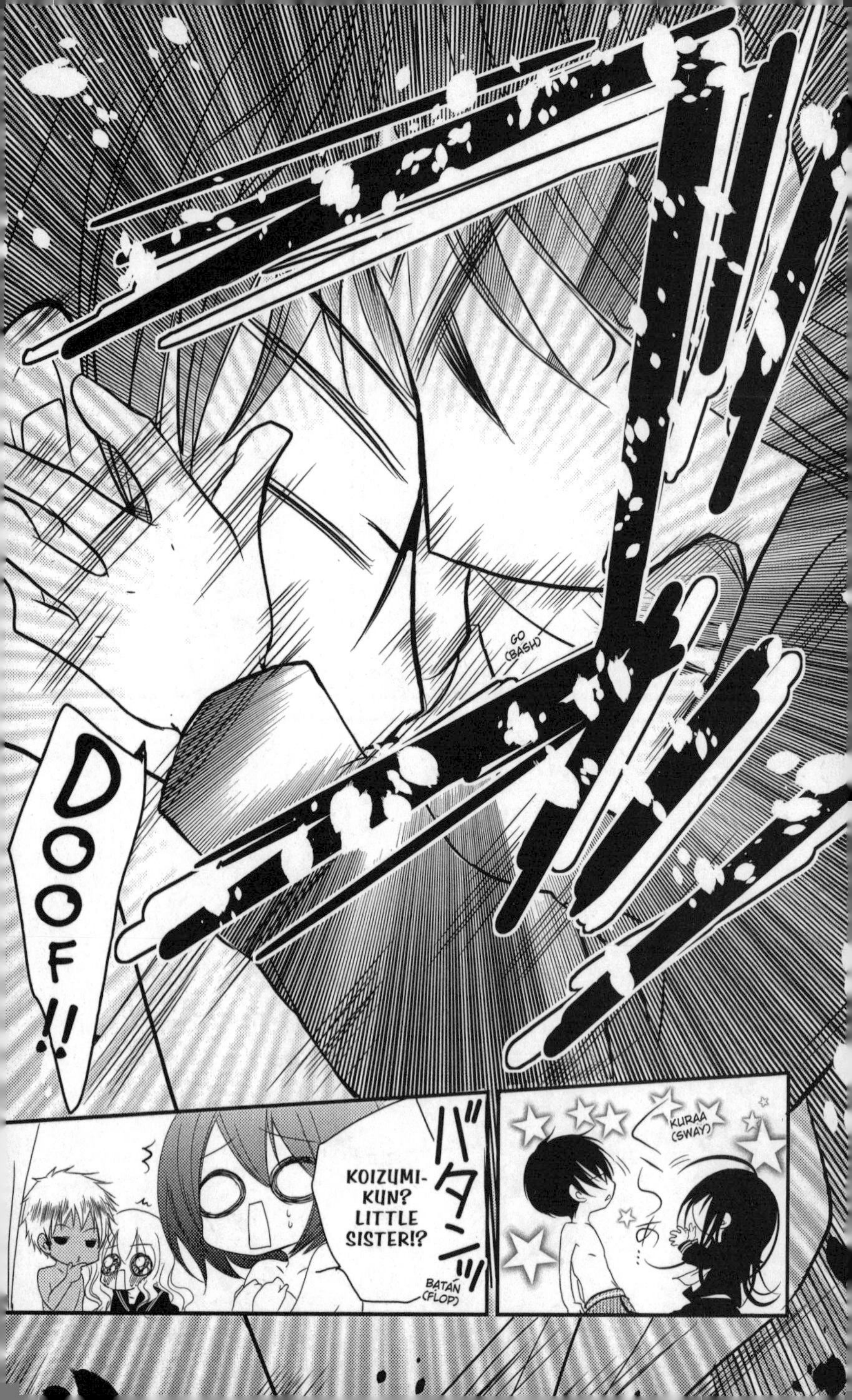
GO (BASH)
DOOF!!
KURAA (SWAY)
バタンッ
BATAN (FLOP)
KOIZUMI-KUN? LITTLE SISTER!?

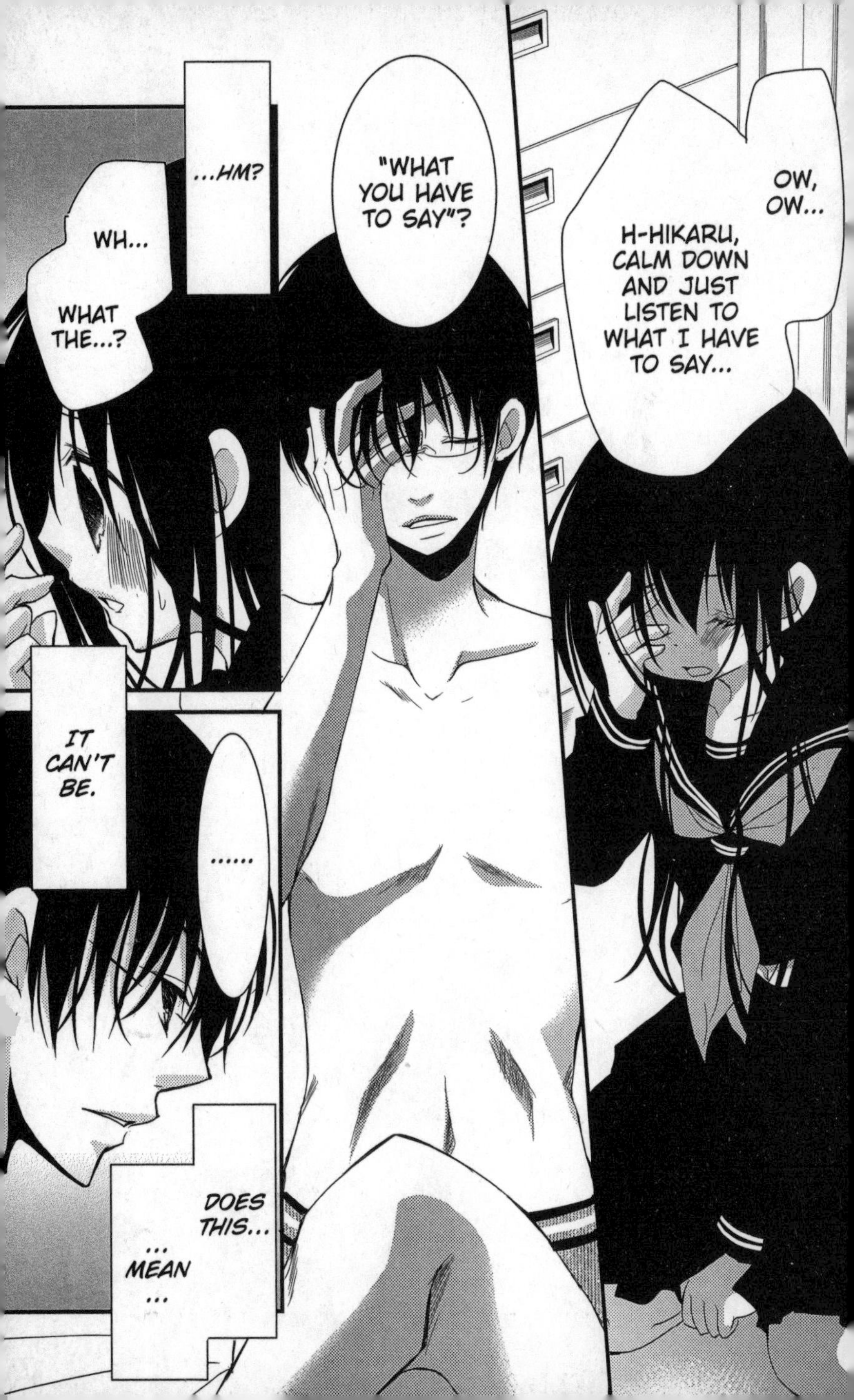
OW, OW...
H-HIKARU, CALM DOWN AND JUST LISTEN TO WHAT I HAVE TO SAY...
"WHAT YOU HAVE TO SAY"?
...HM?
WH...
WHAT THE...?
IT CAN'T BE.
......
DOES THIS...
...MEAN...

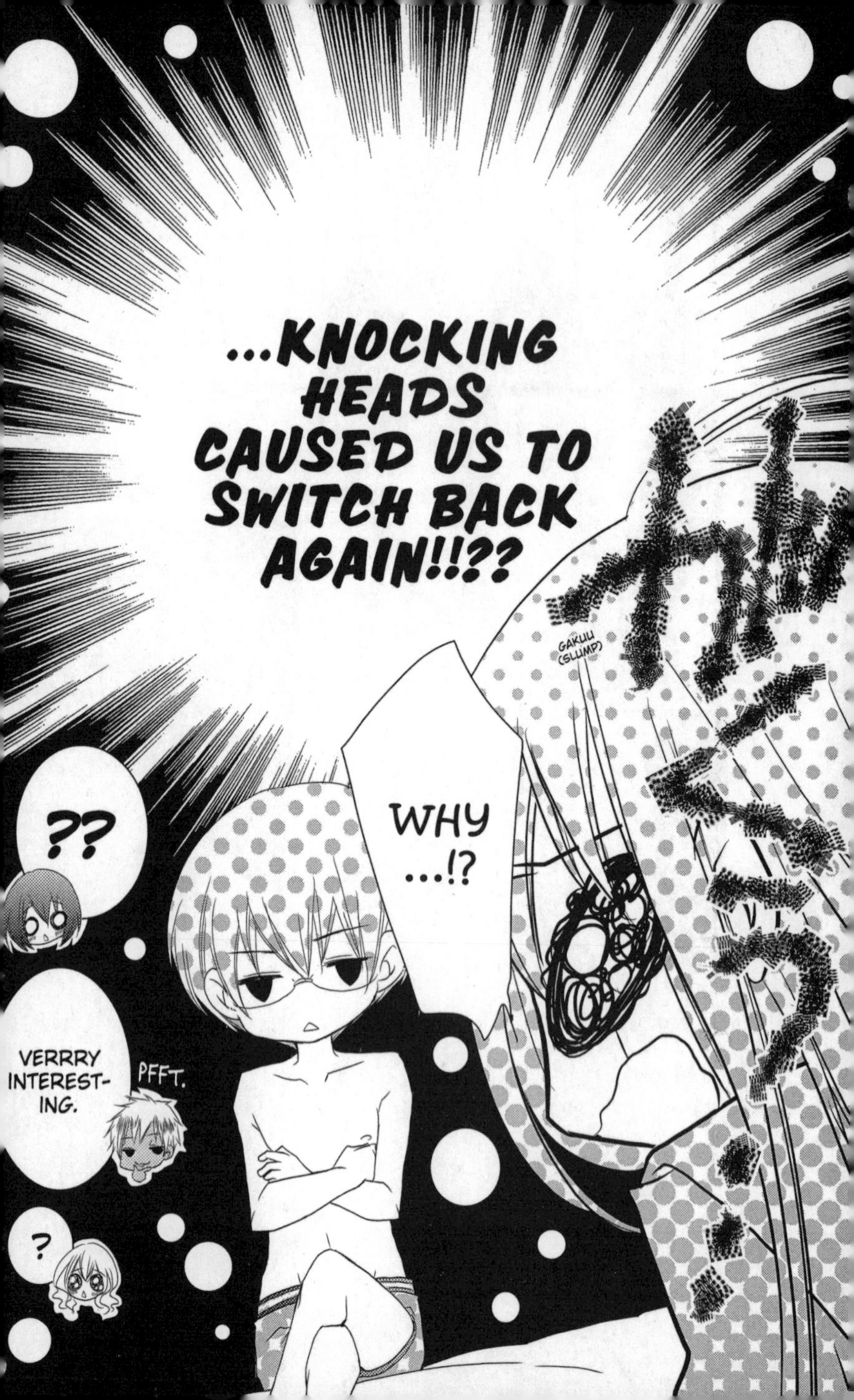
...KNOCKING HEADS CAUSED US TO SWITCH BACK AGAIN!!??
GAKUU (SLUMP)
WHY ...!?
??
VERRRY INTEREST-ING.
PFFT.
?

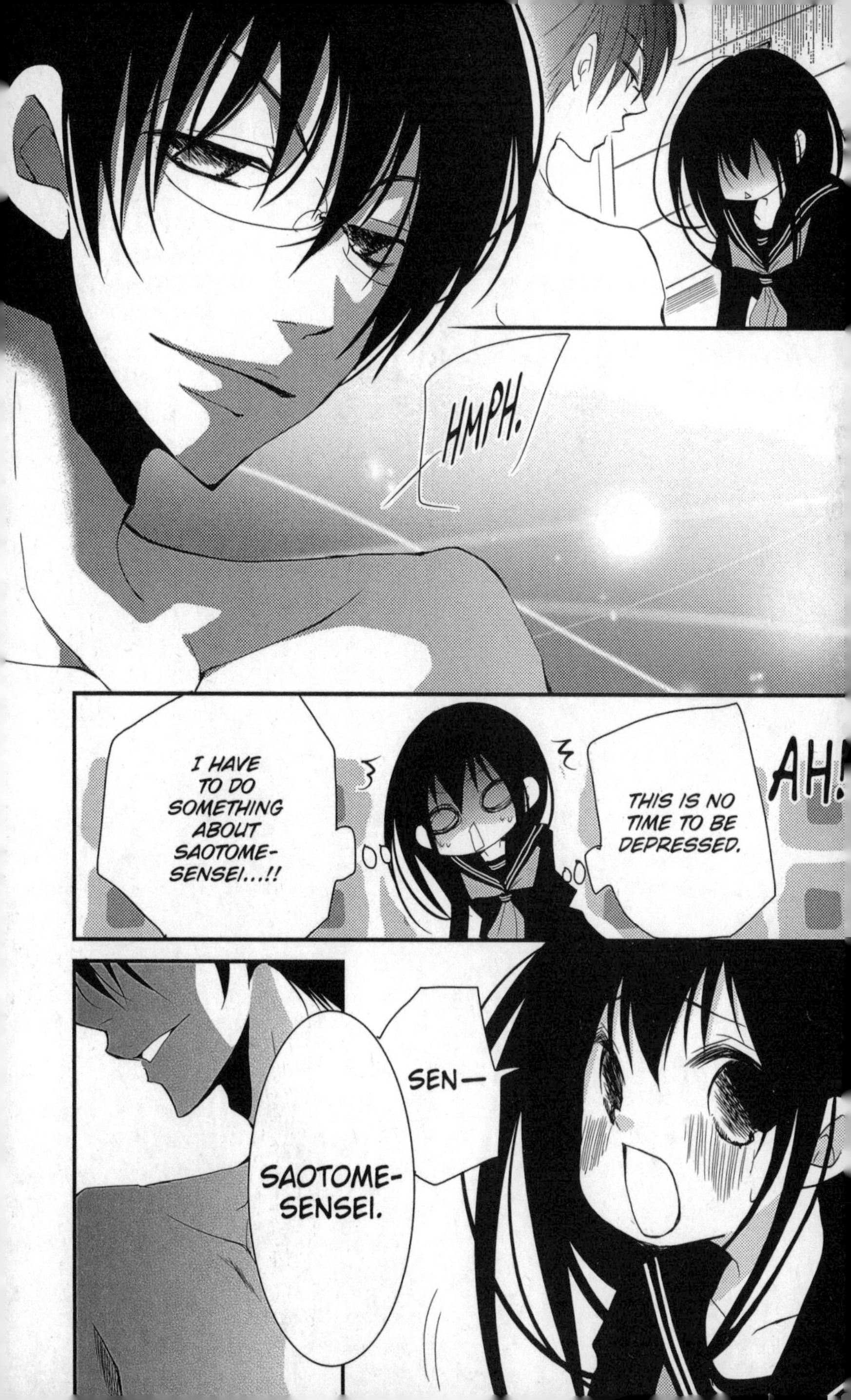
HMPH.
AH!
THIS IS NO TIME TO BE DEPRESSED.
I HAVE TO DO SOMETHING ABOUT SAOTOME-SENSEI...!!
SEN—
SAOTOME-SENSEI.

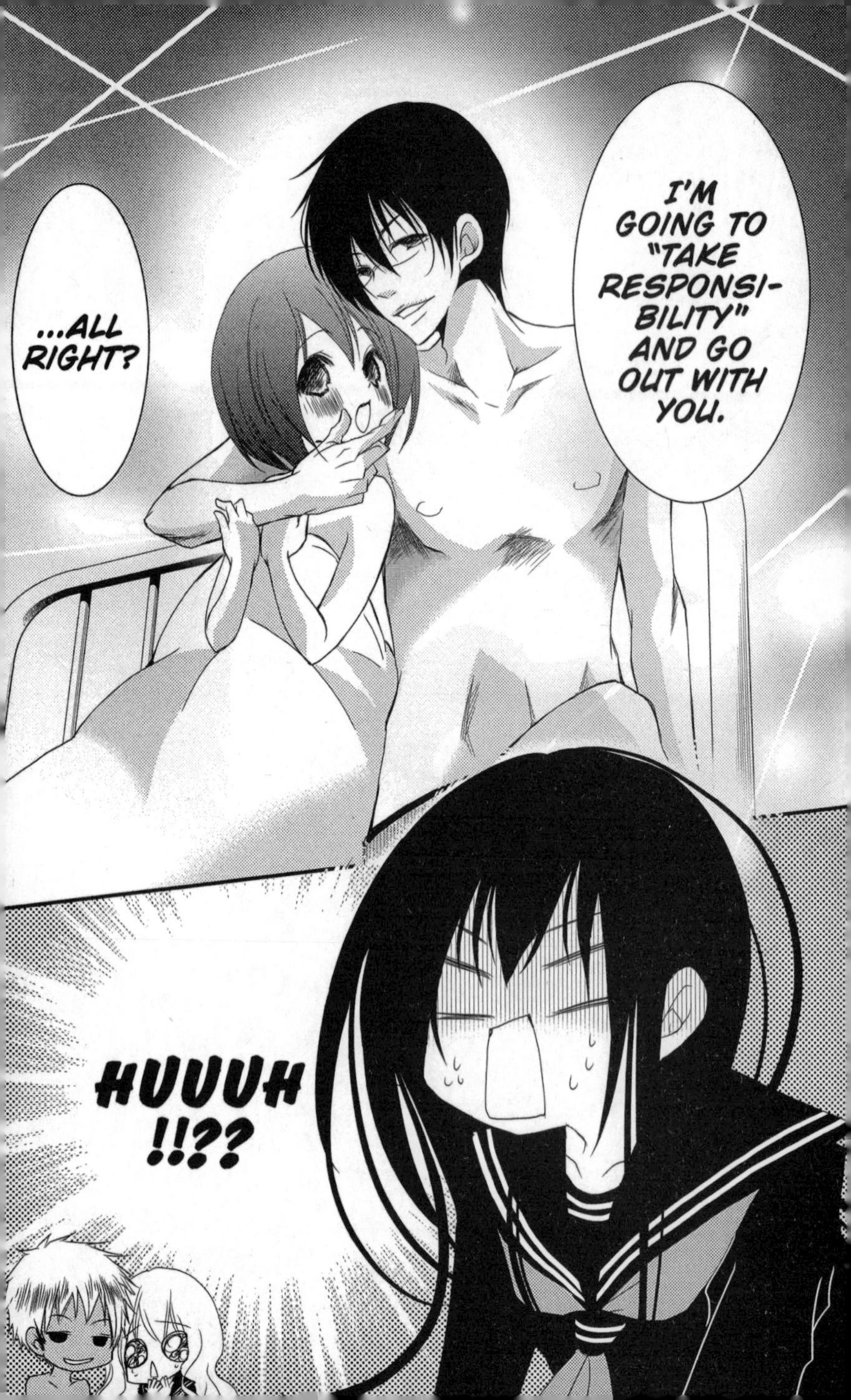
I'M GOING TO "TAKE RESPONSI-BILITY" AND GO OUT WITH YOU.
...ALL RIGHT?
HUUUH !!??

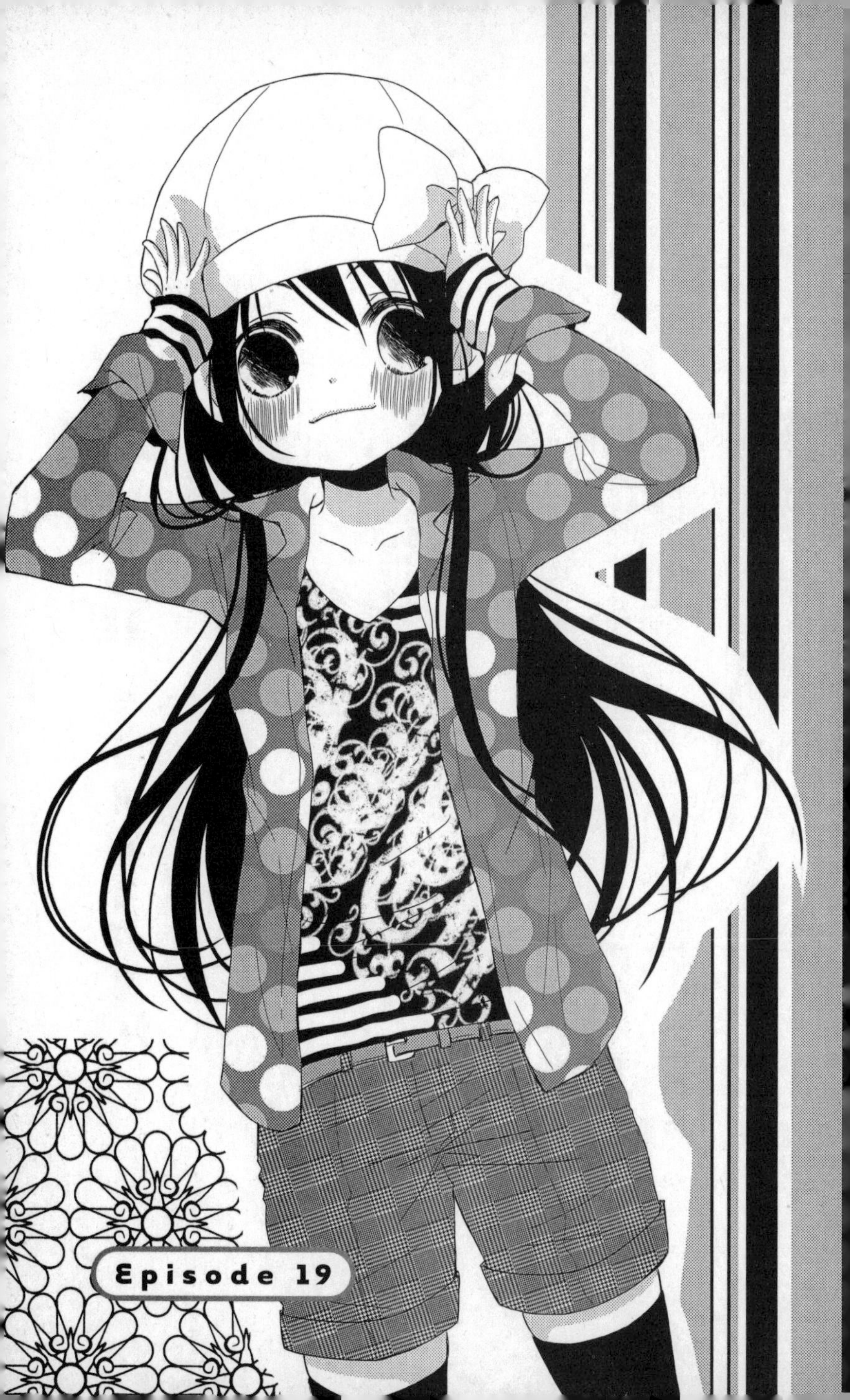
Episode 19

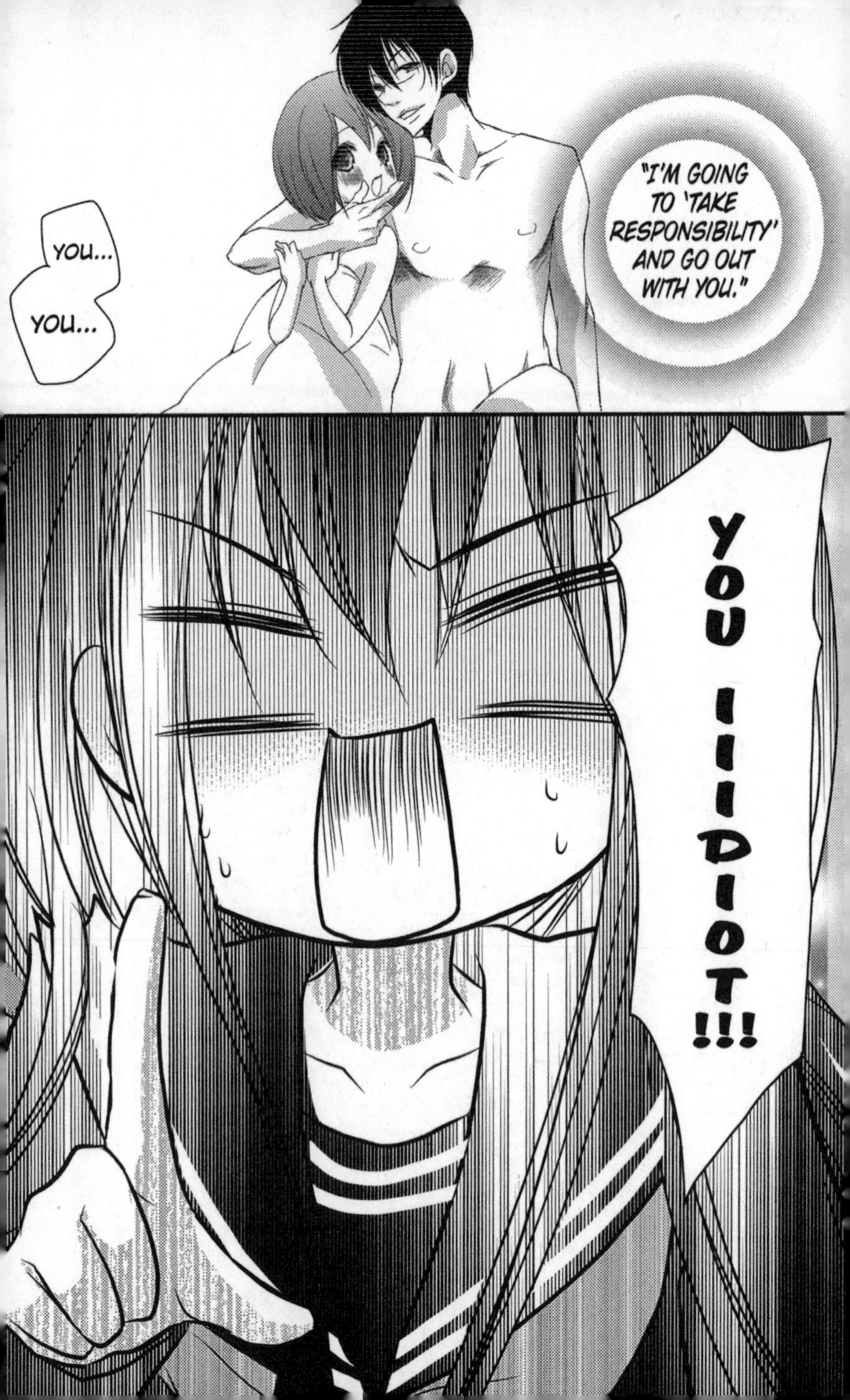
"I'M GOING TO 'TAKE RESPONSIBILITY' AND GO OUT WITH YOU."
YOU...
YOU...
YOU IIIDIOT!!!

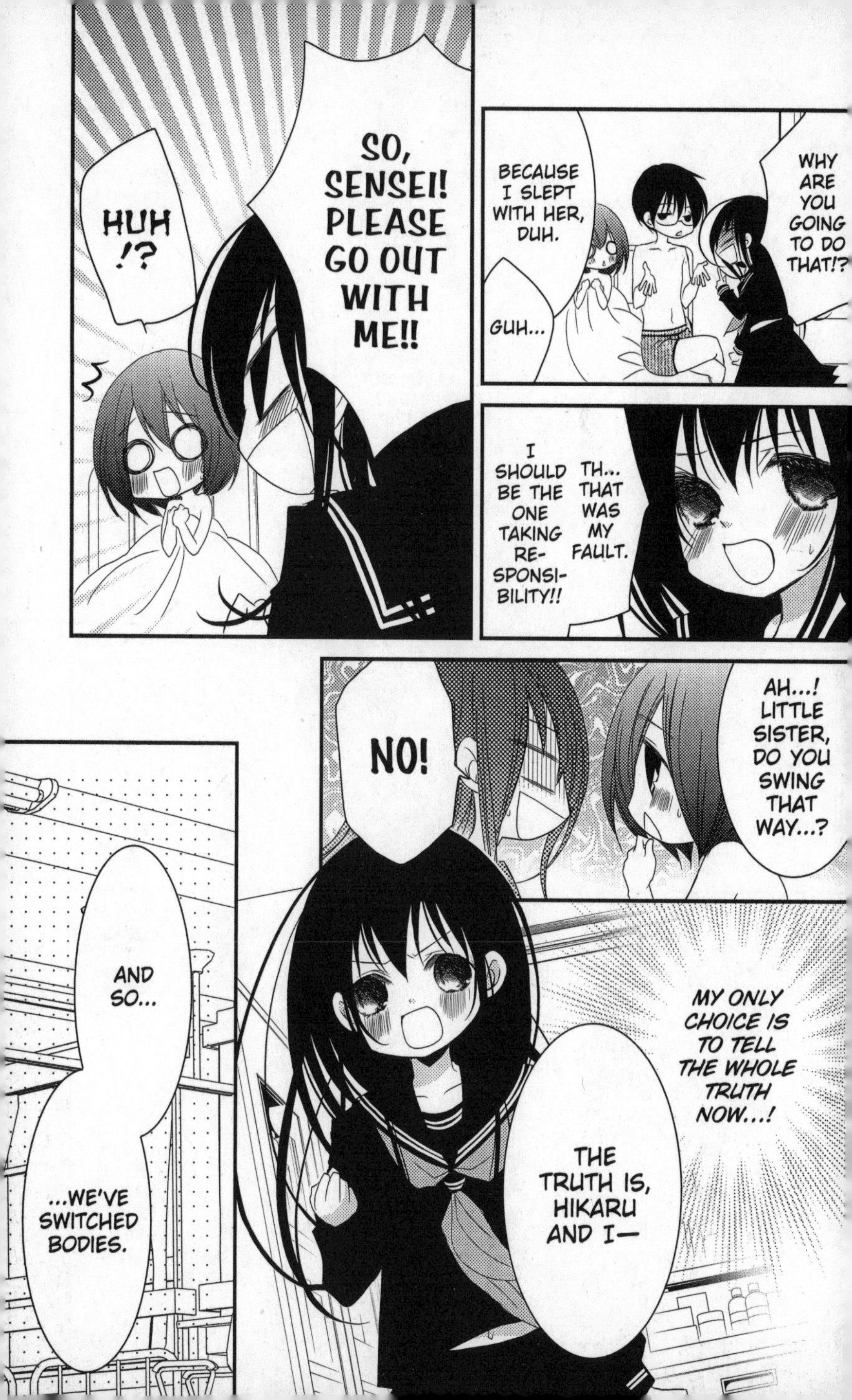
WHY ARE YOU GOING TO DO THAT!?
BECAUSE I SLEPT WITH HER, DUH.
GUH...
TH... THAT WAS MY FAULT.
I SHOULD BE THE ONE TAKING RE-SPONSI-BILITY!!
SO, SENSEI! PLEASE GO OUT WITH ME!!
HUH!?
AH...! LITTLE SISTER, DO YOU SWING THAT WAY...?
NO!
MY ONLY CHOICE IS TO TELL THE WHOLE TRUTH NOW...!
THE TRUTH IS, HIKARU AND I—
AND SO...
...WE'VE SWITCHED BODIES.

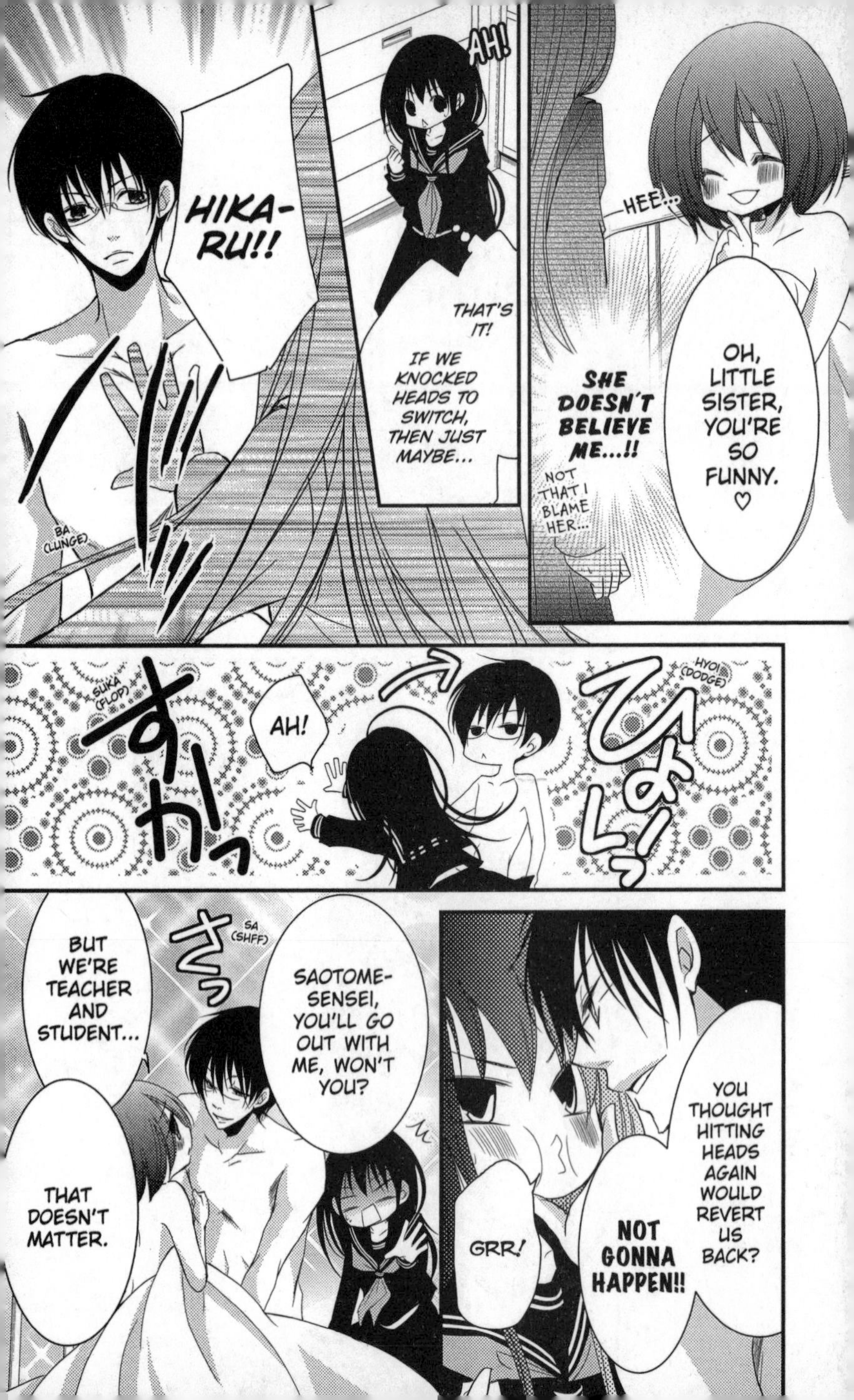
HEE...
OH, LITTLE SISTER, YOU'RE SO FUNNY. ♡
SHE DOESN'T BELIEVE ME...!!
NOT THAT I BLAME HER...
AH!
THAT'S IT!
IF WE KNOCKED HEADS TO SWITCH, THEN JUST MAYBE...
HIKA-RU!!
BA (LUNGE)
HYOI (DODGE)
ひょいっ
AH!
SUKA (FLOP)
すかっ
YOU THOUGHT HITTING HEADS AGAIN WOULD REVERT US BACK?
NOT GONNA HAPPEN!!
GRR!
SAOTOME-SENSEI, YOU'LL GO OUT WITH ME, WON'T YOU?
SA (SHFF)
さっ
BUT WE'RE TEACHER AND STUDENT...
THAT DOESN'T MATTER.

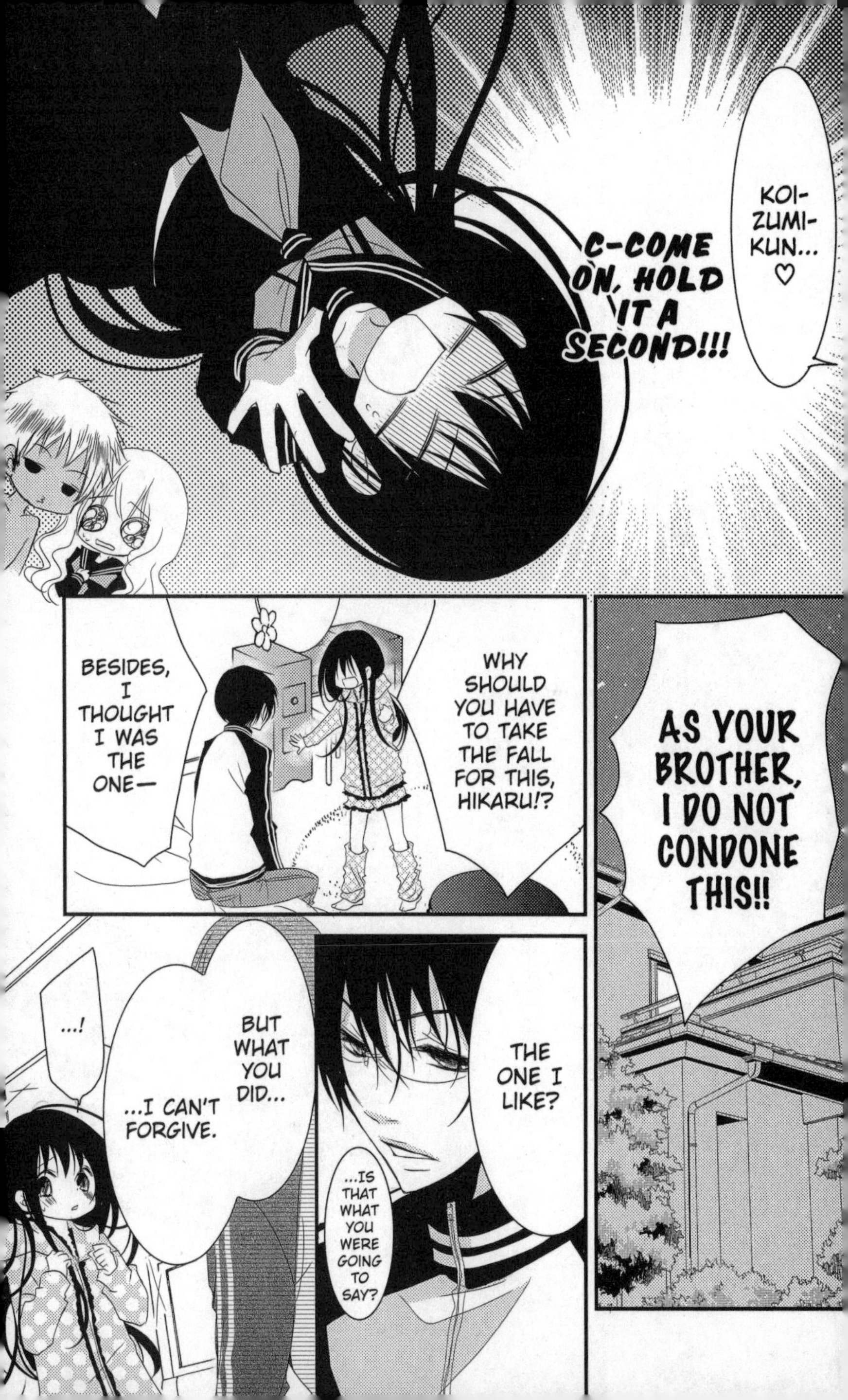
KOI-ZUMI-KUN... ♡
C-COME ON, HOLD IT A SECOND!!!
AS YOUR BROTHER, I DO NOT CONDONE THIS!!
WHY SHOULD YOU HAVE TO TAKE THE FALL FOR THIS, HIKARU!?
BESIDES, I THOUGHT I WAS THE ONE—
THE ONE I LIKE?
...IS THAT WHAT YOU WERE GOING TO SAY?
BUT WHAT YOU DID...
...I CAN'T FORGIVE.
...!

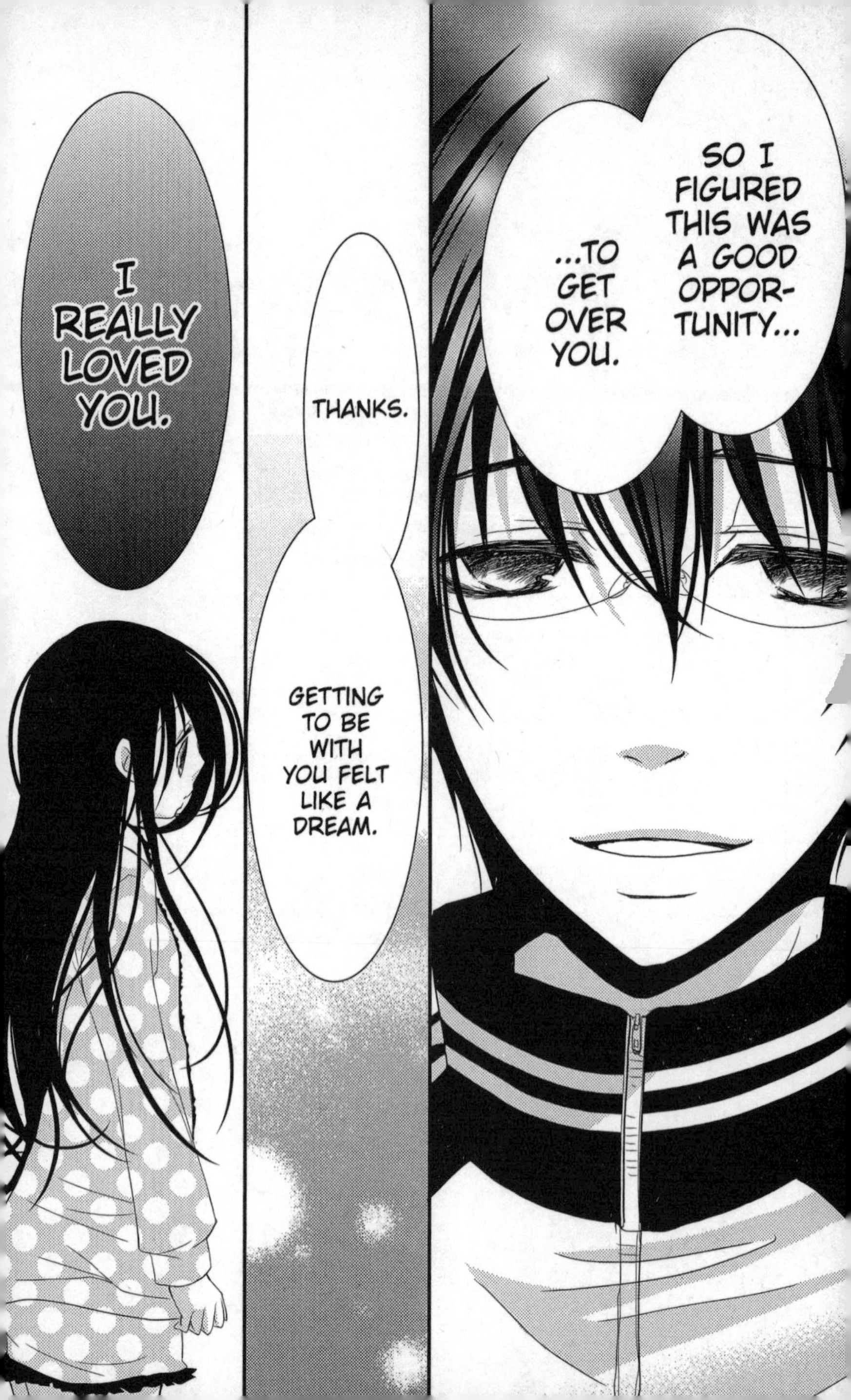
SO I FIGURED THIS WAS A GOOD OPPORTUNITY...
...TO GET OVER YOU.
THANKS.
GETTING TO BE WITH YOU FELT LIKE A DREAM.
I REALLY LOVED YOU.

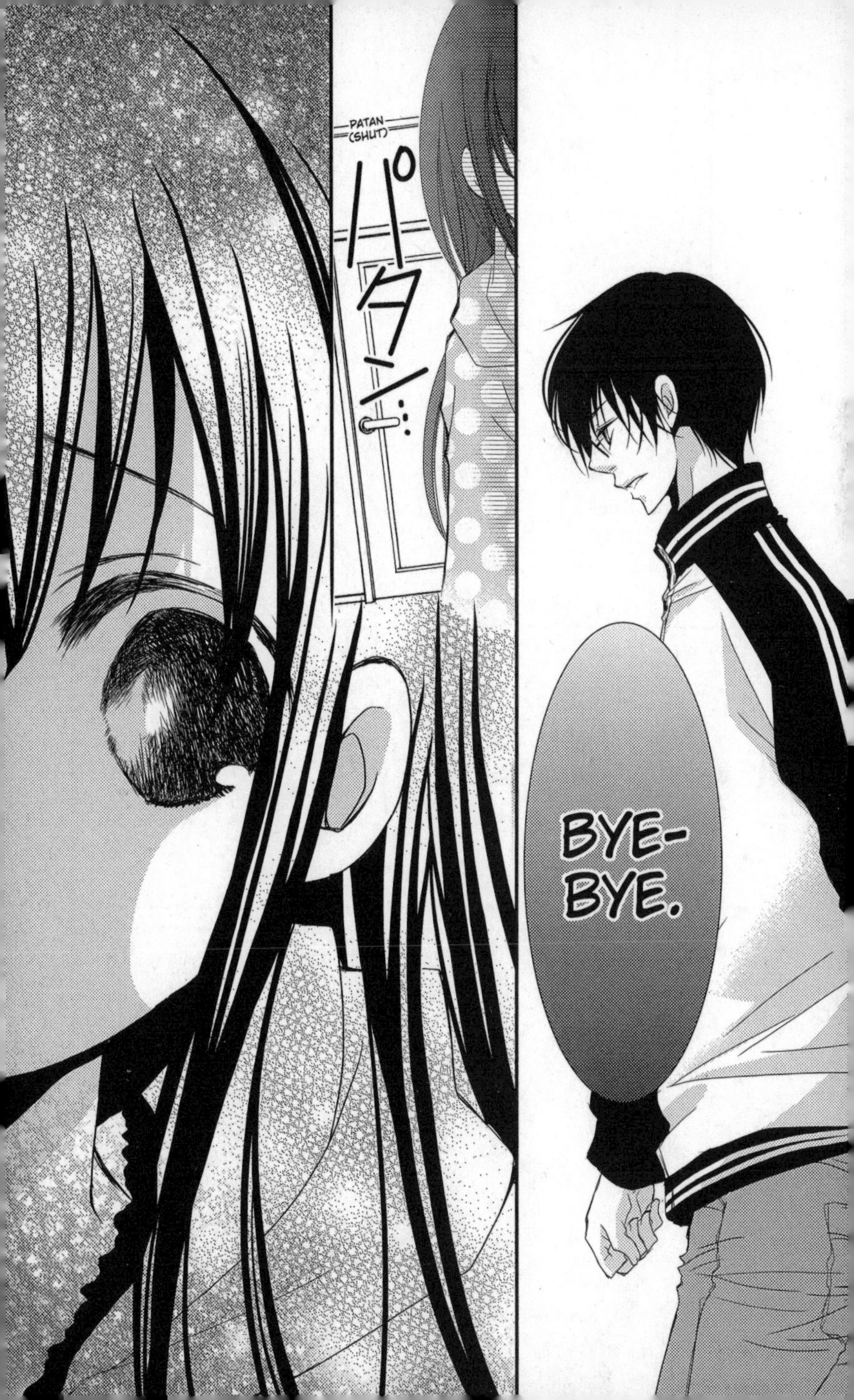
BYE-BYE.
PATAN (SHUT)

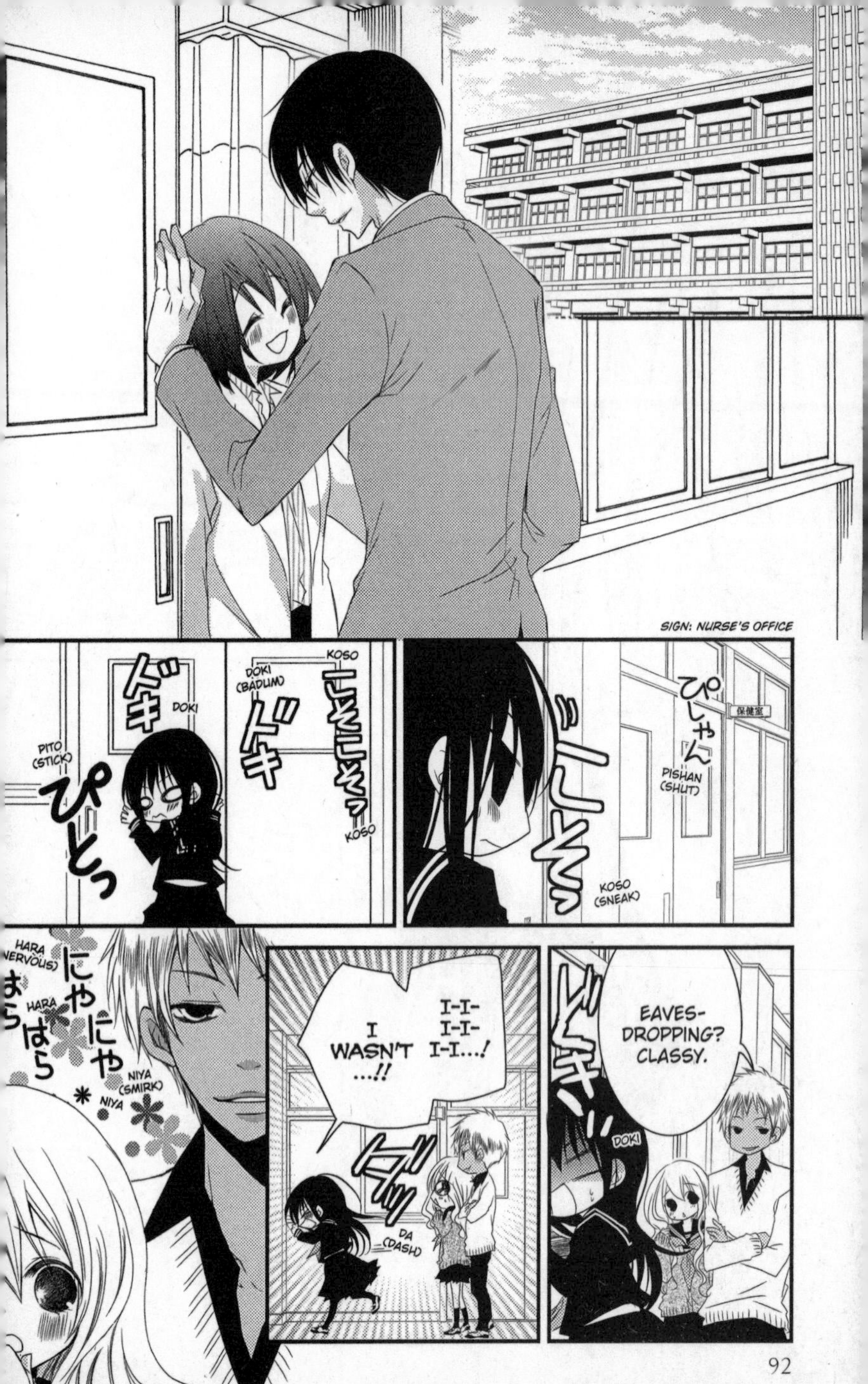
SIGN: NURSE'S OFFICE
ぴしゃん
PISHAN (SHUT)
保健室
こそっ
KOSO (SNEAK)
こそこそっ
KOSO
KOSO
ドキ
DOKI (BADUM)
ドキ
DOKI
ぴとっ
PITO (STICK)
EAVES-DROPPING? CLASSY.
どきーっ
DOKI
I-I-I-I-I-I...!
I WASN'T ...!!
ダッ
DA (DASH)
にやにや
NIYA (SMIRK)
NIYA
はらはら
HARA (NERVOUS)
HARA

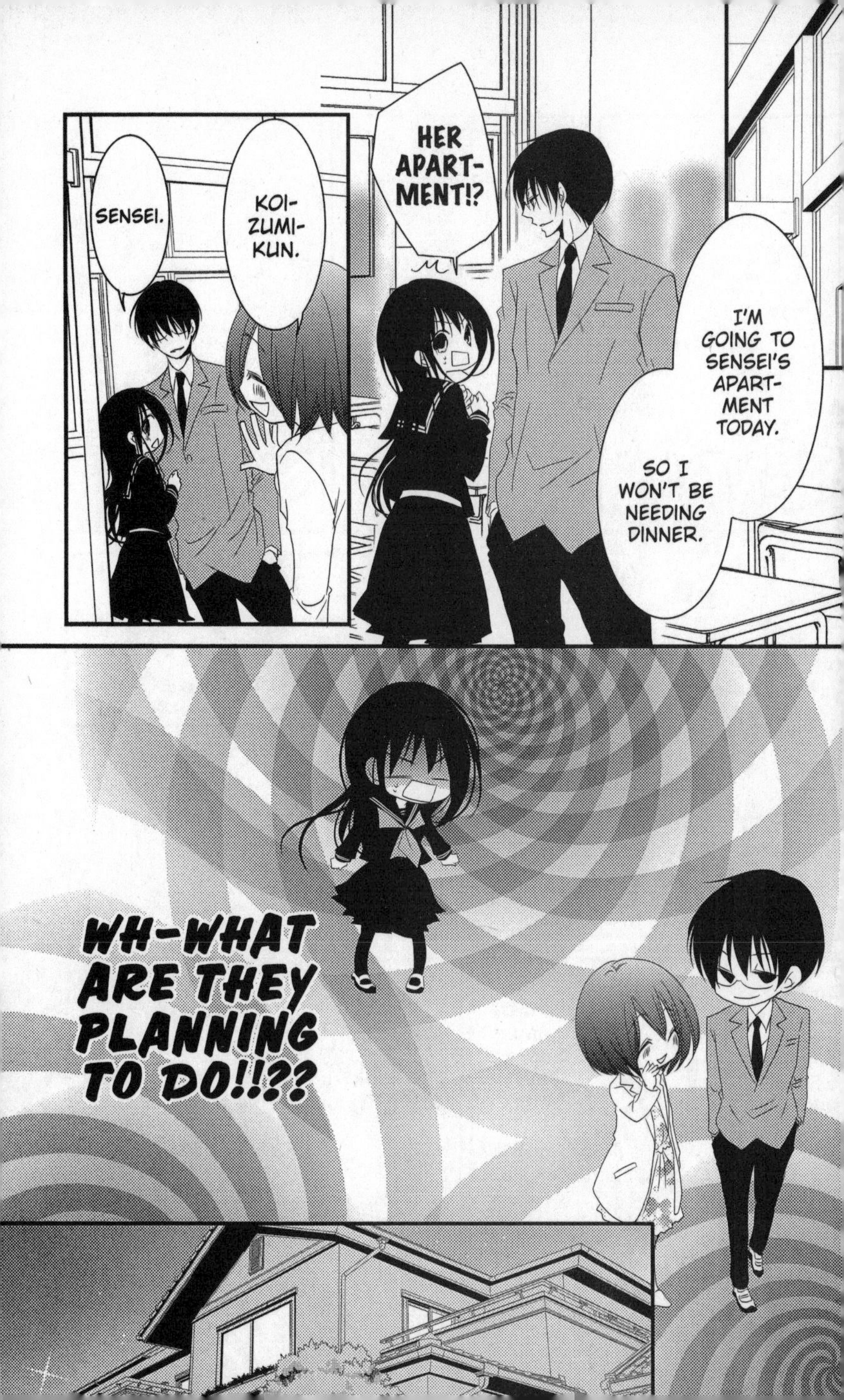
I'M GOING TO SENSEI'S APARTMENT TODAY.
SO I WON'T BE NEEDING DINNER.
HER APARTMENT!?
KOI-ZUMI-KUN.
SENSEI.
WH-WHAT ARE THEY PLANNING TO DO!!??

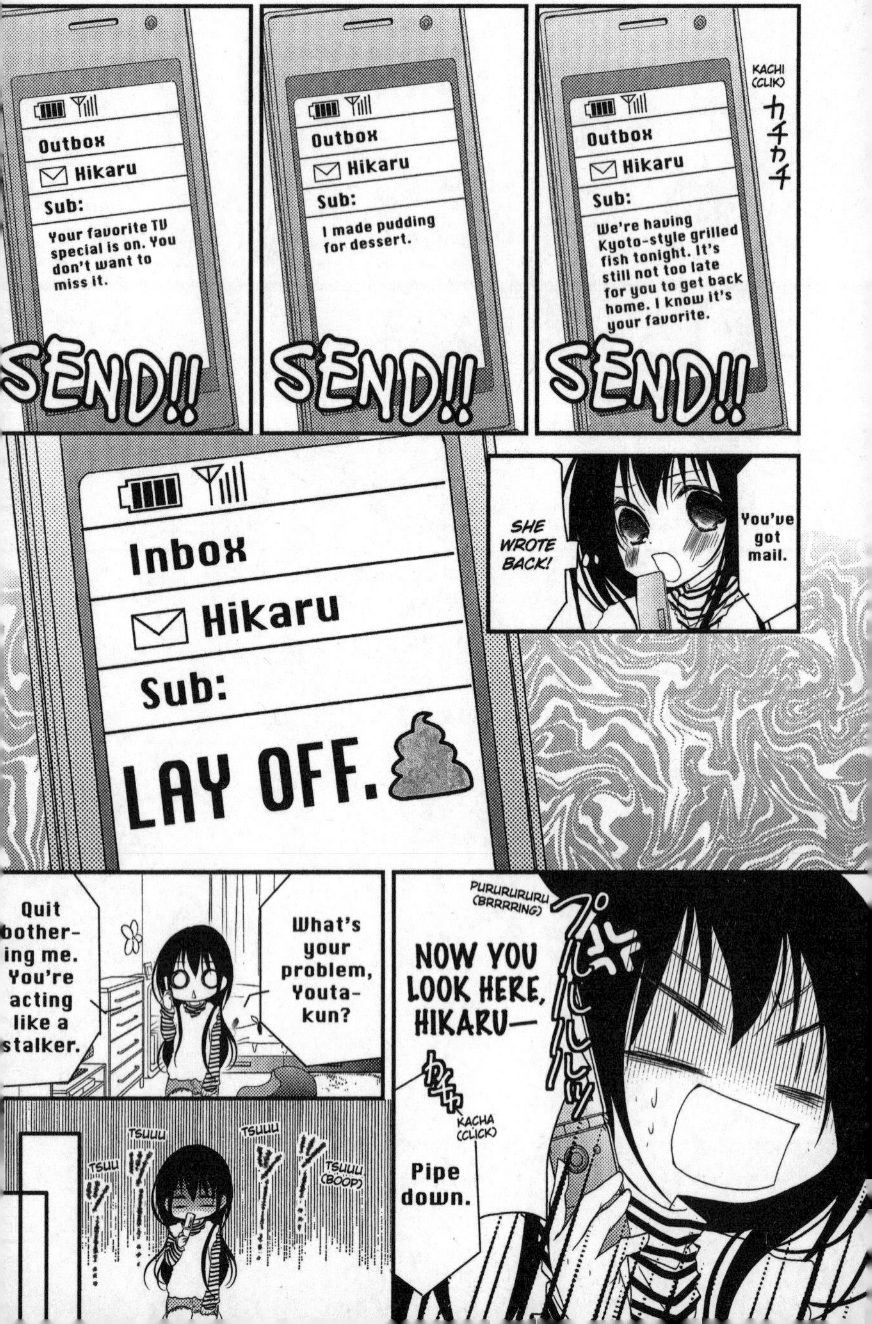
KACHI (CLIK)
カチカチ
Outbox
Hikaru
Sub:
We're having Kyoto-style grilled fish tonight. It's still not too late for you to get back home. I know it's your favorite.
SEND!!
Outbox
Hikaru
Sub:
I made pudding for dessert.
SEND!!
Outbox
Hikaru
Sub:
Your favorite TV special is on. You don't want to miss it.
SEND!!
You've got mail.
SHE WROTE BACK!
Inbox
Hikaru
Sub:
LAY OFF.
PURURURURU (BRRRRING)
NOW YOU LOOK HERE, HIKARU—
KACHA (CLICK)
Pipe down.
What's your problem, Youta-kun?
Quit bothering me. You're acting like a stalker.
TSUUU
TSUUU
TSUU
TSUUU (BOOP)

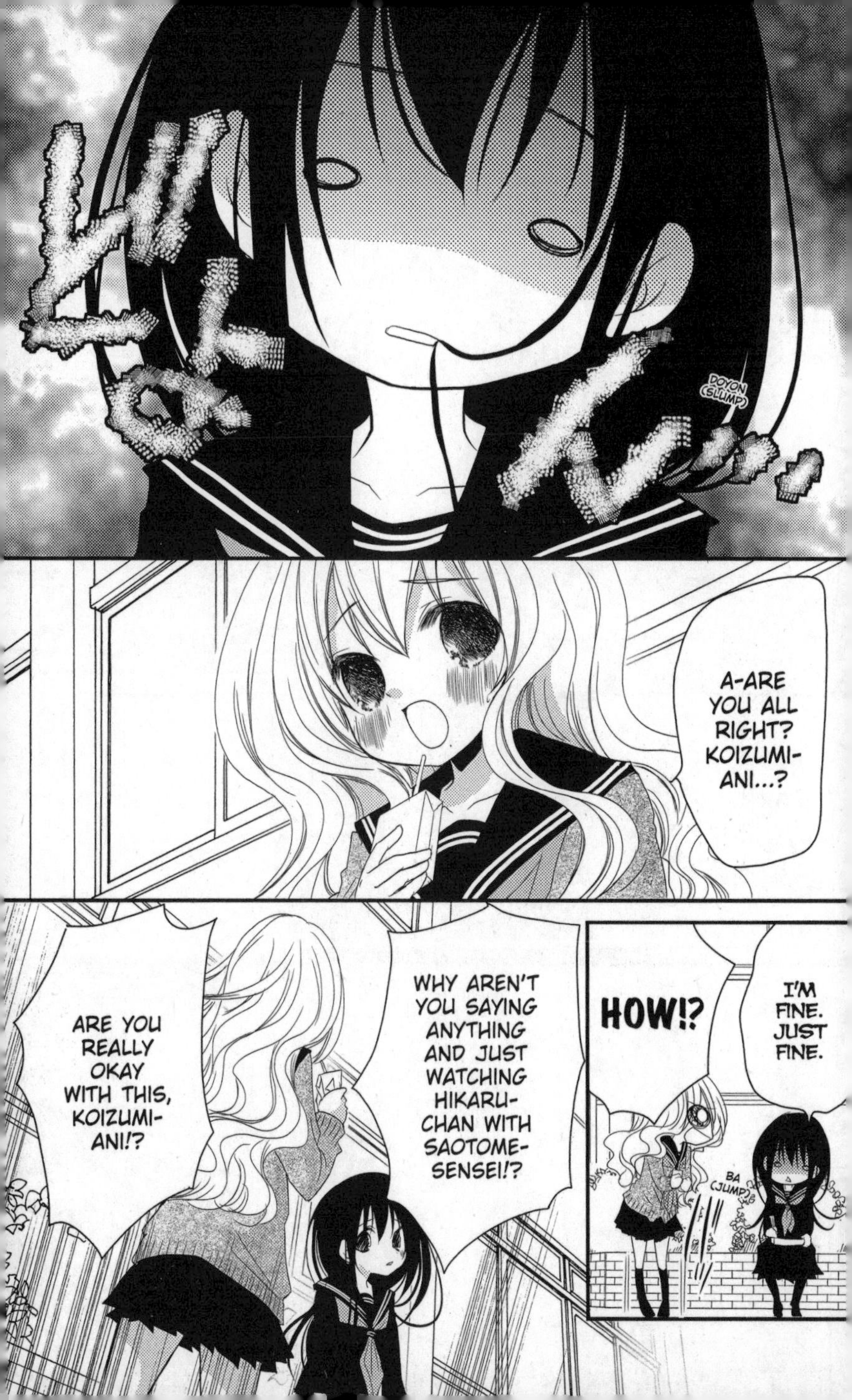
DOYON (SLUMP)
A-ARE YOU ALL RIGHT? KOIZUMI-ANI...?
I'M FINE. JUST FINE.
HOW!?
BA (JUMP)
WHY AREN'T YOU SAYING ANYTHING AND JUST WATCHING HIKARU-CHAN WITH SAOTOME-SENSEI!?
ARE YOU REALLY OKAY WITH THIS, KOIZUMI-ANI!?

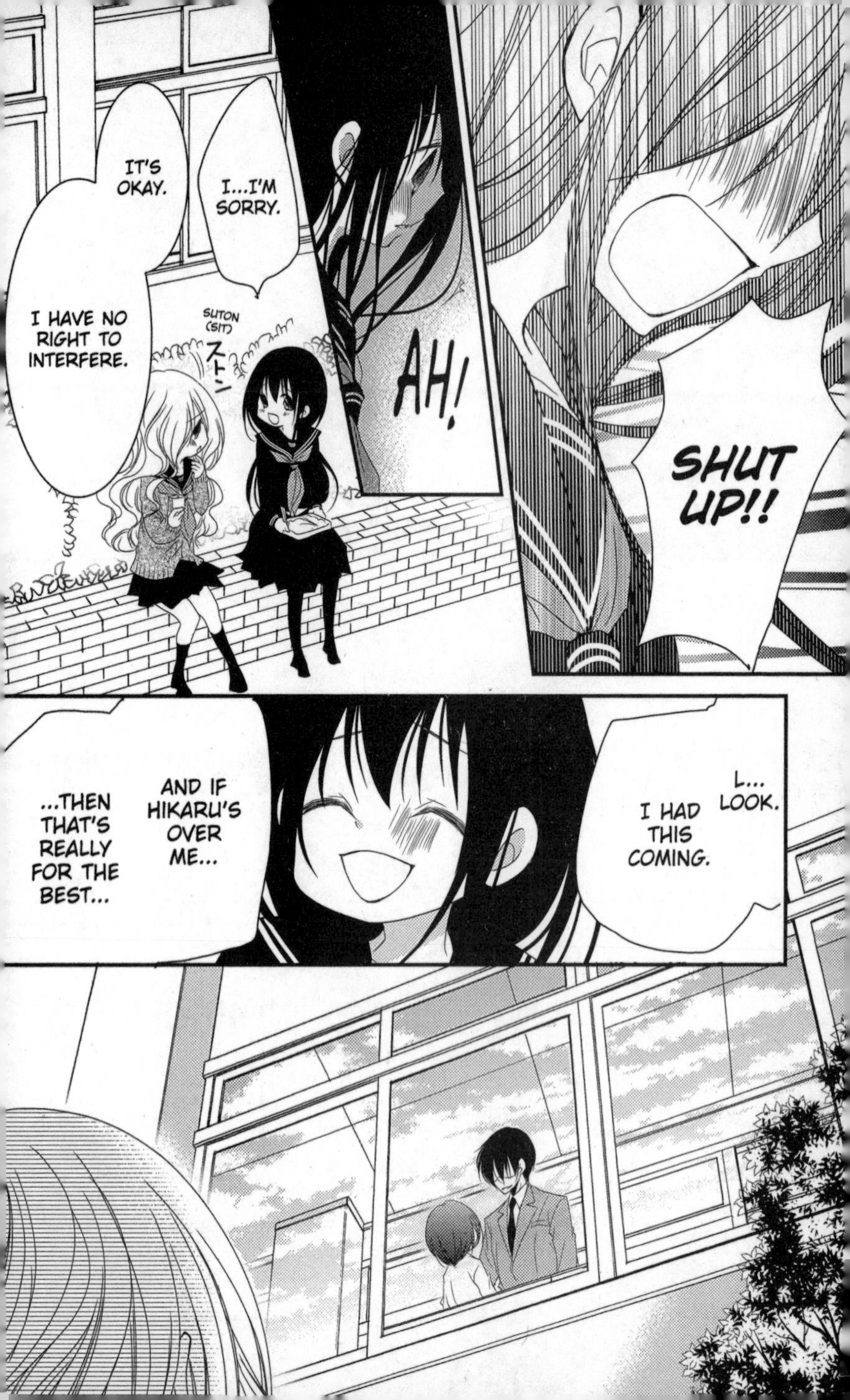
SHUT UP!!
AH!
I...I'M SORRY.
IT'S OKAY.
SUTON (SIT)
ストン
I HAVE NO RIGHT TO INTERFERE.
L... LOOK.
I HAD THIS COMING.
AND IF HIKARU'S OVER ME...
...THEN THAT'S REALLY FOR THE BEST...

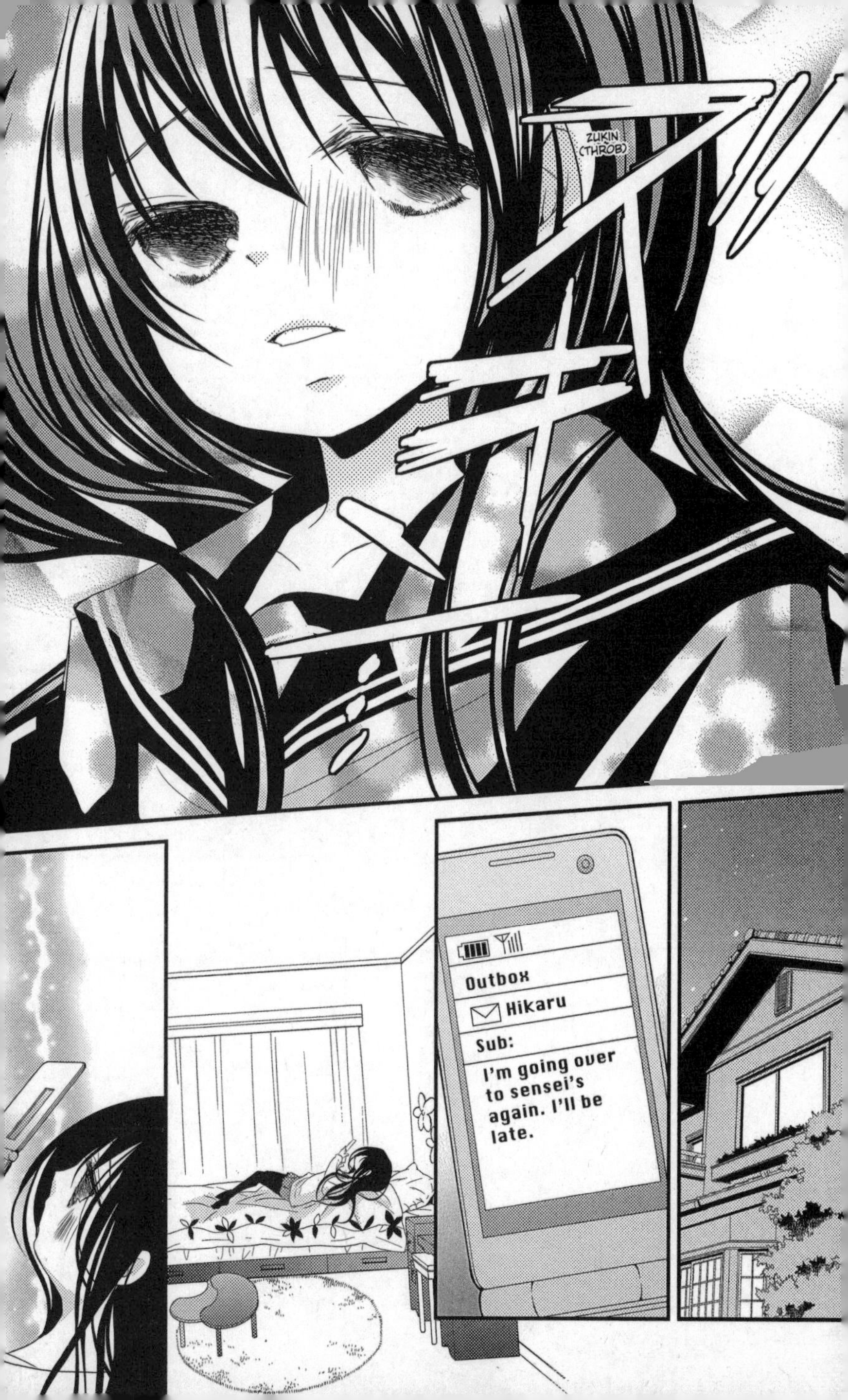
ZUKIN
(THROB)
Outbox
Hikaru
Sub:
I'm going over to sensei's again. I'll be late.

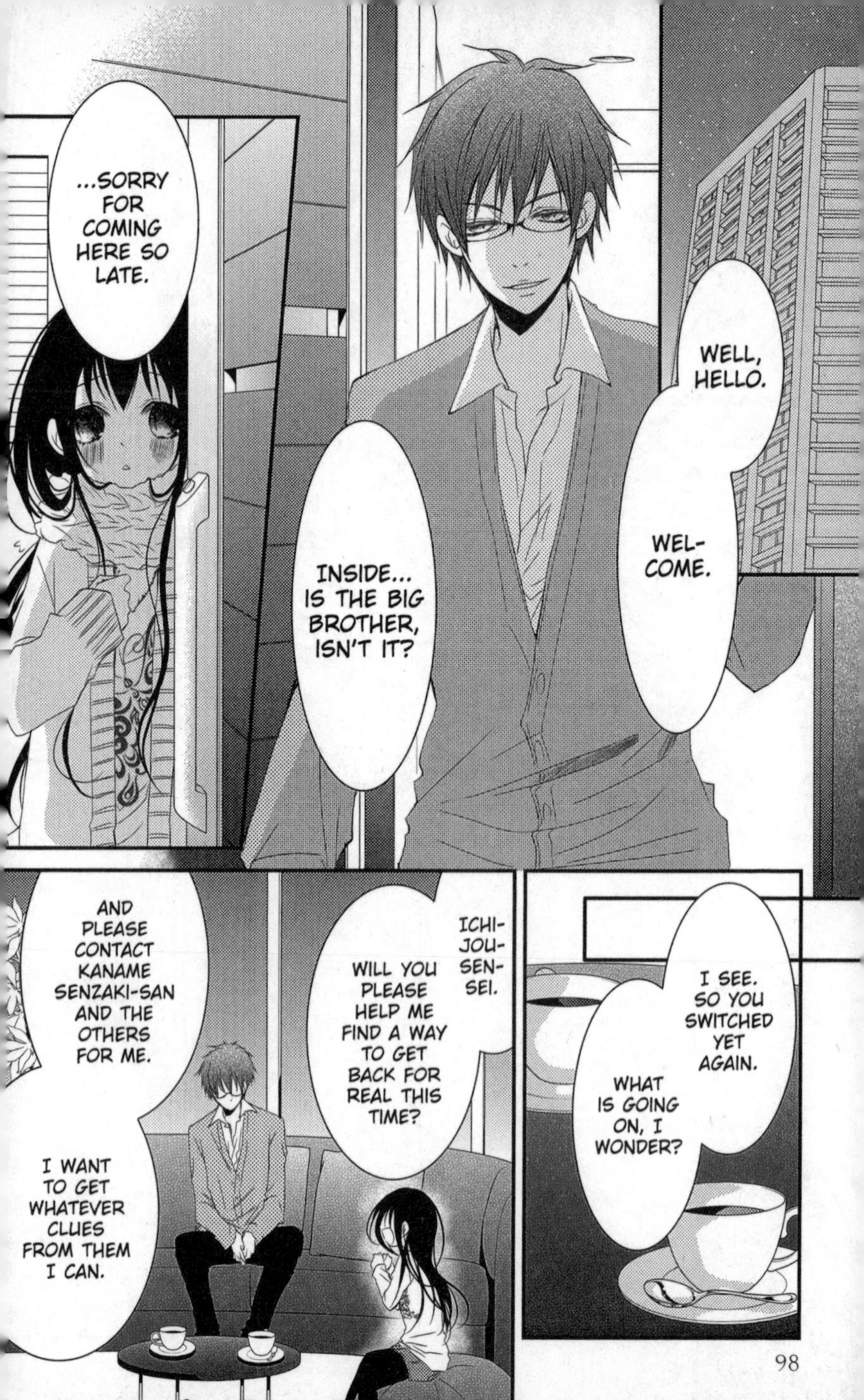
WELL, HELLO.
WEL-COME.
INSIDE... IS THE BIG BROTHER, ISN'T IT?
...SORRY FOR COMING HERE SO LATE.
I SEE. SO YOU SWITCHED YET AGAIN.
WHAT IS GOING ON, I WONDER?
ICHI-JOU-SEN-SEI.
WILL YOU PLEASE HELP ME FIND A WAY TO GET BACK FOR REAL THIS TIME?
AND PLEASE CONTACT KANAME SENZAKI-SAN AND THE OTHERS FOR ME.
I WANT TO GET WHATEVER CLUES FROM THEM I CAN.

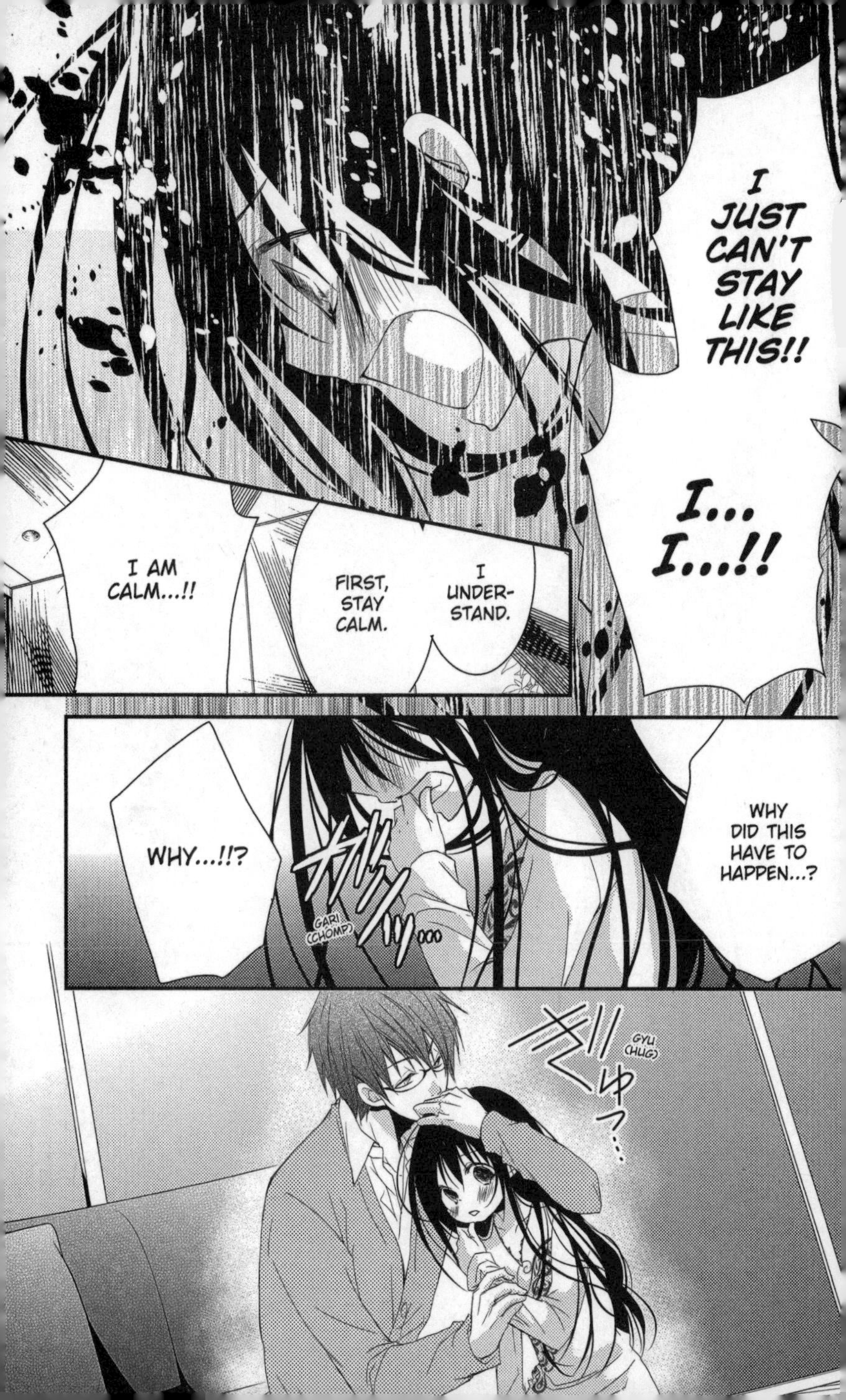
I JUST CAN'T STAY LIKE THIS!!
I... I...!!
I UNDER-STAND.
FIRST, STAY CALM.
I AM CALM...!!
WHY DID THIS HAVE TO HAPPEN...?
WHY...!!?
GARI (CHOMP)
GYU (HUG)

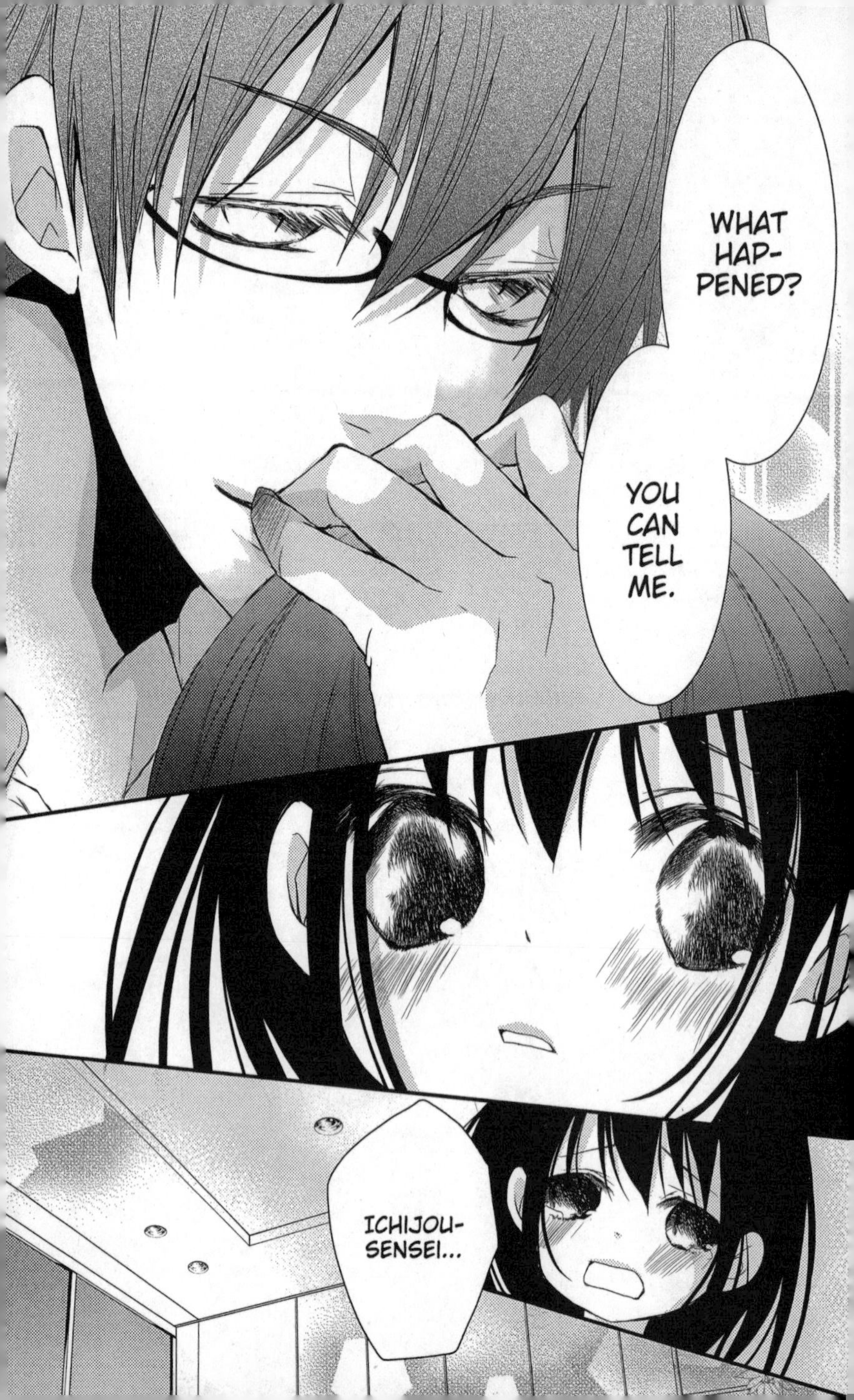
WHAT HAP-PENED?
YOU CAN TELL ME.
ICHIJOU-SENSEI...

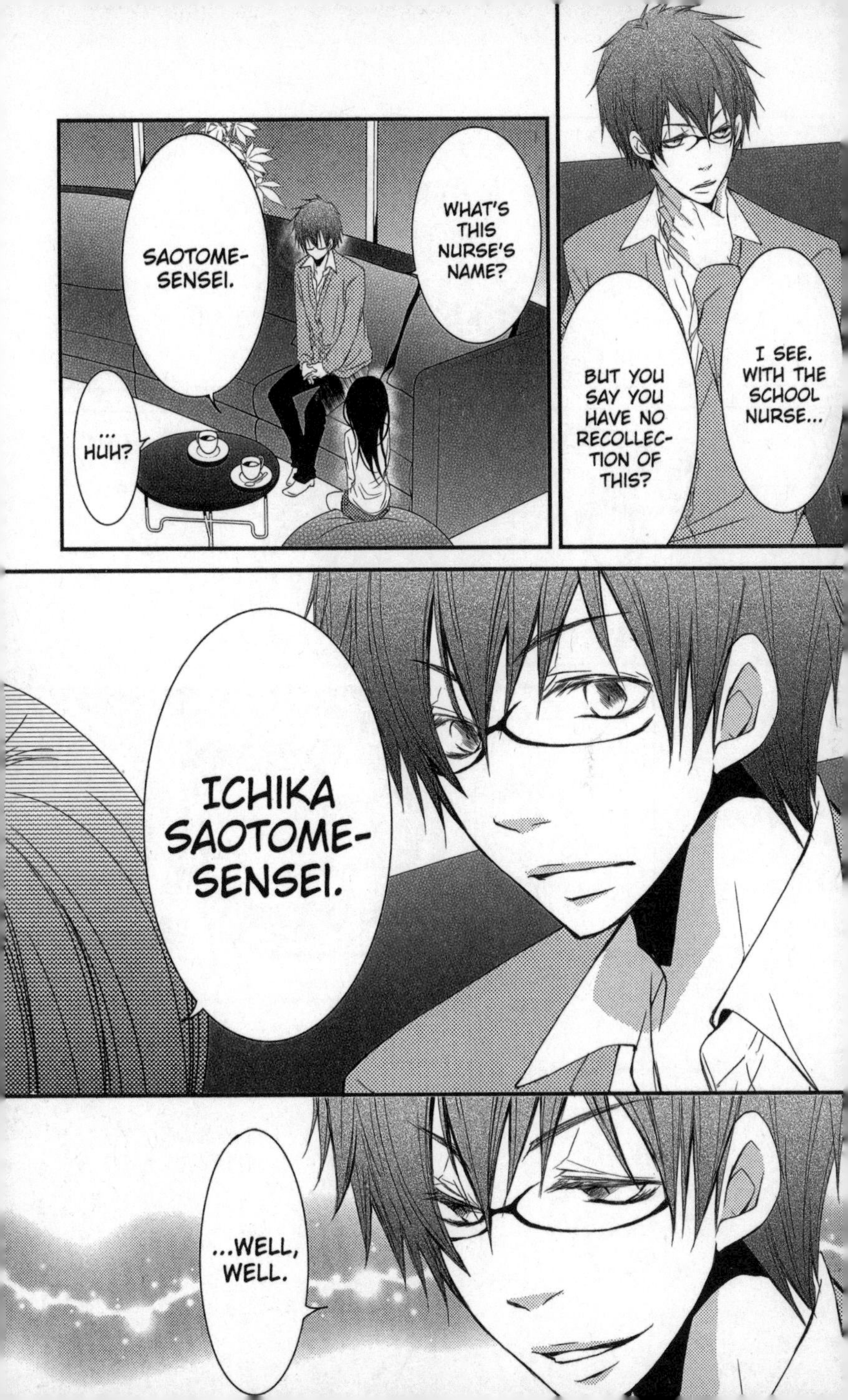
I SEE. WITH THE SCHOOL NURSE...
BUT YOU SAY YOU HAVE NO RECOLLECTION OF THIS?
WHAT'S THIS NURSE'S NAME?
SAOTOME-SENSEI.
...HUH?
ICHIKA SAOTOME-SENSEI.
...WELL, WELL.

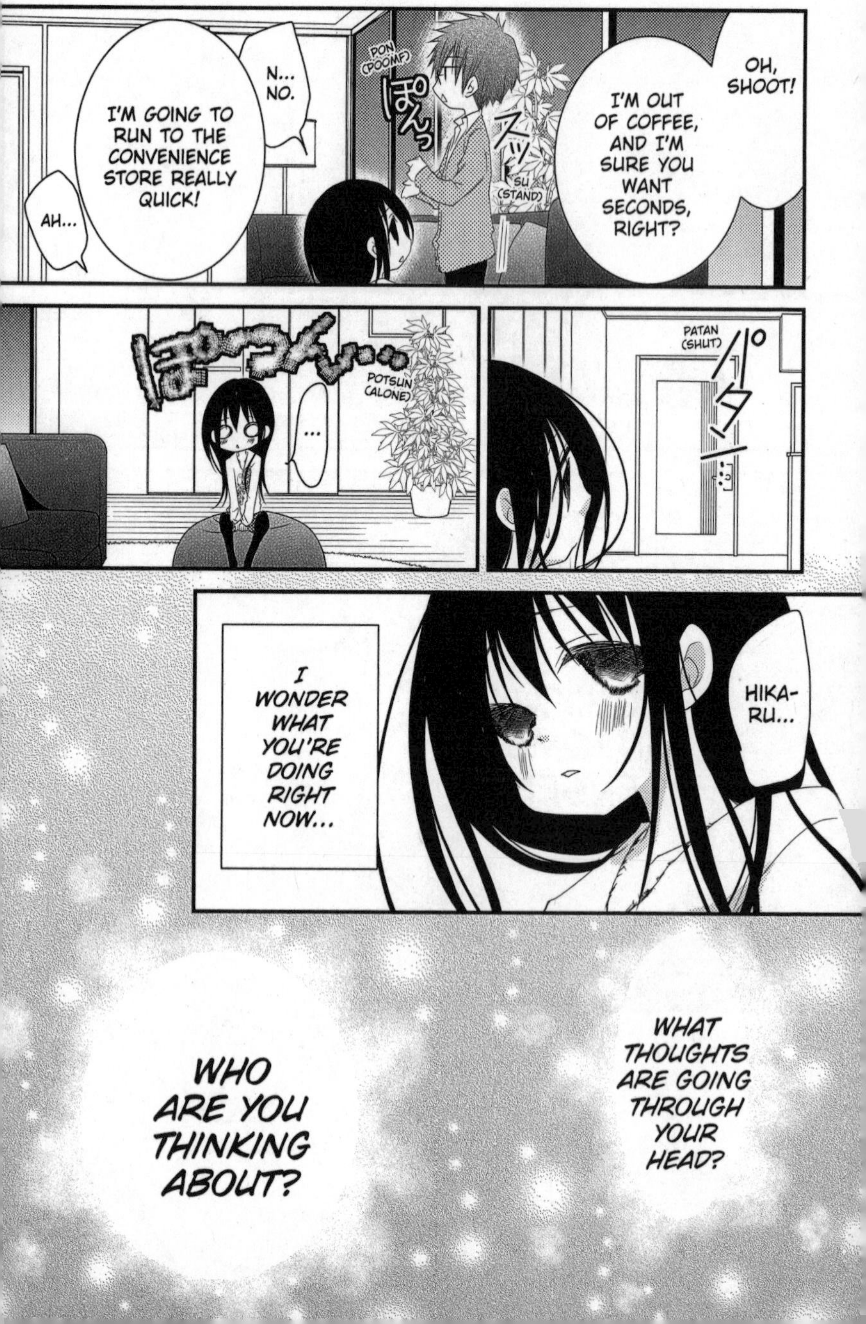
OH, SHOOT!
I'M OUT OF COFFEE, AND I'M SURE YOU WANT SECONDS, RIGHT?
スッ
SU (STAND)
ぽんっ
PON (POOMF)
N... NO.
I'M GOING TO RUN TO THE CONVENIENCE STORE REALLY QUICK!
AH...
パタン
PATAN (SHUT)
POTSUN (ALONE)
...
HIKA-RU...
I WONDER WHAT YOU'RE DOING RIGHT NOW...
WHAT THOUGHTS ARE GOING THROUGH YOUR HEAD?
WHO ARE YOU THINKING ABOUT?

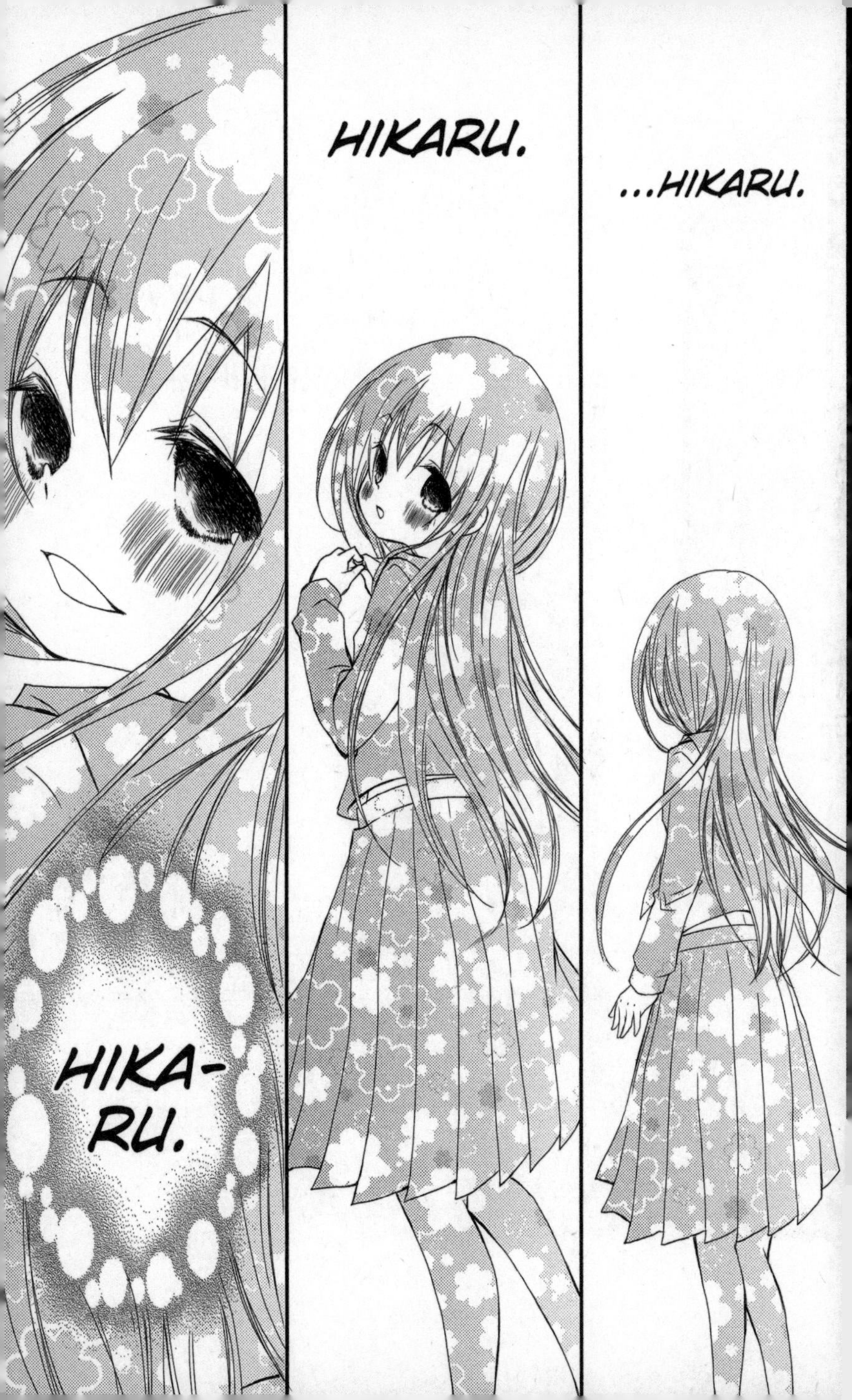
...HIKARU.
HIKARU.
HIKA-
RU.

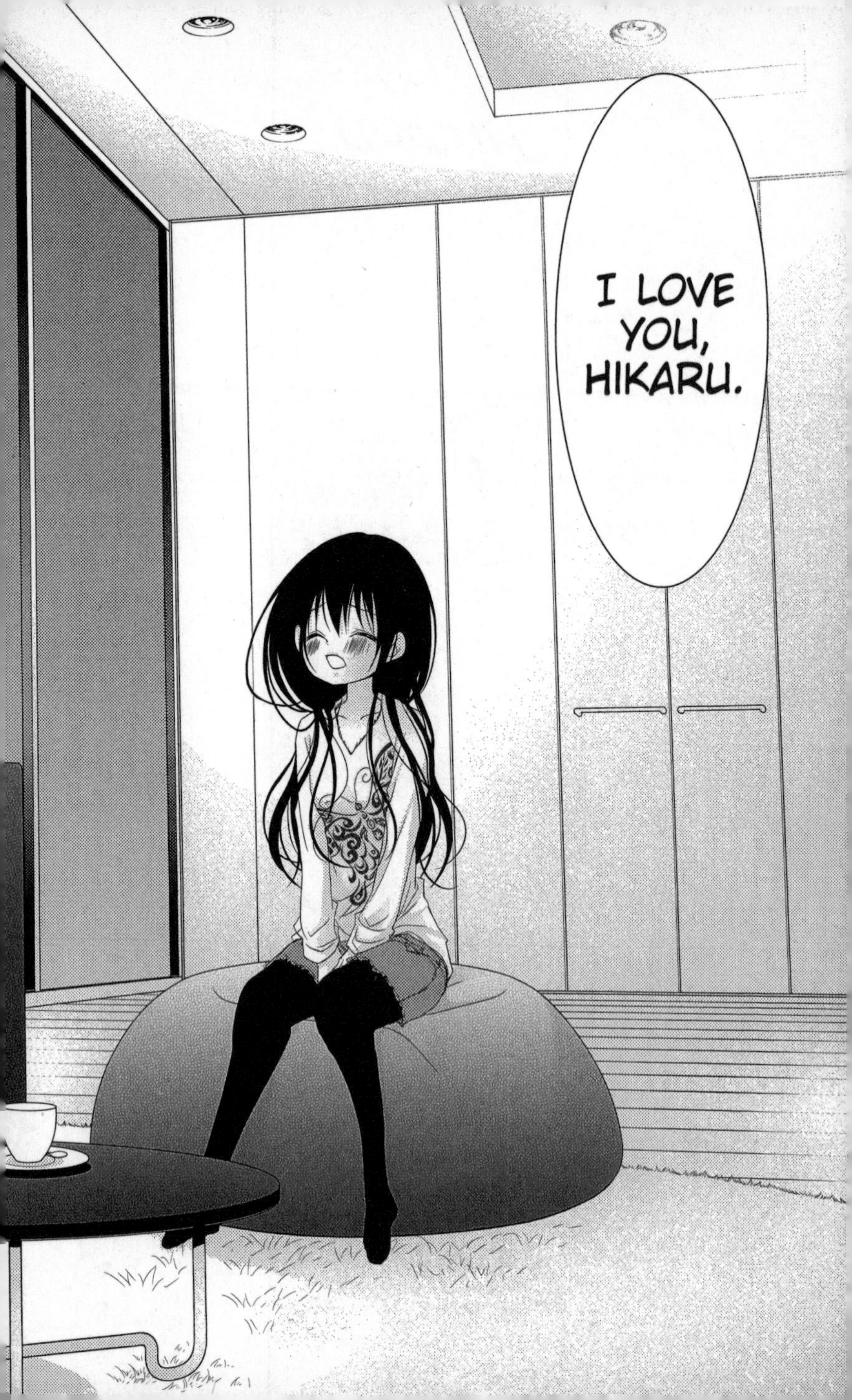
I LOVE YOU, HIKARU.

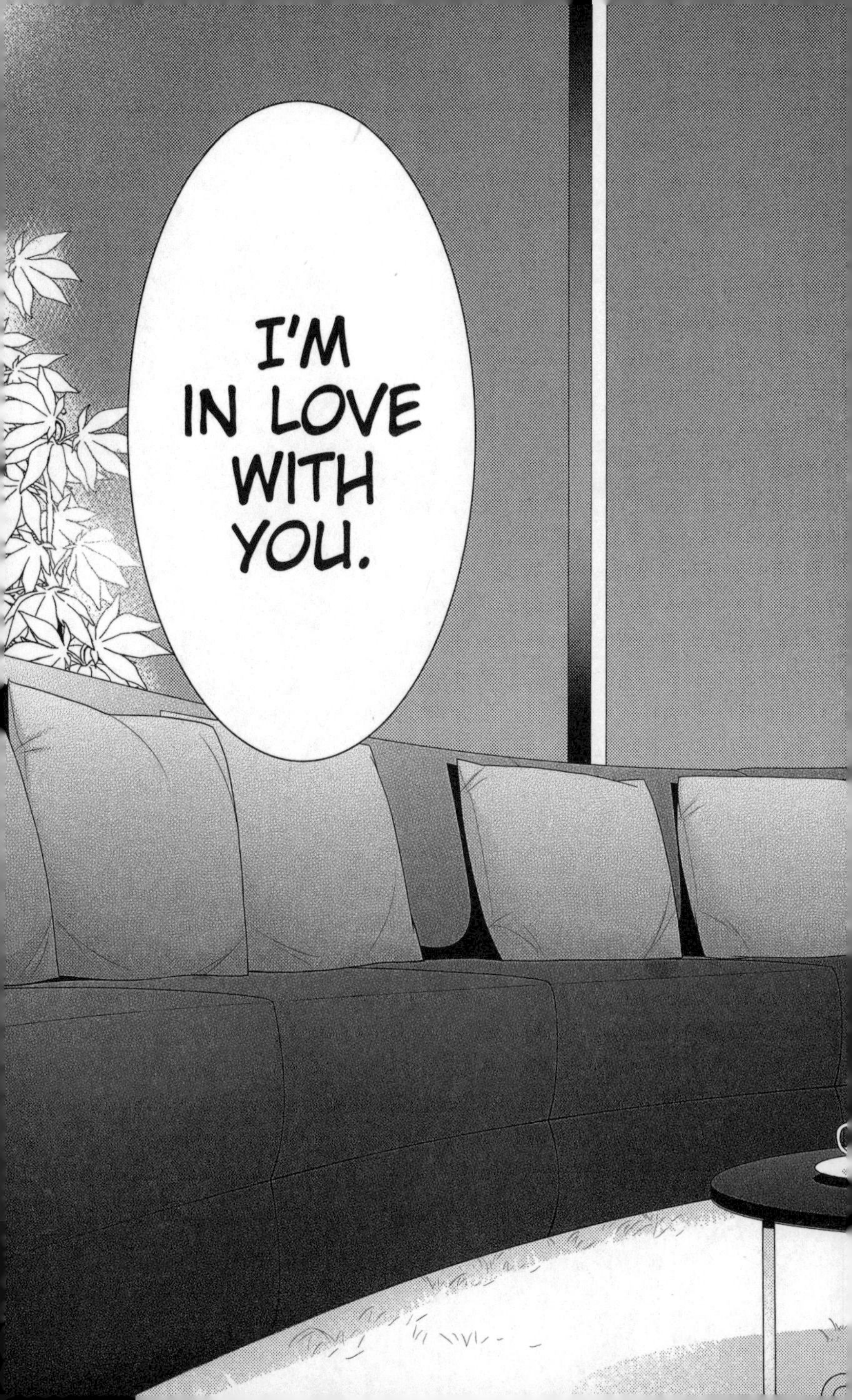
I'M IN LOVE WITH YOU.

—!
BA (FWP)
AH ...
I...
I...
NO MATTER WHAT HAPPENED, I ALWAYS WANTED TO BE WITH HIKARU.
THAT'S WHY I WANTED TO KEEP UP OUR BROTHER AND SISTER RELATIONSHIP.
I...
...AM AN IDIOT.
I NEVER THOUGHT...
...WE'D SPLIT UP LIKE THIS.

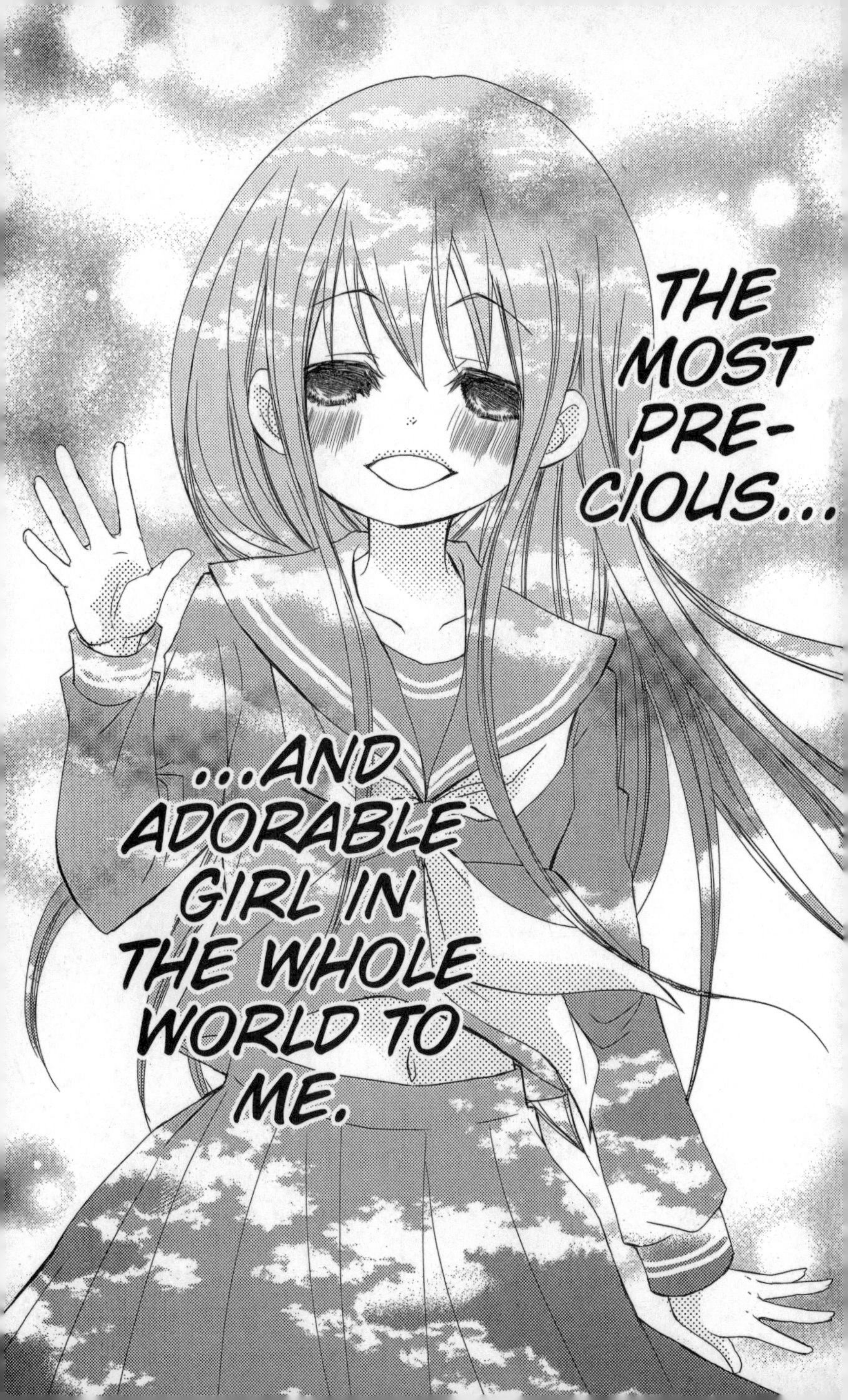
THE MOST PRE-CIOUS...
...AND ADORABLE GIRL IN THE WHOLE WORLD TO ME.

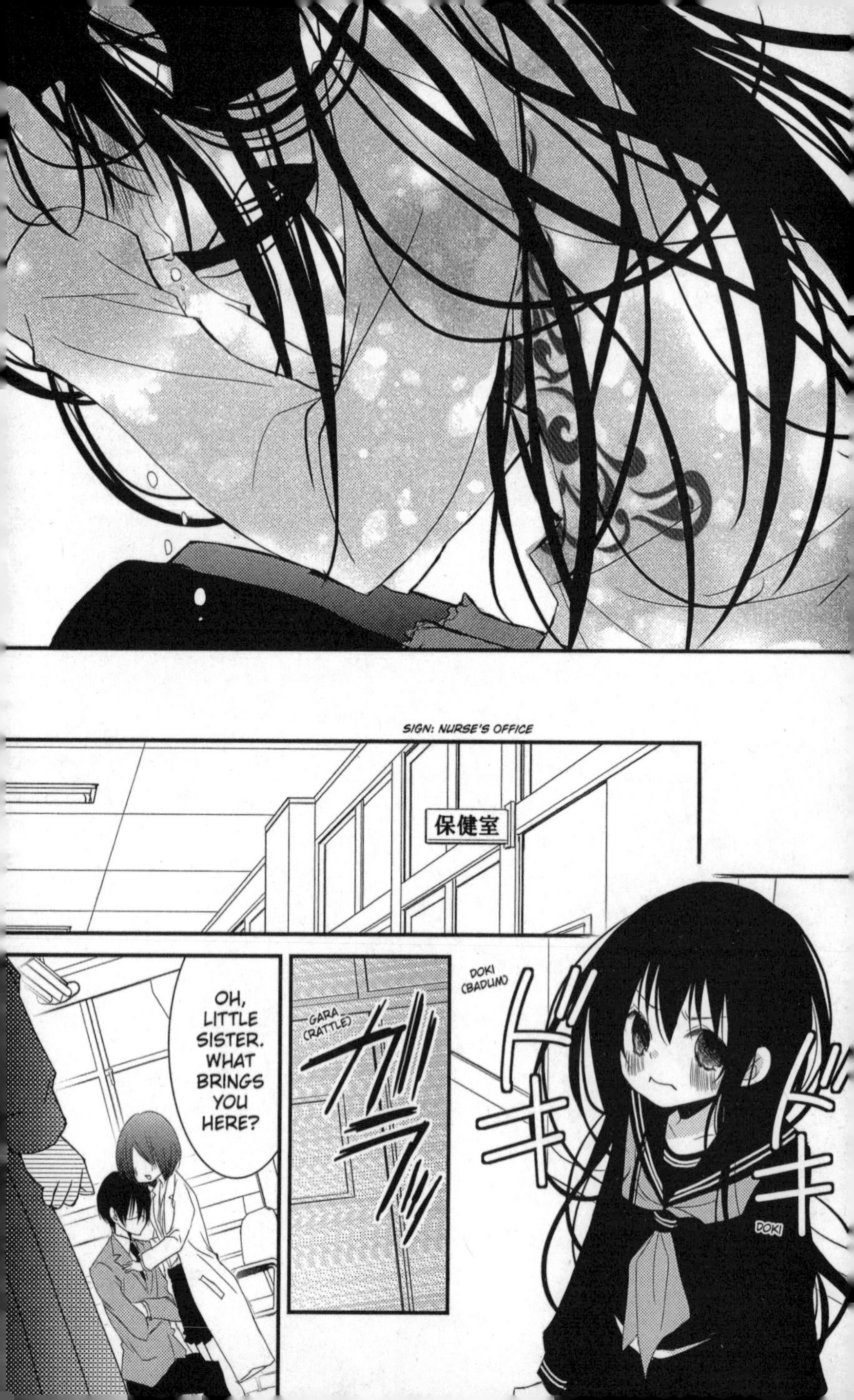
SIGN: NURSE'S OFFICE
保健室
DOKI (BADUM)
DOKI
GARA (RATTLE)
OH, LITTLE SISTER. WHAT BRINGS YOU HERE?

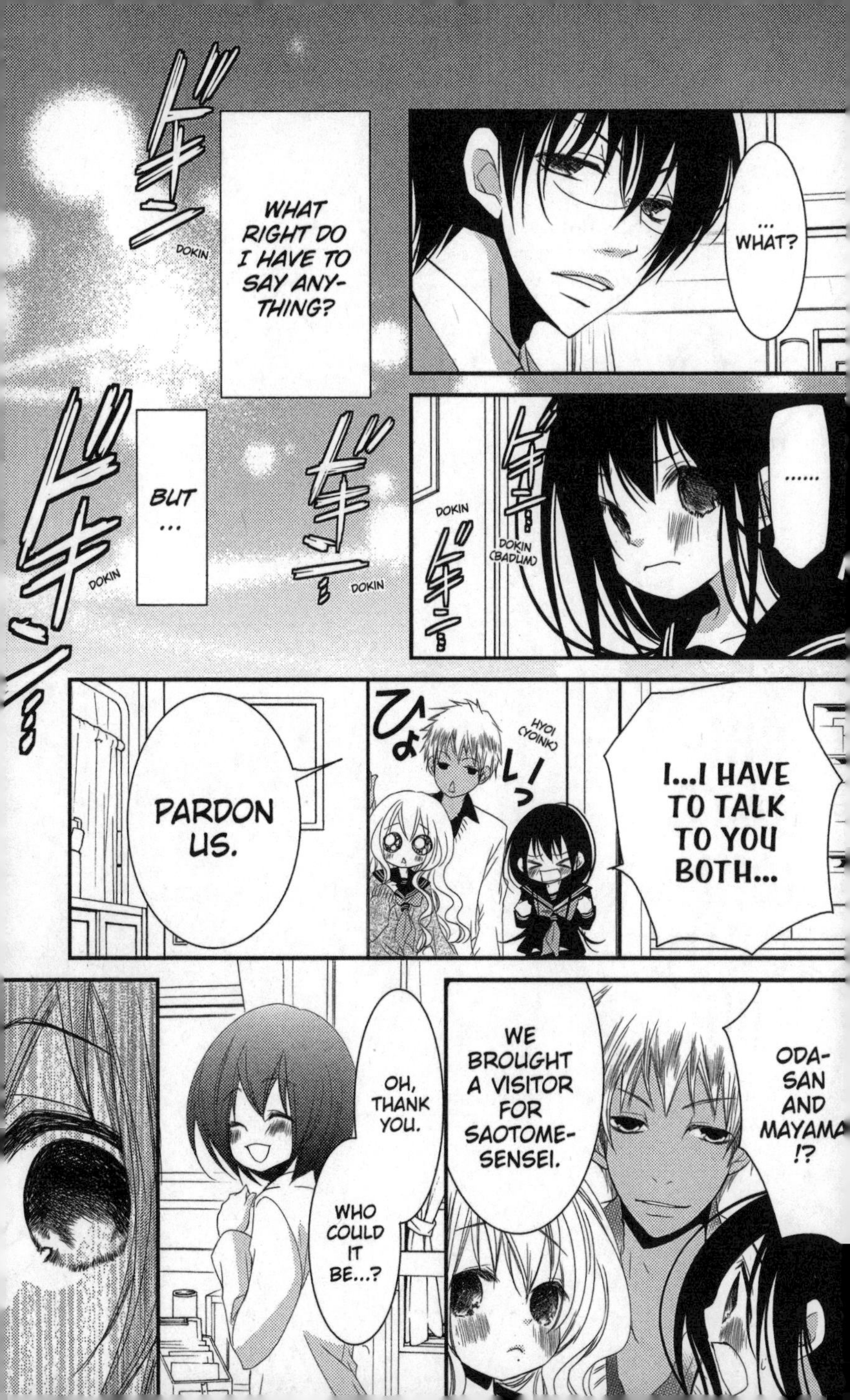

...WHAT?
......
DOKIN
DOKIN (BADUM)
DOKIN
WHAT RIGHT DO I HAVE TO SAY ANYTHING?
BUT...
DOKIN
DOKIN
I...I HAVE TO TALK TO YOU BOTH...
HYOI (YOINK)
PARDON US.
ODA-SAN AND MAYAMA!?
WE BROUGHT A VISITOR FOR SAOTOME-SENSEI.
OH, THANK YOU.
WHO COULD IT BE...?

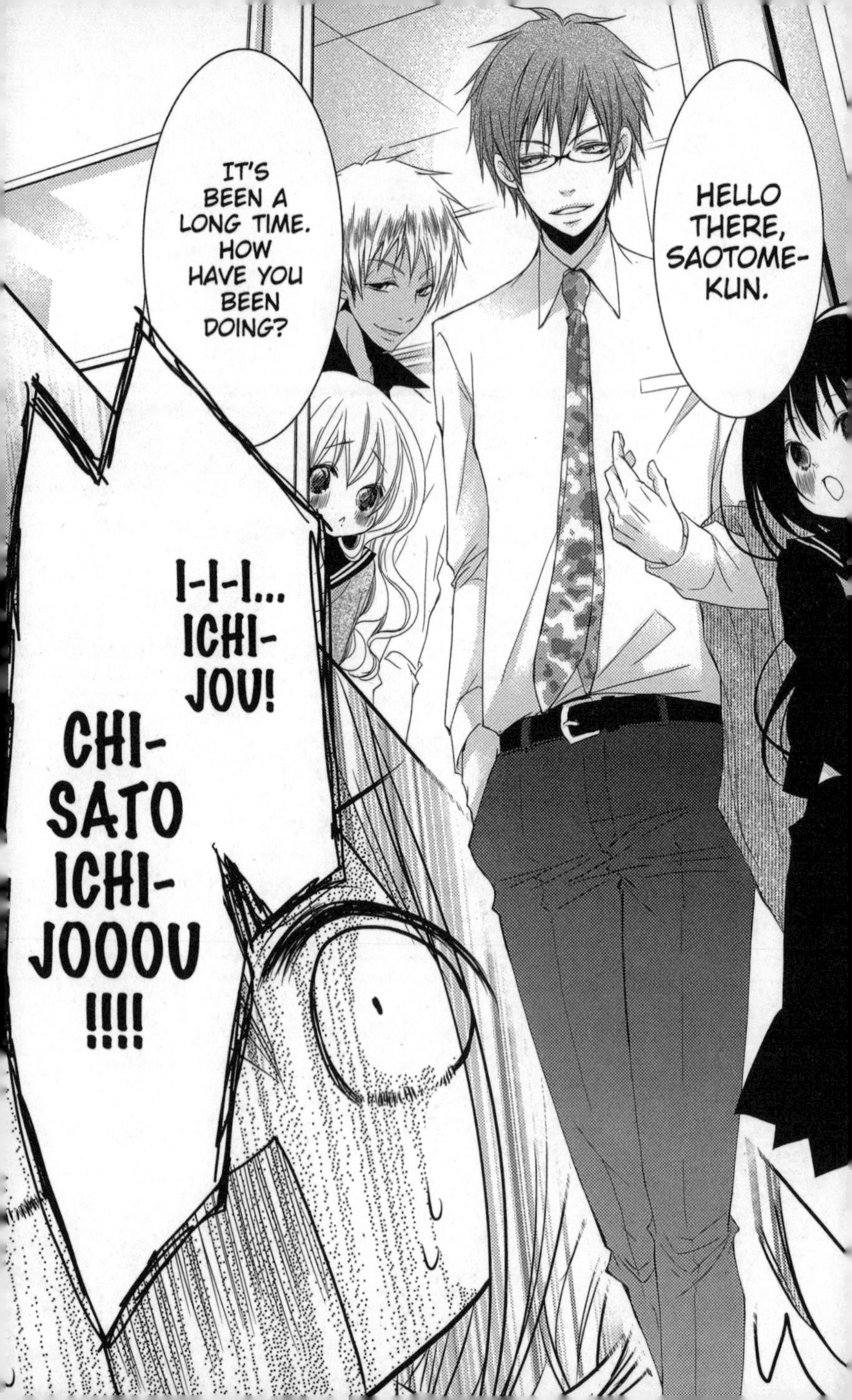
HELLO THERE, SAOTOME-KUN.
IT'S BEEN A LONG TIME. HOW HAVE YOU BEEN DOING?
I-I-I... ICHI-JOU!
CHI-SATO ICHI-JOOOU !!!!

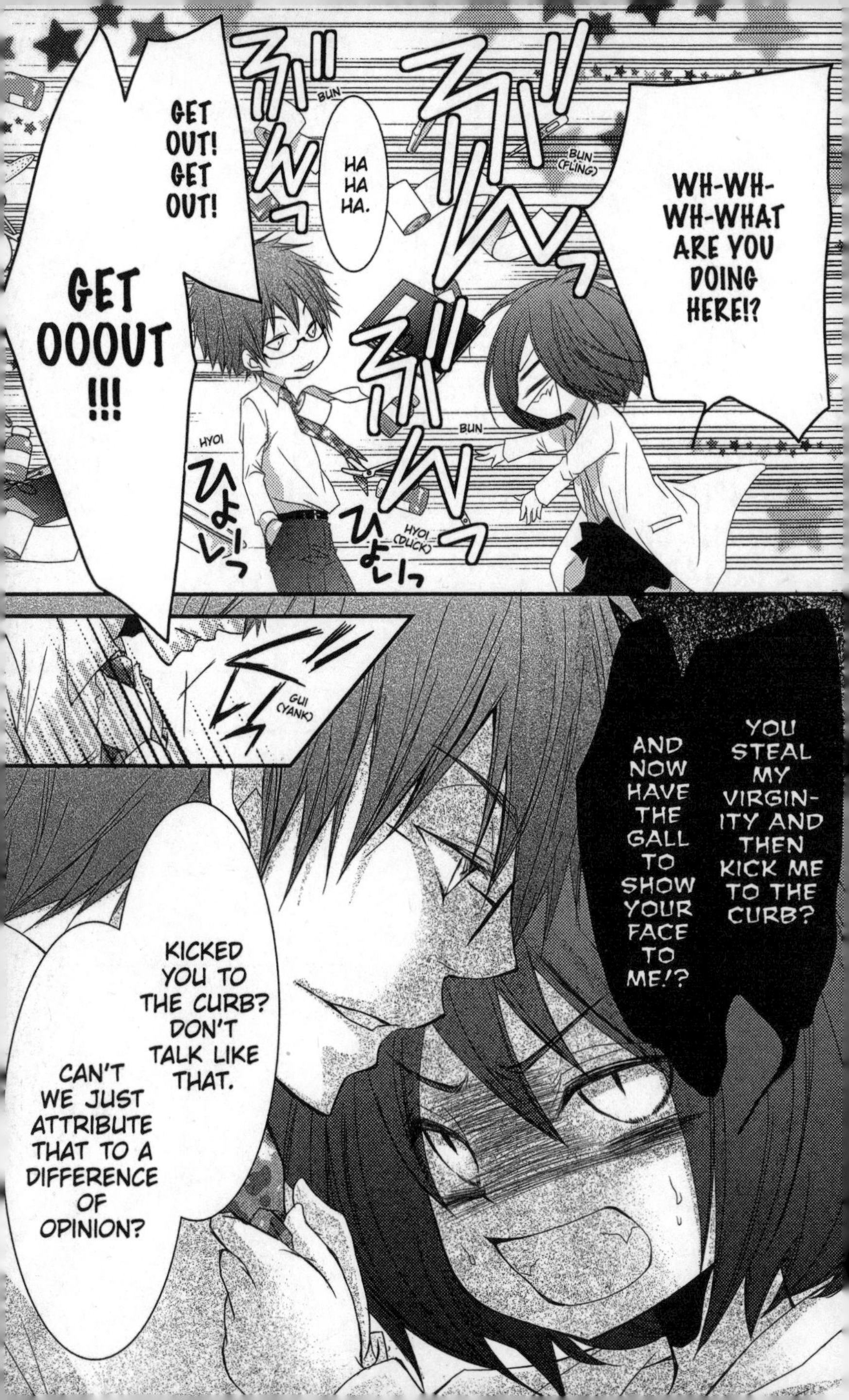
WH-WH-WH-WHAT ARE YOU DOING HERE!?
BUN (FLING)
HA HA HA.
BUN
GET OUT! GET OUT!
GET OOOUT!!!
BUN
HYOI (DUCK)
HYOI
GUI (YANK)
YOU STEAL MY VIRGINITY AND THEN KICK ME TO THE CURB?
AND NOW HAVE THE GALL TO SHOW YOUR FACE TO ME!?
KICKED YOU TO THE CURB? DON'T TALK LIKE THAT.
CAN'T WE JUST ATTRIBUTE THAT TO A DIFFERENCE OF OPINION?

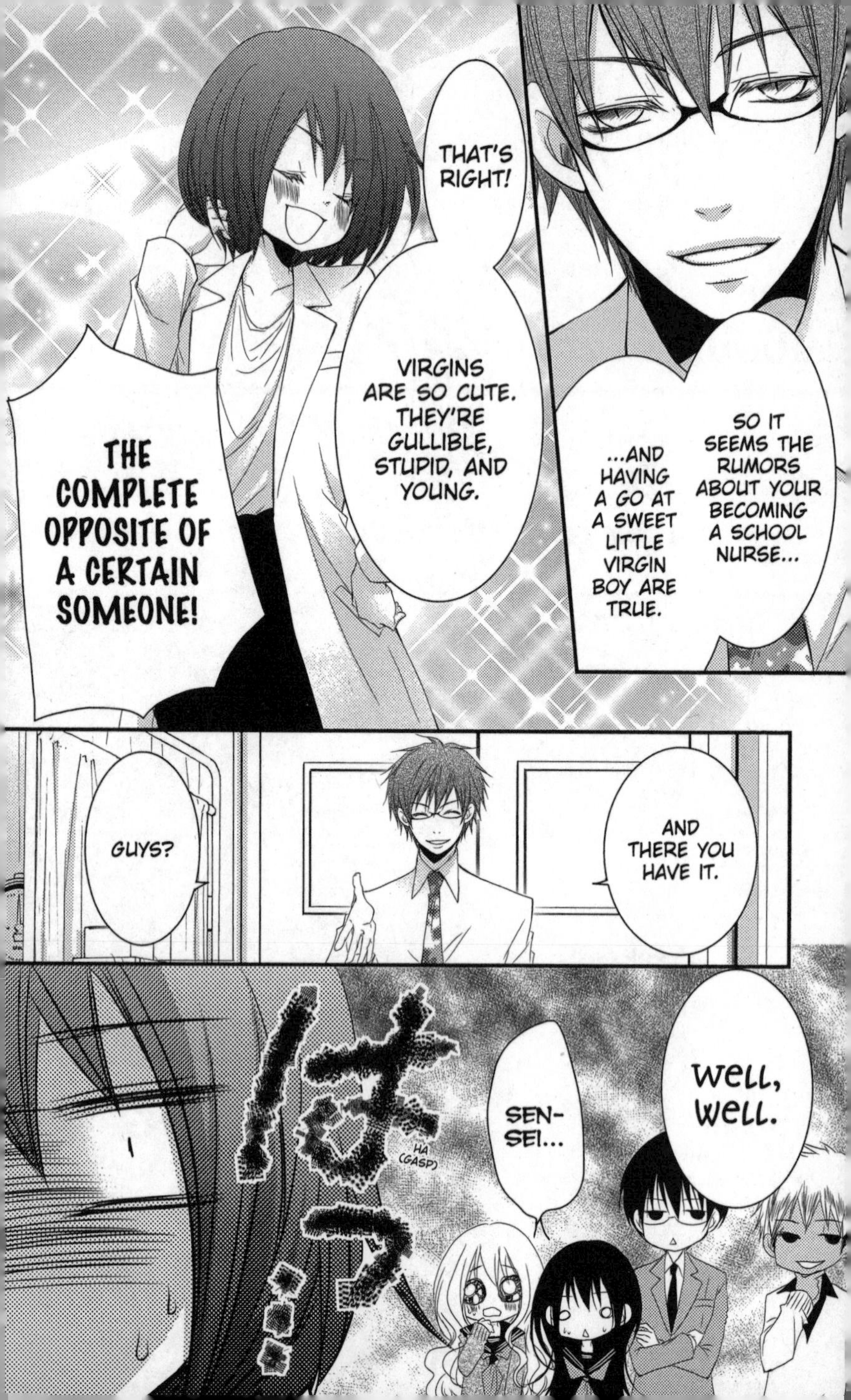
SO IT SEEMS THE RUMORS ABOUT YOUR BECOMING A SCHOOL NURSE...
...AND HAVING A GO AT A SWEET LITTLE VIRGIN BOY ARE TRUE.
THAT'S RIGHT!
VIRGINS ARE SO CUTE. THEY'RE GULLIBLE, STUPID, AND YOUNG.
THE COMPLETE OPPOSITE OF A CERTAIN SOMEONE!
AND THERE YOU HAVE IT.
GUYS?
WELL, WELL.
SEN-SEI...
HA (GASP)

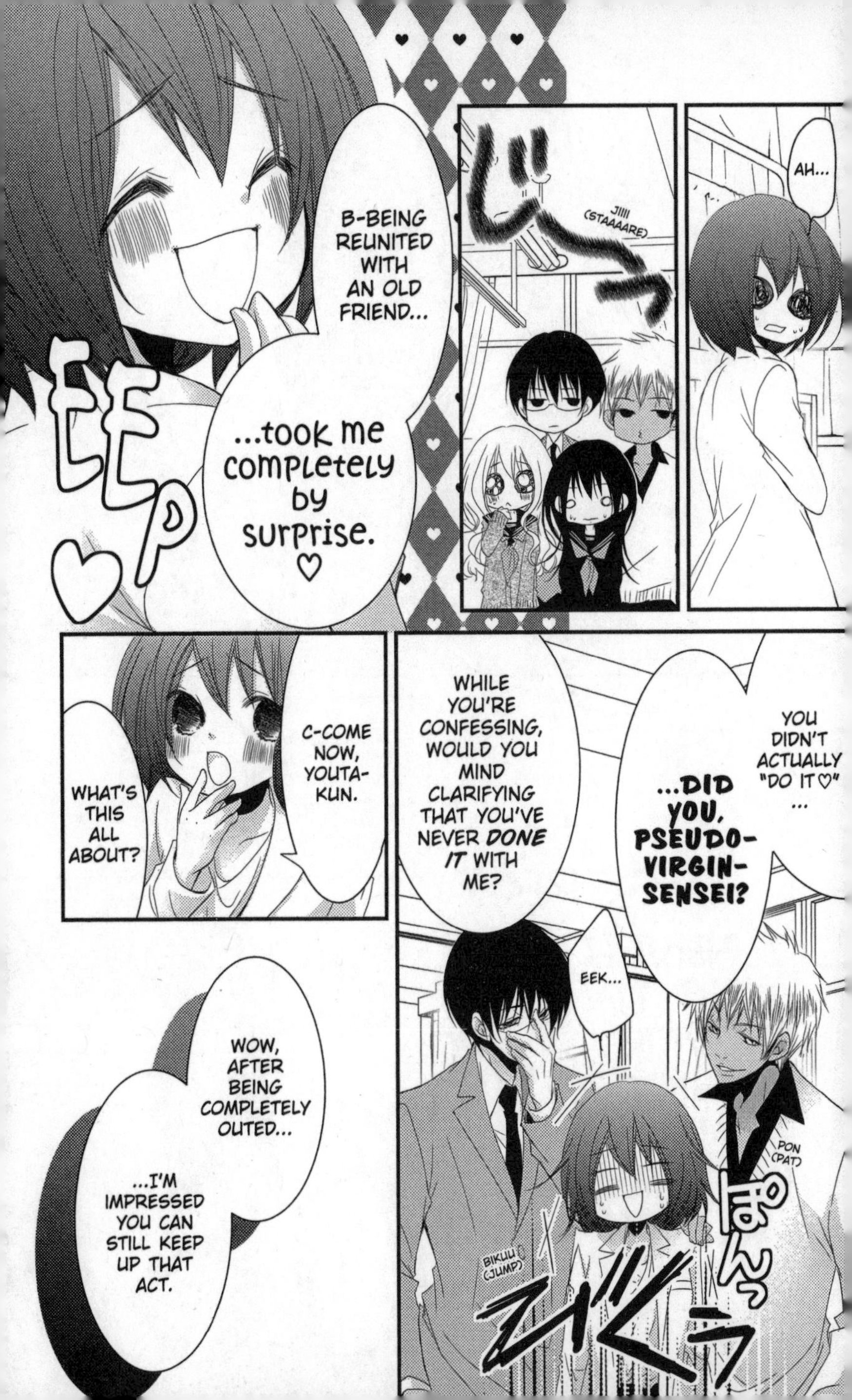
AH...
JIIII (STAAAARE)
B-BEING REUNITED WITH AN OLD FRIEND...
...took me completely by surprise. ♡
EEP ♡
YOU DIDN'T ACTUALLY "DO IT♡" ...
...DID YOU, PSEUDO-VIRGIN-SENSEI?
WHILE YOU'RE CONFESSING, WOULD YOU MIND CLARIFYING THAT YOU'VE NEVER DONE IT WITH ME?
EEK...
PON (PAT)
BIKUU (JUMP)
C-COME NOW, YOUTA-KUN.
WHAT'S THIS ALL ABOUT?
WOW, AFTER BEING COMPLETELY OUTED...
...I'M IMPRESSED YOU CAN STILL KEEP UP THAT ACT.

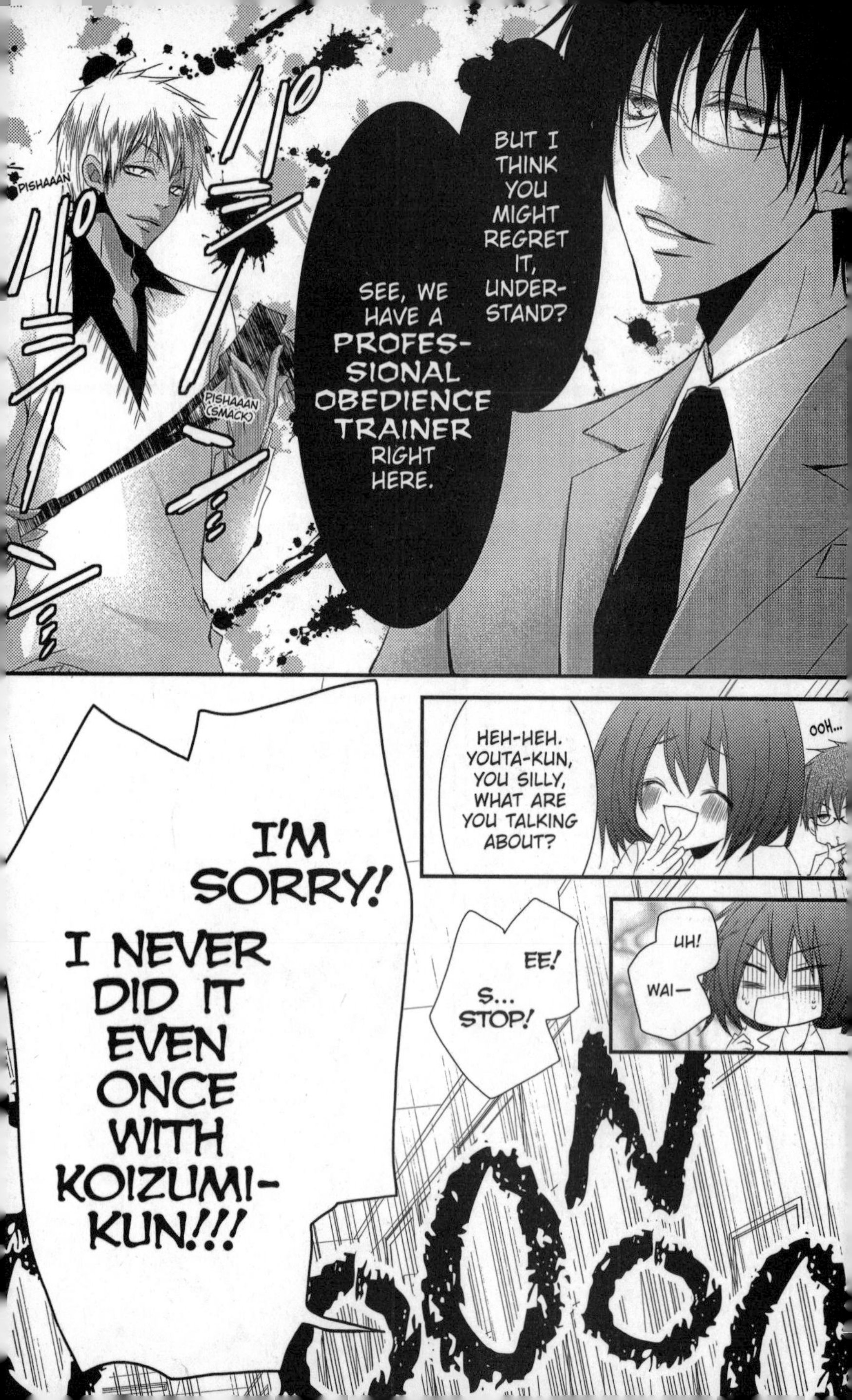
BUT I THINK YOU MIGHT REGRET IT, UNDERSTAND?
SEE, WE HAVE A PROFESSIONAL OBEDIENCE TRAINER RIGHT HERE.
PISHAAAN (SMACK)
PISHAAAN
OOH...
HEH-HEH. YOUTA-KUN, YOU SILLY, WHAT ARE YOU TALKING ABOUT?
UH!
WAI—
EE!
S... STOP!
I'M SORRY!
I NEVER DID IT EVEN ONCE WITH KOIZUMI-KUN!!!

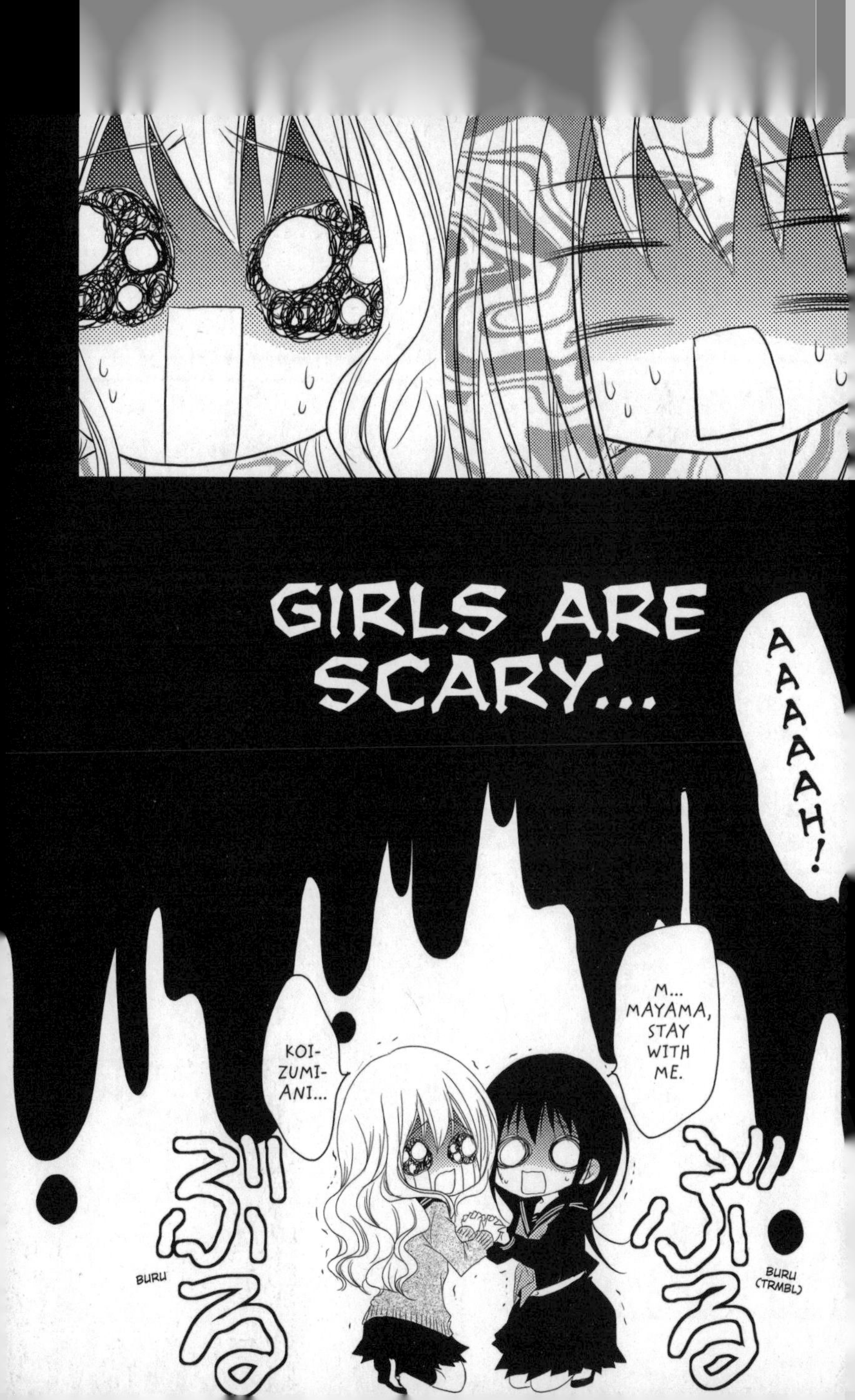
GIRLS ARE SCARY...
AAAAAH!
M... MAYAMA, STAY WITH ME.
KOI-ZUMI-ANI...
ぶる
BURU (TRMBL)
ぶる
BURU

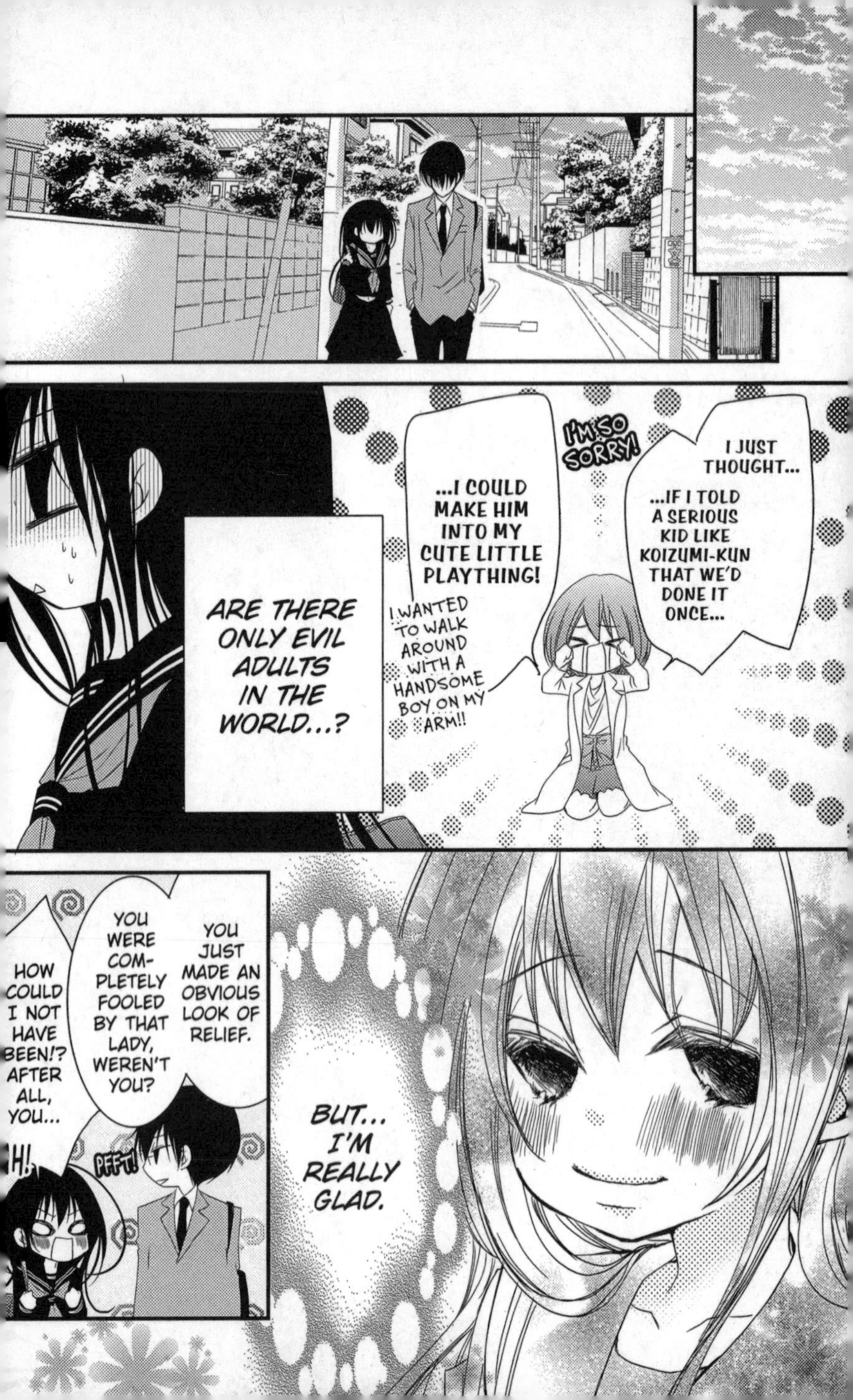
I JUST THOUGHT...
...IF I TOLD A SERIOUS KID LIKE KOIZUMI-KUN THAT WE'D DONE IT ONCE...
I'M SO SORRY!
...I COULD MAKE HIM INTO MY CUTE LITTLE PLAYTHING!
I WANTED TO WALK AROUND WITH A HANDSOME BOY ON MY ARM!!
ARE THERE ONLY EVIL ADULTS IN THE WORLD...?
BUT... I'M REALLY GLAD.
YOU JUST MADE AN OBVIOUS LOOK OF RELIEF.
YOU WERE COM-PLETELY FOOLED BY THAT LADY, WEREN'T YOU?
PFFT!
HOW COULD I NOT HAVE BEEN!? AFTER ALL, YOU...

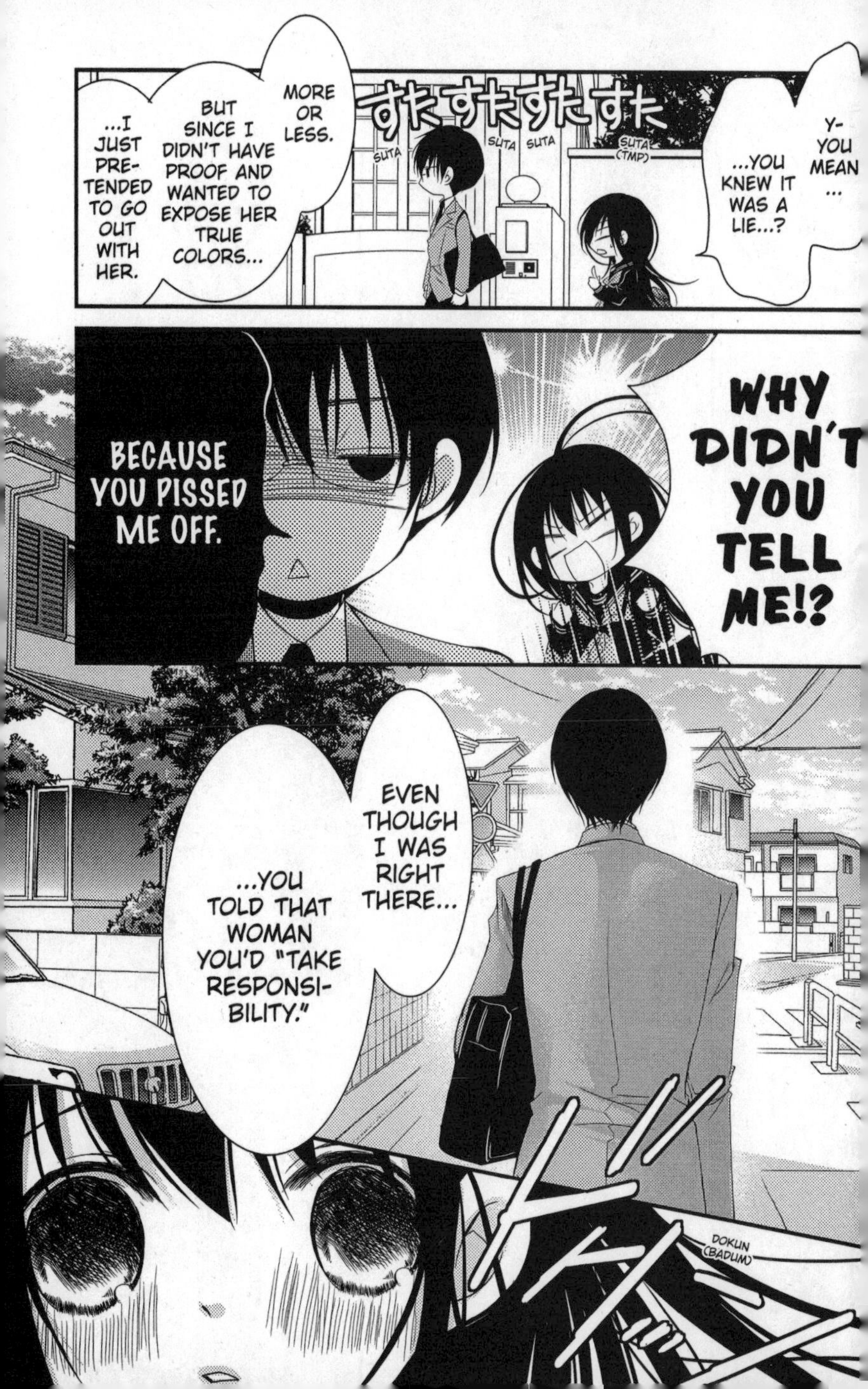
Y-YOU MEAN ...
...YOU KNEW IT WAS A LIE...?
すたすたすたすた
SUTA SUTA SUTA SUTA (TMP)
MORE OR LESS.
BUT SINCE I DIDN'T HAVE PROOF AND WANTED TO EXPOSE HER TRUE COLORS...
...I JUST PRE-TENDED TO GO OUT WITH HER.
WHY DIDN'T YOU TELL ME!?
BECAUSE YOU PISSED ME OFF.
EVEN THOUGH I WAS RIGHT THERE...
...YOU TOLD THAT WOMAN YOU'D "TAKE RESPONSI-BILITY."
DOKUN (BADUM)

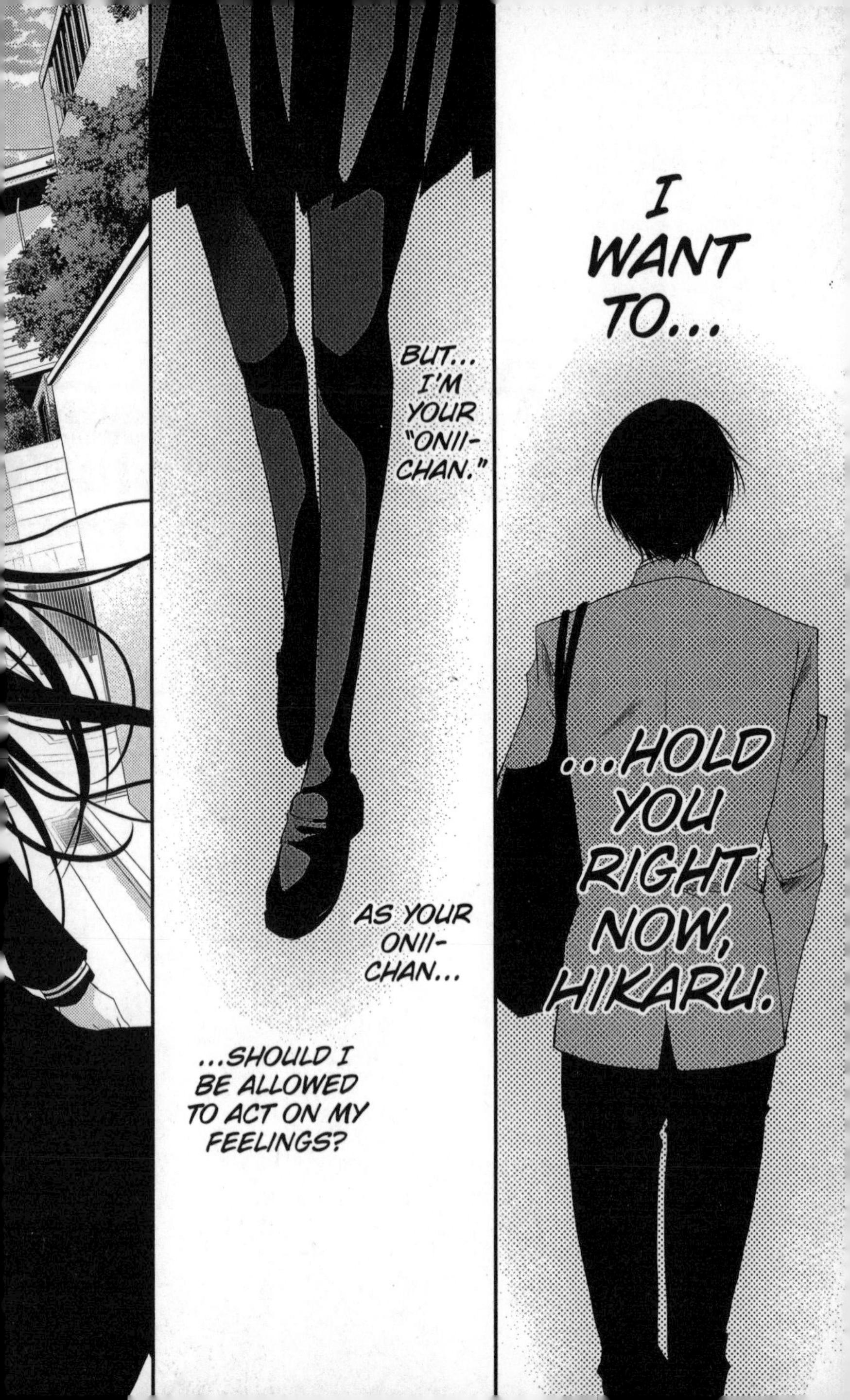
I WANT TO...
...HOLD YOU RIGHT NOW, HIKARU.
BUT... I'M YOUR "ONII-CHAN."
AS YOUR ONII-CHAN...
...SHOULD I BE ALLOWED TO ACT ON MY FEELINGS?

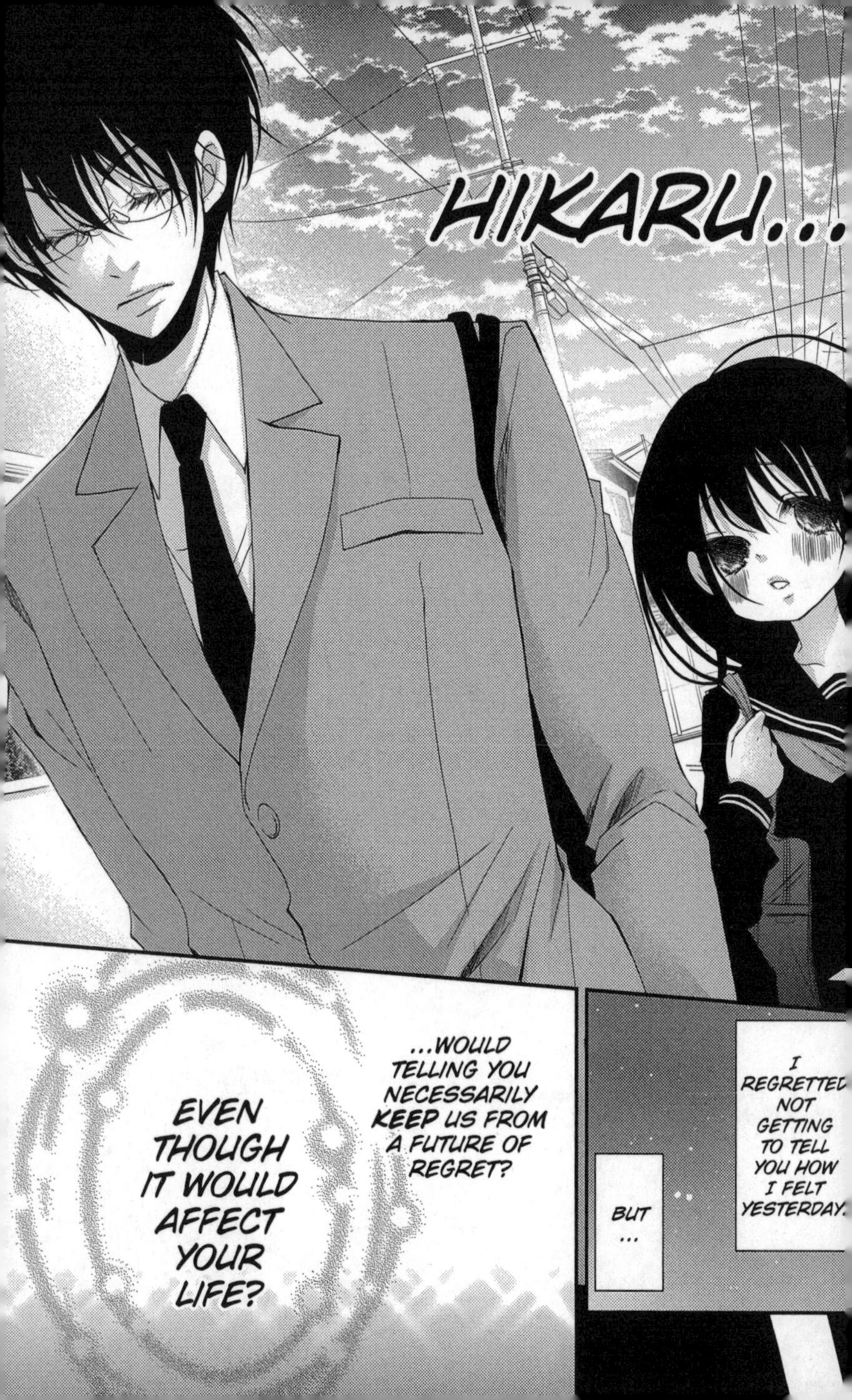
HIKARU...
I REGRETTED NOT GETTING TO TELL YOU HOW I FELT YESTERDAY.
BUT ...
...WOULD TELLING YOU NECESSARILY KEEP US FROM A FUTURE OF REGRET?
EVEN THOUGH IT WOULD AFFECT YOUR LIFE?

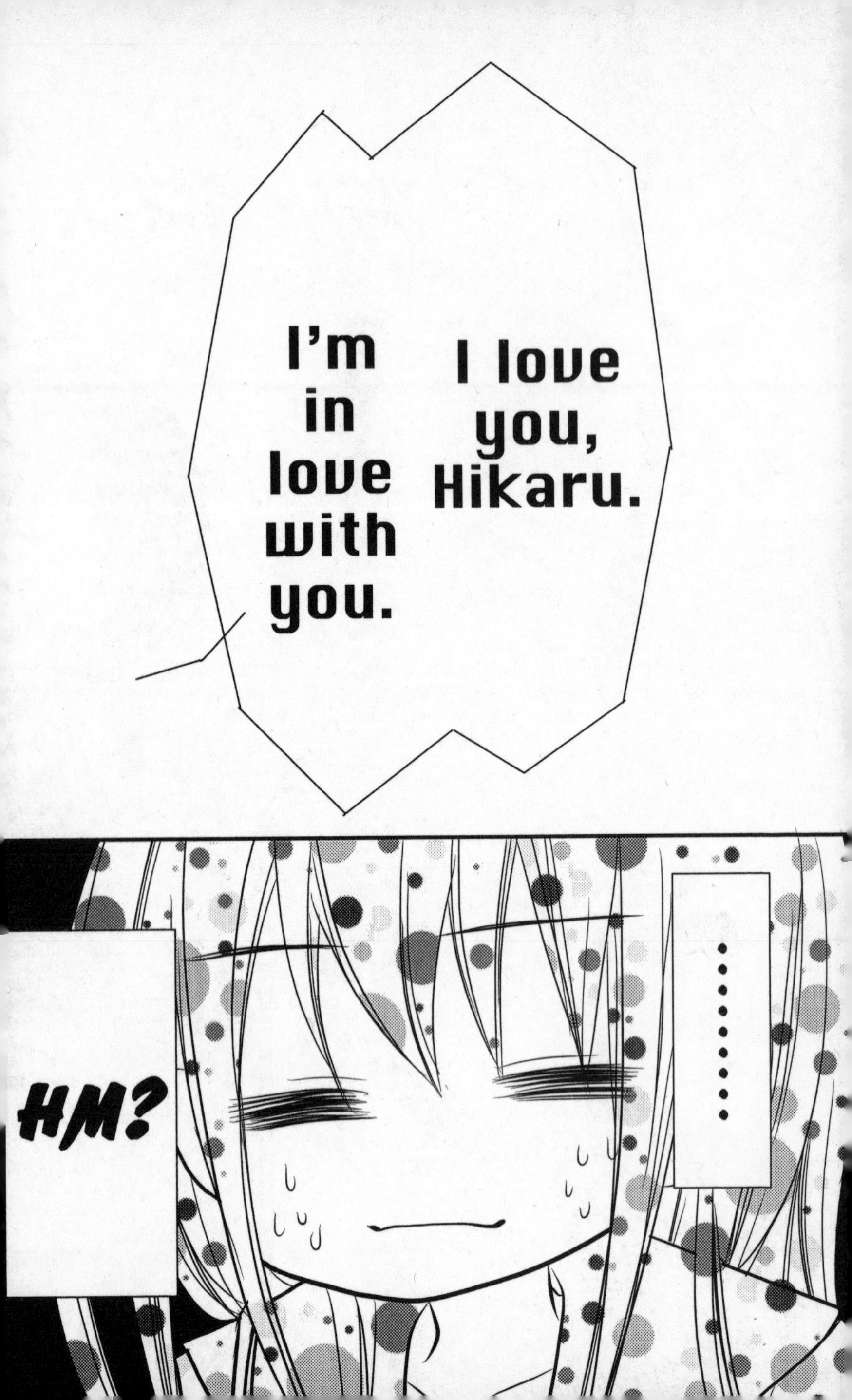
I love you, Hikaru.
I'm in love with you.
……
HM?

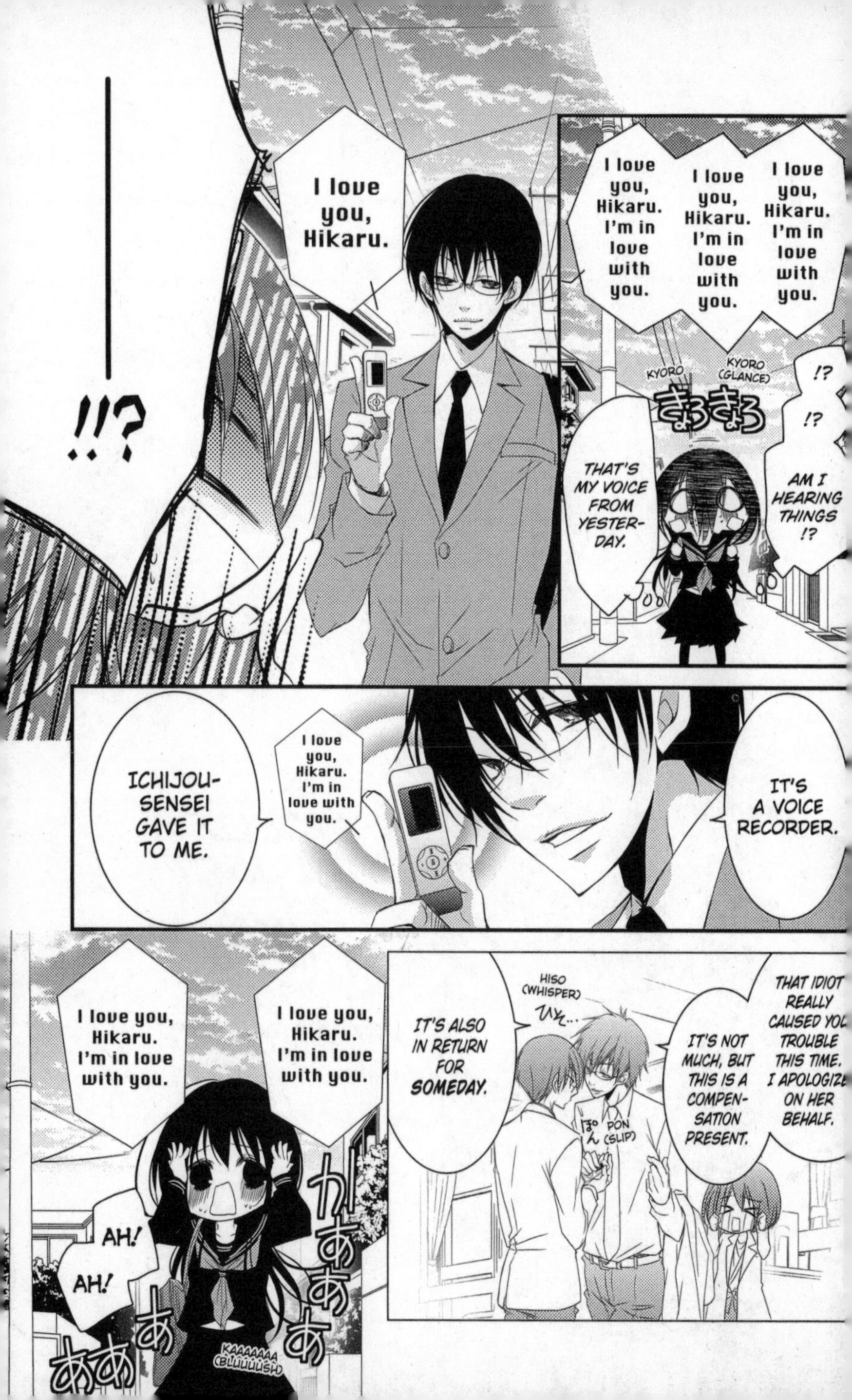

I love you, Hikaru. I'm in love with you.
I love you, Hikaru. I'm in love with you.
I love you, Hikaru. I'm in love with you.
KYORO (GLANCE)
KYORO
きょろきょろ
!?
!?
AM I HEARING THINGS !?
THAT'S MY VOICE FROM YESTERDAY.
I love you, Hikaru.
!!?
IT'S A VOICE RECORDER.
I love you, Hikaru. I'm in love with you.
ICHIJOU-SENSEI GAVE IT TO ME.
THAT IDIOT REALLY CAUSED YOU TROUBLE THIS TIME. I APOLOGIZE ON HER BEHALF.
IT'S NOT MUCH, BUT THIS IS A COMPENSATION PRESENT.
PON (SLIP)
ぽん
HISO (WHISPER)
ひそ…
IT'S ALSO IN RETURN FOR SOMEDAY.
I love you, Hikaru. I'm in love with you.
I love you, Hikaru. I'm in love with you.
かあああ
ああああ
KAAAAAAA (BLUUUUUSH)
AH!
AH!

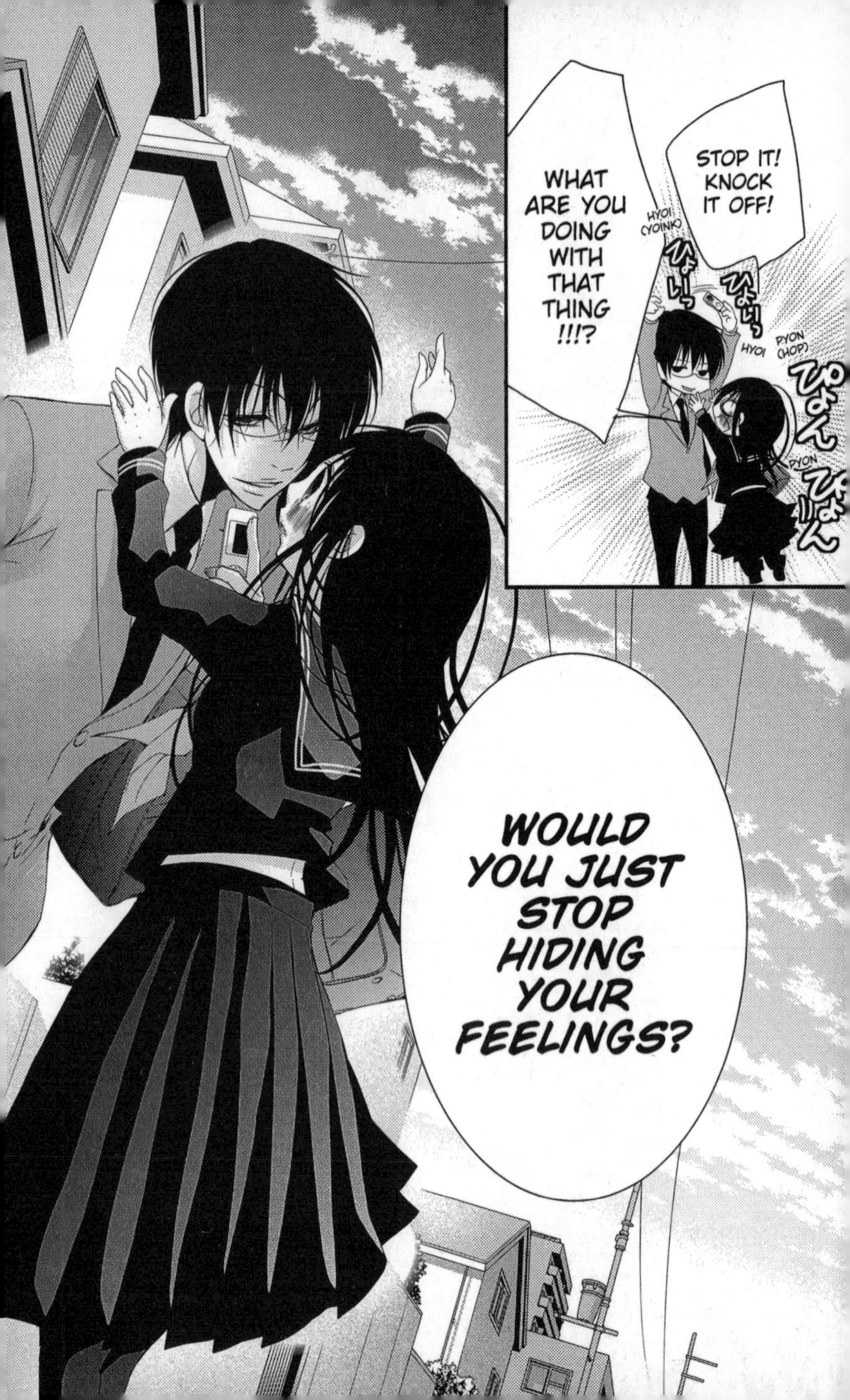
STOP IT! KNOCK IT OFF!
WHAT ARE YOU DOING WITH THAT THING!!!?
HYOI (YOINK) ひょいっ
ひょいっ HYOI
PYON (HOP) ぴょん
ぴょん PYON
WOULD YOU JUST STOP HIDING YOUR FEELINGS?

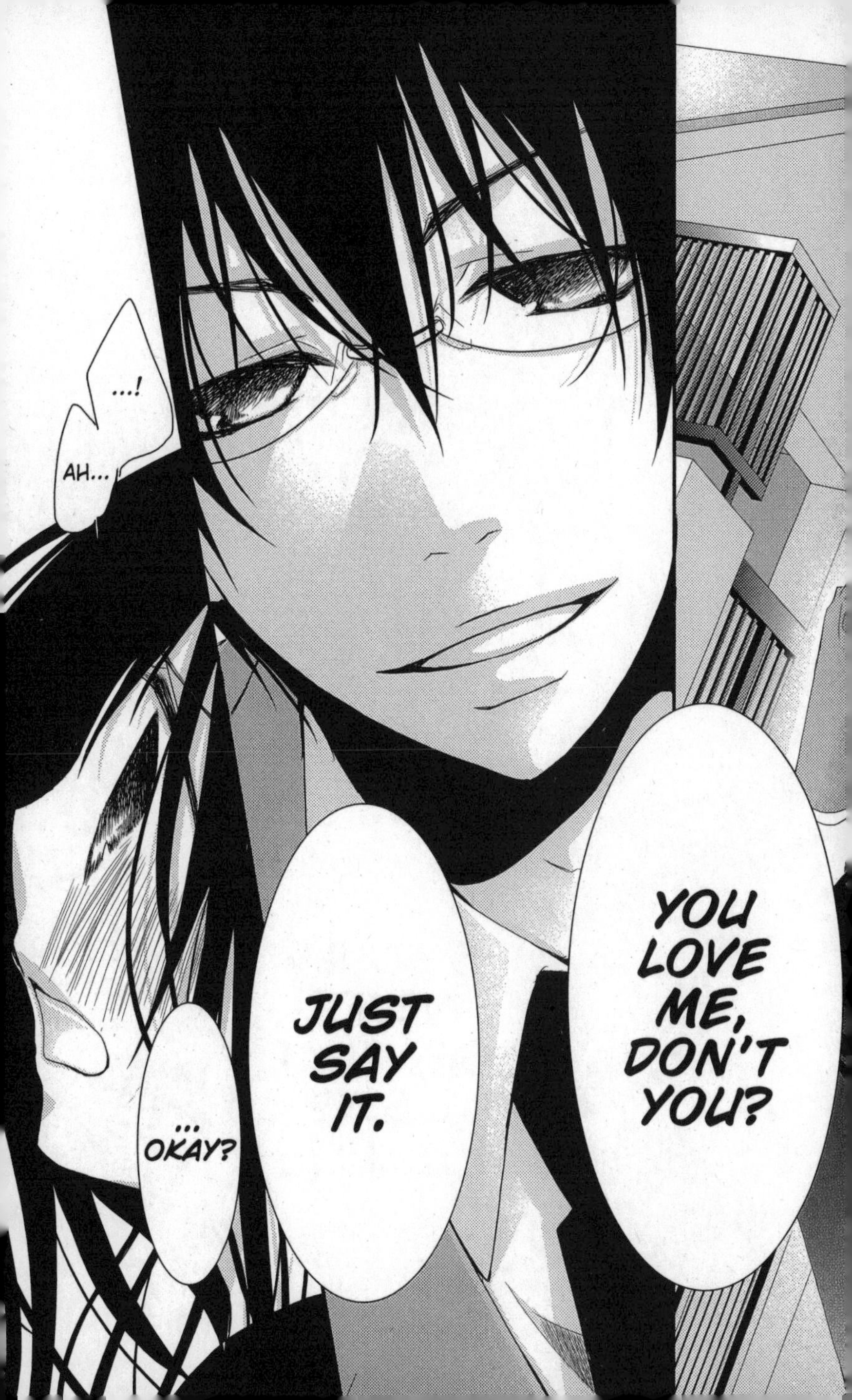
...!
AH...
YOU LOVE ME, DON'T YOU?
JUST SAY IT.
...OKAY?

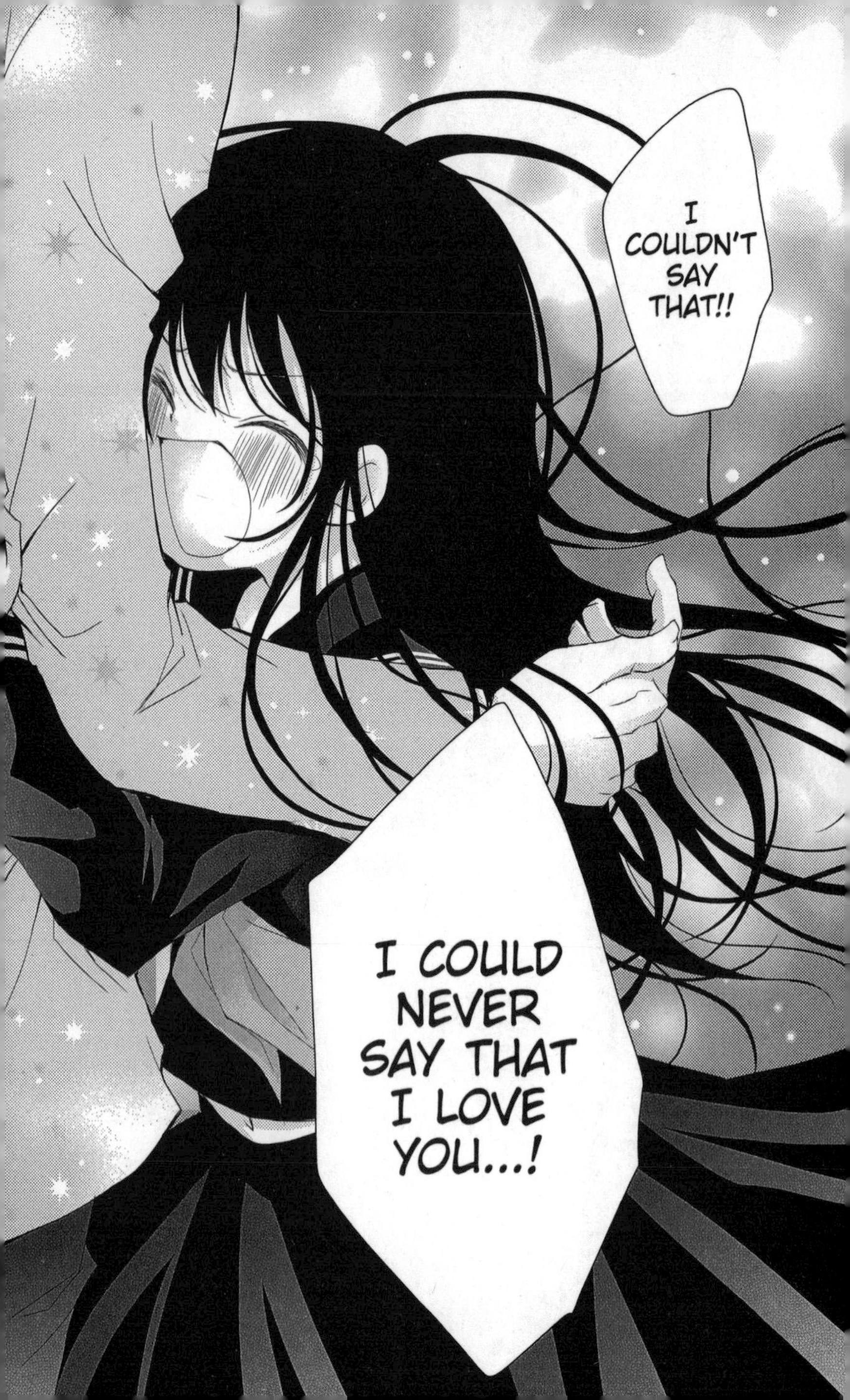
I COULDN'T SAY THAT!!
I COULD NEVER SAY THAT I LOVE YOU...!

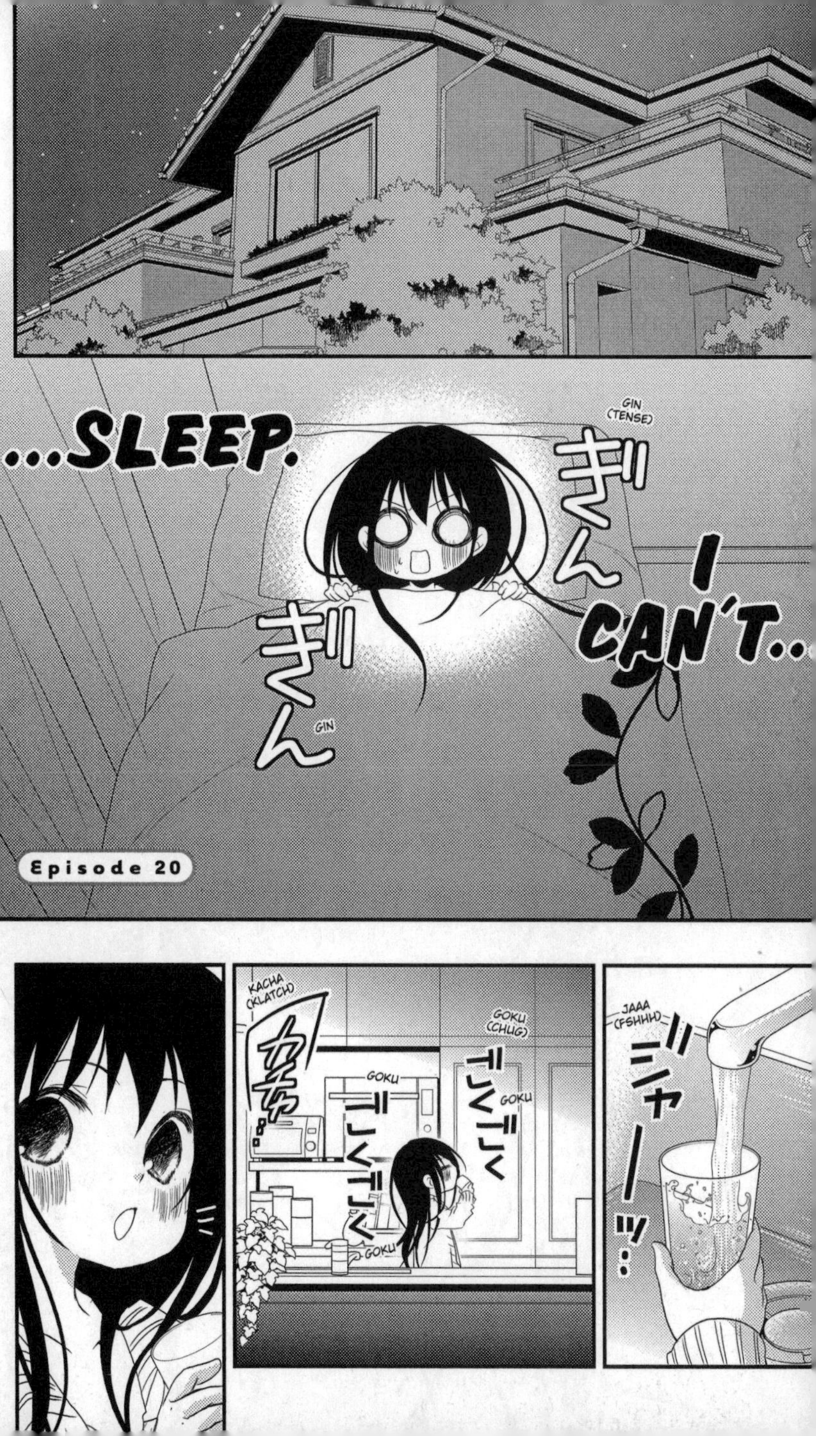
GIN (TENSE)
ぎん
I CAN'T...
...SLEEP.
ぎん
GIN
Episode 20
JAAA (FSHHH)
ジャーーッ..
GOKU (CHUG)
ゴクゴク
GOKU
ゴクゴク
GOKU
GOKU
KACHA (KLATCH)
かちゃ

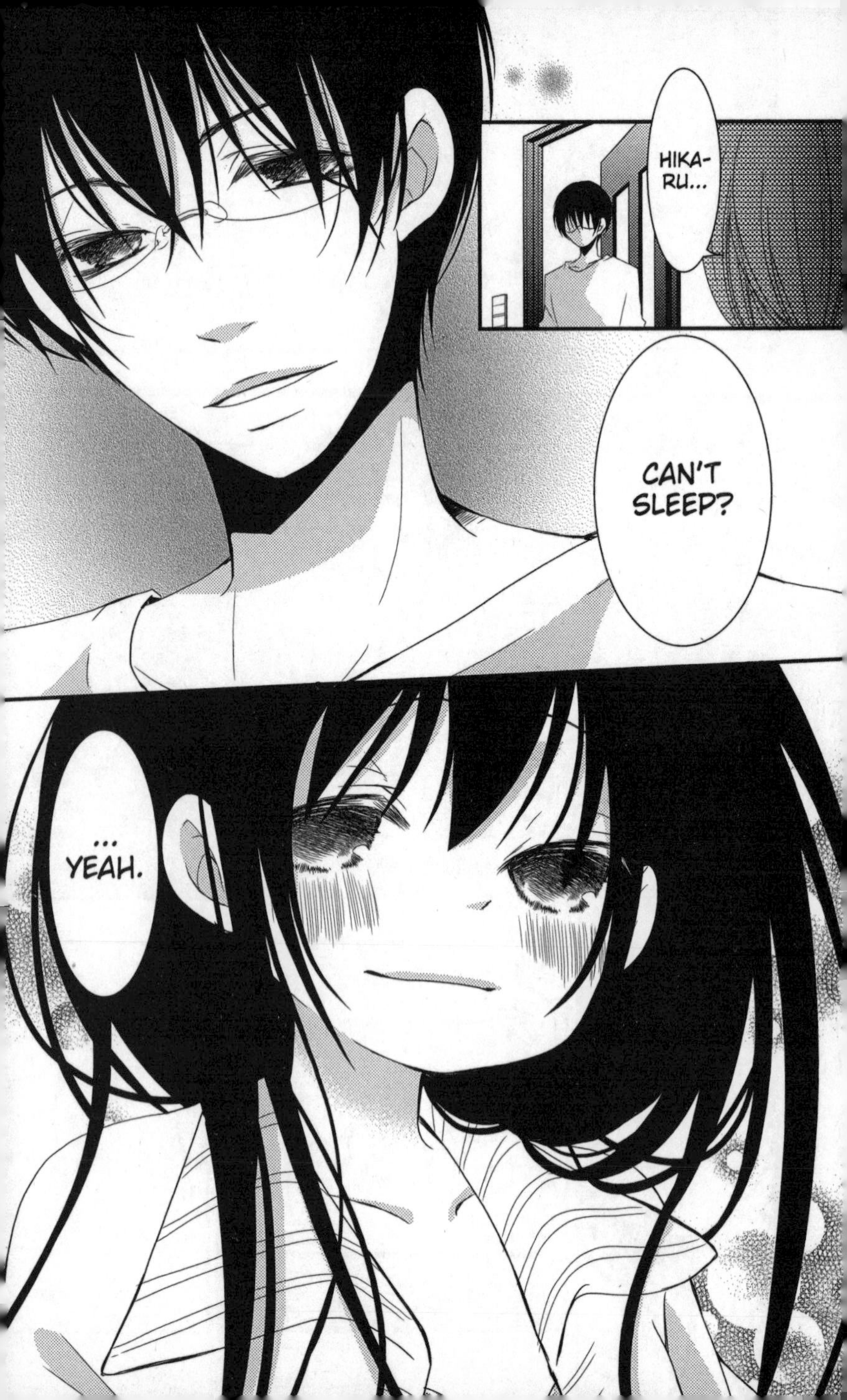
HIKA-RU...
CAN'T SLEEP?
...YEAH.

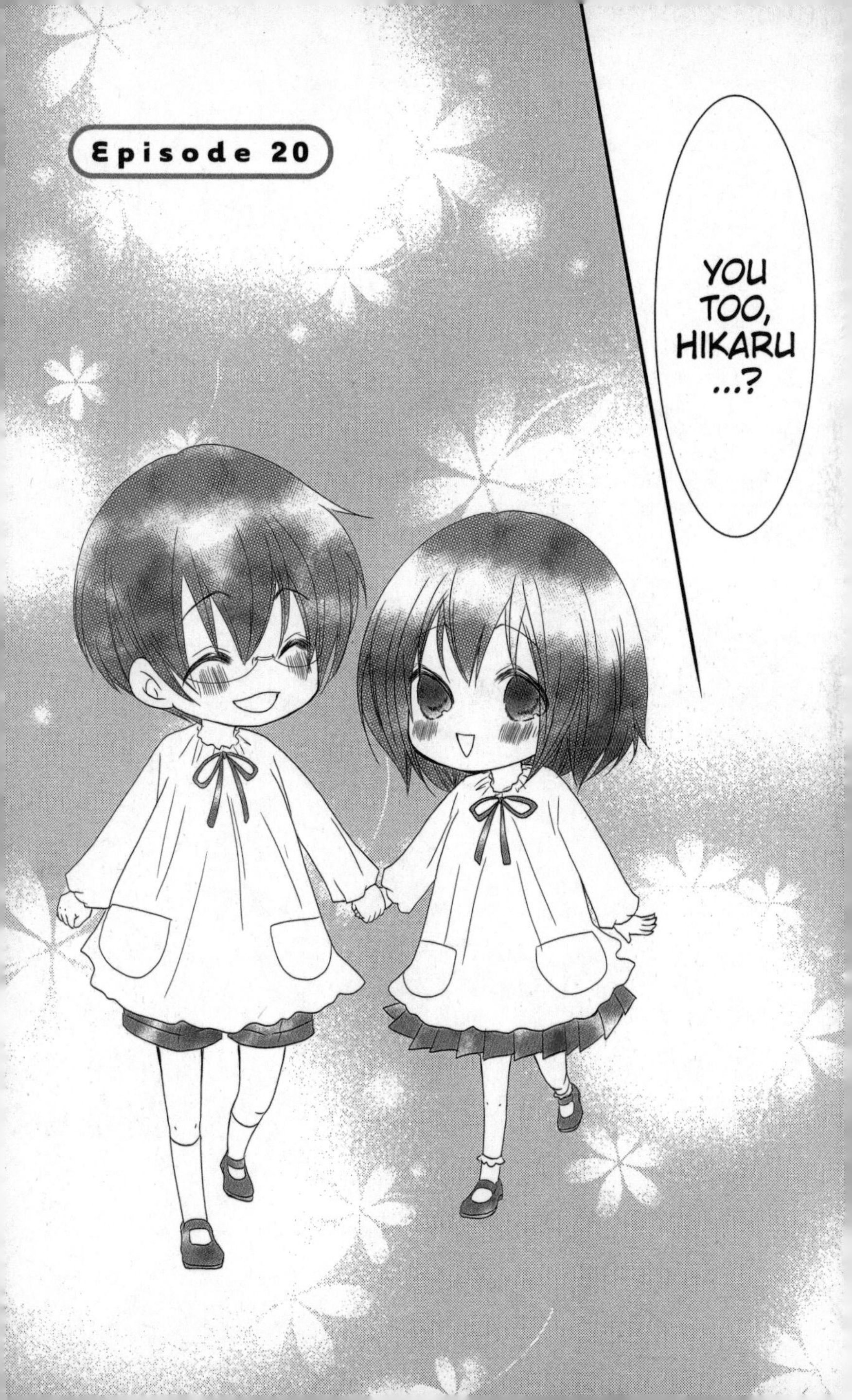
Episode 20
YOU TOO, HIKARU ...?

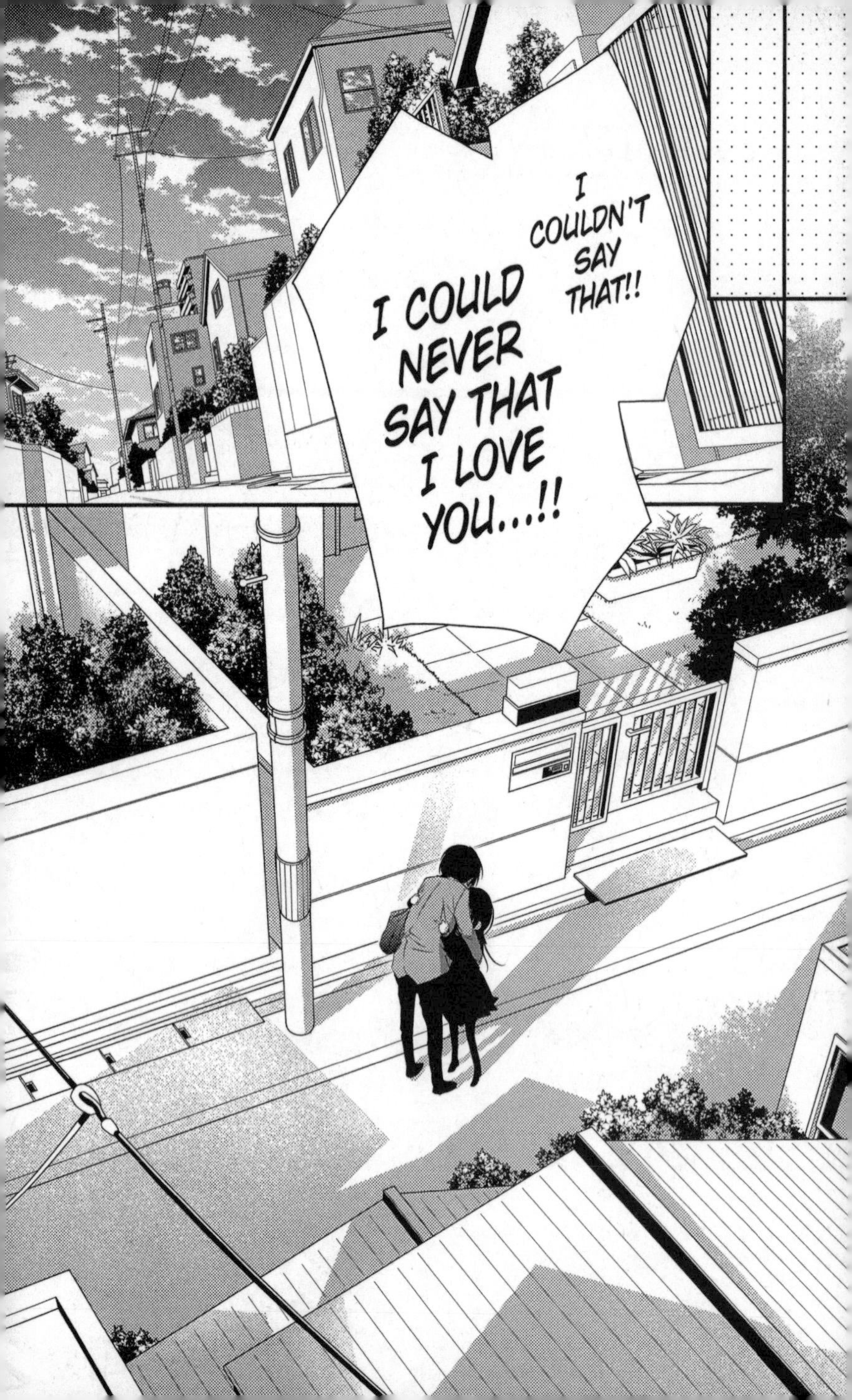
I COULDN'T SAY THAT!!
I COULD NEVER SAY THAT I LOVE YOU...!!

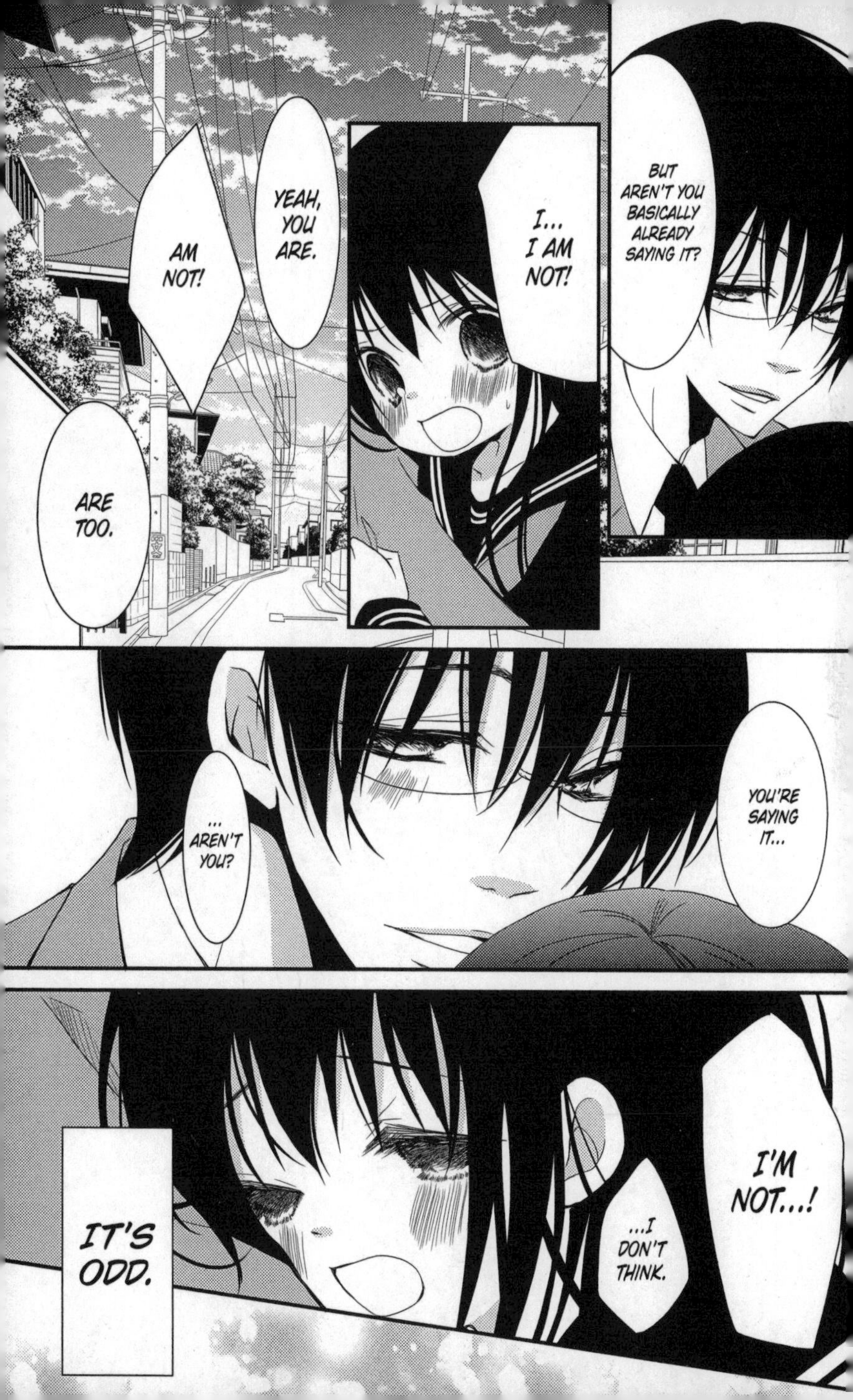
BUT AREN'T YOU BASICALLY ALREADY SAYING IT?
I... I AM NOT!
YEAH, YOU ARE.
AM NOT!
ARE TOO.
YOU'RE SAYING IT...
...AREN'T YOU?
I'M NOT...!
...I DON'T THINK.
IT'S ODD.

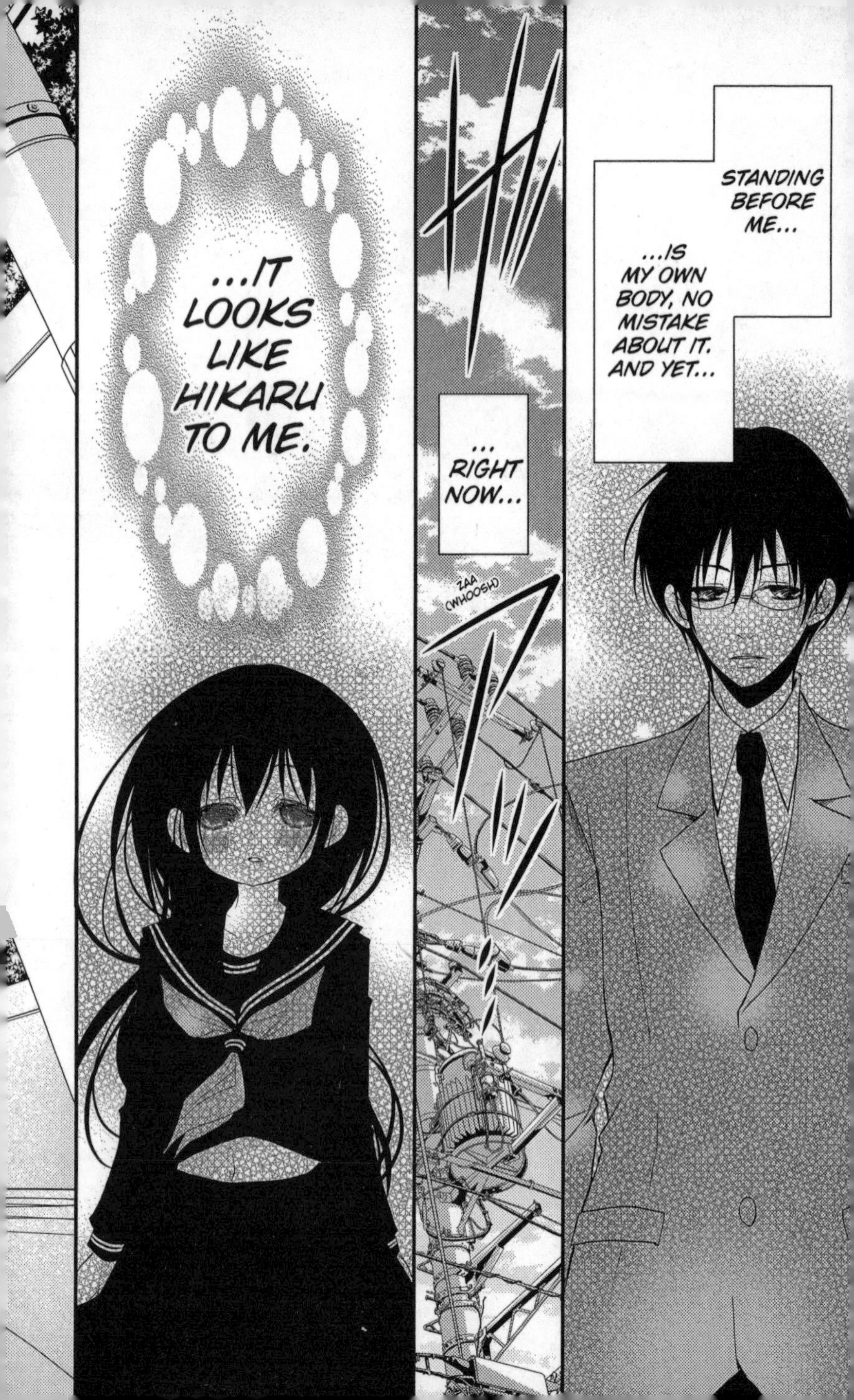
STANDING BEFORE ME...
...IS MY OWN BODY, NO MISTAKE ABOUT IT. AND YET...
... RIGHT NOW...
ZAA (WHOOSH)
...IT LOOKS LIKE HIKARU TO ME.

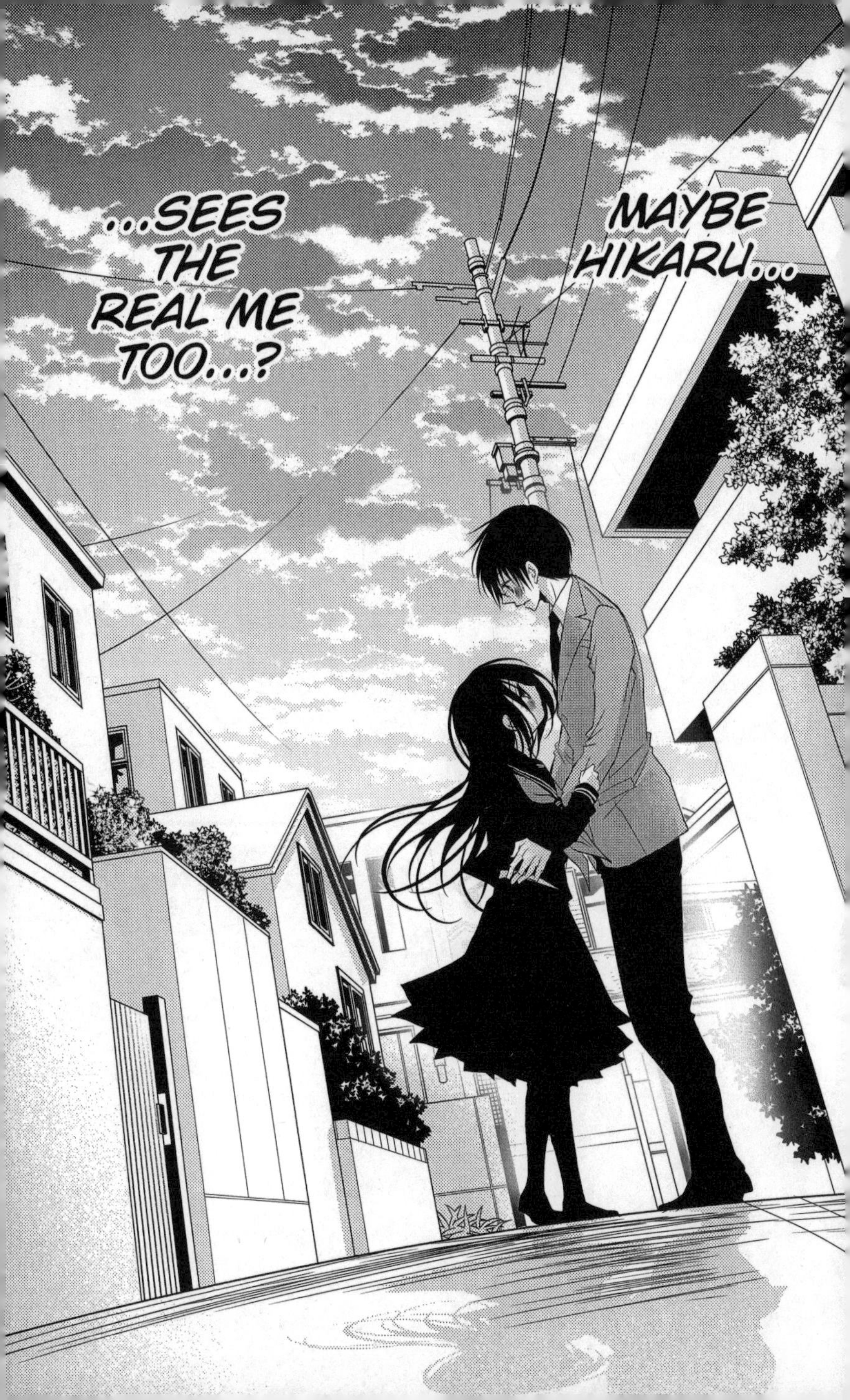
MAYBE HIKARU...
...SEES THE REAL ME TOO...?

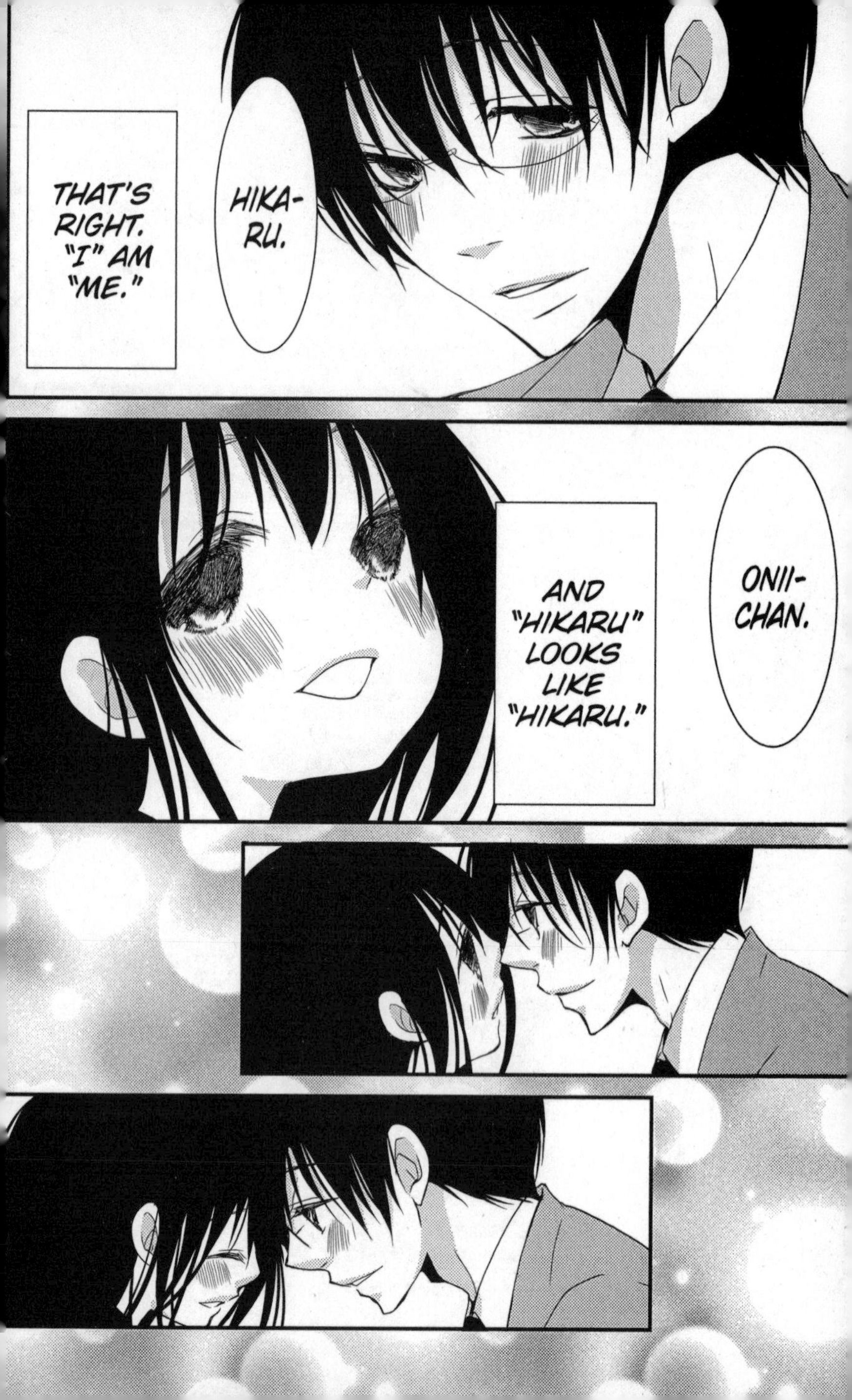
HIKA-RU.
THAT'S RIGHT. "I" AM "ME."
ONII-CHAN.
AND "HIKARU" LOOKS LIKE "HIKARU."

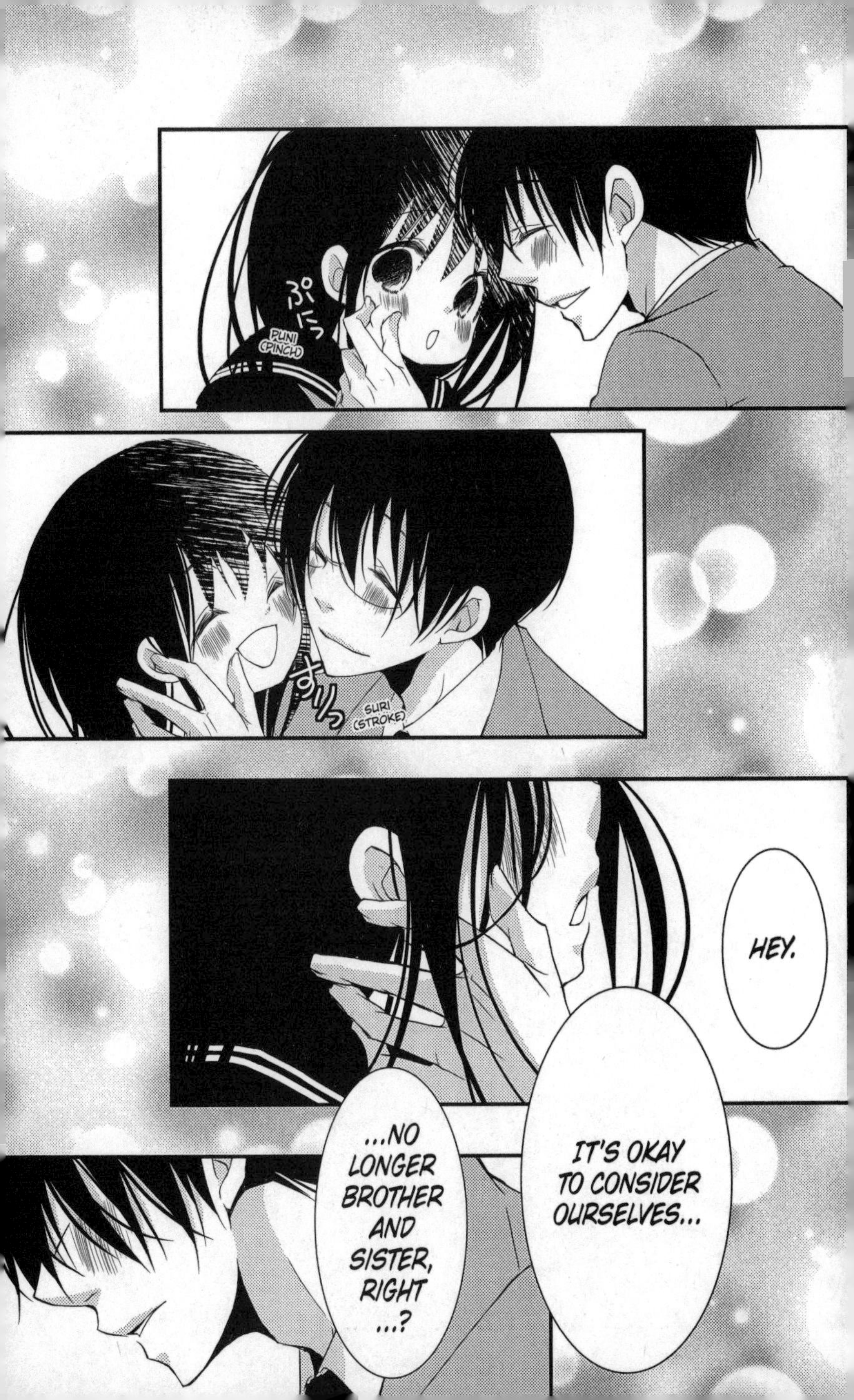
ぷにっ
PUNI (PINCH)
すりっ
SURI (STROKE)
HEY.
IT'S OKAY TO CONSIDER OURSELVES...
...NO LONGER BROTHER AND SISTER, RIGHT ...?

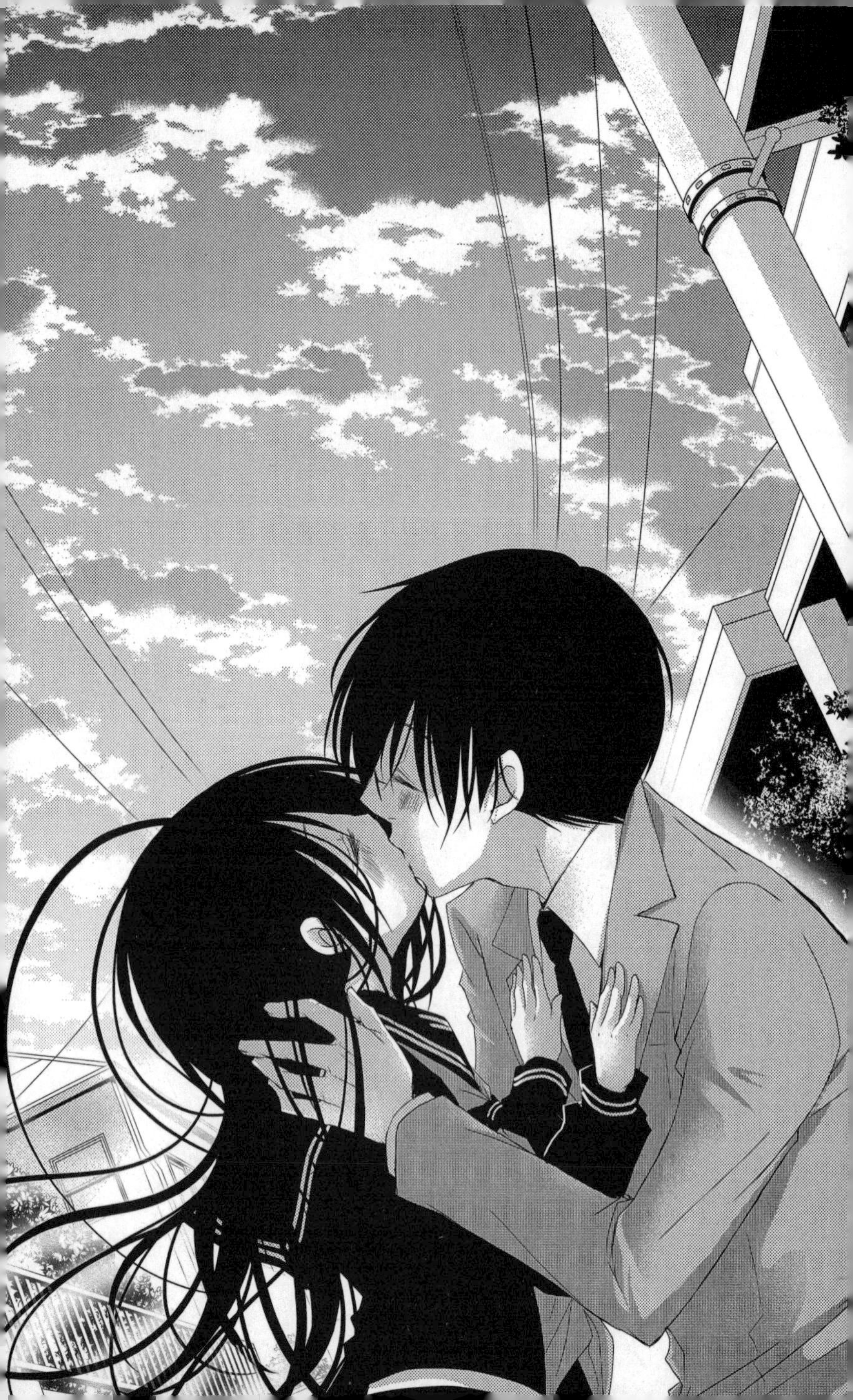

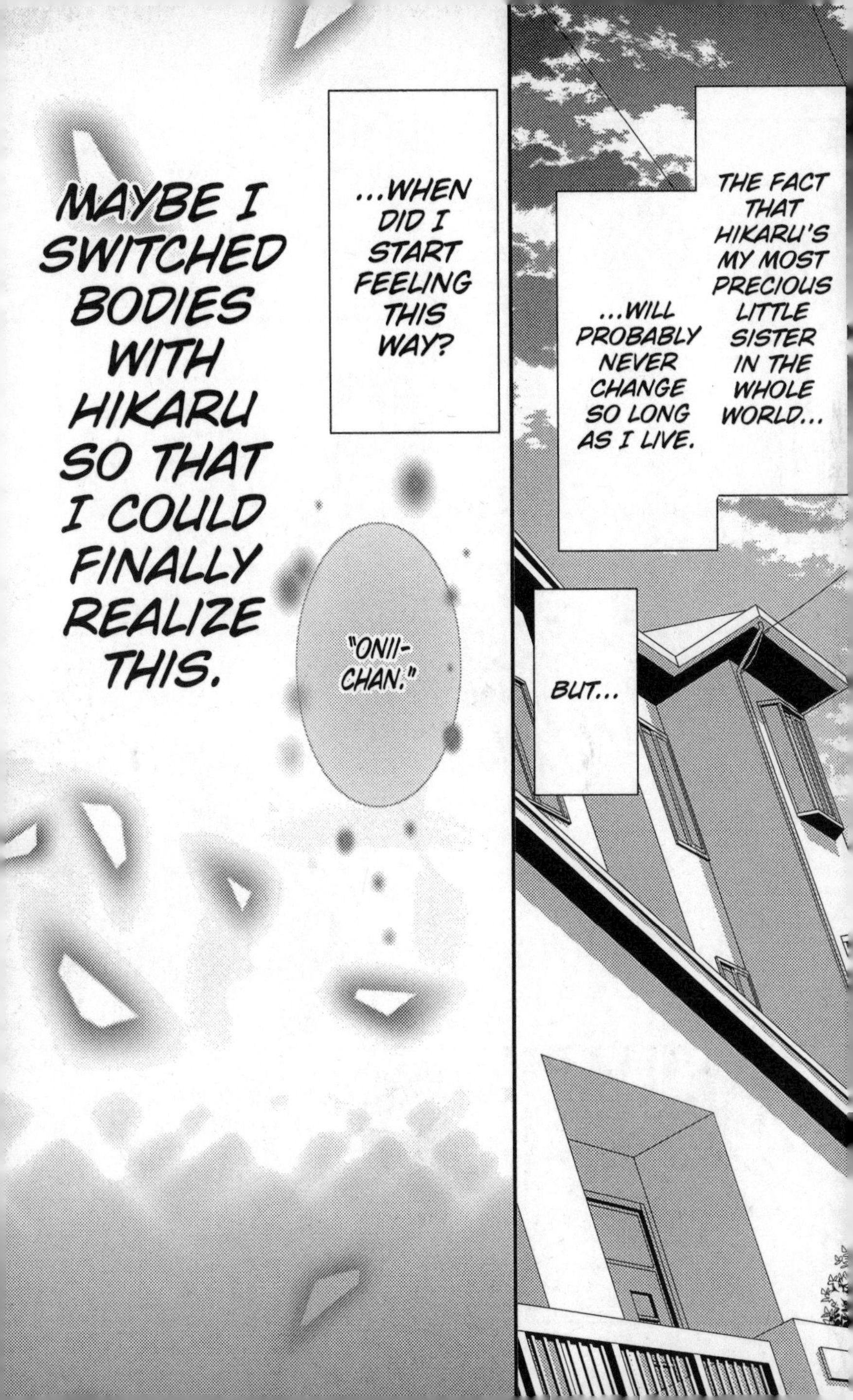
THE FACT THAT HIKARU'S MY MOST PRECIOUS LITTLE SISTER IN THE WHOLE WORLD...
...WILL PROBABLY NEVER CHANGE SO LONG AS I LIVE.
BUT...
...WHEN DID I START FEELING THIS WAY?
"ONII-CHAN."
MAYBE I SWITCHED BODIES WITH HIKARU SO THAT I COULD FINALLY REALIZE THIS.

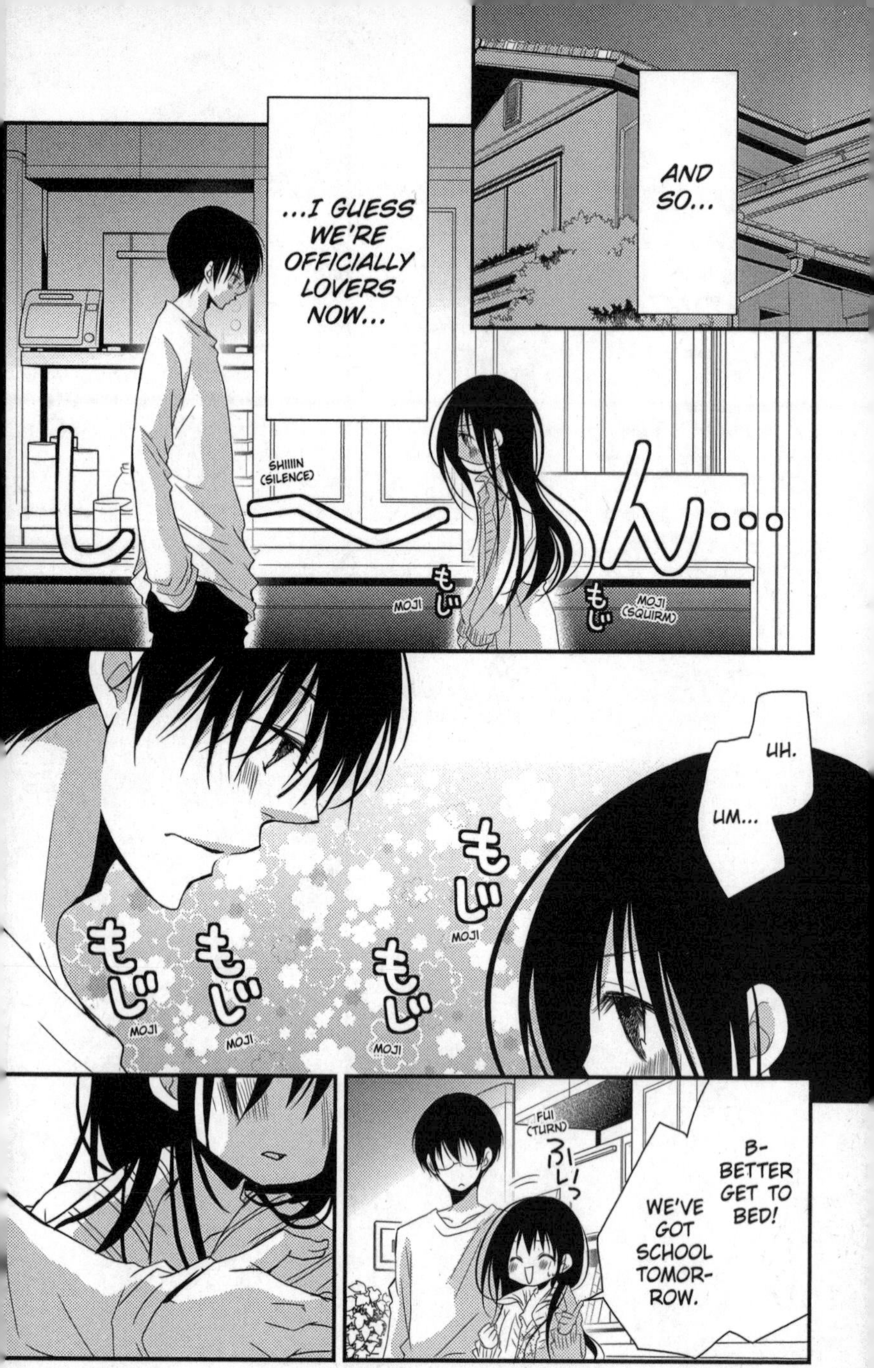
AND SO...
...I GUESS WE'RE OFFICIALLY LOVERS NOW...
SHIIIN (SILENCE)
MOJI (SQUIRM)
MOJI
UH.
UM...
MOJI
MOJI
MOJI
MOJI
FUI (TURN)
B-BETTER GET TO BED!
WE'VE GOT SCHOOL TOMOR-ROW.

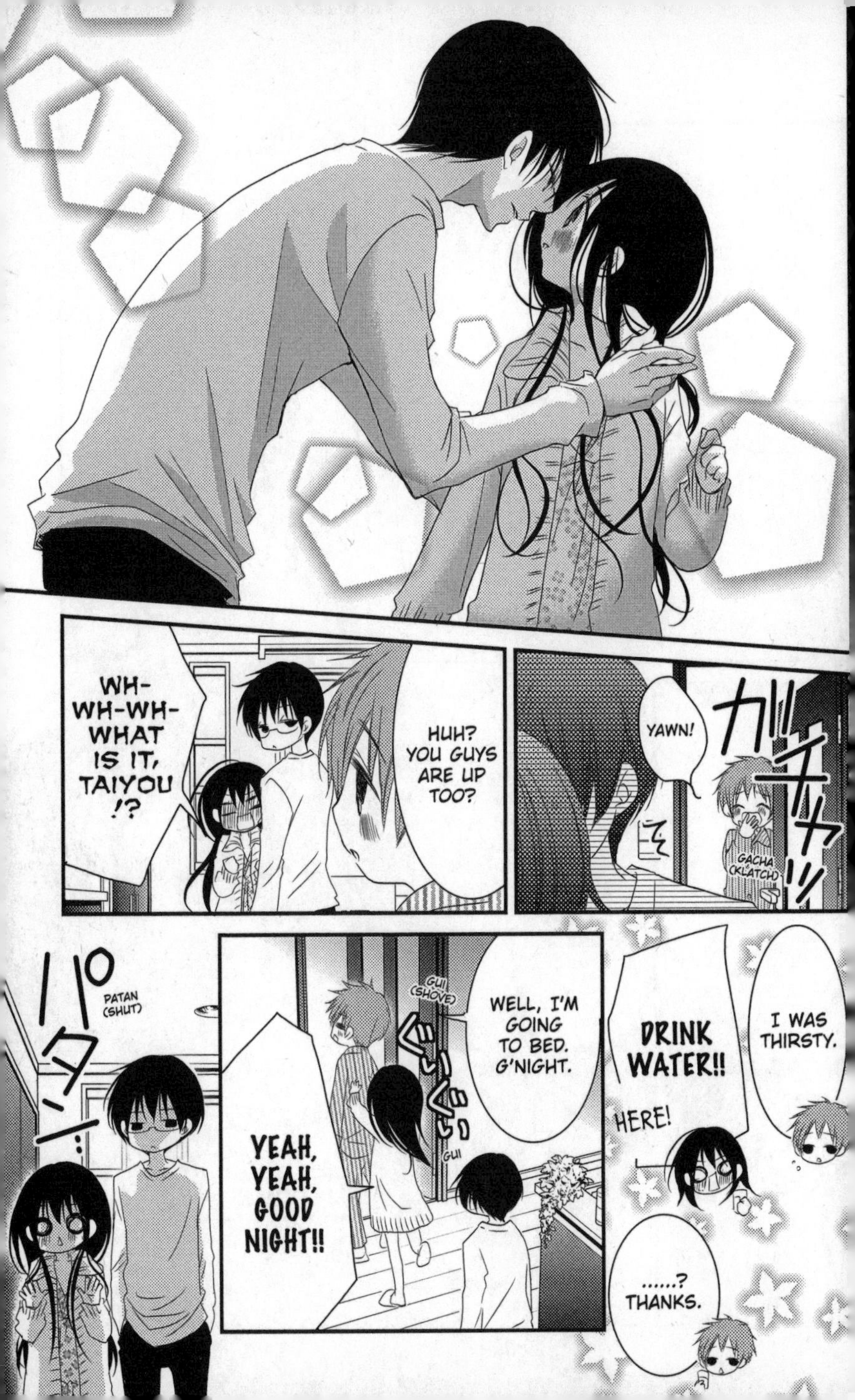
YAWN!
GACHA (KLATCH)
HUH? YOU GUYS ARE UP TOO?
WH-WH-WH-WHAT IS IT, TAIYOU!?
I WAS THIRSTY.
DRINK WATER!!
HERE!
......? THANKS.
WELL, I'M GOING TO BED. G'NIGHT.
GUI (SHOVE)
GUI
YEAH, YEAH, GOOD NIGHT!!
PATAN (SHUT)

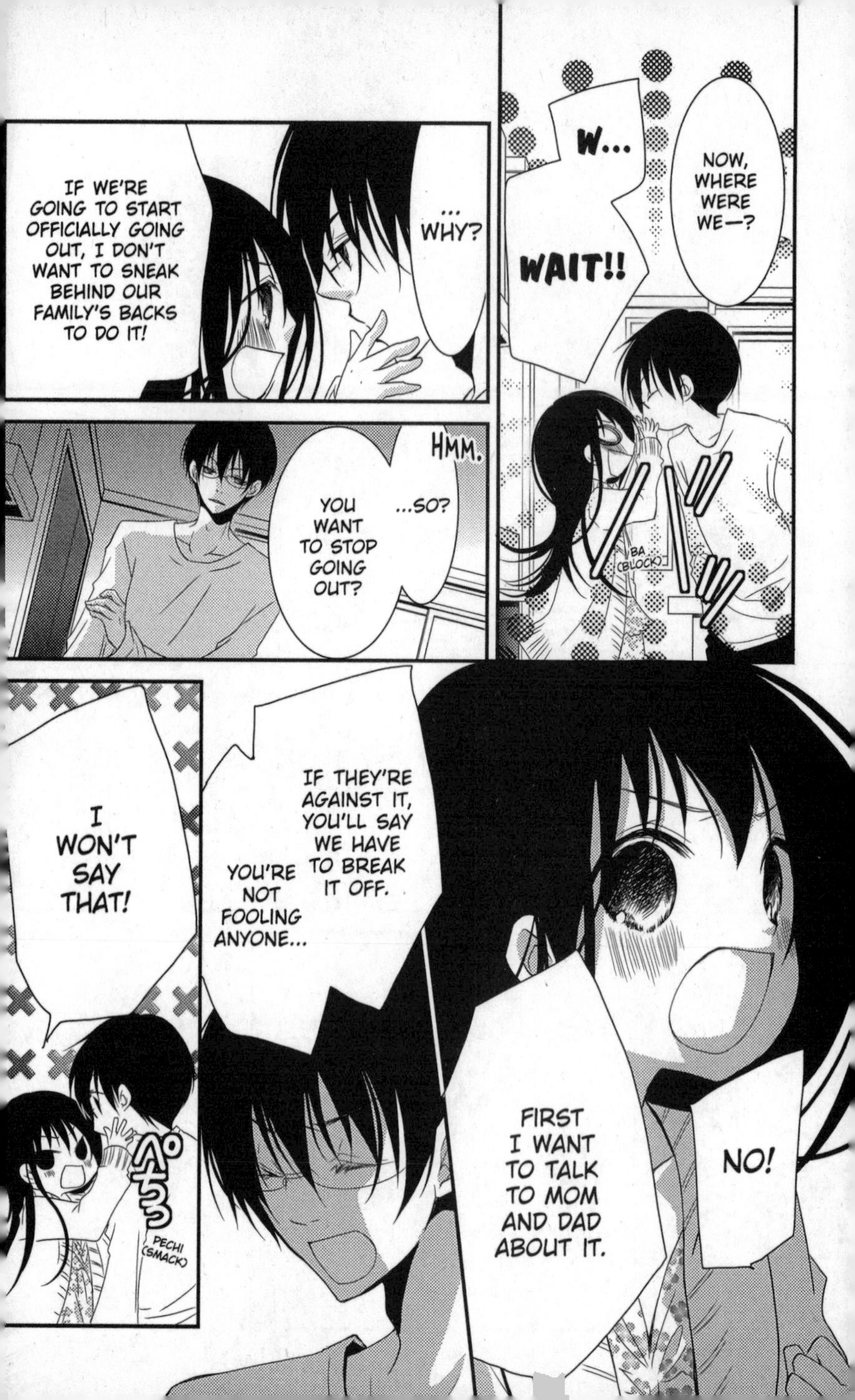
NOW, WHERE WERE WE—?
W... WAIT!!
BA (BLOCK)
... WHY?
IF WE'RE GOING TO START OFFICIALLY GOING OUT, I DON'T WANT TO SNEAK BEHIND OUR FAMILY'S BACKS TO DO IT!
HMM.
...SO?
YOU WANT TO STOP GOING OUT?
NO!
FIRST I WANT TO TALK TO MOM AND DAD ABOUT IT.
IF THEY'RE AGAINST IT, YOU'LL SAY WE HAVE TO BREAK IT OFF.
YOU'RE NOT FOOLING ANYONE...
I WON'T SAY THAT!
ぺちっ
PECHI (SMACK)

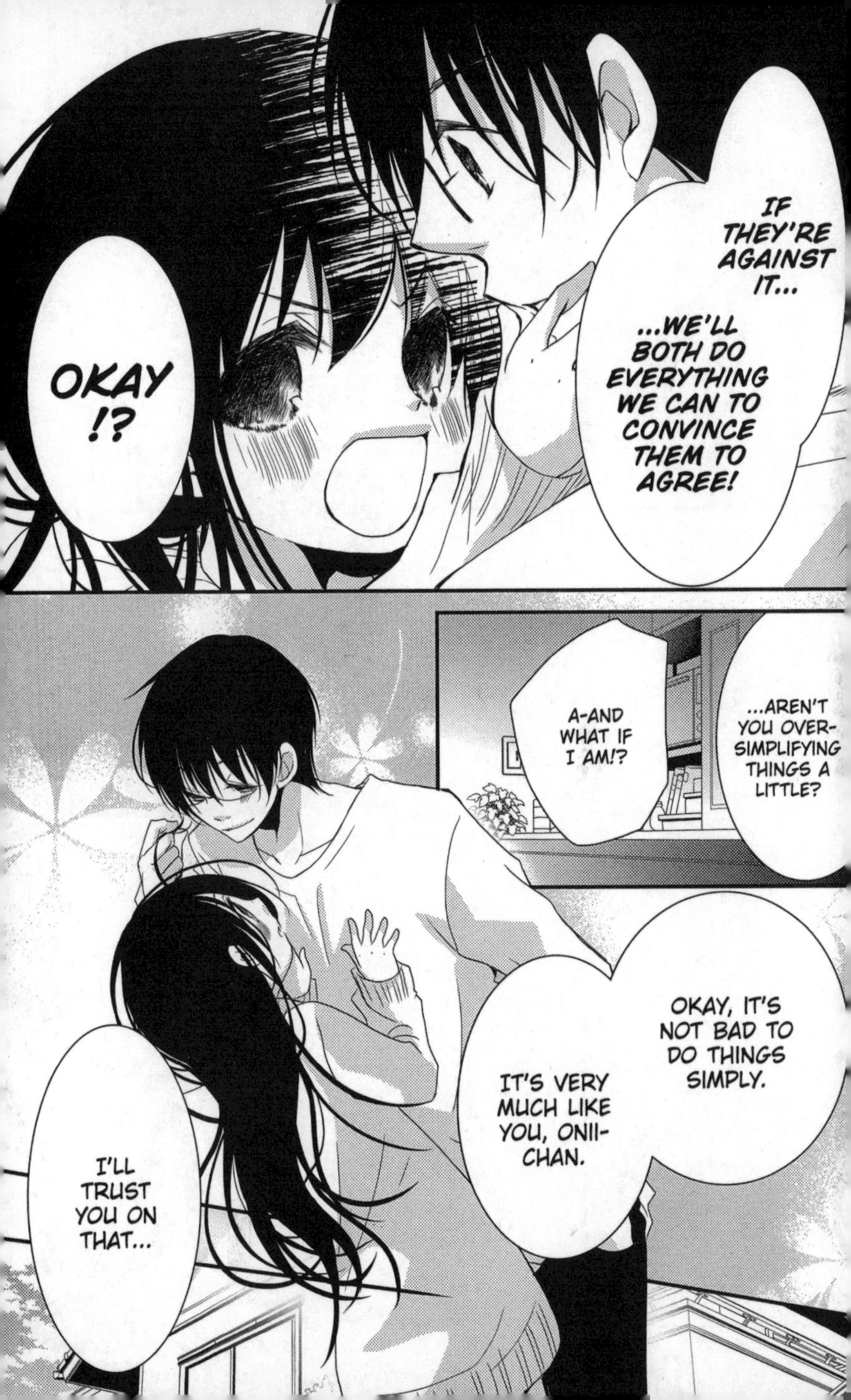
IF THEY'RE AGAINST IT...
...WE'LL BOTH DO EVERYTHING WE CAN TO CONVINCE THEM TO AGREE!
OKAY !?
...AREN'T YOU OVER-SIMPLIFYING THINGS A LITTLE?
A-AND WHAT IF I AM!?
OKAY, IT'S NOT BAD TO DO THINGS SIMPLY.
IT'S VERY MUCH LIKE YOU, ONII-CHAN.
I'LL TRUST YOU ON THAT...

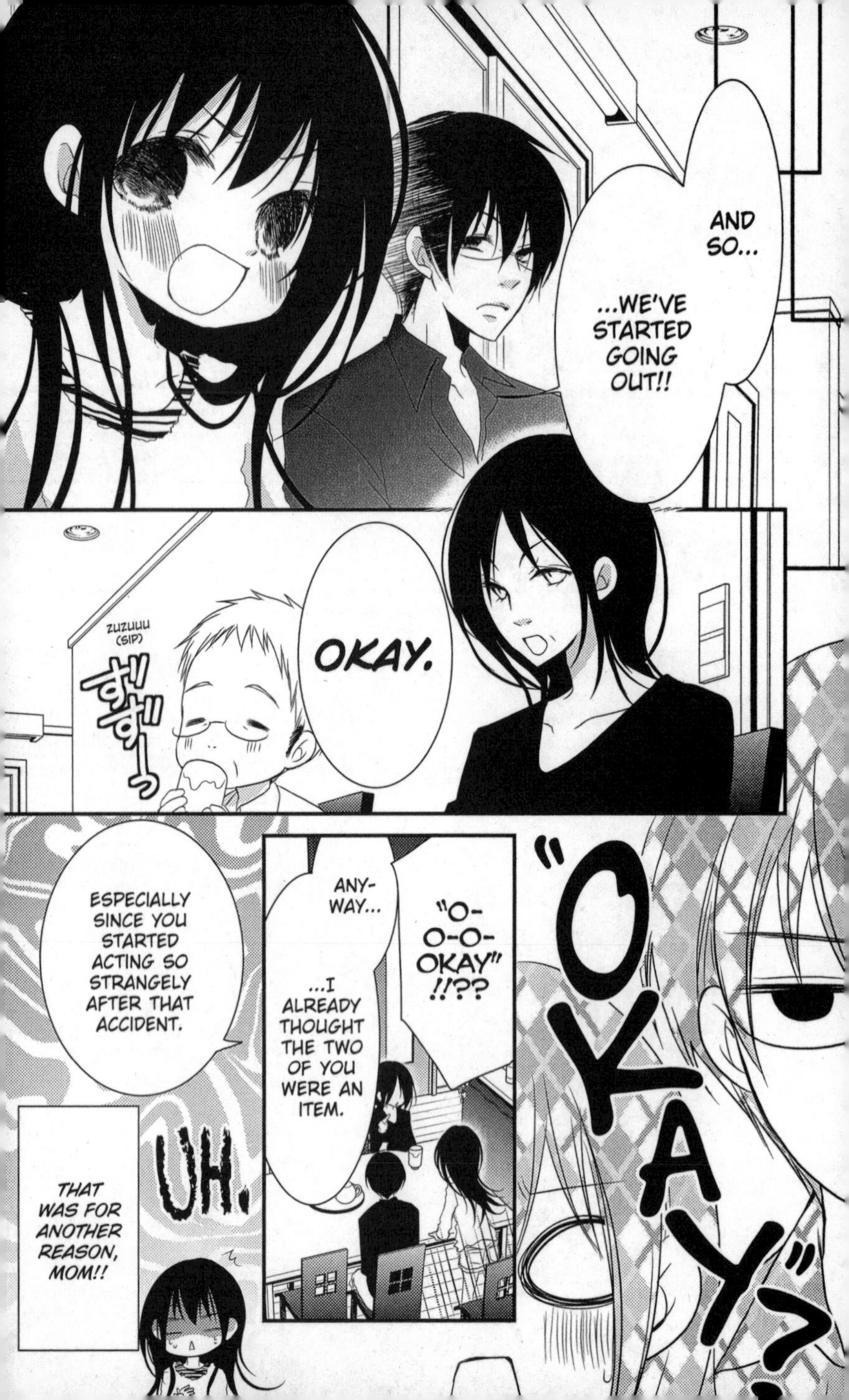
AND SO...
...WE'VE STARTED GOING OUT!!
OKAY.
ZUZUUU (SIP)
ずずーっ
"OKAY"?
"O-O-O-OKAY"!!??
ANY-WAY...
...I ALREADY THOUGHT THE TWO OF YOU WERE AN ITEM.
ESPECIALLY SINCE YOU STARTED ACTING SO STRANGELY AFTER THAT ACCIDENT.
UH.
THAT WAS FOR ANOTHER REASON, MOM!!

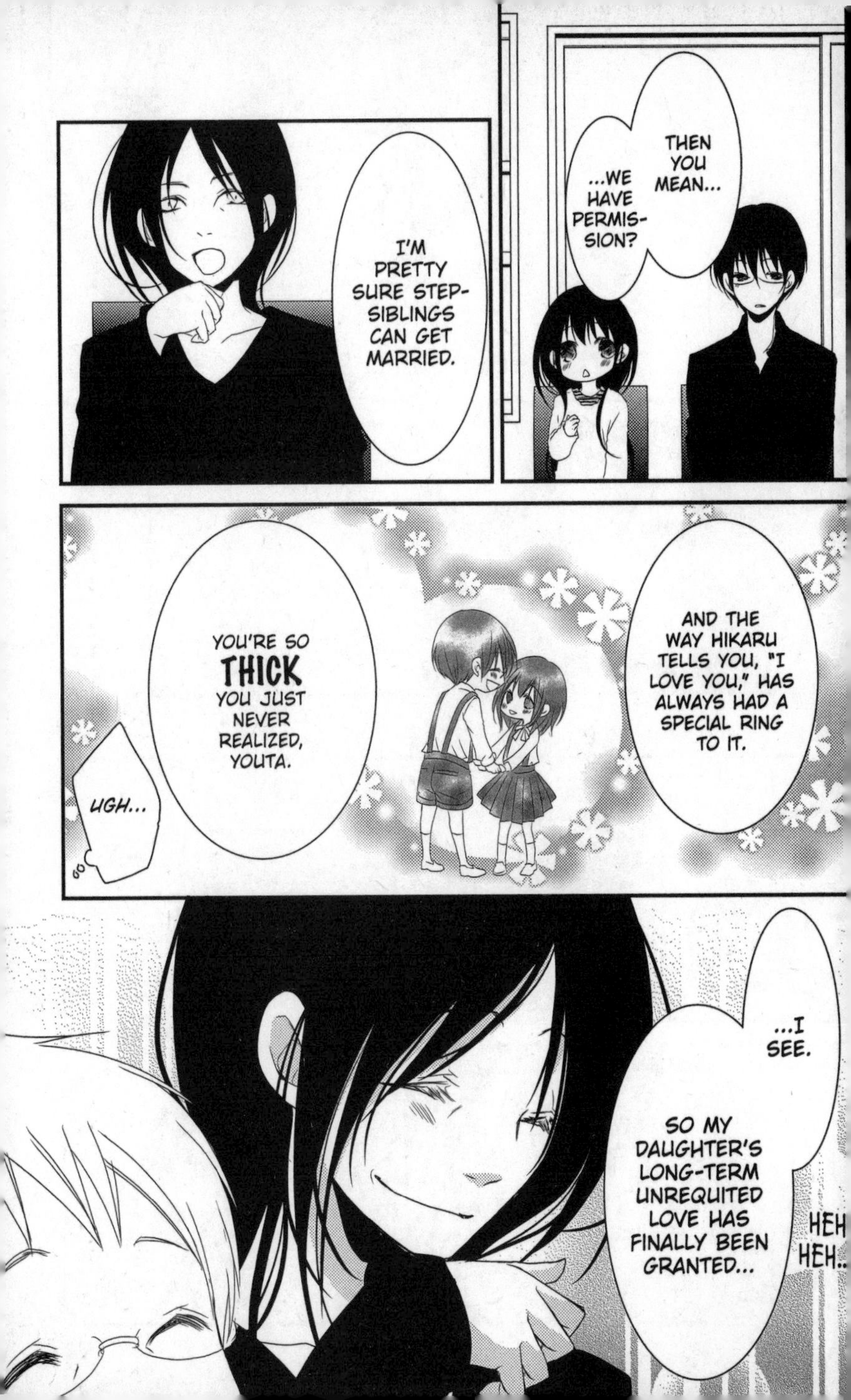
THEN YOU MEAN...
...WE HAVE PERMISSION?
I'M PRETTY SURE STEP-SIBLINGS CAN GET MARRIED.
AND THE WAY HIKARU TELLS YOU, "I LOVE YOU," HAS ALWAYS HAD A SPECIAL RING TO IT.
YOU'RE SO THICK YOU JUST NEVER REALIZED, YOUTA.
UGH...
...I SEE.
SO MY DAUGHTER'S LONG-TERM UNREQUITED LOVE HAS FINALLY BEEN GRANTED...
HEH HEH...

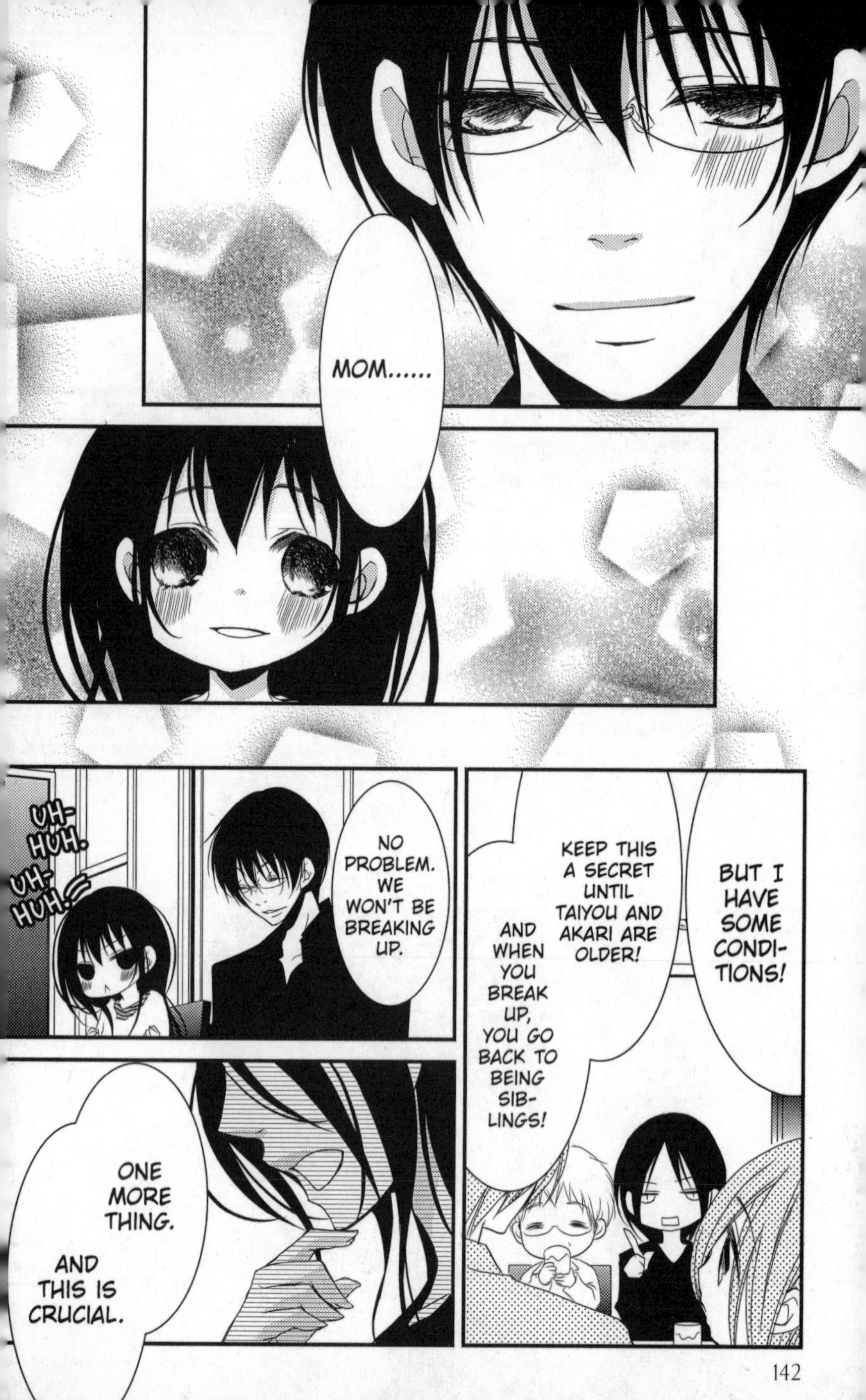
MOM......
BUT I HAVE SOME CONDITIONS!
KEEP THIS A SECRET UNTIL TAIYOU AND AKARI ARE OLDER!
AND WHEN YOU BREAK UP, YOU GO BACK TO BEING SIBLINGS!
NO PROBLEM. WE WON'T BE BREAKING UP.
UH-HUH. UH-HUH.
ONE MORE THING.
AND THIS IS CRUCIAL.

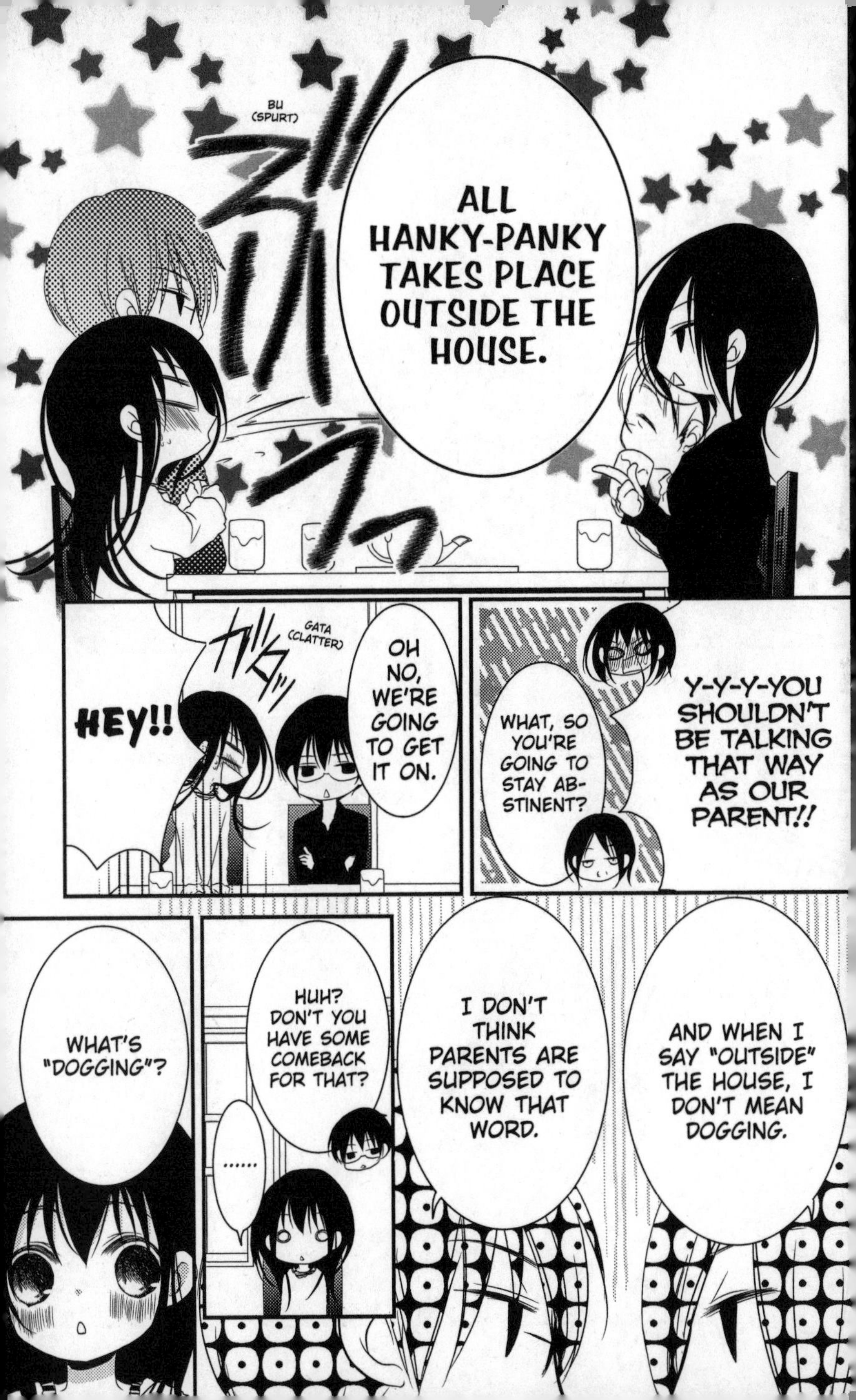
ALL HANKY-PANKY TAKES PLACE OUTSIDE THE HOUSE.
BU (SPURT)
Y-Y-Y-YOU SHOULDN'T BE TALKING THAT WAY AS OUR PARENT!!
WHAT, SO YOU'RE GOING TO STAY AB-STINENT?
OH NO, WE'RE GOING TO GET IT ON.
GATA (CLATTER)
HEY!!
AND WHEN I SAY "OUTSIDE" THE HOUSE, I DON'T MEAN DOGGING.
I DON'T THINK PARENTS ARE SUPPOSED TO KNOW THAT WORD.
HUH? DON'T YOU HAVE SOME COMEBACK FOR THAT?
......
WHAT'S "DOGGING"?

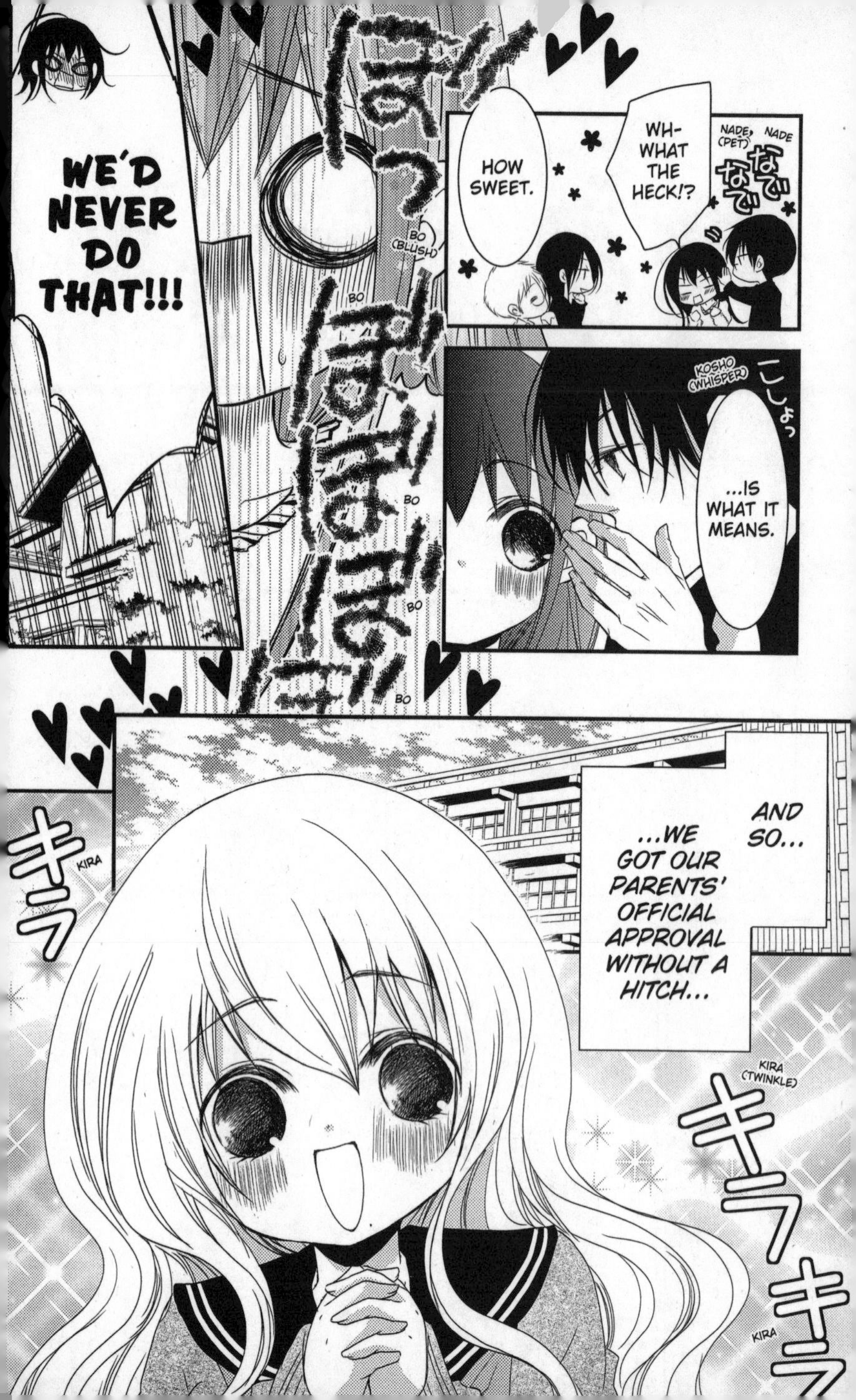

NADE (PET) NADE
なでなで
WH- WHAT THE HECK!?
HOW SWEET.
KOSHO (WHISPER)
こしょっ
...IS WHAT IT MEANS.
BO (BLUSH)
BO
BO
BO
BO
WE'D NEVER DO THAT!!!
AND SO...
...WE GOT OUR PARENTS' OFFICIAL APPROVAL WITHOUT A HITCH...
KIRA (TWINKLE)
キラキラ
KIRA
KIRA
キラ

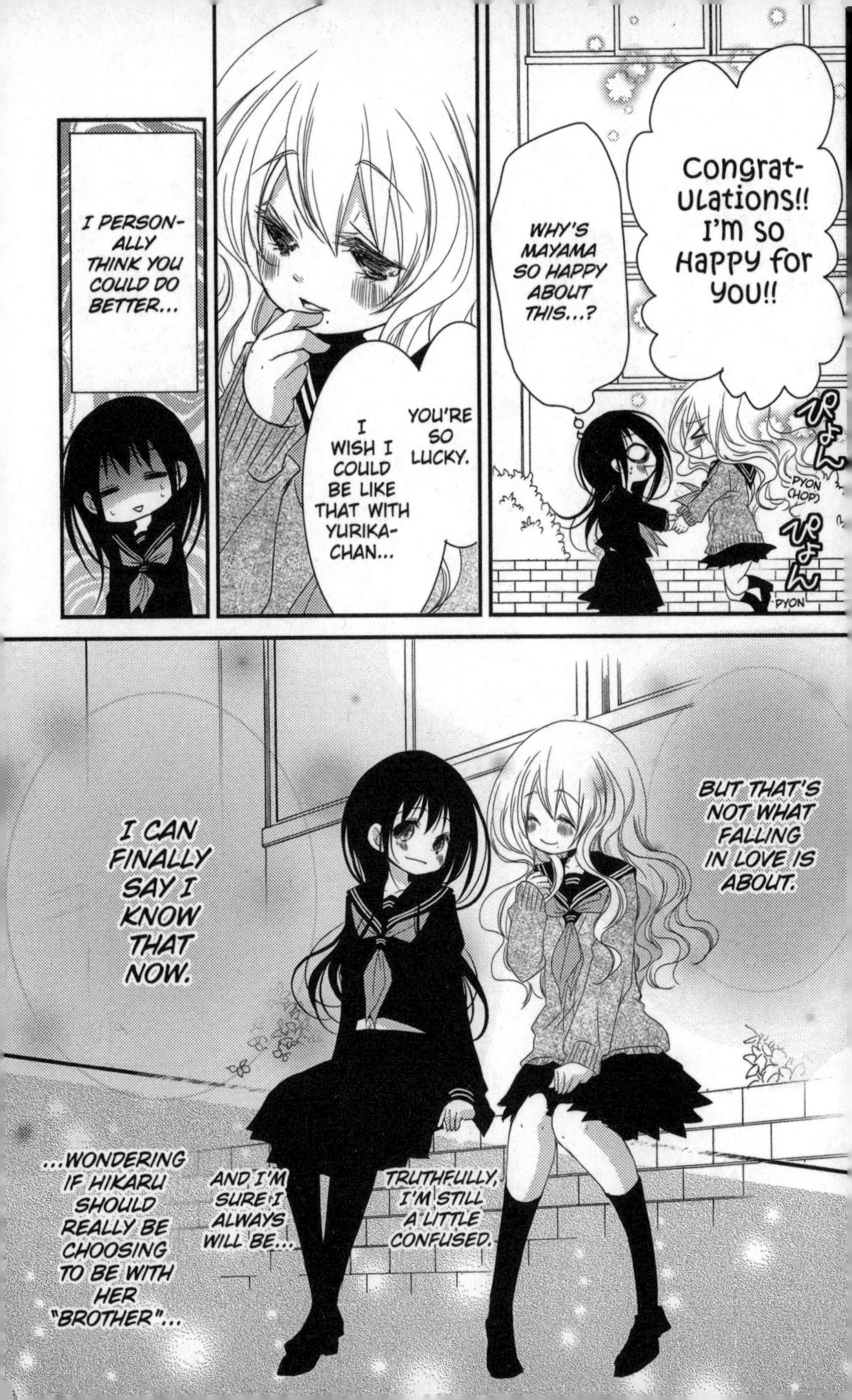
Congrat-ulations!! I'm so happy for you!!
WHY'S MAYAMA SO HAPPY ABOUT THIS...?
ぴょん
PYON (HOP)
ぴょん
PYON
YOU'RE SO LUCKY.
I WISH I COULD BE LIKE THAT WITH YURIKA-CHAN...
I PERSON-ALLY THINK YOU COULD DO BETTER...
BUT THAT'S NOT WHAT FALLING IN LOVE IS ABOUT.
I CAN FINALLY SAY I KNOW THAT NOW.
TRUTHFULLY, I'M STILL A LITTLE CONFUSED.
AND I'M SURE I ALWAYS WILL BE...
...WONDERING IF HIKARU SHOULD REALLY BE CHOOSING TO BE WITH HER "BROTHER"...

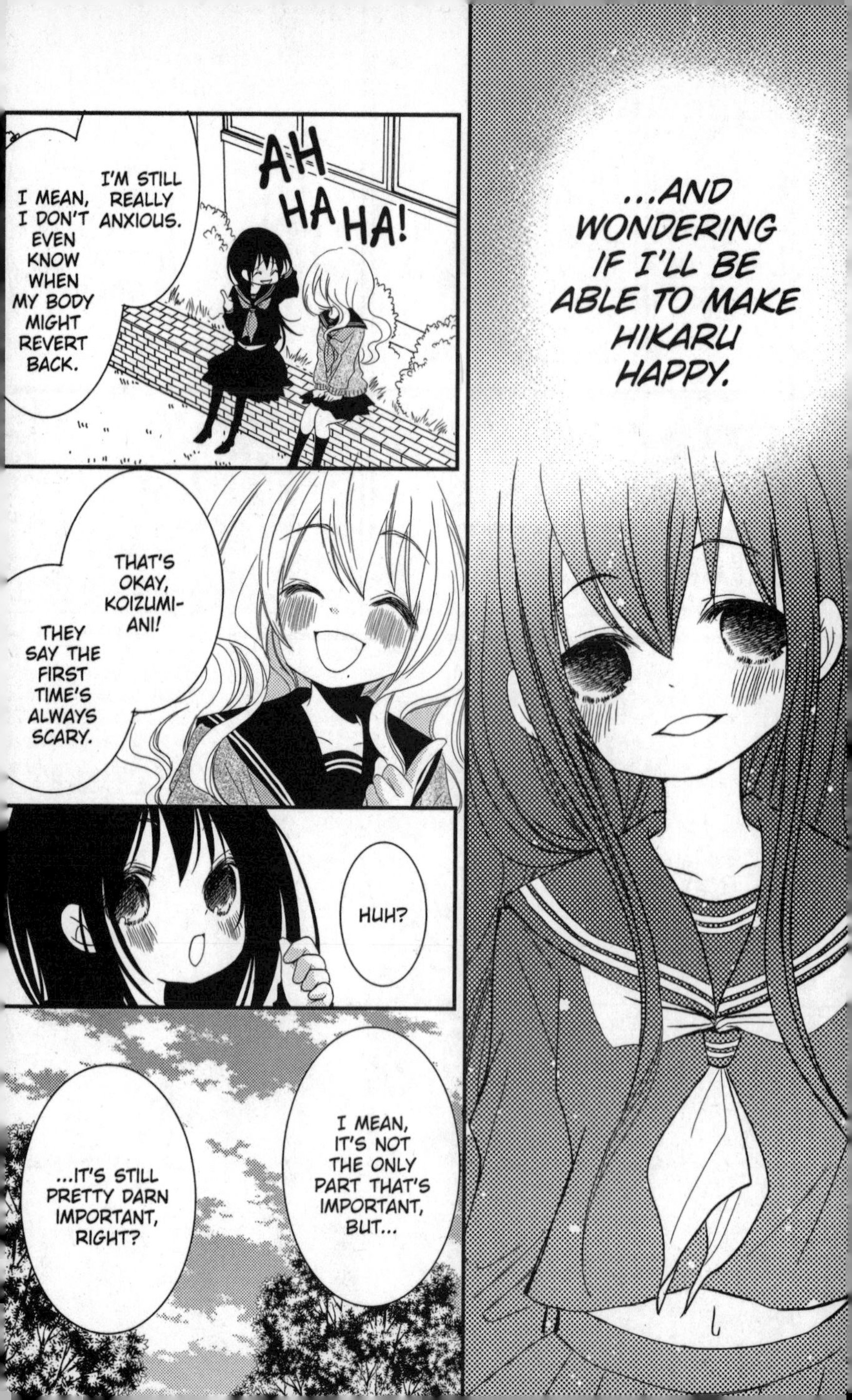
...AND WONDERING IF I'LL BE ABLE TO MAKE HIKARU HAPPY.
AH HA HA!
I'M STILL REALLY ANXIOUS.
I MEAN, I DON'T EVEN KNOW WHEN MY BODY MIGHT REVERT BACK.
THAT'S OKAY, KOIZUMI-ANI!
THEY SAY THE FIRST TIME'S ALWAYS SCARY.
HUH?
I MEAN, IT'S NOT THE ONLY PART THAT'S IMPORTANT, BUT...
...IT'S STILL PRETTY DARN IMPORTANT, RIGHT?

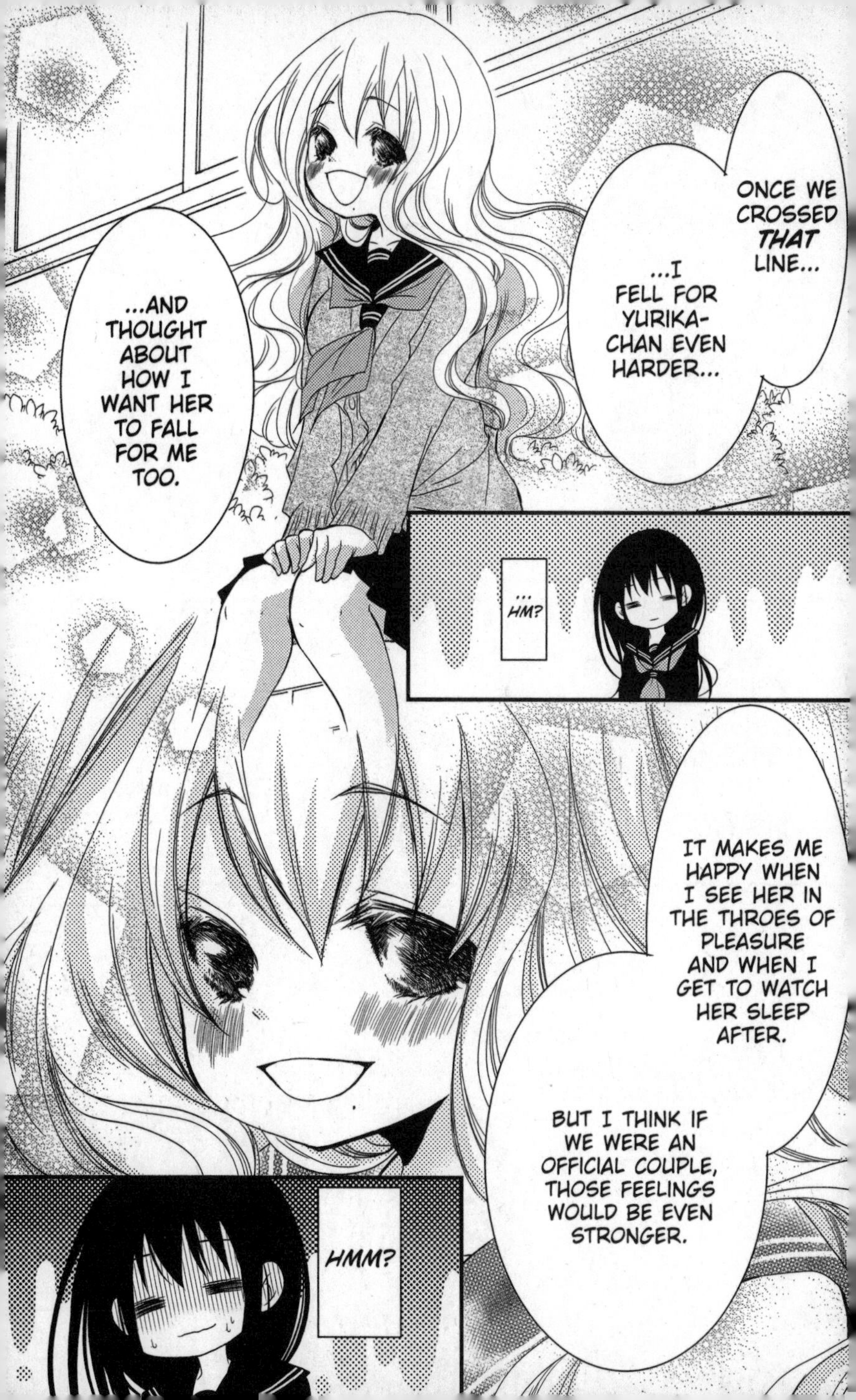
ONCE WE CROSSED *THAT* LINE...
...I FELL FOR YURIKA-CHAN EVEN HARDER...
...AND THOUGHT ABOUT HOW I WANT HER TO FALL FOR ME TOO.
...HM?
IT MAKES ME HAPPY WHEN I SEE HER IN THE THROES OF PLEASURE AND WHEN I GET TO WATCH HER SLEEP AFTER.
BUT I THINK IF WE WERE AN OFFICIAL COUPLE, THOSE FEELINGS WOULD BE EVEN STRONGER.
HMM?

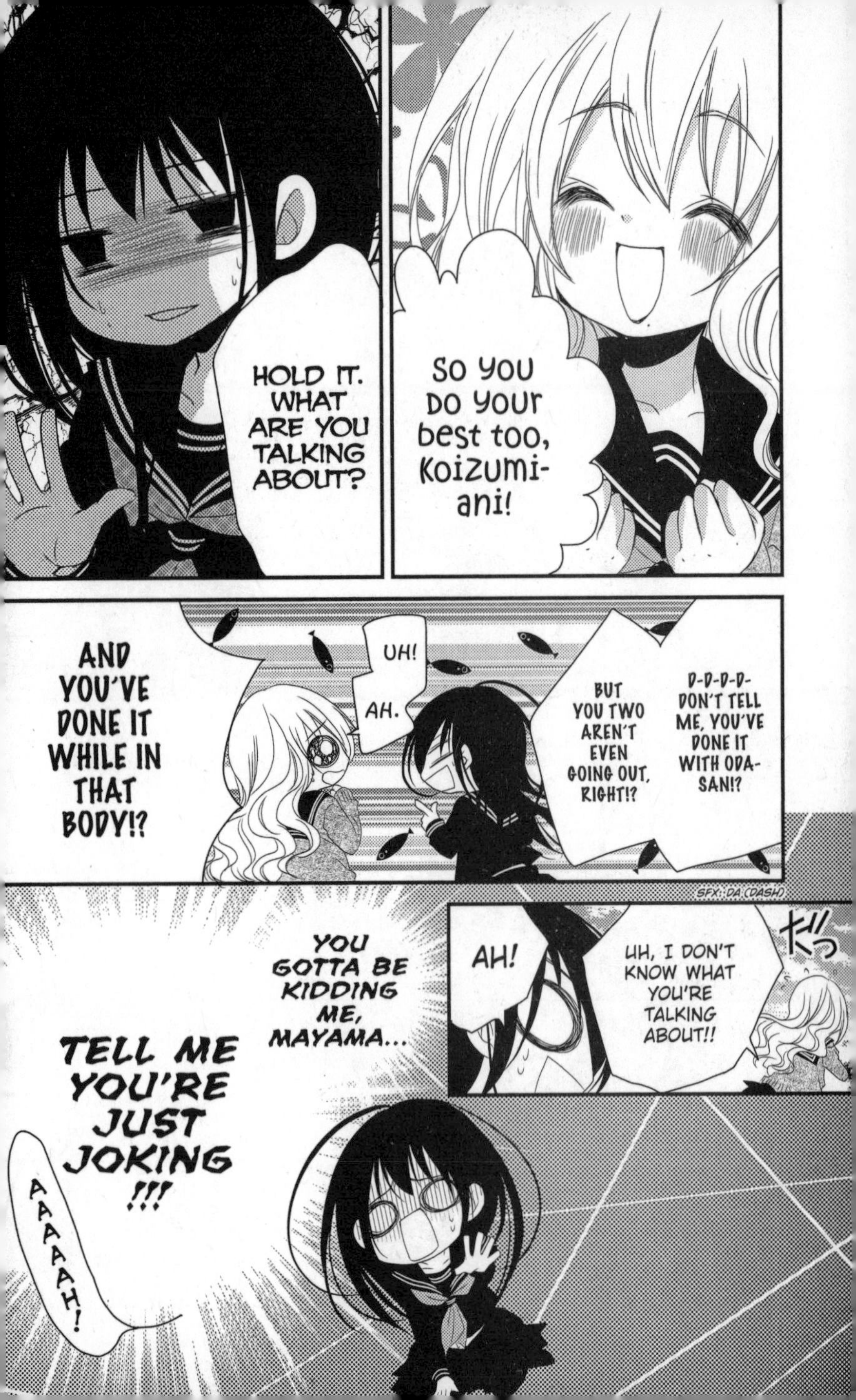
So you do your best too, Koizumi-ani!
HOLD IT. WHAT ARE YOU TALKING ABOUT?
D-D-D-D-DON'T TELL ME, YOU'VE DONE IT WITH ODA-SAN!?
BUT YOU TWO AREN'T EVEN GOING OUT, RIGHT!?
UH!
AH.
AND YOU'VE DONE IT WHILE IN THAT BODY!?
SFX: DA (DASH)
だっ
UH, I DON'T KNOW WHAT YOU'RE TALKING ABOUT!!
AH!
YOU GOTTA BE KIDDING ME, MAYAMA...
TELL ME YOU'RE JUST JOKING !!!
AAAAAH!

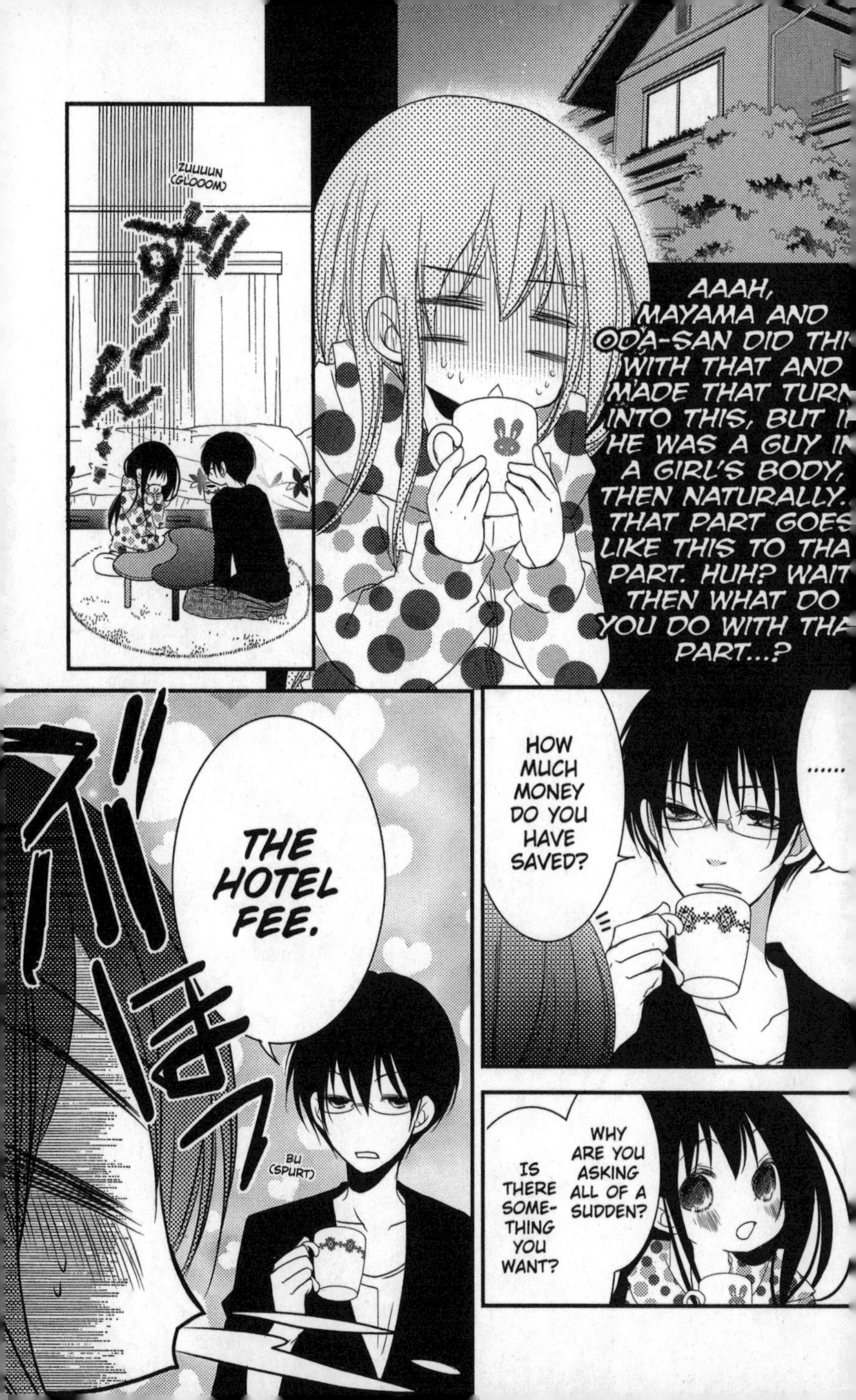

AAAH, MAYAMA AND ODA-SAN DID THI WITH THAT AND MADE THAT TURN INTO THIS, BUT I HE WAS A GUY IN A GIRL'S BODY, THEN NATURALLY. THAT PART GOES LIKE THIS TO THA PART. HUH? WAIT THEN WHAT DO YOU DO WITH THA PART...?
ZUUUUN (GLOOOM)
HOW MUCH MONEY DO YOU HAVE SAVED?
......
WHY ARE YOU ASKING ALL OF A SUDDEN?
IS THERE SOME-THING YOU WANT?
THE HOTEL FEE.
BU (SPURT)

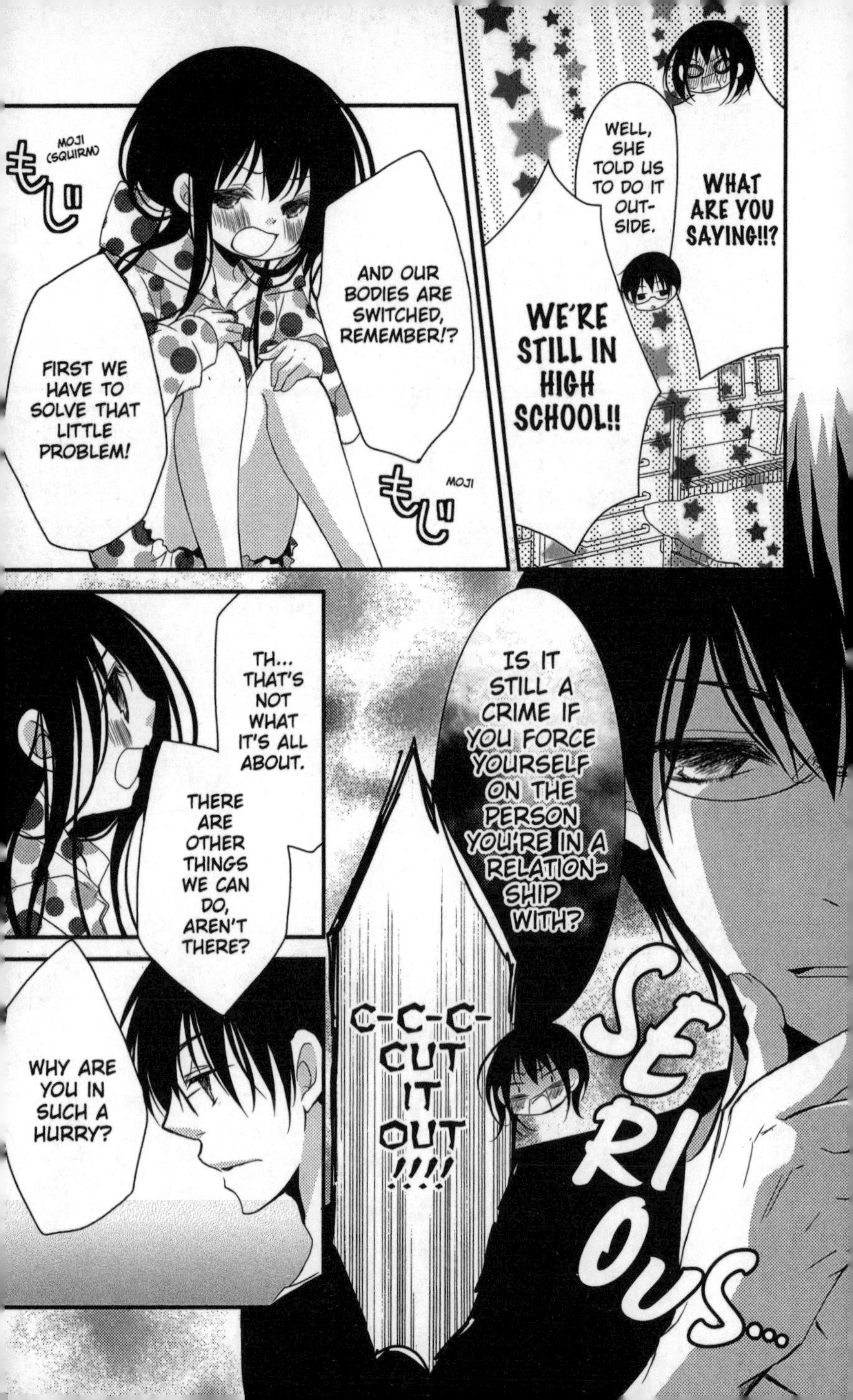
WHAT ARE YOU SAYING!!?
WELL, SHE TOLD US TO DO IT OUT-SIDE.
WE'RE STILL IN HIGH SCHOOL!!
AND OUR BODIES ARE SWITCHED, REMEMBER!?
MOJI (SQUIRM)
FIRST WE HAVE TO SOLVE THAT LITTLE PROBLEM!
MOJI
IS IT STILL A CRIME IF YOU FORCE YOURSELF ON THE PERSON YOU'RE IN A RELATION-SHIP WITH?
SERIOUS...
C-C-C-CUT IT OUT!!!!
TH... THAT'S NOT WHAT IT'S ALL ABOUT.
THERE ARE OTHER THINGS WE CAN DO, AREN'T THERE?
WHY ARE YOU IN SUCH A HURRY?

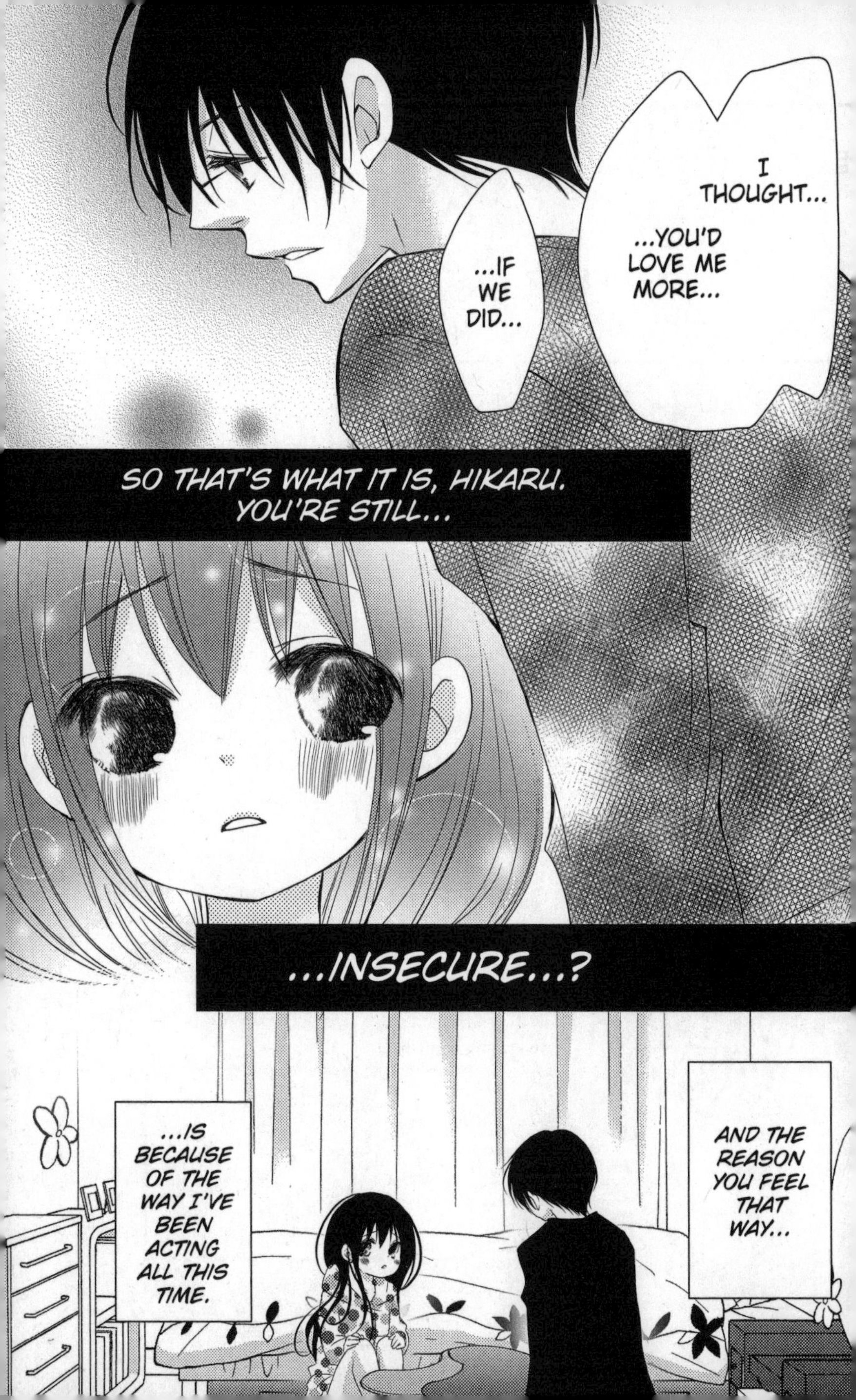
I THOUGHT... ...YOU'D LOVE ME MORE...
...IF WE DID...
SO THAT'S WHAT IT IS, HIKARU. YOU'RE STILL...
...INSECURE...?
AND THE REASON YOU FEEL THAT WAY...
...IS BECAUSE OF THE WAY I'VE BEEN ACTING ALL THIS TIME.

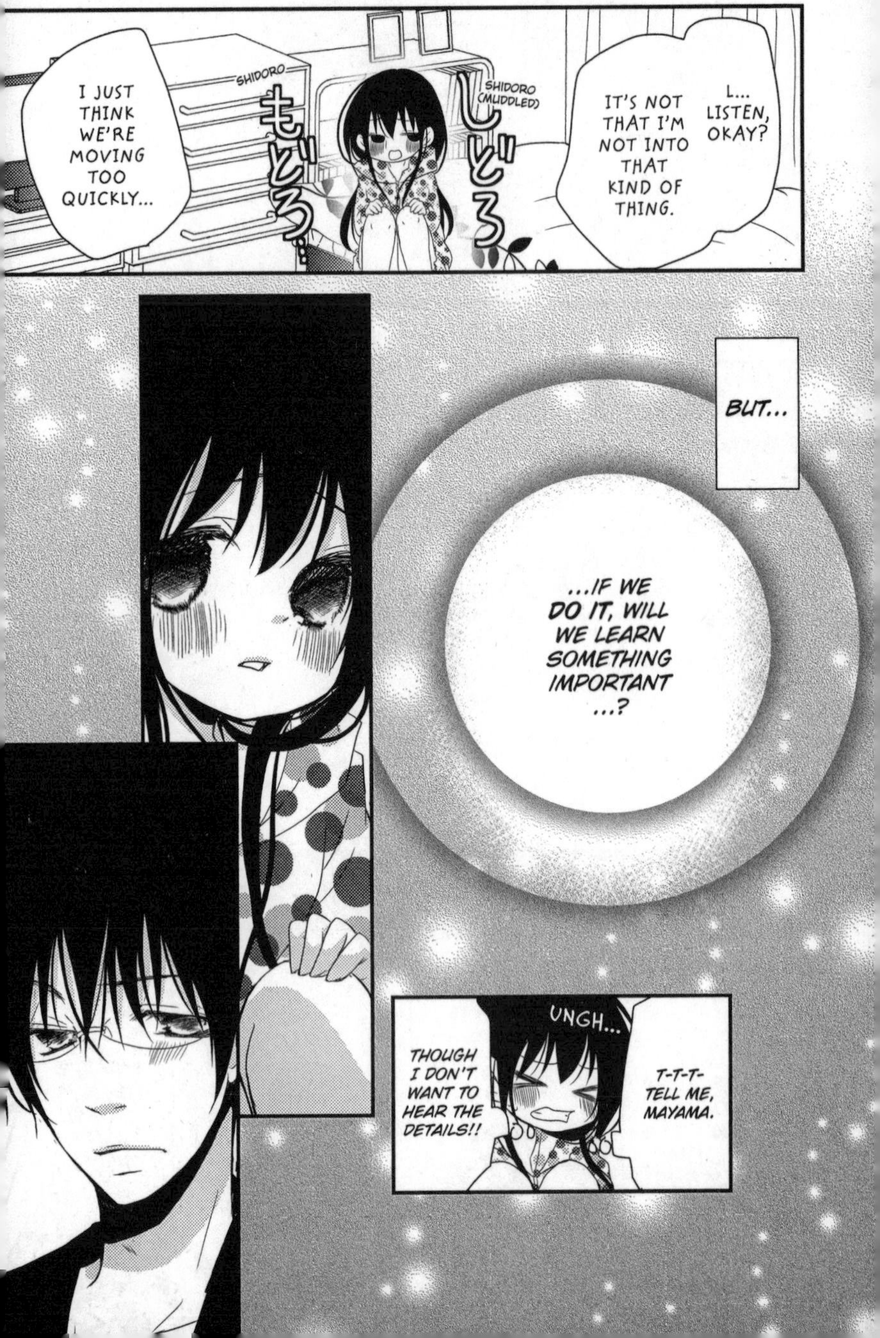
L... LISTEN, OKAY?
IT'S NOT THAT I'M NOT INTO THAT KIND OF THING.
しどろ
SHIDORO (MUDDLED)
もどろ
SHIDORO
I JUST THINK WE'RE MOVING TOO QUICKLY...
BUT...
...IF WE DO IT, WILL WE LEARN SOMETHING IMPORTANT ...?
UNGH...
T-T-T-TELL ME, MAYAMA.
THOUGH I DON'T WANT TO HEAR THE DETAILS!!

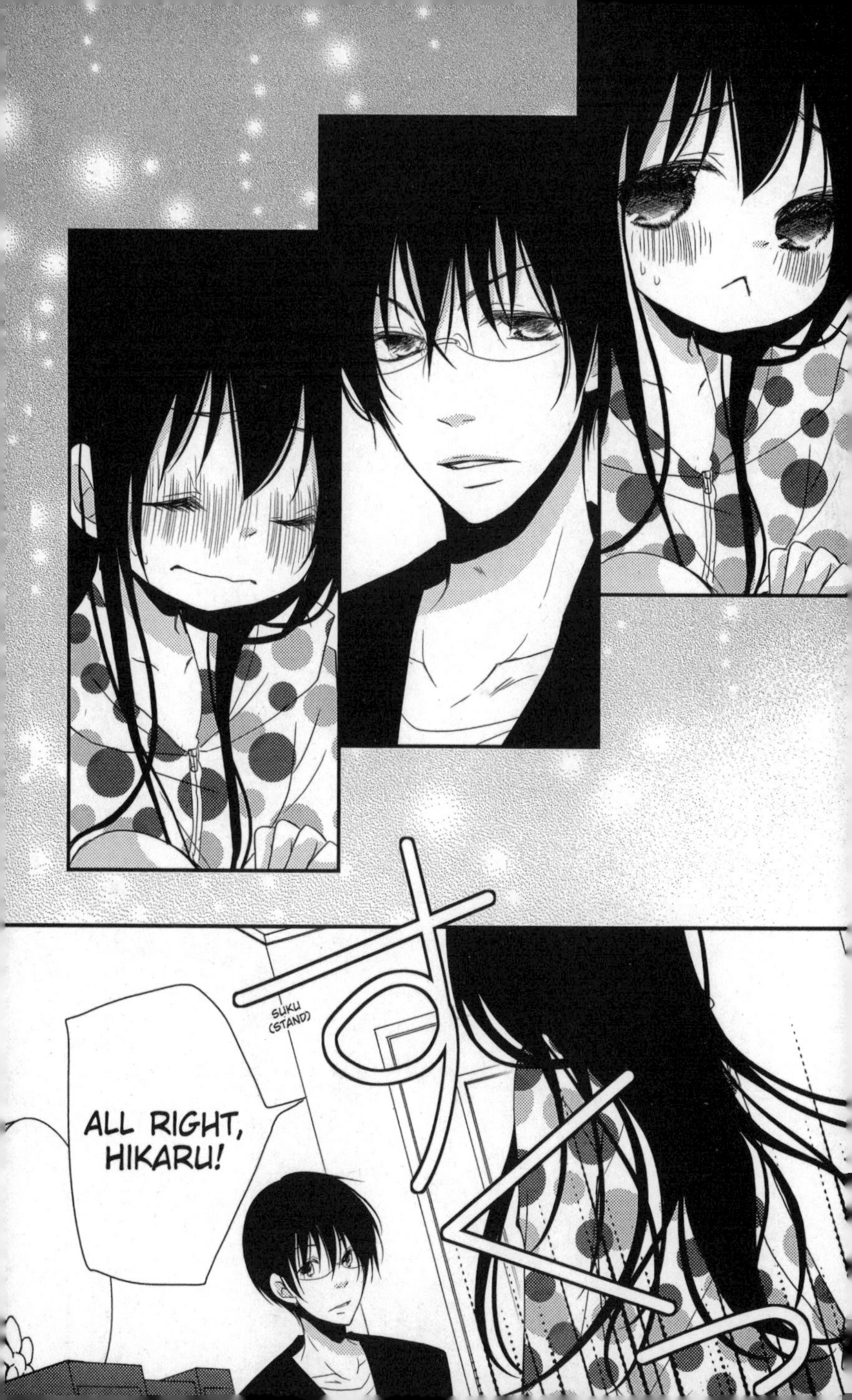
SUKU (STAND)
ALL RIGHT, HIKARU!

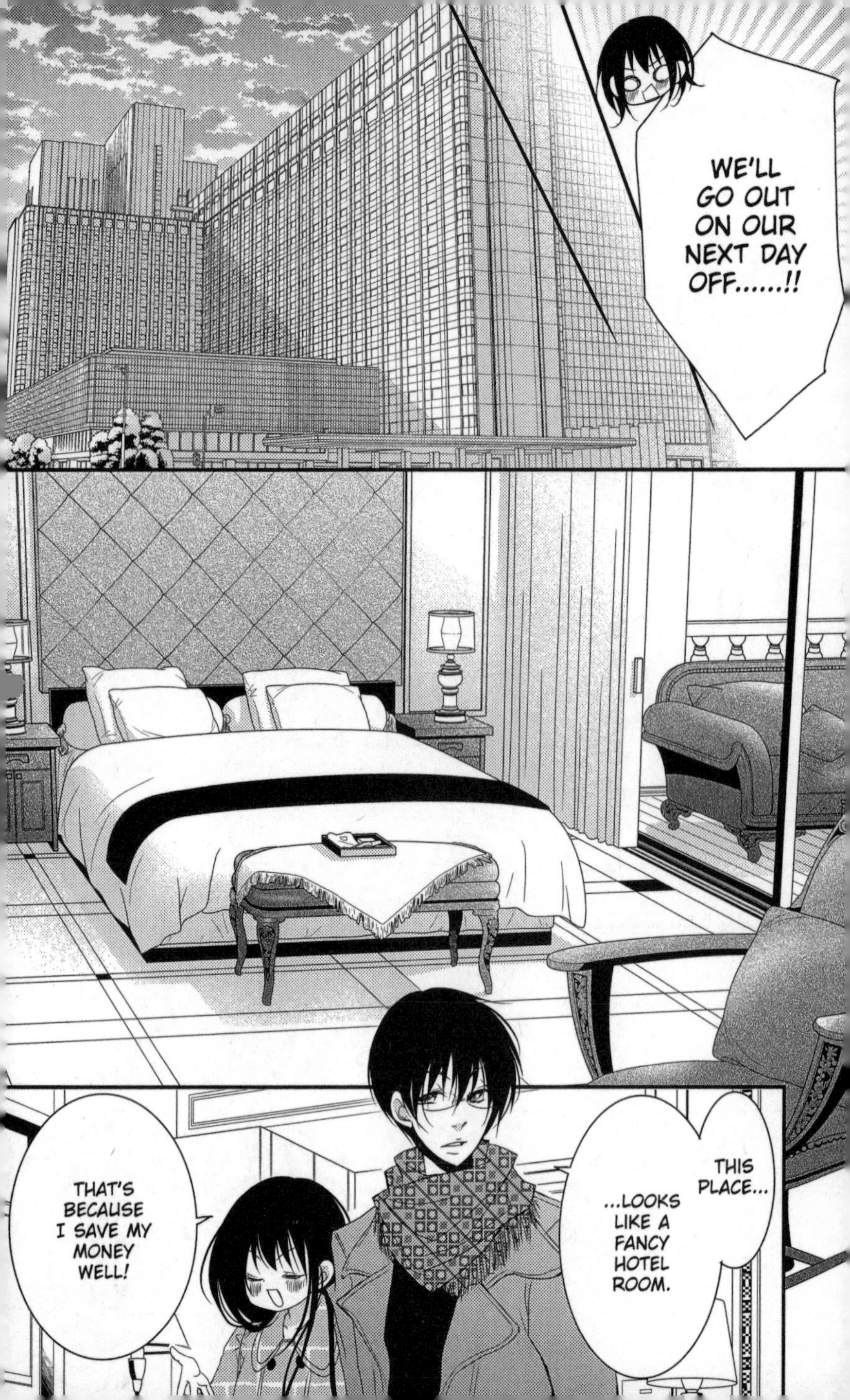
WE'LL GO OUT ON OUR NEXT DAY OFF......!!
THIS PLACE...
...LOOKS LIKE A FANCY HOTEL ROOM.
THAT'S BECAUSE I SAVE MY MONEY WELL!

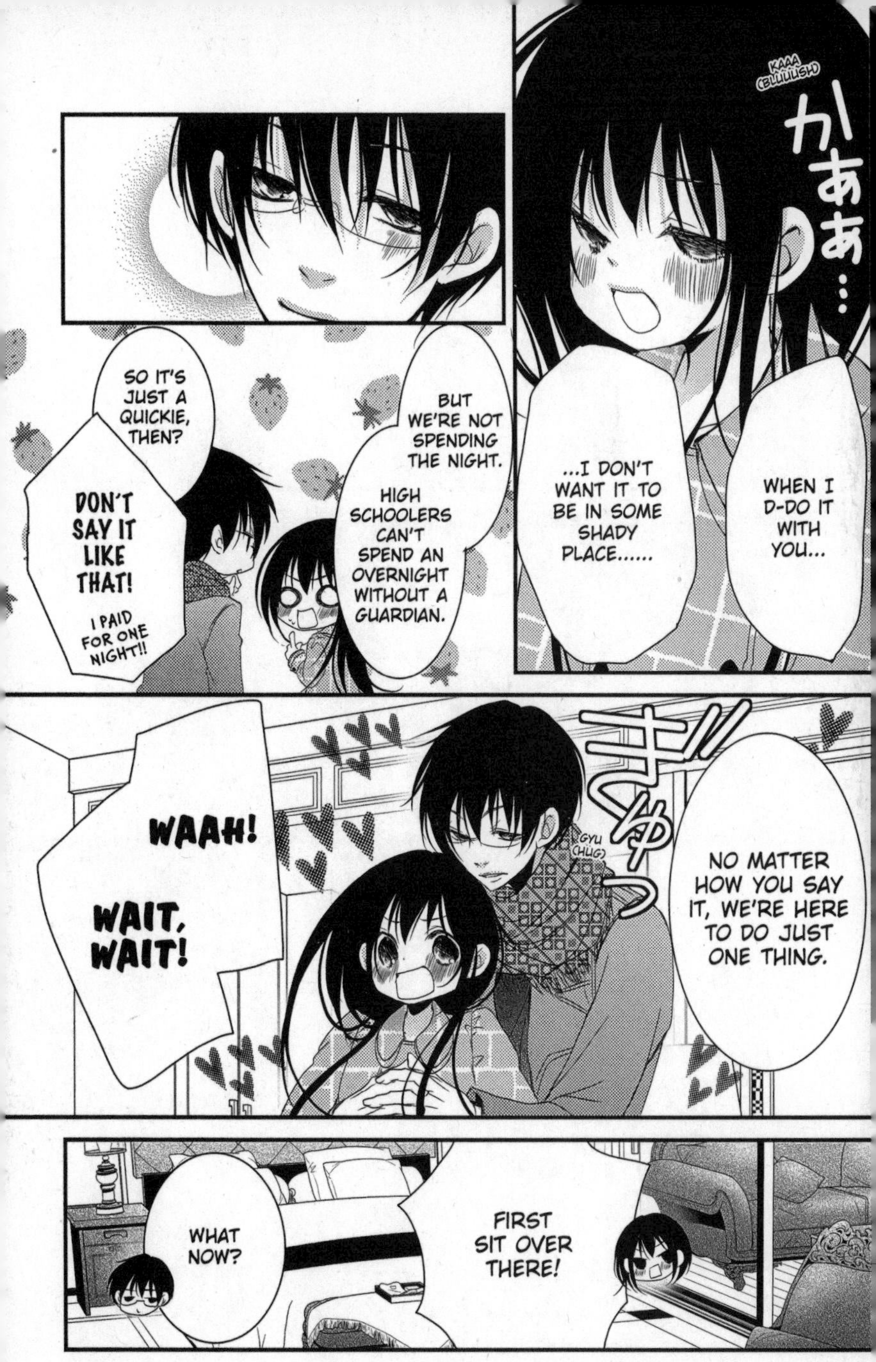
KAAA (BLUUUSH)
かぁぁ…
WHEN I D-DO IT WITH YOU...
...I DON'T WANT IT TO BE IN SOME SHADY PLACE......
BUT WE'RE NOT SPENDING THE NIGHT.
HIGH SCHOOLERS CAN'T SPEND AN OVERNIGHT WITHOUT A GUARDIAN.
SO IT'S JUST A QUICKIE, THEN?
DON'T SAY IT LIKE THAT!
I PAID FOR ONE NIGHT!!
ぎゅっ
GYU (HUG)
NO MATTER HOW YOU SAY IT, WE'RE HERE TO DO JUST ONE THING.
WAAH!
WAIT, WAIT!
FIRST SIT OVER THERE!
WHAT NOW?

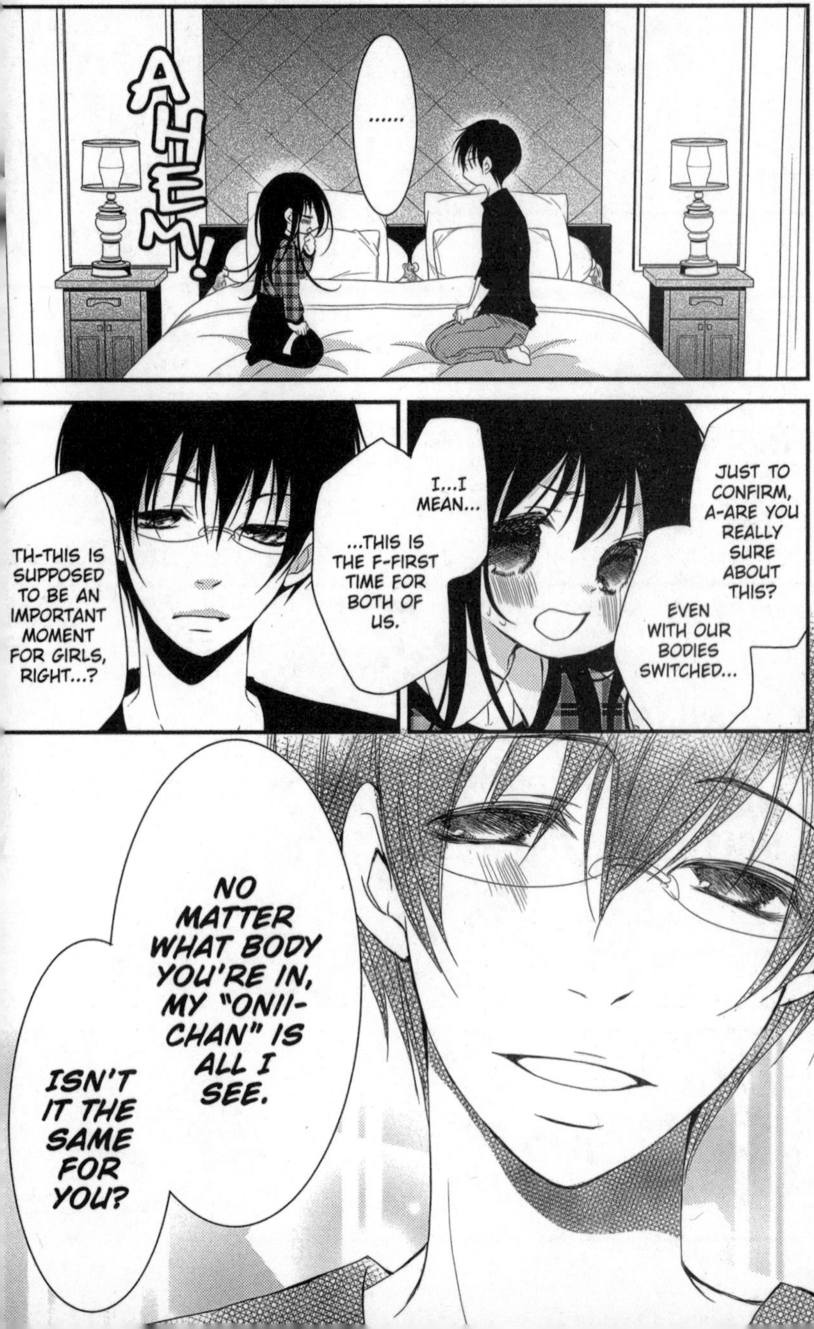
......
AHEM!
JUST TO CONFIRM, A-ARE YOU REALLY SURE ABOUT THIS?
EVEN WITH OUR BODIES SWITCHED...
I...I MEAN...
...THIS IS THE F-FIRST TIME FOR BOTH OF US.
TH-THIS IS SUPPOSED TO BE AN IMPORTANT MOMENT FOR GIRLS, RIGHT...?
NO MATTER WHAT BODY YOU'RE IN, MY "ONII-CHAN" IS ALL I SEE.
ISN'T IT THE SAME FOR YOU?

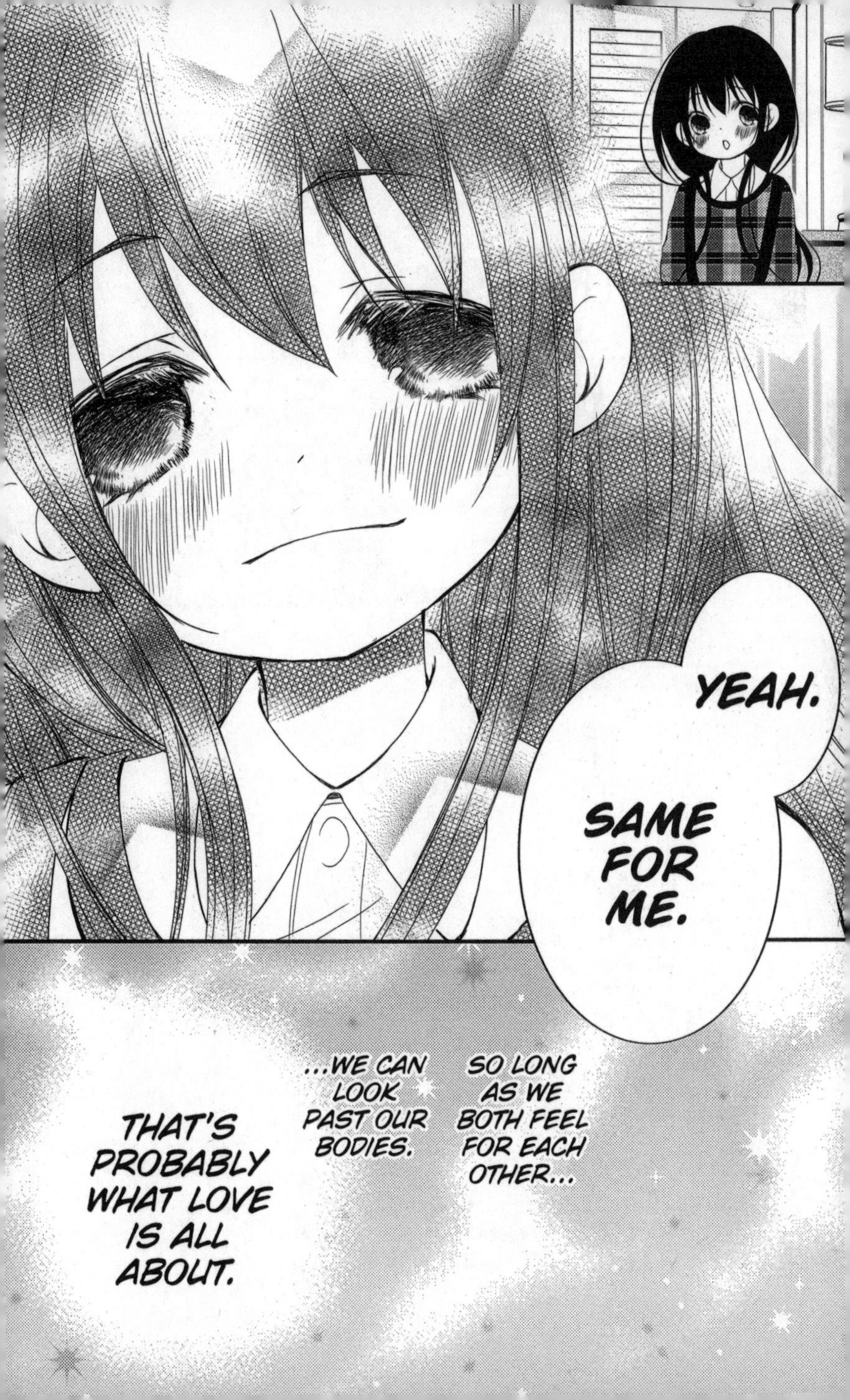
YEAH.
SAME FOR ME.
SO LONG AS WE BOTH FEEL FOR EACH OTHER...
...WE CAN LOOK PAST OUR BODIES.
THAT'S PROBABLY WHAT LOVE IS ALL ABOUT.

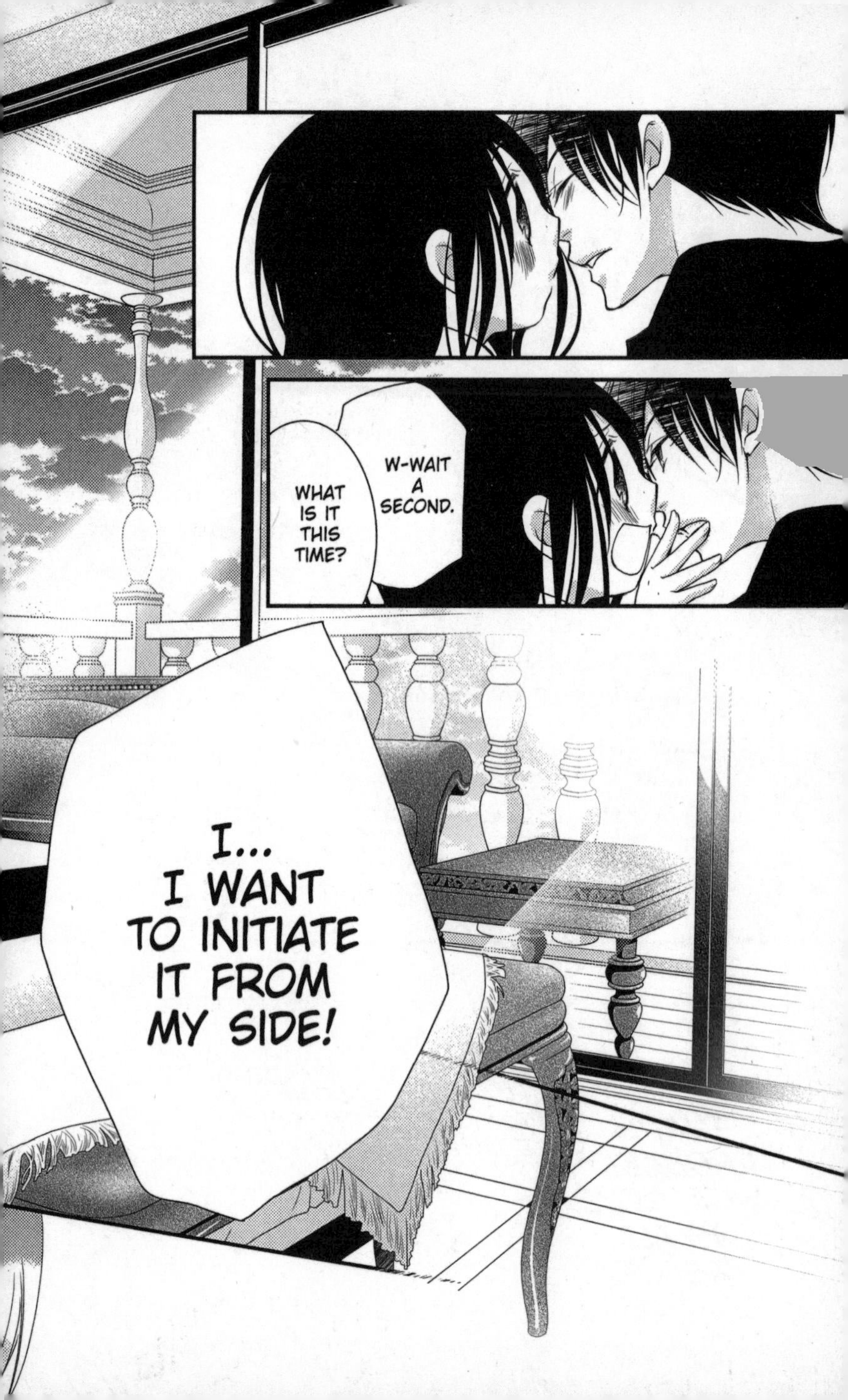
W-WAIT A SECOND.
WHAT IS IT THIS TIME?
I... I WANT TO INITIATE IT FROM MY SIDE!

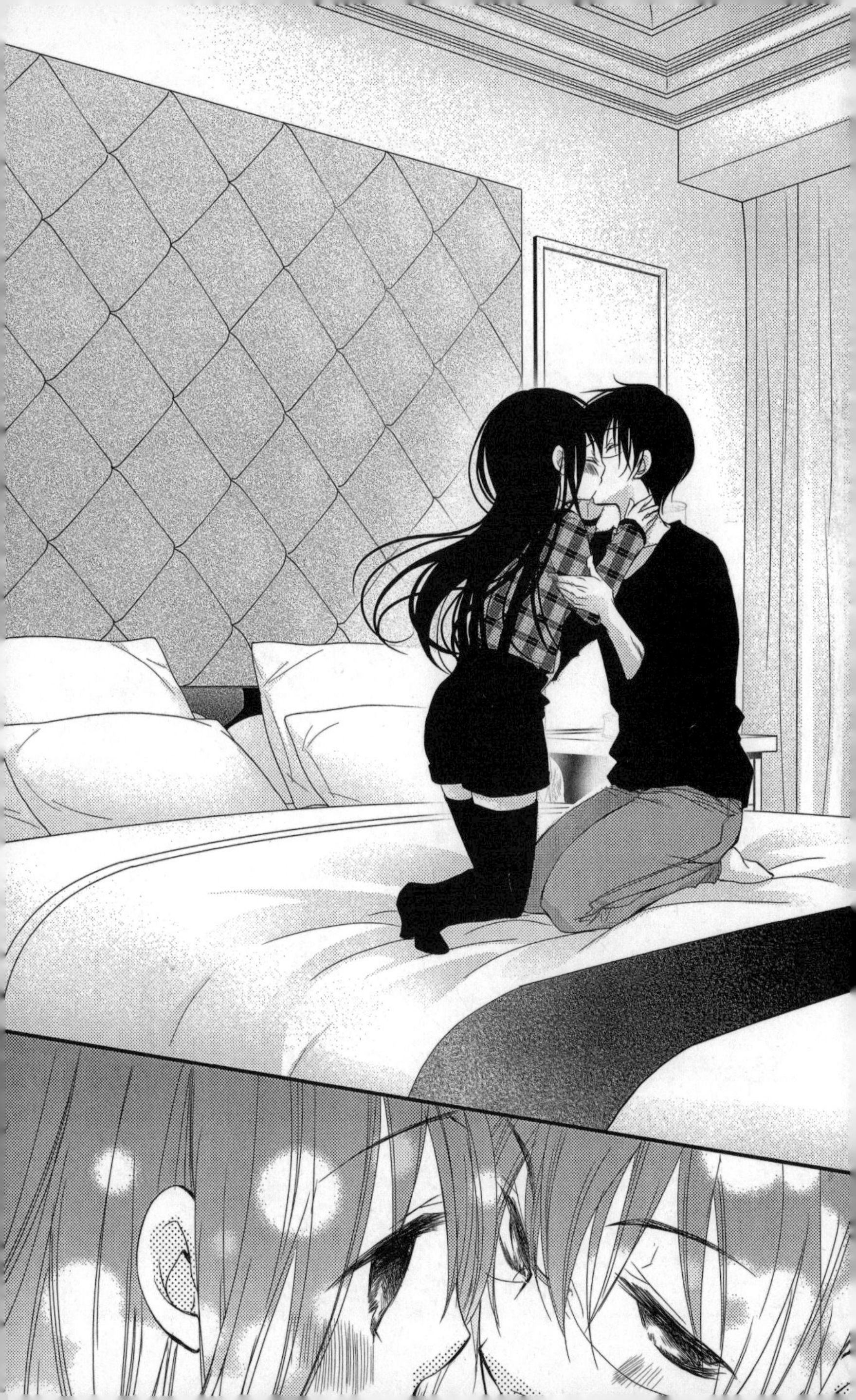

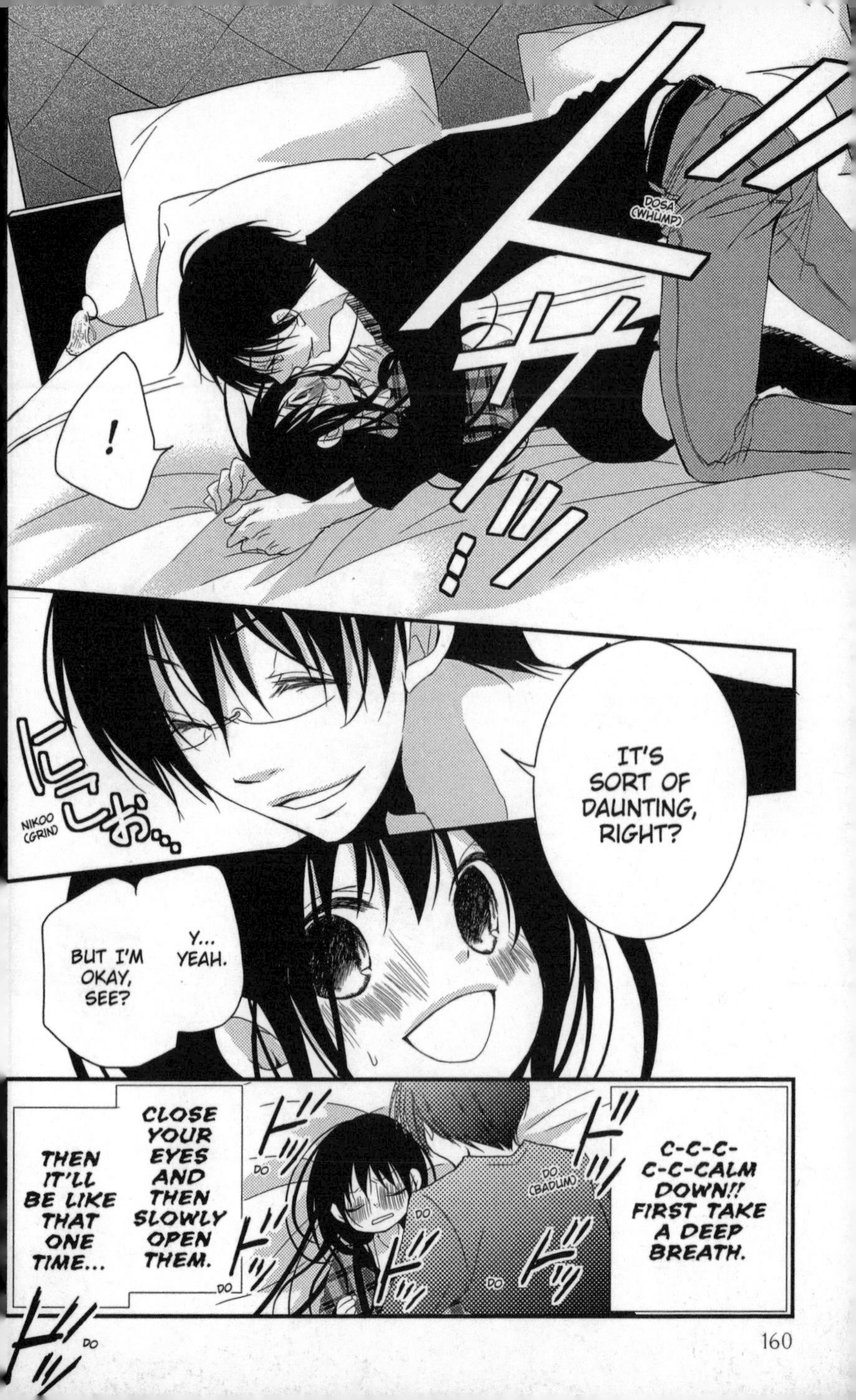
DOSA (WHUMP)
!
IT'S SORT OF DAUNTING, RIGHT?
NIKOO (GRIN)
Y... YEAH.
BUT I'M OKAY, SEE?
C-C-C-C-C-CALM DOWN!! FIRST TAKE A DEEP BREATH.
DO (BADUM)
DO
DO
CLOSE YOUR EYES AND THEN SLOWLY OPEN THEM.
DO
THEN IT'LL BE LIKE THAT ONE TIME...
DO
DO

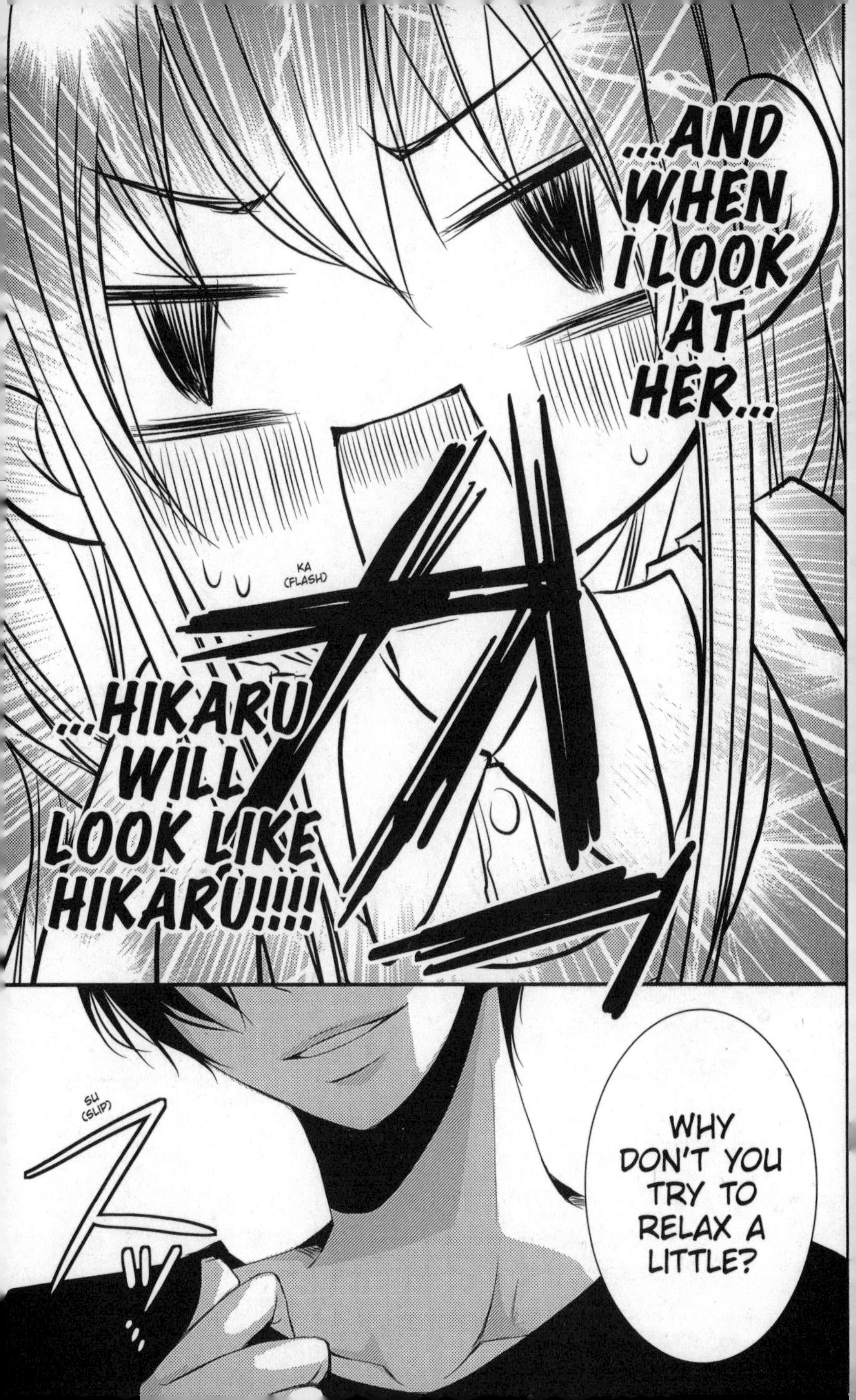
...AND WHEN I LOOK AT HER...
KA (FLASH)
...HIKARU WILL LOOK LIKE HIKARU!!!!
WHY DON'T YOU TRY TO RELAX A LITTLE?
SU (SLIP)

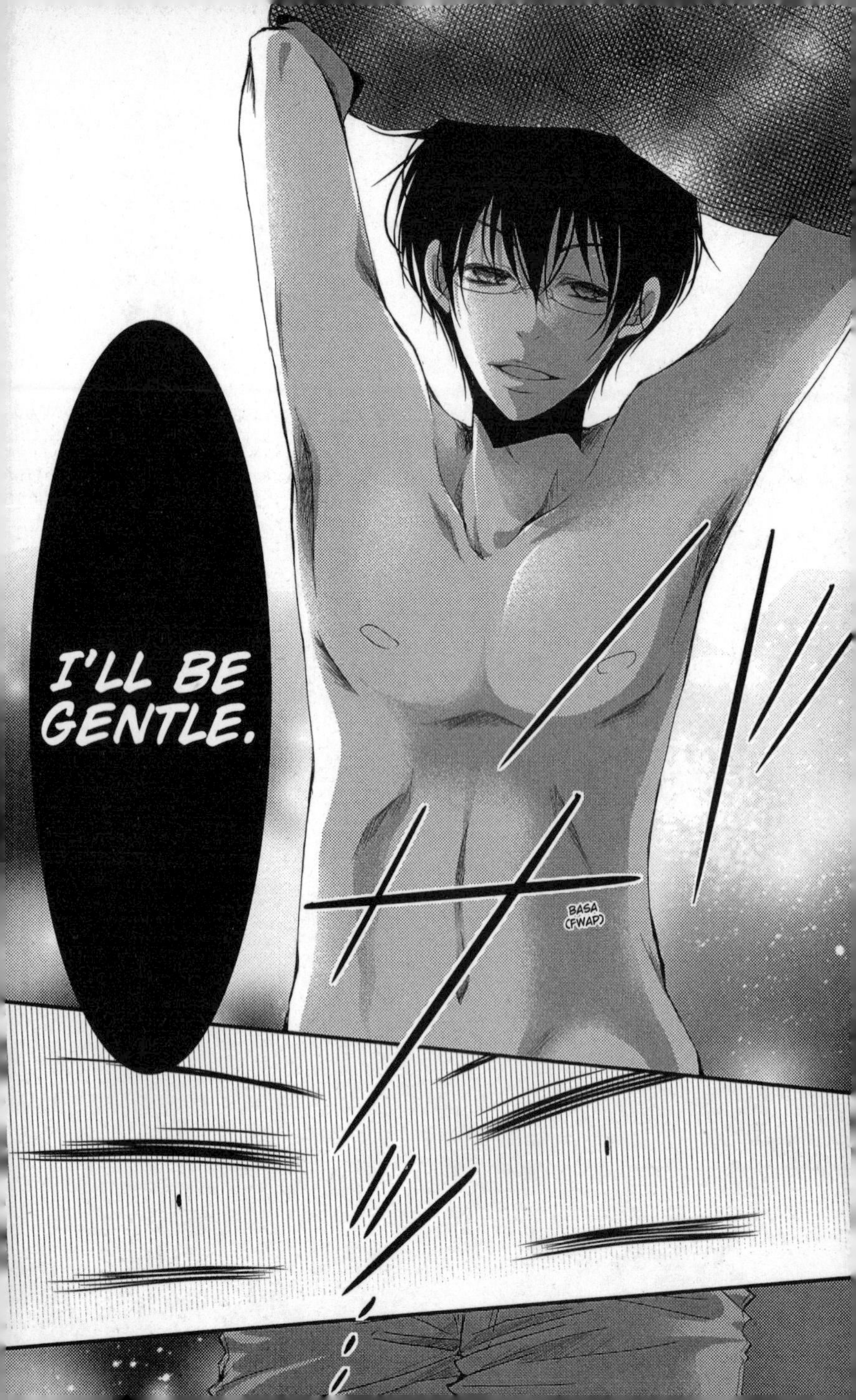
I'LL BE GENTLE.
BASA (FWAP)

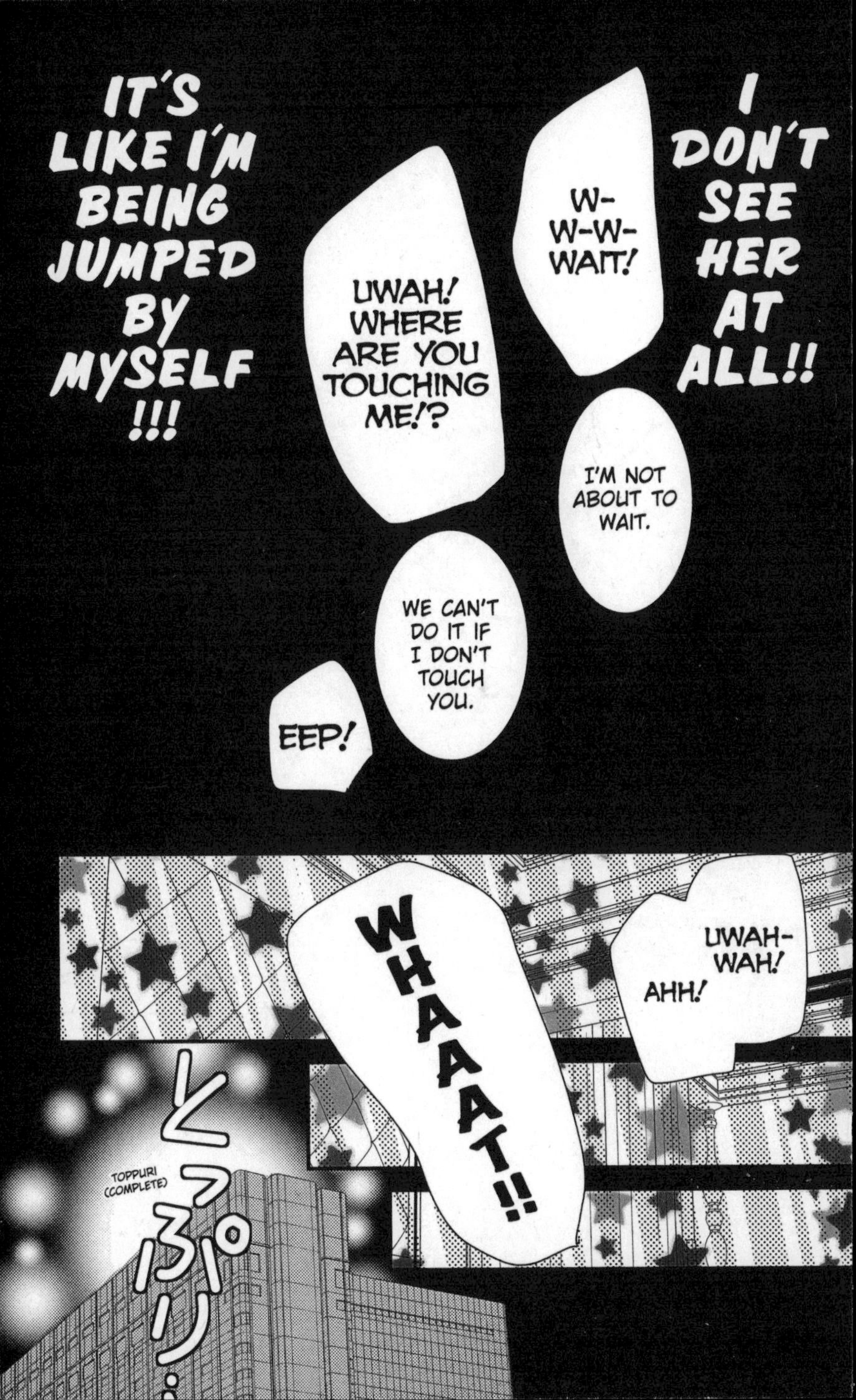
I DON'T SEE HER AT ALL!!
W-W-W-WAIT!
UWAH! WHERE ARE YOU TOUCHING ME!?
I'M NOT ABOUT TO WAIT.
WE CAN'T DO IT IF I DON'T TOUCH YOU.
EEP!
IT'S LIKE I'M BEING JUMPED BY MYSELF!!!
UWAH-WAH!
AHH!
WHAAAAT!!
とっぷり…
TOPPURI (COMPLETE)

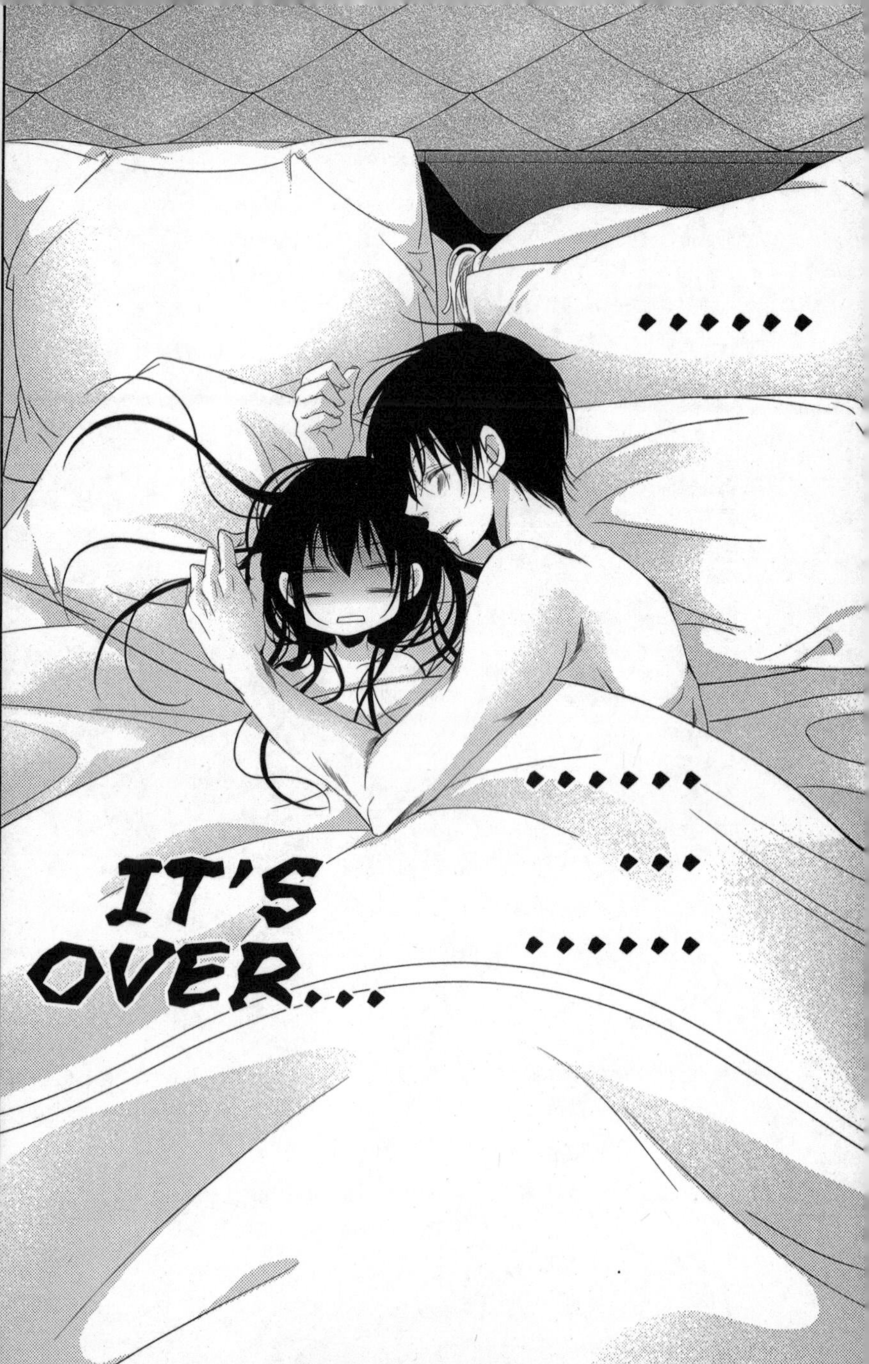
......
......
...
......
IT'S OVER...

Continued in Volume 6

Translation Notes

Common Honorifics:

no honorific: Indicates familiarity or closeness; if used without permission or reason, addressing someone in this manner would constitute an insult.

-san: The Japanese equivalent of Mr./Mrs./Miss. If a situation calls for politeness, this is the fail-safe honorific.

-sama: Conveys great respect; may also indicate that the social status of the speaker is lower than that of the addressee.

-kun: Used most often when referring to boys, this indicates affection or familiarity. Occasionally used by older men among their peers, but it may also be used by anyone referring to a person of lower standing.

-chan: An affectionate honorific indicating familiarity used mostly in reference to girls; also used in reference to cute persons or animals of either gender.

-senpai: A suffix used to address upperclassmen or more experienced coworkers.

-sensei: A respectful term for teachers, artists, or high-level professionals.

-oniisan, onii-san, aniki, etc.: Terms used to address an elder brother or brother-like figure.

-oneesan, onee-san, aneki, etc.: Terms used to address an elder sister or sister-like figure.

Page 27
Saotome
The two characters in Saotome's name mean "early virgin."

[Ani-Imo]
Big Brother becomes Little Sister;
Little Sister becomes Big Brother.

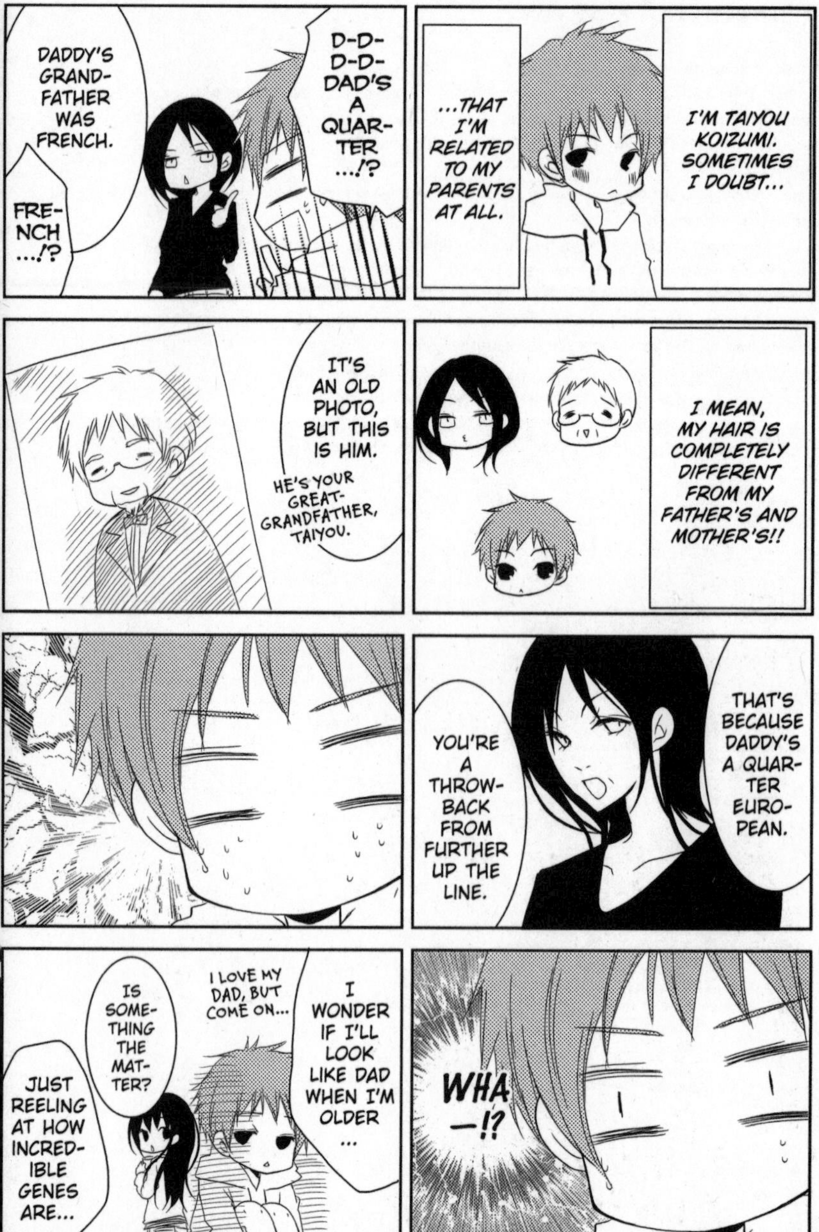
I'M TAIYOU KOIZUMI. SOMETIMES I DOUBT...
...THAT I'M RELATED TO MY PARENTS AT ALL.
I MEAN, MY HAIR IS COMPLETELY DIFFERENT FROM MY FATHER'S AND MOTHER'S!!
THAT'S BECAUSE DADDY'S A QUARTER EUROPEAN.
YOU'RE A THROWBACK FROM FURTHER UP THE LINE.
WHA—!?
D-D-D-D-DAD'S A QUARTER...!?
DADDY'S GRANDFATHER WAS FRENCH.
FRENCH...!?
IT'S AN OLD PHOTO, BUT THIS IS HIM.
HE'S YOUR GREAT-GRANDFATHER, TAIYOU.
I WONDER IF I'LL LOOK LIKE DAD WHEN I'M OLDER...
I LOVE MY DAD, BUT COME ON...
IS SOMETHING THE MATTER?
JUST REELING AT HOW INCREDIBLE GENES ARE...

HELLO. THIS IS HARUKO KURUMATANI. THANK YOU FOR PICKING UP VOLUME 5. AT LONG LAST, OUR CHARACTERS HAVE ARRIVED AT THIS MOMENT— SO HOW DID YOU ALL ENJOY IT? I'M GOING TO WORK HARD ON VOLUME 6 TOO, SO UNTIL THEN!

HARUKO KURUMATANI
C/O YEN PRESS
1290 AVENUE OF THE AMERICAS
NEW YORK, NY 10104

http://kurumatani.jugem.jp/
Twitter ID: @kurumatani_h

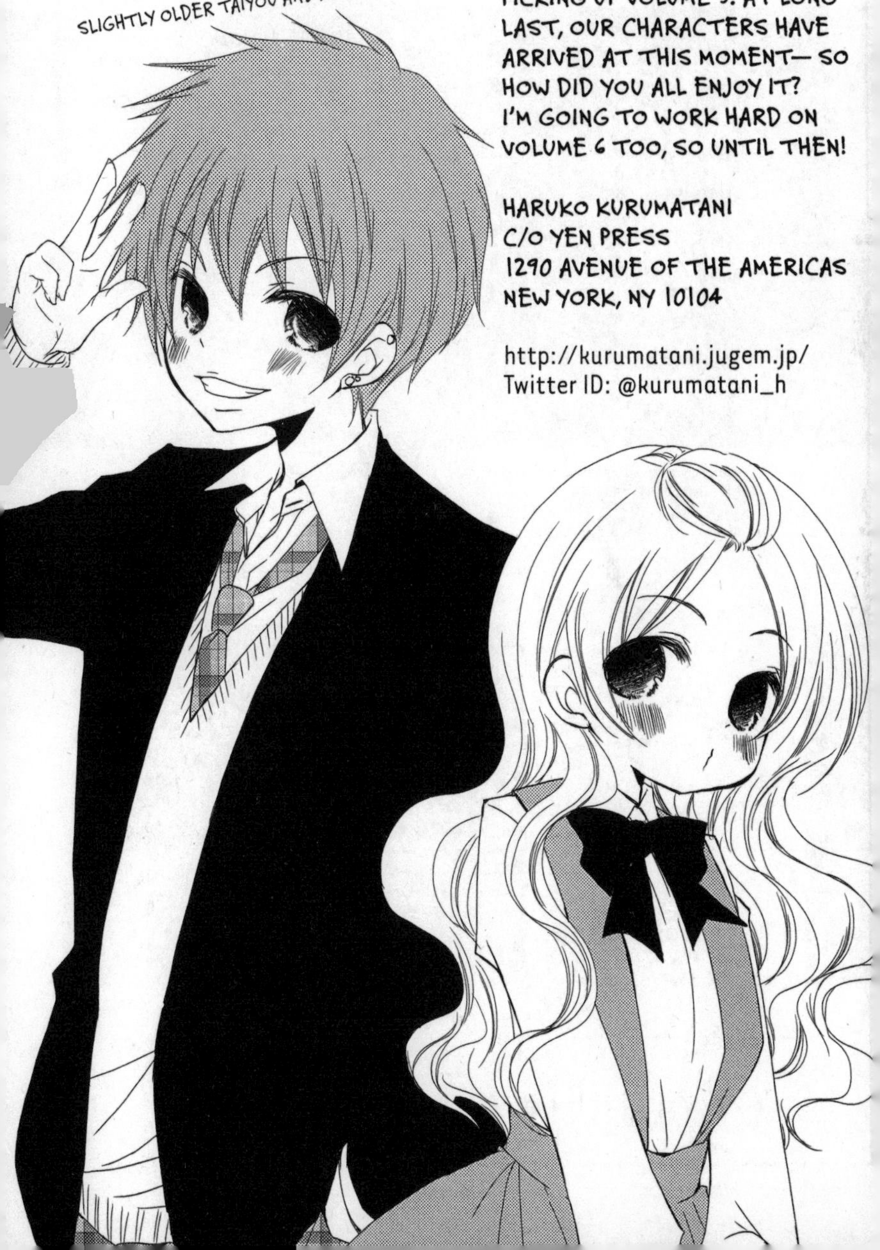

SLIGHTLY OLDER TAIYOU AND AKARI

Next Issue

WHAT WILL HAPPEN TO THESE TWO NOW THAT THEY'VE FINALLY DONE IT...?

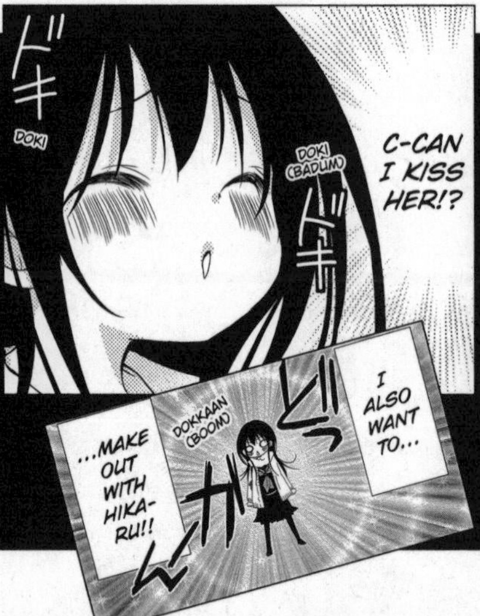
C-CAN I KISS HER!?
DOKI (BADUM)
DOKI
I ALSO WANT TO...
DOKKAAN (BOOM)
...MAKE OUT WITH HIKA-RU!!

FORGET **THAT.** I WANT TO MAKE OUT WITH HIKARU SOME MORE!

AND **HIKARU'S** COOL AS A CUCUMBER—NOT EVEN A LITTLE JEALOUS.

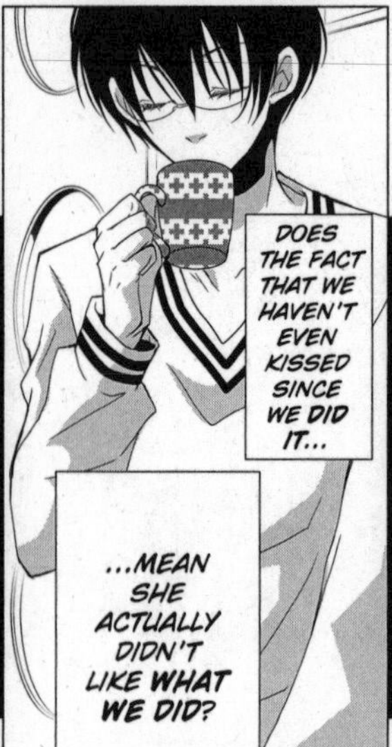
DOES THE FACT THAT WE HAVEN'T EVEN KISSED SINCE WE DID IT...
...MEAN SHE ACTUALLY DIDN'T LIKE WHAT WE DID?

Available February 2016

NOW THAT WE'VE JOINED IN BODY AND SPIRIT, I FEEL EVEN MORE STRONGLY...

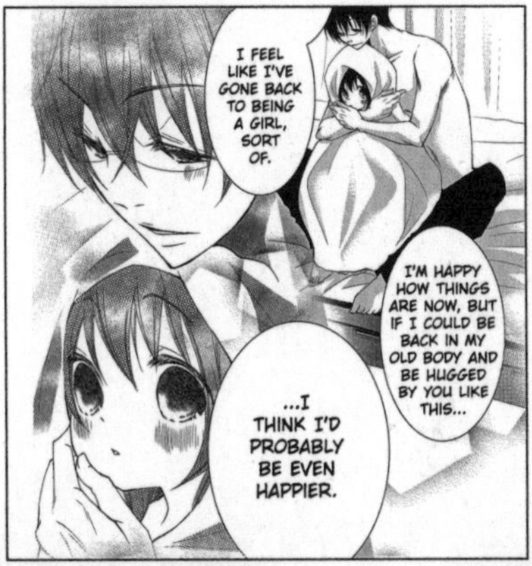
I FEEL LIKE I'VE GONE BACK TO BEING A GIRL, SORT OF.
I'M HAPPY HOW THINGS ARE NOW, BUT IF I COULD BE BACK IN MY OLD BODY AND BE HUGGED BY YOU LIKE THIS...
...I THINK I'D PROBABLY BE EVEN HAPPIER.

...ABOUT WANTING TO RETURN TO MY ORIGINAL BODY.

THEN OUR BODY-SWAPPING SENPAIS...

...GIVE US A SHOCKING...

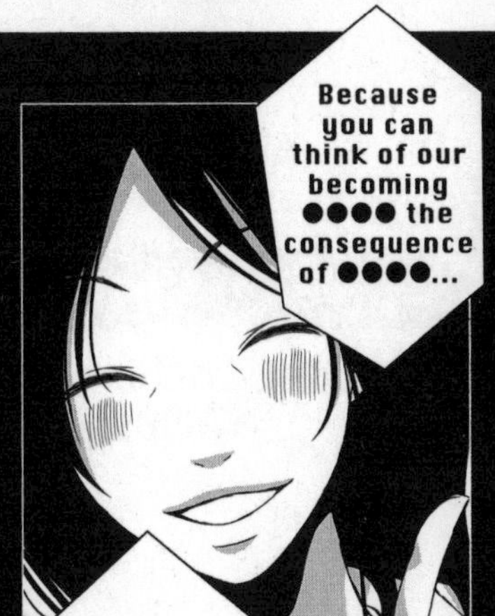
Because you can think of our becoming ●●●● the consequence of ●●●●...
...under no circumstances are you to ●●●● with ●●●●. ☆

...PIECE OF NEWS!!?

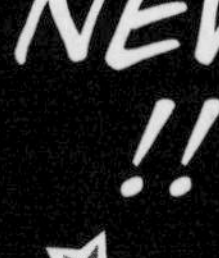

Ani-Imo (6)

Ani-Imo (6)

Sneak Peek

Read on for an early look at Volume 6,
available February 2016.

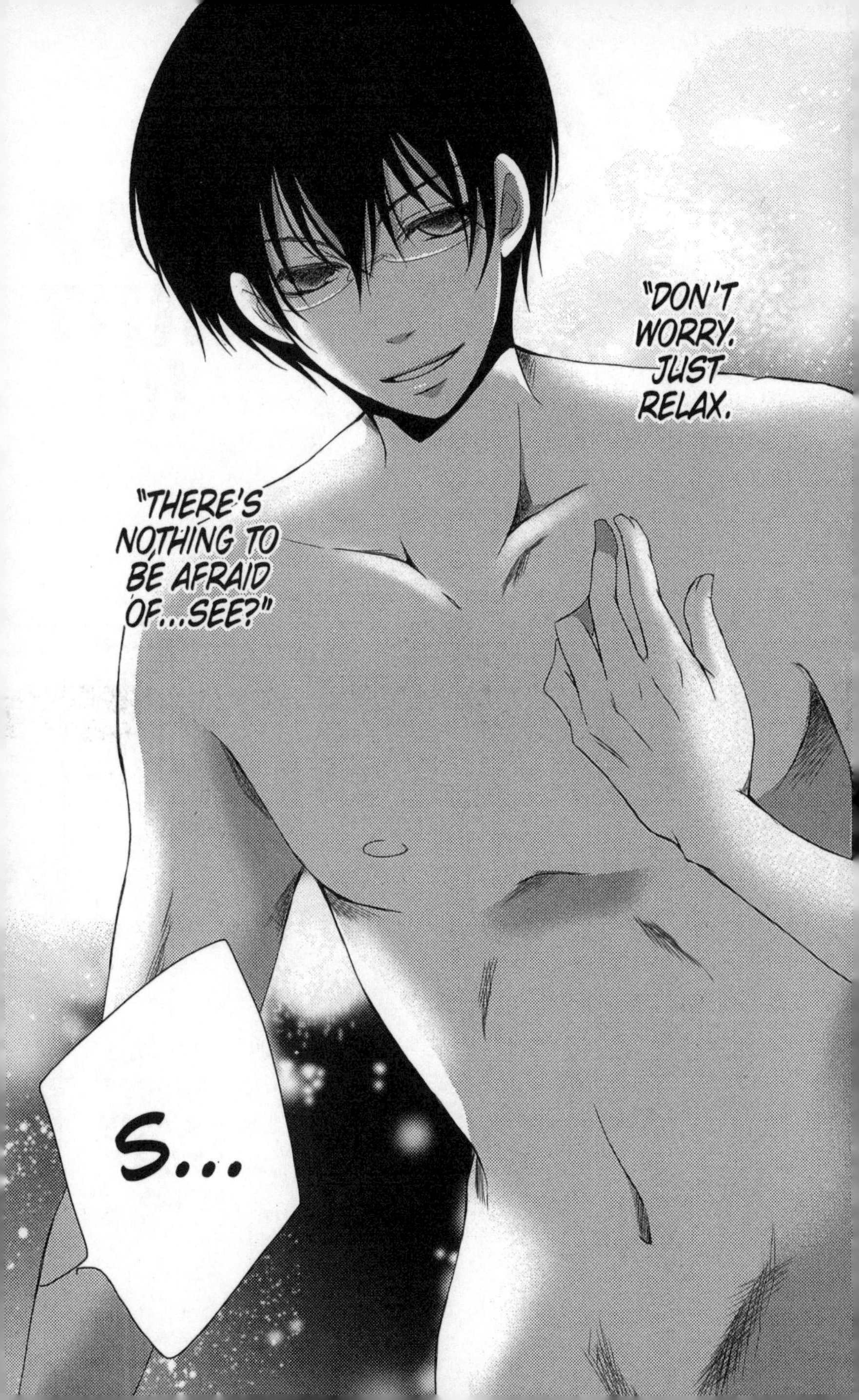
"DON'T WORRY. JUST RELAX.
"THERE'S NOTHING TO BE AFRAID OF...SEE?"
S...

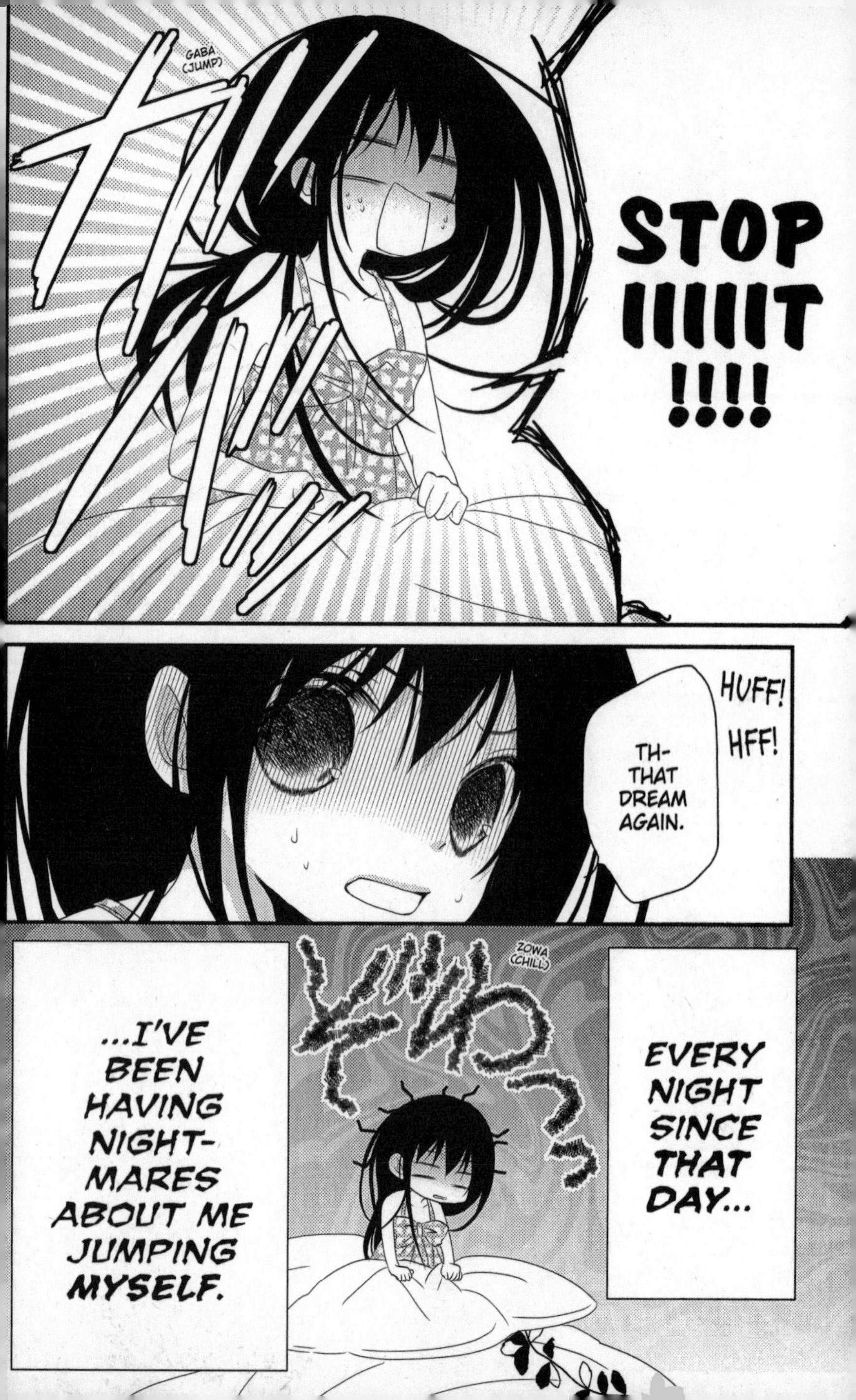
GABA (JUMP)
STOP IIIIIT !!!!
HUFF! HFF!
TH-THAT DREAM AGAIN.
EVERY NIGHT SINCE THAT DAY...
ZOWA (CHILL)
...I'VE BEEN HAVING NIGHT-MARES ABOUT ME JUMPING MYSELF.

TO BE HONEST, I DON'T QUITE REMEMBER EVERYTHING THAT HAPPENED.
IT WAS ALL OVER BY THE TIME I'D GOTTEN PAST THE PANIC...
ONE THING I REMEMBER DISTINCTLY IS...
HAAH...
"DOES IT HURT...? I'M SORRY."
EEEE! I DON'T WANT TO REMEMBER THAT!!!
IF I EVER HAD TO GO THROUGH WITH THAT AGAIN...
がばっ
GABA (DUCK)
...I MIGHT...
...DIE.

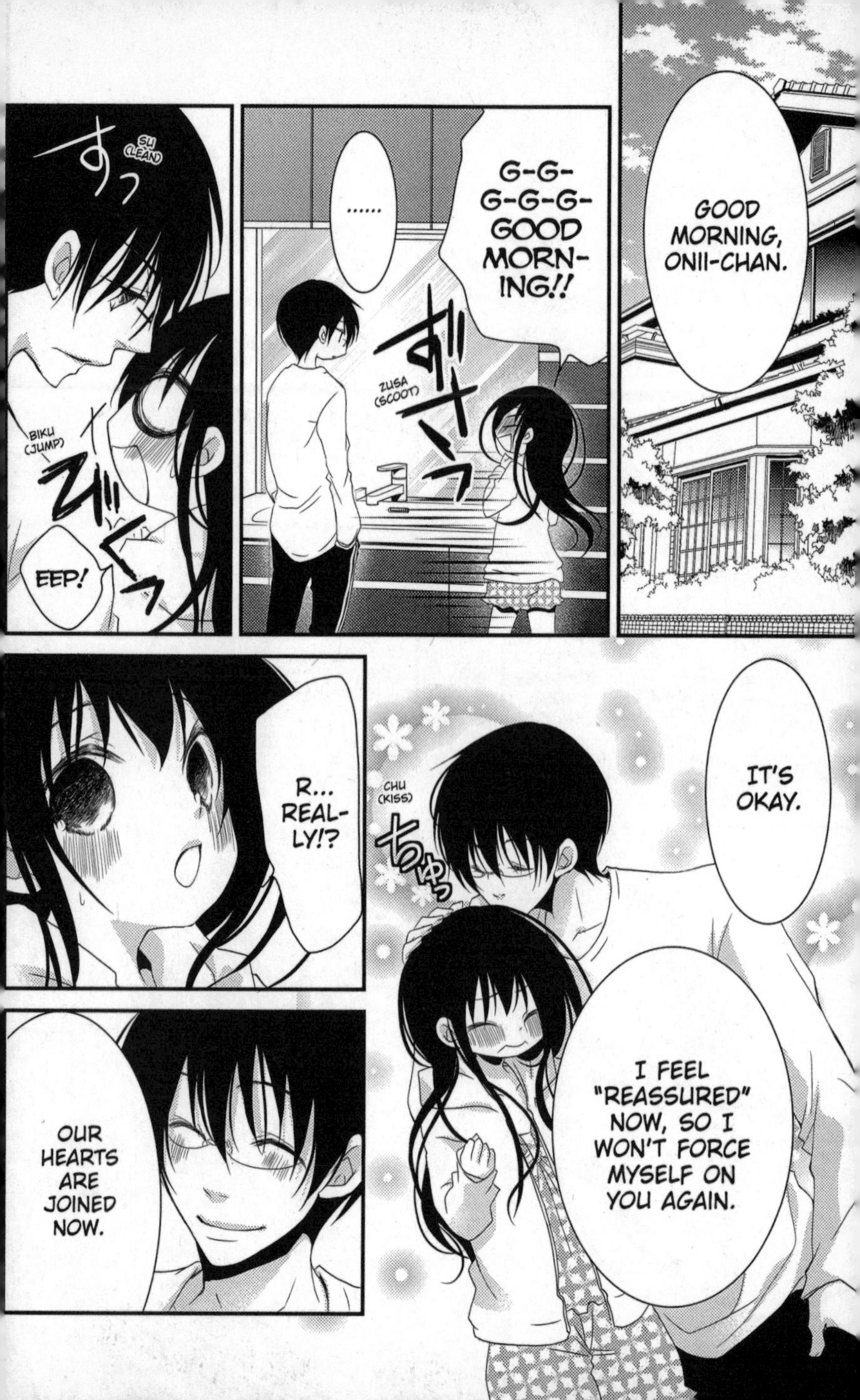
GOOD MORNING, ONII-CHAN.
G-G-G-G-G-GOOD MORN-ING!!
......
ずさっ
ZUSA (SCOOT)
すっ
SU (LEAN)
BIKU (JUMP)
びくっ
EEP!
IT'S OKAY.
CHU (KISS)
ちゅっ
I FEEL "REASSURED" NOW, SO I WON'T FORCE MYSELF ON YOU AGAIN.
R... REAL-LY!?
OUR HEARTS ARE JOINED NOW.

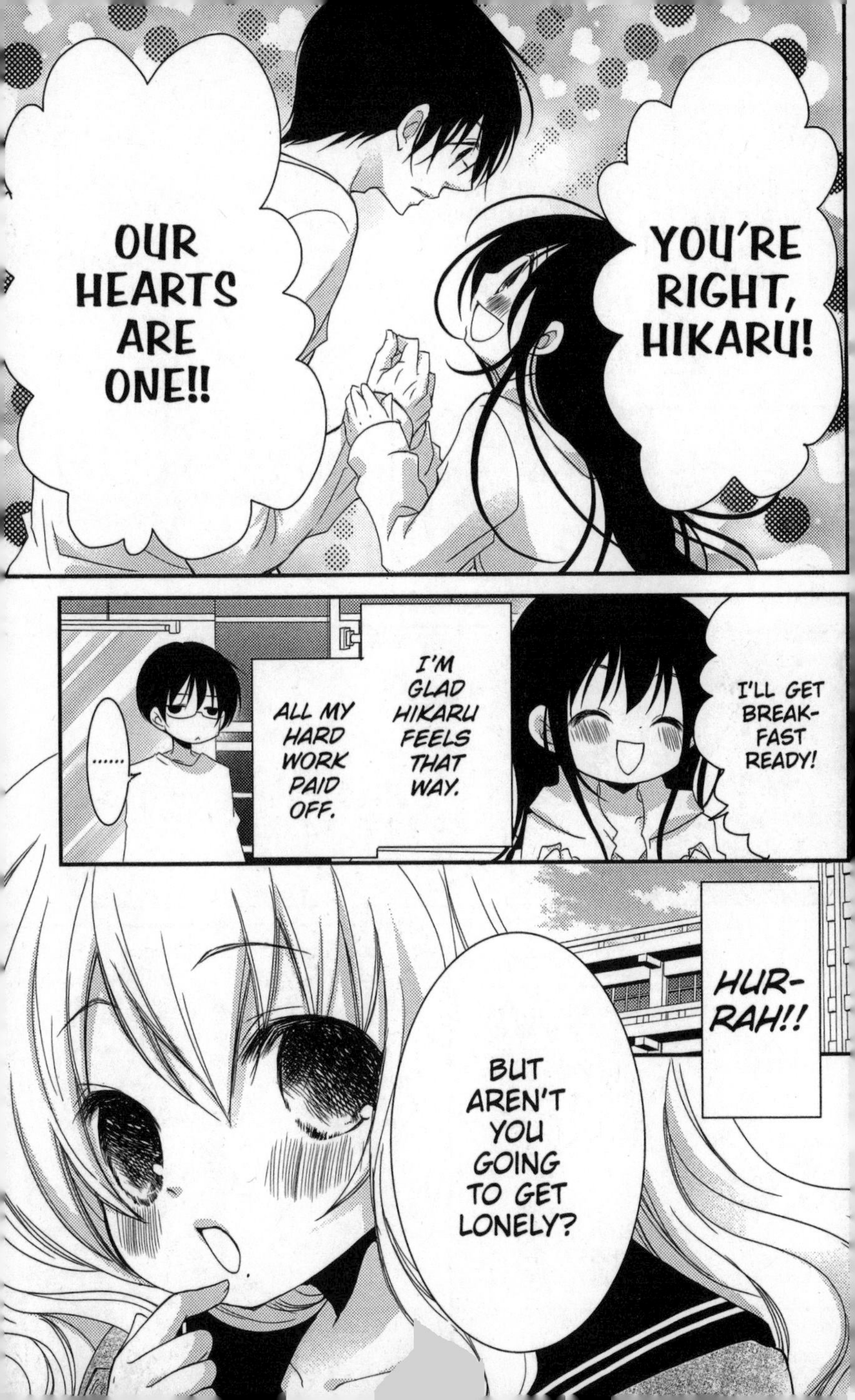
YOU'RE RIGHT, HIKARU!
OUR HEARTS ARE ONE!!
I'LL GET BREAK-FAST READY!
I'M GLAD HIKARU FEELS THAT WAY.
ALL MY HARD WORK PAID OFF.
......
HUR-RAH!!
BUT AREN'T YOU GOING TO GET LONELY?

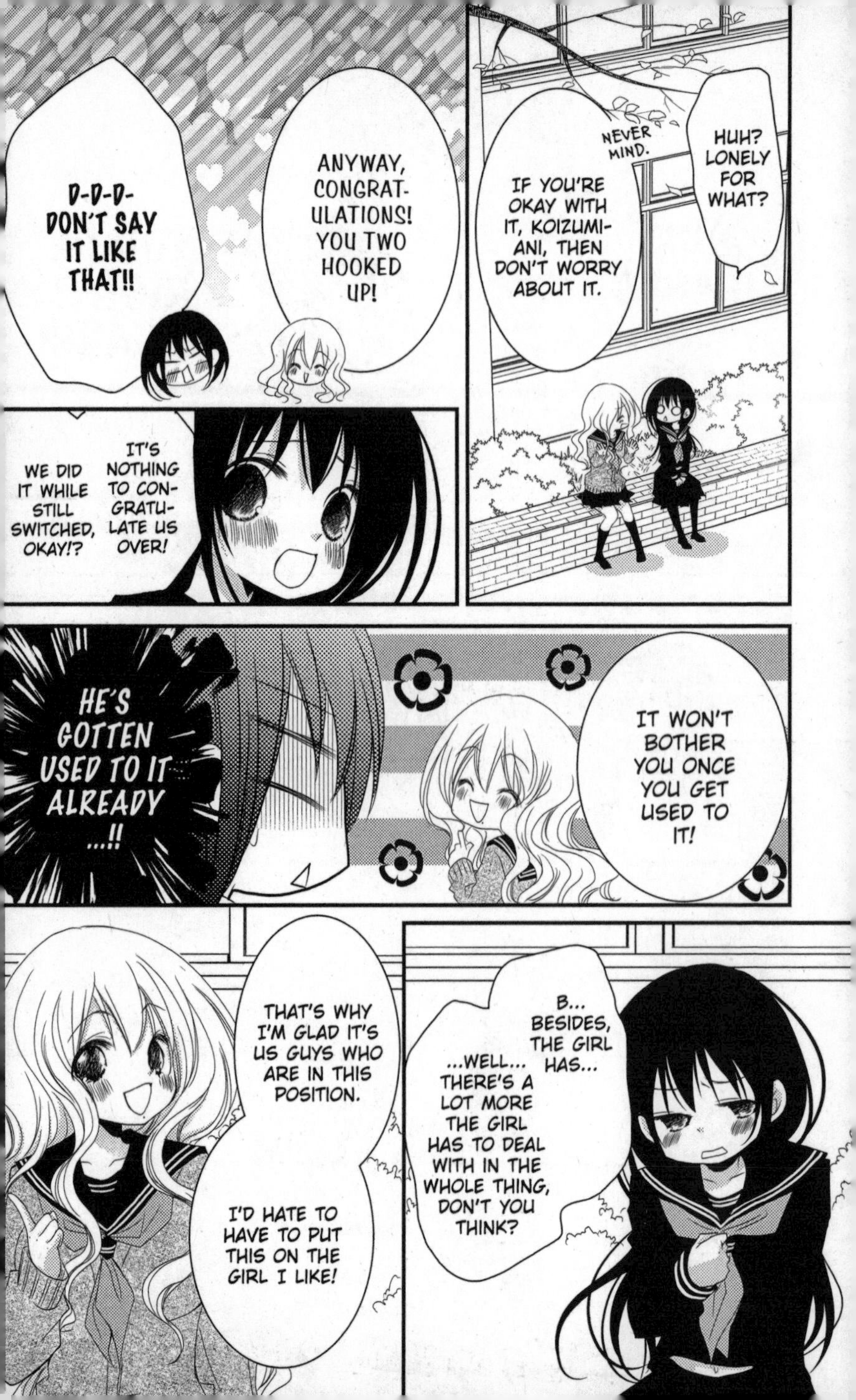
HUH? LONELY FOR WHAT?
NEVER MIND.
IF YOU'RE OKAY WITH IT, KOIZUMI-ANI, THEN DON'T WORRY ABOUT IT.
ANYWAY, CONGRAT-ULATIONS! YOU TWO HOOKED UP!
D-D-D-DON'T SAY IT LIKE THAT!!
IT'S NOTHING TO CON-GRATU-LATE US OVER!
WE DID IT WHILE STILL SWITCHED, OKAY!?
IT WON'T BOTHER YOU ONCE YOU GET USED TO IT!
HE'S GOTTEN USED TO IT ALREADY ...!!
B... BESIDES, THE GIRL HAS...
...WELL... THERE'S A LOT MORE THE GIRL HAS TO DEAL WITH IN THE WHOLE THING, DON'T YOU THINK?
THAT'S WHY I'M GLAD IT'S US GUYS WHO ARE IN THIS POSITION.
I'D HATE TO HAVE TO PUT THIS ON THE GIRL I LIKE!

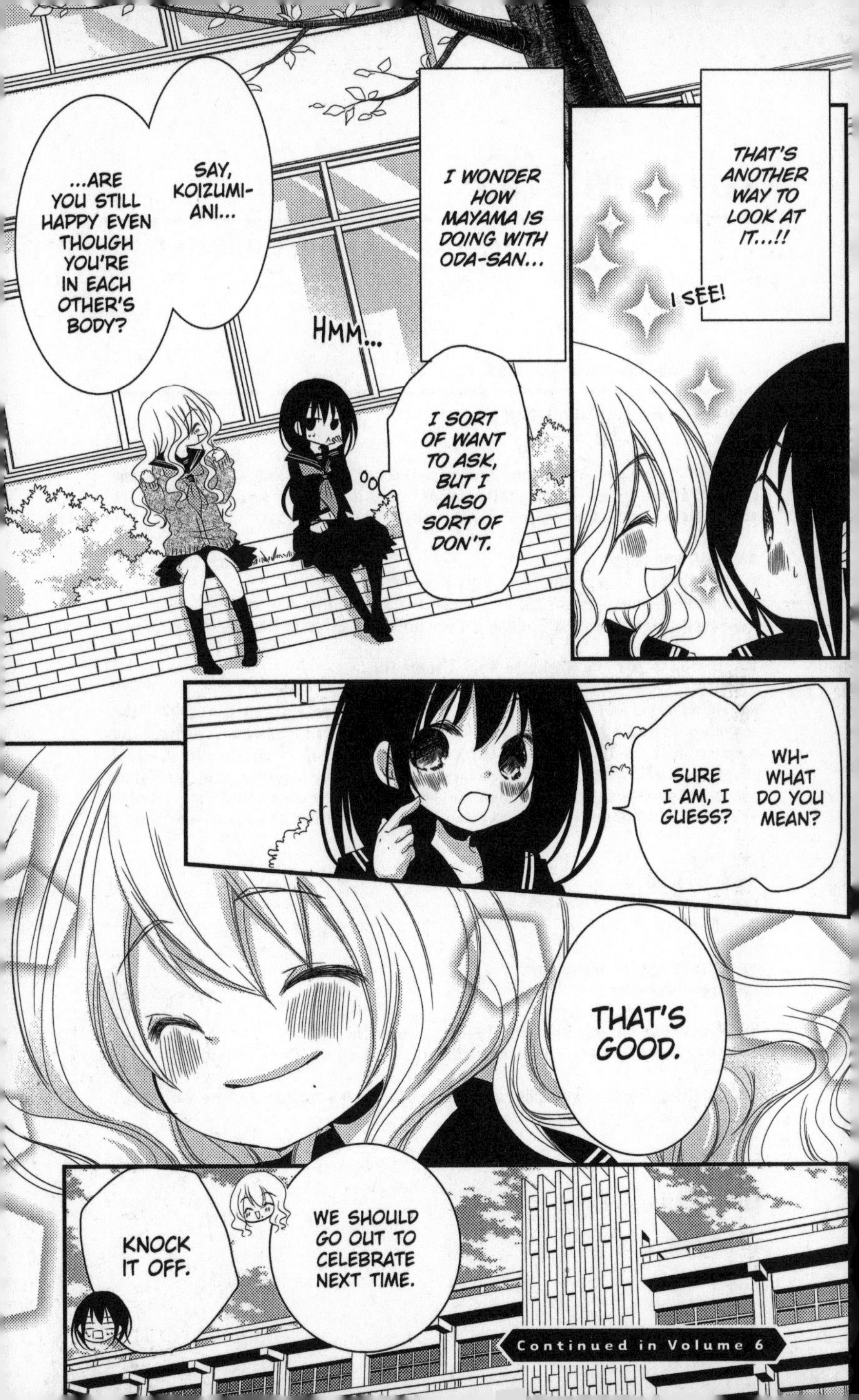
THAT'S ANOTHER WAY TO LOOK AT IT...!!
I SEE!
I WONDER HOW MAYAMA IS DOING WITH ODA-SAN...
SAY, KOIZUMI-ANI...
...ARE YOU STILL HAPPY EVEN THOUGH YOU'RE IN EACH OTHER'S BODY?
HMM...
I SORT OF WANT TO ASK, BUT I ALSO SORT OF DON'T.
WH-WHAT DO YOU MEAN?
SURE I AM, I GUESS?
THAT'S GOOD.
WE SHOULD GO OUT TO CELEBRATE NEXT TIME.
KNOCK IT OFF.
Continued in Volume 6

ANI-IMO(5)

HARUKO KURUMATANI

Translation: Christine Dashiell

Lettering: Abigail Blackman

ANI-IMO Volume 5
© 2014 Haruko Kurumatani. All rights reserved.
First published in Japan in 2014 by Kodansha, Ltd., Tokyo.
Publication rights for this English edition arranged through Kodansha Ltd. Tokyo.

Translation © 2015 by Hachette Book Group, Inc.

Yen Press
Hachette Book Group
1290 Avenue of the Americas
New York, NY 10104

www.hachettebookgroup.com
www.yenpress.com

Yen Press is an imprint of Hachette Book Group, Inc.
The Yen Press name and logo are trademarks of Hachette Book Group, Inc.

The publisher is not responsible for websites (or their content) that are not owned by the publisher.

First Yen Press Edition: November 2015

ISBN: 978-0-316-34574-3

10 9 8 7 6 5 4 3 2 1

BVG

Printed in the United States of America